Christian L. Glossner is Lecturer in Political Communication at the Université de Fribourg and was formerly Lecturer in Political Economy and European History at the University of Oxford. He previously held a Europaeum Research Fellowship at the Institut Universitaire de Hautes Études Internationales (IUHEI) in Geneva and worked for the Directorate-General for Economic and Financial Affairs (ECFIN) of the European Commission in Brussels. He is a graduate from the Université de Fribourg as well as the London School of Economics and Political Science (LSE) and received his D.Phil. (PhD) on political history and economic theory from the University of Oxford.

AF765701

THE MAKING OF THE GERMAN POST-WAR ECONOMY

Political Communication and Public Reception of the Social Market Economy after World War II

Christian L. Glossner

I.B. TAURIS
LONDON · NEW YORK

New paperback edition published in 2013 by I.B.Tauris & Co Ltd
6 Salem Road, London W2 4BU
175 Fifth Avenue, New York NY 10010
www.ibtauris.com

First published in hardback in 2010 by Tauris Academic Studies, an imprint of I.B.Tauris & Co Ltd

Copyright © 2010, 2013 Christian L. Glossner

The right of Christian L. Glossner to be identified as the author of this work has been asserted by the author in accordance with the Copyright, Designs and Patents Act 1988.

All rights reserved. Except for brief quotations in a review, this book, or any part thereof, may not be reproduced, stored in or introduced into a retrieval system, or transmitted, in any form or by any means, electronic, mechanical, photocopying, recording or otherwise, without the prior written permission of the publisher.

ISBN 978 1 78076 421 4

A full CIP record for this book is available from the British Library
A full CIP record for this book is available from the Library of Congress

Library of Congress catalog card: available

For Anna, Lies' and Ina

For You

CONTENTS

LIST OF TABLES AND FIGURES

LIST OF ABBREVIATIONS

ACDP	Archiv der Christlich-Demokratischen Politik
ACSP	Archiv für Christlich-Soziale Politik
ADAV	Allgemeiner Deutscher Arbeiterverein
ADL	Archiv des Liberalismus
AdsD	Archiv der sozialen Demokratie
AfDR	Akademie für Deutsches Recht
AG CDU/CSU	Arbeitsgemeinschaft der CDU/CSU Deutschlands
AG EvB	Arbeitsgemeinschaft Erwin von Beckerath
AG VWB	Volkswirtschaftliche Arbeitsgemeinschaft für Bayern
AG VWL	Arbeitsgemeinschaft Volkswirtschaftslehre
ALES	Archiv der Ludwig-Erhard-Stiftung
AMZON	American Zone
AOC	Archives de l'Occupation Française en Allemagne et en Autriche, Colmar
AOZ	American Occupation Zone
AP	Arbeiterpartei
ASM	Aktionsgemeinschaft Soziale Marktwirtschaft
AVBRD	Akten zur Vorgeschichte der Bundesrepublik Deutschland
BA	Bundesarchiv
BayHStA	Bayerisches Hauptstaatsarchiv
BayStKA	Akten der Bayerischen Staatskanzlei
BBC	British Broadcasting Corporation
BCSV	Badisch Christlich-Soziale Volkspartei
BDV	Bremer Demokratische Volkspartei
BE	British Element
BGBl.	Bundesgesetzblatt
BGS	Bundesgeschäftsstelle
BHE	Block der Heimatvertriebenen u. Entrechteten

BHE/DG	Block der Heimatvertriebenen u. Entrechteten/ Deutsche Gemeinschaft
BICO	Bipartite Control Office
BKU	Bund Katholischer Unternehmer
BL	Basic Law
BNG	Bewirtschaftungsnotgesetz
BOZ	British Occupation Zone
BP	Bayernpartei
BPA	Bundespresseamt
BR	Bayerischer Rundfunk
BSP	Bayerischer Staatspartei
BTW	Bundestagswahl
BuBa	Bundesbank
BuBa HA	Bundesbank Historisches Archiv
BVerfGE	Bundesverfassungsgerichtsentscheid
BVP	Bayerische Volkspartei
CAG	Christliche Arbeitsgemeinschaft
CCG	Control Commission for Germany
CDB	Christlich-Demokratischer Block
CDP	Christlich-Demokratische Partei
CDU	Christlich-Demokratische Union
CDUB	Christlich-Demokratische Union Baden
CDUD	Christlich Demokratische Union Deutschlands
CDVB	Christlich-Demokratischer Volksbund
CNU	Christlich-Nationale Union
COEE	Centre d'Organisation et d'Etudes Economiques de Fribourg/Breisgau
CSU	Christlich-Soziale Union
CSUP	Christlich-Soziale Unionspartei
CSVD	Christlichsozialer Volksdienst
CSVP	Christlich-Soziale Volkspartei
CU	Christliche Union
CVP	Christliche Volkspartei des Saarlandes
DA	Demokratischer Aufbruch
DAG	Deutsche Angestellten-Gewerkschaft
DANA	Deutsche Allgemeine Nachrichtenagentur
DAP	Deutsche Aufbau-Partei
DB	Deutscher Block
DBt PA	Deutscher Bundestag, Parlamentsarchiv
DDB	Der Deutsche Block
DDP	Deutsche Demokratische Partei
DDZ	*Die Deutsche Zeitung*

DENA	Deutsche Nachrichtenagentur
DG	Deutsche Gemeinschaft
DGB	Deutscher Gewerkschaftsbund
DHM	Deutsches Historisches Museum
DIAS	Drahtfunk im amerikanischen Sektor
DigAM	Digitales Archiv Marburg
DISCC	District Information Services Control Command
DKP/DRP	Deutsche Konservative Partei/Deutsche Rechtspartei
DM	Deutsche Mark
DNVP	Deutschnationale Volkspartei
DP	Deutsche Partei
DPA	Deutsche Presse-Agentur
dpd	Deutscher Pressedienst
DPD	Demokratische Partei Deutschlands
DPRP	Demokratische Partei Rheinland-Pfalz
DPS	Demokratische Partei Saar
DRA	Stiftung Deutsches Rundfunkarchiv
DS	Drucksache
DSJ	*Das Sozialistische Jahrhundert*
DSU	Deutsche Soziale Union
DUD	Deutschland-Union-Dienst
DVP	Demokratische Volkspartei
DZ	*Deutsche Zeitung*
DZP	Deutsche Zentrumspartei (Zentrum)
EC	Economic Council
ECA	Economic Cooperation Act/Administration
ECO	Economic Council Ordinance
ERP	European Recovery Program (Marshall-Plan)
e.V.	eingetragener Verein
EVD	Evangelischer Volksdienst
FAZ	Frankfurter Allgemeine Zeitung
FDP	Freie Demokratische Partei
FES	Friedrich-Ebert-Stiftung
FH	*Frankfurter Hefte*
FL	Flugblatt
FOZ	French Occupation Zone
FRG	Federal Republic of Germany
FRUS	Foreign Relations of the United States
FS	Flugblattsammlung
Fslg.	Flugblattsammlung
GARIOA	Government Aid for Recovery in Occupied Areas
GB	Gesamtdeutscher Block

GDP	Gesamtdeutsche Partei
GG	Grundgesetz
HA	Handakte
HHStA	Hessisches Hauptstaatsarchiv
HSS	Hanns-Seidel-Stiftung
HStA	Hauptstaatsarchiv
ICD	Information Control Division
IfD	Institut für Demoskopie
IfZ	Institut für Zeitgeschichte
IHK	Industrie- und Handelskammer
IPCOG	Informal Policy Committee on Germany
IStGF	Institut für Stadtgeschichte Frankfurt am Main
IUHEI	Institut Universitaire de Hautes Études Internationales
JCS	Joint Chiefs of Staff
JEIA	Joint Export-Import Agency
KAS	Konrad-Adenauer-Stiftung
KP	Kommunistische Partei
KPD	Kommunistische Partei Deutschlands
LABW	Landesarchiv Baden-Württemberg
LDP	Liberal-Demokratische Partei
LDPD	Liberal-Demokratische Partei Deutschlands
LeMO	Lebendiges virtuelles Museum Online
LGF	Landesgeschäftsführer
LT SB	Stenographische Berichte der Verhandlungen des Bayerischen Landtags
LTW	Landtagswahl
MdWR	Mitglied des Wirtschaftsrats
Mitt.	Mitteilungen des Nordwestdeutschen Zeitungsverleger-Vereins e.V. für die britische Zone (Zeitschrift)
MPS	Mont Pèlerin Society
MWi	Akten des Bayerischen Staatsministeriums für Wirtschaft und Verkehr
n.d.	no date, undated
NDP	Nationaldemokratische Partei
n.l.	no location
NL	Nachlass
NLP	Niedersächsische Landespartei
n.n.	no name
n.p.a.	no party affiliation
n.s.	no signature
n.t.	no title
NV	*Neuer Vorwärts*

NWDR	Nordwestdeutscher Rundfunk
NZZ	*Neue Zürcher Zeitung*
OMGUS	Office of Military Government for Germany (United States)
OWI	Office of War Information
PD	Pressedokumentation
PFD	Partei Freier Demokraten
PS	Plakatsammlung
Pslg.	Plakatsammlung
PT	Parteitag
PV	Parteivorstand
PWD	Psychological Warfare Division
RB	Radio Bremen
RHEINA	Rheinische Nachrichtenagentur
RIAS	Radiosender im amerikanischen Sektor
RPD	Republikanische Partei Deutschlands
RSF	Radikal-Soziale Freiheitspartei
SAP	Sozialistische Arbeiterpartei Deutschlands
SDAP	Sozialdemokratische Arbeiterpartei
SDR	Süddeutscher Rundfunk
SDS	Sozialistischer Deutscher Studentenbund
SED	Sozialistische Einheitspartei Deutschlands
SGK	Sonderstelle Geld und Kredit
SHAEF	Supreme Headquarters Allied Expeditionary Force
SHB	Schleswig-Holstein Block
SM	*Sozialistische Monatshefte*
SMAD	Sowjetische Militäradministration in Deutschland
SME	Social Market Economy
SMW	Soziale Marktwirtschaft
SP	Sozialdemokratische Partei
SPD	Sozialdemokratische Partei Deutschlands
spd	Sozialdemokratischer Pressedienst
SPF	Sozialdemokratische Partei Flensburg
SPS	Sozialdemokratische Partei Saar
SSV/SSW	Südschleswigscher Verein/Südschleswigscher Wählerverband
StAB	Stadtarchiv Bonn
StAF	Staatsarchiv Freiburg
StAK	Stadtarchiv Köln
StBKAH	Stiftung Bundeskanzler-Adenauer-Haus
SÜDENA	Süddeutsche Nachrichtenagentur
SVHP	Sozialer Volksbund Hessen-Pfalz

SWF	Südwestfunk
StBA	Statistisches Bundesamt Deutschland
StLA	Statistisches Landesamt
StZ	*Stuttgarter Zeitung*
StVW	Stadtverwaltung
SZ	*Süddeutsche Zeitung*
USFET	US Forces European Theater
VBH	Vaterstädtischer Bund Hamburg
VfW	Verwaltung für Wirtschaft
VfZ	Viertelsjahreshefte für Zeitgeschichte
VV WR	Vollversammlung des Wirtschaftsrates
VWG	Vereinigtes Wirtschaftsgebiet
VZ	*Vossische Zeitung*
WAV	Wirtschaftlicher Aufbauverein
WB	Wörtliche Berichte und Drucksachen des Wirtschaftsrats
WB VfW	Wissenschaftliche Beirat bei der Verwaltung für Wirtschaft
WB VV	Wörtliche Berichte über die 1.-40. Vollversammlung des Wirtschaftsrates des Vereinigten Wirtschaftsgebietes
WDR	West-Deutscher-Rundfunk
WEA	Walter Eucken Archiv, Frankfurt a. Main
WEI	Walter Eucken Institut, Freiburg i. Breisgau
WiGBl.	Gesetz- und Verordnungsblatt der Verwaltung des Vereinigten Wirtschaftsgebiets
WipoG	Wirtschaftspolitische Gesellschaft von 1947 e.V.
WR	Wirtschaftsrat
Z	Deutsche Zentrumspartei or Zentrum (*pol.*)
ZA	Zonenausschuss
ZAS	Zeitungsausschnittsammlung

CHRONOLOGY

23 May 1945	Former Reich Government are imprisoned by Allies after unconditional surrender on 8 May
5 June	Allies claim governmental authority in Germany
10 June	Soviet military authorities permit the foundation of anti-fascist parties and unions
17 June	Rhenish CDU is founded
1 July	*Kölner Leitsätze* as programmatic foundation of CDU are adopted
17 July–2 Aug	Potsdam Conference (Berlin Conference)
30 July	First meeting of Control Council in Berlin
6 Aug	Field Marshal Montgomery (GB) and Gen. Eisenhower (USA) declare to foster political parties in Germany
1 Sep	Approval of democratic political parties in the Anglo-American zone
11 Sep–2 Oct	First Conference of Allied Ministers of Foreign Affairs in London
19 Sep	American Military Government form Hesse, Bavaria and Wuerttemberg
13 Oct	Formation of the CSU in Bavaria
30 Oct	First nationalisations in Soviet occupation zone
6 Nov	*Länderrat* constitutes (Bavaria, Hesse, Wuerttemberg)
14–16 Dec	'*Reichstreffen*' in Bad Godesberg: Christian democratic parties form CDU
20 Jan 1946	First municipal elections in American occupation zone
27 Jan	First communal and local elections in Bavaria and Wuerttemberg-Baden

1 Mar	CDU Party Convention in Neheim-Hüsten: Konrad Adenauer is elected as chairman of the CDU in British occupation zone
1 Apr	First edition of *Frankfurter Hefte*
19 Apr	Communists and Social Democrats form SED in Soviet zone
25 Apr–12 July	Second Conference of Allied Ministers of Foreign Affairs in Paris: James F. Byrnes (US Secretary of State) requests the consolidation of the four zones; only Great Britain accepts (29 July)
28 Apr	Communal and local elections in Bavaria, Hesse, Wuerrtemberg-Baden
9–11 May	First party convention of the SPD in the western zones (Hanover) elects Kurt Schumacher as chairman, Erich Ollenhauer elected representative chairman
26 May	Communal and local elections in Bavaria and Hesse
5 June	Winston Churchill speaks of 'Iron Curtain'
21/22 June	German economic experts and politicians convene in Hamburg in order to discuss economic direction of post-war Germany
28/29 Aug	*Arbeitsgemeinschaft der CDU/CSU in Deutschland* convenes in Königstein
6 Sep	Speech by US Secretary of State James F. Byrnes in Stuttgart
15 Sep	First communal and local elections in Baden, Lower Saxony, North Rhine-Westphalia, Rhineland-Palatinate, Schleswig-Holstein, Wuerttemberg-Hohenzollern and the Saarland
13 Oct	Communal and local elections in Baden, Bremen, Hamburg, North Rhine-Westphalia, Rhineland-Palatinate, Schleswig-Holstein, Wuerttemberg-Hohenzollern
20 Oct	Local elections in Berlin
4 Nov–11 Dec	Third Conference of Allied Ministers of Foreign Affairs in New York
24 Nov	First democratic *Landtag* elections in Wuerttemberg-Baden
1 Dec	First *Landtag* elections in Bavaria and Hesse
2 Dec	Signing of the Bevin–Byrnes Agreement Bavarian Constitution proclaimed
11 Dec	Hessian Constitution proclaimed

1 Jan 1947	American and British occupation zones form Bizone
3 Feb	*Ahlener Programm* (CDU) adopted by the CDU
5/6 Feb	*Arbeitsgemeinschaft der CDU/CSU Deutschlands* constituted
10 Mar–24 Apr	Fourth Conference of Allied Ministers of Foreign Affairs in Moscow
12 Mar	Proclamation of the Truman Doctrine
20 Apr	First democratic *Landtag* elections in Lower Saxony, North Rhine-Westphalia, Schleswig-Holstein
18 May	First democratic *Landtag* elections in Baden, Rhineland-Palatinate, Wuerttemberg-Hohenzollern
29 May	'Agreement for Reorganisation of Bizonal Economic Agencies' signed by Military Governors Lucius D. Clay and Sir Brian Robertson
5 June	George C. Marshall outlines his economic plan at Harvard University
6–8 June	Prime Ministers Conference in Munich
10 June	'Agreement for Reorganisation of Bizonal Economic Agencies' becomes effective
25 June	Economic Council convenes in Frankfurt am Main
15 July	JCS 1067 abrogated
24 July	Election of Director of the VfW in the Economic Council; SPD decides to go in opposition because of disagreement with conservatives
29 Aug	Revised *Industrieplan* for the Bizone
5 Oct	First democratic *Landtag* elections in Saarland
12 Oct	Local elections in Bremen
25 Nov–15 Dec	Fifth Conference of Allied Ministers of Foreign Affairs in London
7 Dec	Communal and local elections in Wuerttemberg-Baden
7/8 Jan 1948	US and GB military governors convene with Prime Ministers and representatives of the Bizone to discuss reform of Bizone
24 Jan	Johannes Semler dismissed as Director of the Administration for Economics
9 Feb	'Frankfurt Charta' becomes effective: duplication of delegates in the Economic Council (104 members), *Länderrat* as second chamber (instead of Economic Committee), power of veto and initiation of legislation, Administrative Council with *Oberdirektor* as quasi-parliament

24 Feb	First plenary meeting of second or enlarged Economic Council
1 Mar	Foundation of *Bank deutscher Länder* (later *Bundesbank*) by military governors of the three western zones in Frankfurt am Main
2 Mar	Second election of directors in the Economic Council; Ludwig Erhard becomes Director of the VfW
20 Apr–8 June	German currency experts prepare insulated (conclave of Rothwesten) and under Allied instructions technical implementation of currency reform
21 Apr	Keynote address of Ludwig Erhard in Economic Council
25 Apr	Communal and local elections in Bavaria and Hesse
30 May	Communal elections in Bavaria
17/18 June	*Gesetz über Leitsätze für die Bewirtschaftung und Preispolitik nach der Geldreform* passed by Economic Council
18 June	Currency reform in West Germany Berlin Blockade
19 June	Currency reform in Soviet occupation zone
21 June	Erhard declares programmatic reorganisation of the economy
22 June	Double currency in Berlin
1 July	Handing over of *Frankfurt Documents* to Prime Ministers
7 July	*Rittersturz* Conference
14 July	Prime Ministers of American zone of occupation meet with Gen. Lucius D. Clay
10–23 Aug	*Herrenchiemsee* Convent drafts Constitution for Germany
1 Sep	Parliamentary Council assembles
2 Sep	Periodical publication of price comparison list started
7 Oct	*Gesetz gegen Preistreiberei* passed
17 Oct	Communal and local elections in North Rhine-Westphalia
24 Oct	Communal and local elections in Schleswig-Holstein
3 Nov	Abolition of pay freeze
5 Nov	Communal and local elections in Wuerttemberg-Hohenzollern
10 Nov	Second motion of no confidence against Erhard fails
12 Nov	General strike (9.2 million workers demonstrate for 24 hours)
14 Nov	Communal and local elections in Baden, Rhineland-Palatinate, Wuerttemberg-Hohenzollern
16 Nov	Formation of Price Council

28 Nov	Communal and local elections in Lower Saxony
2 Dec	First *Lastenausgleichsgesetz* (*'Soforthilfegesetz'*) adopted
5 Dec	Local elections in West Berlin
11 Dec	Formation of the FDP in the western occupation zones
28 Jan 1949	Formation of *Sozialpolitische Arbeitsgemeinschaft des VWG* (later: *Bundesvereinigung der deutschen Arbeitgeberverbände*)
29 Jan	Formation of *Deutscher Beamtenbund* (after 1950: *Deutscher Beamtenbund – Gewerkschaft der Berufsbeamten*)
27 Mar	*Landtag* elections in Saarland
8 Apr	Accession of French zone of occupation to Bizone forms Trizone
4 May	End of Berlin Blockade
23 May	Promulgation of Basic Law in Bonn
15 July	*Arbeitsgemeinschaft der CDU/CSU Deutschlands* adopts *Düsseldorfer Leitsätze*
14 Aug	First *Bundestag* elections
16 Aug	Final meeting between the representatives of the bizonal administration with the Allied Military Governors
18 Aug	News agencies of the three western zones of occupation (dena, dpd, südena) form dpa
12 Sep	Theodor Heuss elected first president of Federal Republic of Germany
15 Sep	First *Bundestag* convenes and elects Konrad Adenauer to Chancellor
20 Sep	Formation of coalition government by CDU/CSU, FDP and DP
13 Oct	Foundation of *Deutscher Gewerkschaftsbund* (DGB)
16 Oct	*Landtag* elections in Hamburg
19 Oct	Formation of *Ausschuss für Wirtschaftsfragen industrieller Verbände* (after 1950: *Bundesverband der Deutschen Industrie*)

ACKNOWLEDGEMENTS

It is rather surprising to recall how many people have helped in many different ways with the completion of this monograph, based on my interdisciplinary study at the University of Oxford, incorporating elements of economic, political and communication research. This is my opportunity to express my gratitude, and I am delighted to take it.

For inspiring discussions, I would like to thank Dieter Roth (*Forschungsgruppe Wahlen* Mannheim) and Frank Brettschneider (University of Hohenheim), to whom I owe the very initiative to undertake this research. While Elisabeth Noelle-Neumann (IfD Allensbach) provided me with comprehensive data regarding public opinion, I am most indebted to Hartmut J. O. Pogge von Strandmann (University College) for the conceptual design, constructive criticism and continual support.

Archival research is possible only if access both to archives and to particular sources is granted: it is here that I record my gratitude to Andreas Müller-Armack and Christine Blumenberg-Lampe. Spending weeks in the archives, often partnerships and even friendships develop. For most fruitful and productive co-operation, I should like to thank Nils Goldschmidt (WEI), Hans-Jürgen Klegraf (ADCP), Christoph Stamm (AdsD), Renate Höpfinger (ACSP), Andreas Schirmer (ALES), Brigitte Nelles (DBt PA), Hans-Joachim Bödler (BA), Karl-Ulrich Gelberg (BayHstA), Elisabeth Skrip (BPA), and Konrad Schneider (IStGF).

Carrying out archival research in Germany was accompanied by seminars at the University of Bonn and the *Institut Universitaire de Hautes Études Internationales* (IUHEI) in Geneva, where I held an EUROPAEUM research fellowship in 2004/2005. There, the discussions with Günther Schulz and Pierre du Bois (†) proved to be enormously enriching.

For supportive advice on specific aspects of this study, I give my thanks to Günter Grosche (European Commission), Ernst Bollinger (†), Louis Bosshart and Anne-Marie Carrel (*Université de Fribourg*), Robert Jeremy A. I. Catto and Ian Forrest (Oriel College), Patricia Clavin (Jesus College), Keith Tribe (University of Sussex) and Niall Ferguson (Harvard).

In addition to academic support, financial assistance was provided by the University of Oxford, Peter de H. Collett and Ernest Nicholson from Oriel College, and the Sir Richard Stapley Educational Trust.

For editing and constuctive criticism, I thank Joanna Godfrey. More thanks are due to Jane Caplan (European Studies Centre, St Antony's College), Penelope and Francis Warner (St Peter's College) as well as to Joanna Dennison (Oxford Tutorial College), for whom I taught in all my years in Oxford; and, not to be overlooked, to my fellow students and friends Jens-Wilhelm Wessels (†), Jochen W. Klingelhöfer, Camilla Oxley, Theresa D'Aligny, Christoffer Koch, Dennis Lehmkuhl, Josef C. Karl, Matthias Uhl, Julia DeClerck-Sachsse, Charley Choe, Almuth Wietholtz, Thomas Schmelzer, Florian Sturm and Parnesh Sharma, who were constant reminders of how productive and valuable it can be to work close to someone who shares the same academic idiosyncrasies and obsessions. It would prolong this acknowledgement intolerably if I were to name all those friends who have in one way or another, by drawing my attention to sources which I had overlooked or by discussing the problems of the period, provided me with fresh material and stimulus. I hope they forgive me for acknowledging their generous help in this global and anonymous expression of thanks, which is nonetheless sincere.

I am also most grateful to Javier Cuadriello-Rodriguez, Timothy J. Durkin, Nils Baus, Philippe Sacher, Markus Kitzmüller, Christina Franca Berger, Karin Christina Längle, Heiko J. Trautwein, Mario Gstrein, Sven Mangels, Edmund Fono (†) and Michael Schmauser, who proved to be a source of constant encouragement, sound advice, and genuine friendship.

Finally, emotional support is as important as intellectual stimulus. Anna, Lies' and Christina as well as my father Ludwig and my brothers Thomas and Stefan provided both. To them I dedicate this book with love and thanks for keeping faith in me.

Academic protocol and tradition require that I absolve all from culpability for any errors or omissions, which remain; they deserve praise without responsibility.

PREFACE

The phenomena of increasing so-called economic globalisation, Europeanisation with the quest for a European social contract, and German unification have called into question the much praised German triad of democracy, market economy, and welfare state. Mainly free market capitalism exerts pressure on the Social Market Economy, which has been Germany's distinguished 'Third Way' of regulatory policy between centralist socialism and unbridled capitalism. Although intended to be a flexible system able to adapt to changing economic conditions, the model is undergoing a major revision. Thus, more than sixty years after its entry into force, the economic and socio-political concept is once more subject to debate. Unlike then, today parties across the political spectrum adhere to the Social Market Economy and the so-called *Ökonomisierungsdebatte* (debate on the (ir)reconcilability between social responsibility and capitalist profit seeking) in politics and public alike is on corporate governance and the form of capitalism. Whereas today the discussion in the *Bundestag* centres on capitalism versus capitalism, the debate in the first post-war parliament and progenitor of the German *Bundestag*, the Economic Council, in the years of German economic reorganisation was on capitalism versus socialism.

In view of the continuing debate regarding the *reformation* of the economic system, it is interesting to examine the public debate and opinion at the time of the *formation* of the Social Market Economy. Although there is considerable literature on German post-war history, the communication of policy, public opinion and civil engagement during the period of economic and political reconstruction have been largely neglected in academic research. This study on the economic reconstruction of post-war West Germany traces the development of ideas about economic and socio-political publicity, and their gradual absorption by mainstream politicians, officials and the general public during the period of transition between 1945 and 1949. In those years, several German think tanks, political parties and individuals gave impulse to and then shaped the development of a viable socio-political and economic alternative between the extremes of *laissez-faire* capitalism and the collectivist planned economy. In their endeavours to bring into effect their particular economic ideas – often diametrically opposed to one another – the parties of left and right stimulated not only academic and political but also public debate about the political and economic reconstruction of occupied post-war Germany. While all the various neo-liberal approaches attached to the people sovereign and decisive status in the institutional economic order, and recognised the interdependence of politics, economics and the public, one particular school of economic thought outpaced the others in communicating a model of coordinated economic and social policy, namely the Social Market Economy. This research investigates whether or not it was primarily the subtlety of the political campaign for this model that led to its implementation by the then Economic Council and eventual validation by the German electorate. In this connection, the programmes published by the principal academic and political groups of the time and the practical day-to-day decisions of the first parliament in post-war Germany are analysed with reference to popular preferences. By examining both the constitutive involvement of German parties in post-war reconstruction and the role of the public during the process of economic liberalisation, this study provides alternative explanations for why the Social Market Economy prevailed as the socio-political and economic model for the Federal Republic of Germany.

Christian L. Glossner

INTRODUCTION

The history of the Federal Republic of Germany is mainly its economic policy. Nothing shaped the West German state more than its economic-political development. The economy not only created the foundation for the emergence of stable forms of democracy but also for the international emancipation of the legal successor of the Third Reich; the economy was vehicle for national identification and self-conception.[1]

(Werner Abelshauser, 1983)

The constitutional and economic foundations of the Federal Republic of Germany (FRG), and in particular the introduction of the Basic Law and the Social Market Economy, have received general praise. Whereas the constitutional developments in the Parliamentary Council have been much studied, economic developments in general and the Economic Council in particular, West Germany's first post-war legislative parliament and progenitor of the German *Bundestag*, have received considerably less attention. The current political and public debate on the reformation of Germany's socio-political and economic arrangements and the recent constitutional anchoring of the Social Market Economy in the Treaty establishing a Constitution for the European Union,[2] however, draw attention to the formation of the distinctive German model of economic and social policy and to the constitutive forces behind the political and economic reconstruction of occupied post-war Germany. While undoubtedly the Allies set the political, economic and institutional framework in this transition period between the imprisonment of the last Reich Government in May 1945 and the swearing-in of the democratically elected Adenauer cabinet in autumn 1949, some confusion remains about the extent of German involvement in the political and economic reorganisation of post-war West Germany. Despite the widely held perception that economic policy was imposed by the occupying powers and that Germans were mere objects of Allied policy,[3] there is concrete evidence of the active involvement of several German academics and of the main political parties in the post-war economic reconstruction. Often overlooked, the various conceptions by German parties gave impulse to and shaped political and economic developments.

For many years, however, the prehistory of the Federal Republic and the constitutive period between 1945 and 1949 were predominantly examined in relation to international politics and the dominant role of the Allies.[4] The assumptions in many scholarly works that the conflict over socio-political systems among the four victorious Allied nations had a predetermining effect on the socio-political and economic (re)formation of defeated Germany, and further that the occupying powers constituted the fundamental factor in subsequently shaping the political and economic developments has meant that the contribution of German parties to the reorganisation of post-war West Germany has been neglected in historical and political research.[5] The prime reason for the paucity of German academics writing about the prehistory of Federal Germany can be seen in their initial reservations about confronting their own shameful national history, aggravated by the allegations made by the 1960s student protesters that the old political and economic elites had been partly, albeit covertly, restored. Eventually, growing consciousness of their own constitutional past detached from the self-inflicted disaster of the inglorious Third Reich, with its painful and soul-destroying consequences for the German people, along with the gradual accessibility of archival sources, prompted an increasing interest in the socio-political and economic developments during the Allied occupation which is expressed in later accounts and editions;[6] no longer could the prehistory of the Federal Republic of Germany be considered the blind spot of research as described by Hans-Peter Schwarz in 1966.[7] Most studies, however, concentrate on political and constitutional developments[8] and relatively few publications recount the economic reorganisation and resurgence of post-war West Germany. While some of these argue that the post-war German economic 'miracle' had its roots in the policies of the former Minister for Armaments and War Production, Albert Speer, and the investments of the Nazis in the 1930s,[9] others built on the restoration paradigm by denying that the economic resurgence was initiated by German parties but rather by the international trading system and by the fact that the nation fell into longer-term trends of twentieth-century economic growth.[10] More balanced accounts have weighed the relative importance of domestic approaches and policies versus the importance of international and historical economic patterns determining West Germany's economic reconstruction.[11] In examining German influence in the course of post-war West Germany's socio-political and economic reorganisation and resurgence, however, historians, economists and political scientists have focused on Ludwig Erhard and his policies encapsulated in the concept of the Social Market Economy.[12] This meant that other German parties' ideas and efforts to influence the post-war economic reconstruction were widely eclipsed.

This study seeks to illuminate the individual academic and political approaches of that time. However, this research is confined to the activities of the three most influential schools of economic thought, namely the academically little researched *Arbeitsgemeinschaft Erwin von Beckerath* (AG_{EvB}) within the Freiburg Circles,[13] the often misleadingly equated but distinctly different ordo-liberal Freiburg School with its main proponent Walter Eucken,[14] and, finally, the Cologne School of Economics around Alfred Müller-Armack.[15] The reason for this confinement is that other economic programmes and doctrines, principally Marxism or communism, were either prevented by the occupying powers or were discredited and thus their influence remained negligible. Apart from German think tanks and individuals, naturally the major political parties gave impulse to and then shaped economic developments in occupied Germany. Thus, this book includes the economic and socio-political conceptions of the socialist *Sozialdemokratische Partei Deutschlands* (SPD),[16] the conservative *Christlich-Demokratische Union* (CDU)[17] as well as the programmatically and organisationally different Bavarian *Christlich-Soziale Union* (CSU). While the first two *Volksparteien* (people's parties) and their respective economic philosophies are relatively well researched, the socio-political and economic programme of the latter has received considerably less attention with a few notable though incomplete exceptions.[18] Largely, this desideratum with regard to the CSU and Bavaria's economic reconstruction seems due to the fact that more and more regional responsibilities were passed to the bizonal then trizonal Economic Council and to the widespread misconception that the CDU and CSU shared the same economic policy.[19] Moreover, the liberal *Freie Demokratische Partei* (FDP) and the *Kommunistische Partei Deutschlands* (KPD) must be acknowledged as political alternatives distinct from the above-mentioned parties; but, both being small in size and with varying degrees of potential importance, they have received relatively little attention in academic research,[20] and informative publications on their socio-political and economic concepts are still missing. With regard to the political parties and their respective *Fraktionen*, i.e. parliamentary party groups in the first legislative parliament in the Anglo-American Bizone, the emerging Economic Council is also subject to examination. Although this research could draw on the edited minutes of the caucuses of the SPD[21] and CDU/CSU,[22] one should not forget that these records had to be submitted for approval to the Allied military authorities; therefore, changes of wording – if traceable – need to be observed. While the stance of the SPD on the formulation and implementation of an economic model for post-war Germany has been extensively examined,[23] a detailed study on the CDU/CSU parliamentary group and a lengthy monograph on the Bizonal Economic Council in general are still missing. In examining the respective academic and political ambitions to influence the economic policy in post-war West Germany and to eventually implement their particular economic system for the emerging Federal Republic of Germany entering force in 1949, the focus has been on neither the genesis nor the theoretical definition of individual economic concepts but on their respective communication to both the political classes and the public.

Despite increasing research and interest on the formation of the German post-war economic model,[24] the communications of academic concepts and party programmes to the public and the involvement of the German people in political and economic decision-making have not been adequately explored. Anton Riedl's doctoral thesis on the backing given to Ludwig Erhard's politics by liberal sectors of opinion forms a prominent exception; but it is rather selective in its study of the media, and is focused on the post-1949 era.[25] Similarly, Mark E. Spicka's examination of election propaganda and various public relations campaigns, reflecting new electioneering techniques borrowed from the United States, such as public opinion polling and advertising techniques, is confined to conservative political and economic groups seeking to construct and sell a political meaning of the Social Market Economy and the economic miracle in West Germany during the 1950s.[26] Thus, by examining the role of the public as actual sovereign in the formation and implementation of a particular socio-political and economic model for post-war Germany, this research aims to fill this gap in popular and academic writing, and to contribute to the historical understanding of the economic reconstruction of post-war Germany.

Both the Allies and German political parties aimed to design a democratic economic system consistent with the preferences of the citizens. In view of the inhumane totalitarianism and militarism of National Socialism, any new socio-political and economic order was supposed to be democratic and foster a humane and free society based on Christian values. In this regard, Immanuel Kant's postulate for solidarity and Georg Wilhelm Friedrich Hegel's accentuation of reconciliation and of the dialectic abolition of inequalities became the categorical imperatives. Although the German idea of the state had historically been formulated by Johann Gottlieb Fichte, Ferdinand Lassalle, and Johann Karl Rodbertus, as a *Volksgemeinschaft* (people's community) in which the individual has less rights but rather duties, rejecting the interventionist state of the Third Reich and protecting the individual from collectivism necessarily meant adding the principle of subsidiarity. In this respect, the sovereignty of the solidary citizen became *the* fundamental normative principle and public acceptance became *the* relevant legitimising criterion for any political action. Thus, in line with these claims, the public were doubly the focal point: according to Ludwig Erhard, the principles of solidarity, subsidiarity, and sovereignty could be achieved only if the public were determined to ascribe them priority;[27] economic policy, being contingent on public acceptance, likewise had to ascribe priority to the people. In this connection, the triad of solidarity, subsidiarity, and sovereignty tended to lead to a 'Third Way' between *laissez-faire* capitalism and collectivist socialism not only in socio-political and economic terms, but also in philosophical ones.[28] Rejecting capitalist individualism and socialist collectivism alike, this so-called 'solidarism' or 'personalism'[29] became characteristic of any socio-political and economic concept put forth, and in particular the Social Market Economy. Starting from the premise that its theoretical foundation, i.e. ordo-liberalism, aimed to underpin a framework that encouraged ordinary people to pursue their own interests together with the common good, Walter Eucken *et al.* elaborated the interdependence of politics, economics and the public, which finally became both the foundation and subject of institutional and constitutional economics. It is the examination of this interdependence between politics and the public that constitutes the conceptual architecture of this research.

In order to assess the political communication as well as public reception of emerging socio-political and economic models for post-war Germany, this book is divided into two sections: while the first one discusses the various academic and political concepts of economic policy and their respective communication to both the political classes and the public, the second section is concerned with the subsequent political implementation of the prevailing Social Market Economy and the public reception of economic liberalisation. This process of political communication, defined as transmission of policy between political elites and the public,[30] not only reveals the statements by those who became active in post-war German politics and the reflections of what they considered to be the popular mood, but it eventually accommodates the posit for democratic action. In order to provide an accurate assessment of the various academic and political models of economic policy and their respective communication to the public, all then available channels for the transmission of economic and political content are evaluated: publications by academics and policy-makers, newspapers and party press, radio and election campaigns, press conferences, and, additionally, posters and pamphlets or political leaflets as underestimated but by all means informative documentation illustrating abstracted political ideas. In doing so, it is of particular importance to, initially, examine and consider both the economic difficulties and the restricted political circumstances inherent in times of occupation. Furthermore, the political aspect carries another dimension, namely the rejection of authoritarianism and the diminished credibility of political authorities and the media. These factors shaped the prevailing mentality of the German people; this, in turn, had a predetermining effect on both the character and the promotion of any economic ideas.

The process of political communication examined in the first section not only considers the demand for democratic political action, but also shows that governance emphasising communication and thus discussion was decisive in the formation of public opinion. Citizens' preferences and orientations towards issues of political substance, in turn, formed guidelines for political conduct. Such a Habermasian deliberative, discursive or participative democracy, however, required the informed citizen to commit himself to public deliberation and political affairs.[31] It is in this context of government *for* the people but also of government *by* the people, and in accordance with the axiom of David Hume that government is founded on public opinion,[32] that Article 20 paragraph 2 of the Basic Law for the Federal Republic of Germany – '*Alle Staatsgewalt geht vom Volke aus*' (all state authority shall be derived from the people) – must be viewed.[33] Due to this commitment and the importance of public acceptance as prerequisite for democracy, and thus also the implementation of the Social Market Economy as a democratic economic model for post-war Germany, one may therefore fundamentally expect an increased government responsiveness to public will. With regard to public opinion both about economic liberalisation and about the policy responsiveness of the first parliament, i.e. the Economic Council, in post-war West Germany between 1945 and 1949, ambiguity exists even in scholarly writings and academic research; what little there is appears contradictory and incomplete.[34]

Thus, the second section concerned with the subsequent implementation of the prevailing Social Market Economy assesses public opinion regarding the most salient aspects of economic liberalisation and investigates whether the conduct of the Economic Council was in accordance with the preferences of the German public. Where traceable, the influence of interest groups and the general public on the political decision-making process will be considered. In order quantitatively and qualitatively to gauge both representative public opinion and policy responsiveness over time, this research considers in the first instance the extensive public opinion polls conducted by the United States' Office of Military Government for Germany (OMGUS) as well as opinion surveys by German public opinion research institutions, namely the *Institut für Demoskopie* (IfD) (Institute for Public Opinion Polling) and the institute for the *Erforschung der öffentlichen Meinung, Marktforschung, Nachrichten, Informationen und Dienstleistungen* (EMNID) (Ascertainment of Opinion, Market Research, News, Information and Services). Taking into account the arguable methodological shortcomings of public opinion polling regarding empirical validity, this study includes petitions and resolutions by German organisations and individuals sent to the Economic Council and its delegates. Furthermore, the numerous articles and reports on economic affairs in licensed daily newspapers are vital sources for indicating the resonance of political decisions. Next to official intra-party discussion papers and minutes of the respective caucuses in the Economic Council as well as reports by various local governments on the perceived public sentiment regarding economic issues, the public debate accompanying the then economic policy is often reflected in political actors' private memoirs, diaries and notes. While the general public's attitude towards economic liberalisation and its consequences occasionally found its expression in strikes and protests, it eventually became manifest in the results of democratic elections on a local, regional and federal level. In its claim for a thorough and scholarly assessment, this research not only incorporates new archival material and primary sources but also methods not applied before. The archival sources and academic literature on this subject are more by necessity than by deliberate focus primarily German in source. Furthermore material in other languages is scarce, as this topic does not appear to have invited much study by British and other non-German scholars.

Historical awareness is not an inherent value but rather a necessary intellectual corrective. By examining both the constitutive involvement of German parties in post-war reconstruction and the role of the public during the process of economic liberalisation, this research seeks to complete the study of the little explored interplay and mutual interdependence between politics and the public at that time. A better historical understanding of this reciprocal process also reveals the actors and factors which proved to be formative in the implementation and eventual validation of the Social Market Economy as the principal socio-political and economic model for the Federal Republic of Germany.

PART I

CONCEPTION AND COMMUNICATION

We will work, be happy with our lot, modest – and trust in God. Maybe one day there will be a new, admirable Germany again.[1]

(Ursula von Kardorff, 1945)

In May 1945 German administration virtually disintegrated and any reconstruction of governmental and institutional structures[2] could come only from outside. Initially, however, there was a vacuum not only in German government, but also in Allied policy regarding the economic and political reorganisation of post-war Germany. Although the occupying powers' determination to reform German policy, economy and society was resolute, there was neither a common Allied approach, due to a lack of consensus, nor were there singular and coherent individual plans on how to best achieve these goals.[3] The conferences of Casablanca, Teheran, and Yalta did not make statements on these subjects, but instead proclaimed the supremacy of the Allied Control Council,[4] and demanded the Germans' full and unconditional compliance with its instructions.

First the communiqué of the Potsdam Conference, released on 2 August 1945, contained detailed, indeed inconsistent, declarations which had a decisive impact on the development of German political life and thus on the reorganisation and development of the economy in post-war Germany. The agreement, or proclamation, on policy for the occupation and reconstruction aimed at outlawing National Socialism and abolishing its ramified system. In its place, the Potsdam Agreement sought to restore local self-government throughout Germany on democratic principles, and, in particular, through elective councils. Therefore, democratic parties with the right of assembly and public discussion were to be allowed and encouraged. Further, representative and elective principles were to be introduced into regional, provincial and *Länder* or state[5] administration as rapidly as might be justified by the successful application of these principles in local self-government.[6] However, German government at national level was to be limited to the establishment of certain essential central administrative departments particularly in the fields of finance, transport, communications, foreign trade and industry, headed by State Secretaries under the immediate supervision of the Allied Control Council.[7] Although the Allies rejected the dismemberment of Germany and considered the four occupation zones as 'a single economic unit',[8] the Council never succeeded in establishing these agencies for the administration of Germany as a whole. Hence, decisions had to be implemented separately and independently in each zone by its military governor.[9] As the United States, the United Kingdom, and France could not agree with the Soviet Union on the form and scope of a government for all of Germany, and were unwilling to delay further the return of responsibilities to the German people, the Allied effort to rule Germany by unanimous agreement of the representatives of the four occupying powers failed. However, while the Potsdam Agreement provided the formal basis for the most significant development of the time, i.e. German self-government, ironically, the disagreement among and intensified tensions between the Allies acted as a powerful impetus in the formation of old and new political parties and democratic institutions in post-war West Germany.

When it came to the acknowledgement and licensing of the newly (re)founded political parties, however, the approach and procedure in the various zones of occupation varied notably, and once more it was difficult for the occupying powers to arrive at rational and consistent policies.[10] Whereas the Soviet military authorities permitted and promoted the foundation of anti-fascist parties and unions, namely the KPD followed by the SPD, the CDU, and the *Liberal-Demokratische Partei Deutschlands* (LDPD), in their zone, which was formed by the *Länder* Brandenburg, Mecklenburg, Saxony, Saxony-Anhalt, Thuringia plus the Berlin boroughs of Mitte, Prenzlauer Berg, Pankow, Weissensee, Friedrichshain, Lichtenberg, Treptow and Köpenick, as early as June 1945, the occupying authorities in the French zone were more restrictive, not allowing the formation of political parties until the end of 1945. On 13 December 1945, a proclamation of the French Military Government granted political parties in the *Länder* Baden, Rhineland-Palatinate, Saarland, and Wuerttemberg-Hohenzollern, as well as in the boroughs of Wedding and Reinickendorf in Berlin, the right to register and campaign. In the following, on 16 December 1945, the *Badisch Christlich-Soziale Volkspartei* (BCSV) was formed but not approved until early February 1946; later, in

April 1947, the BCSV merged in the *CDU Baden* (CDUB), which was licensed in March 1946. The Liberals in the French zone of occupation, constituted of the *Liberal-Demokratische Partei* (LDP) and the *Sozialer Volksbund Hessen-Pfalz* (SVHP) which both formed the *Demokratische Partei Rheinland-Pfalz* (DPRP), appeared not before early 1947. However, the development of political parties beyond the borders of the French zone was hindered by the fact that visitors needed a special pass to enter that was difficult to obtain and often intentionally issued late with the consequence that appointments could not be met. The American and British authorities pursued a middle course by declaring, on 6 August, that the foundation of German parties (and unions) was to be fostered in their zones of occupation, which consisted of the *Länder* Bavaria, Bremen, Hesse, and Wuerttemberg-Baden and additionally, the boroughs of Neukölln, Kreuzberg, Tempelhof, Schöneberg, Steglitz and Zehlendorf on the one side, and the *Länder* Hamburg, Lower Saxony, North Rhine-Westphalia, Schleswig-Holstein, and the Berlin boroughs of Tiergarten, Charlottenburg, Wilmersdorf and Spandau on the other side.[11] Although further directives concretised the *modus operandi* concerning the authorisation of political parties, the first political parties that were initially cooperating through informal working committees were already formed in May 1945. The first local and municipal reestablishments of the western SPD organisation were initiated by Kurt Schumacher on 6 May 1945. While the CDU, which initially appeared under different names, was founded in Cologne on 17 June, and as the *Christlich-Demokratische Partei* (CDP) in Frankfurt on 15 September 1945 (later renamed CDU), it is difficult to pinpoint the precise date of formation of the Bavarian CSU between 12 September and 13 October 1945. However, the CSU received provisional permission by the Office of Military Government for Bavaria on 8 January 1946. The FDP, not offering a nationwide representation before the 11 December 1948, has its roots in the *Partei Freier Demokraten* (PFD) in Hamburg, the LDP in Hesse, the SVHP in Rhineland-Palatinate, and the *Demokratische Volkspartei* (DVP) in Wuerttemberg-Baden, which were (re)established in September, and finally in its immediate predecessor, the *Demokratische Partei Deutschlands* (DPD), founded on 17 March 1947. Finally, the *Niedersächsische Landespartei* (NLP) appeared in Lower Saxony and Bremen on 20 July 1945; the regional party was renamed *Deutsche Partei* (DP) in July 1947. These formal organisations were approved on a zone-wide basis in both territories of occupation in September 1945.[12] In doing so, only 'democratic' parties, namely those that had continued to exist in exile and/or had actively resisted the Third Reich, were initially licensed.[13] Essentially, despite an intended party pluralism in view of the exclusive domination of one governing party in the preceding years, generally only four political parties which had received supra-regional prominence were admitted in the three western zones of occupation: the oldest party, the socialist SPD, the communist KPD, the politically progressive and economically conservative FDP, and the conservative CDU. Without doubt, the Bavarian CSU needs to be added here; often misunderstood due to the fact that it widely cooperated with the CDU, it formally and organisationally constituted an independent party. Thus five parties, which could claim representative character at a zonal level, received a licence.[14] Among those, particularly the two people's parties SPD and the CDU held pre-eminent positions with regard to the formation and final implementation of the Social Market Economy in post-war West Germany.

As the western and eastern zones embarked on their steadily divergent economic and political paths, occupiers and occupied formed an increasingly close, albeit still unequal, partnership. Although one cannot necessarily infer that party formation meant that the supreme authority of the occupying powers was at an end, as suggested by Peter Pulzer,[15] it enabled and facilitated the emancipation of German politics. In particular the American authorities opted for a more cooperative approach and conciliatory attitude towards the West German people, which was reflected in the speech given by US Secretary of State, James F. Byrnes, in Stuttgart on 6 September 1946:

> When the ruthless Nazi dictatorship was forced to surrender unconditionally, there was no German government with which the Allies could deal. [...] It never was the intention of the American Government to deny to the German people the right to manage their own internal affairs as soon as they were able to do so in a democratic way with genuine respect for human rights and fundamental freedoms. [...] It is the view of the American Government that the German people throughout Germany, under proper safeguards, should now be given the primary responsibility for the running of their own affairs.[16]

On 11 July 1947, Washington issued new guidelines that replaced the former 'Directive 1067 by the Joint Chiefs of Staff (JCS) to the Commander-in-Chief of the US Forces of Occupation Regarding the Military Government of Germany in the Period Immediately Following the Cessation of Organised Resistance'. Whereas the latter temporary wartime document, issued on 26 April 1945, stated that 'no political activities of any kind shall be countenanced unless authorized,'[17] the new Directive 1779 articulated the determination to rehabilitate Germany and affirmed the new American goal to establish stable political and economic conditions in Germany to enable the country to make a maximum contribution to European recovery.[18] Thus, the American authorities encouraged German self-government and sought to establish a political organisation which derived from the people and was subject to their control, which operated in accordance with democratic electoral procedures and which was dedicated to uphold the basic civil and human rights of the individual.[19] Within these principles, the ultimate constitutional form of German political life was supposed to be left to the decision of the German people made freely in accordance with democratic processes. In doing so, all political parties whose programmes, activities and structure demonstrated their allegiance to democratic principles were encouraged, none enjoying a privileged status.[20] Thus the first occupying power to provide the essentials for a democratic structure was the US administration.[21] Initially, however, German politicians were recruited into the American governmental machinery[22] rather than democratically elected. On 28 May 1945, the former member of the conservative *Bayerische Volkspartei* (BVP) and founding member of the CSU, Fritz Schäffer, was appointed Prime Minister of Bavaria. Although he was arbitrarily dismissed just four months later, there were *Land* governments headed by appointed German politicians throughout the American occupation zone by the end of 1945. In order to provide for growing coherence of the individual *Länder* as policy-making units within the federal organised American sovereign territory, a so-called '*Länderrat*' (Council of States), composed of the respective Prime Ministers of the states in the American zone, was established in Stuttgart on 5 October 1945. Although the institution, designed primarily to coordinate the efforts of the governments of Bavaria, Hesse, Wuerttemberg-Baden, and Bremen in their attempts to reconstruct the economic and social system of their *Länder*, was not given executive authority, the *Länderrat*'s agreements, when approved by the Military Government, could be issued as decrees in each state. Nevertheless, the German officials were still appointees of the occupying authority and were neither selected by nor responsible to the German people. In making the German administration responsible to the people, the American Military Government for Germany argued for public elections to be held progressively from the village to the state level.

Regarding the electoral system, all western occupation powers virtually left the decision to the Germans in their respective zones while the Soviet occupiers resorted to the so-called 'unity list' system which pre-arranged quotas for the individual quotas to secure Communist dominance. Due to historical experience and in order to stabilise support for the emerging democratic political parties, seven of the originally eleven West German states, as well as the later Federal Republic as a whole, introduced electoral systems constituting compromises between majority vote and proportional representation; the four remaining states and West Berlin adopted the latter.[23] The idea of these mixed electoral systems, which aimed to combine the advantages inherent both in the majority vote system and proportional representation, was to elect a certain percentage of delegates directly by simple majority, and to take the votes cast for the defeated parties, which would otherwise be lost, and combine them on a higher level where they were used to allot the remaining seats to the representative party tickets.

Although for many it seemed too early in the occupation for the voters to have developed a real political interest which would draw them to the polls, the first elections were called in *Gemeinden* (villages) with fewer than 20,000 inhabitants in Hesse on 20 and 27 January, and in Bavaria and Wuerttemberg-Baden on 27 January 1946.[24] The elections for *Landkreise* (county councils) and councils in larger towns were held in April and the elections for *Stadtkreise* (city councils) took place in May.[25] In June, elections were held for constituent assemblies and by December of that year, the first *Land* constitutions were proclaimed in Bavaria and Hesse. The first *Landtag* elections (state legislature elections) were held in Wuerttemberg-Baden on 24 November and in Bavaria and Hesse on 1 December. As elections progressed, the *Länderrat* became increasingly conscious of its lack of a popular base and thus asked for permission to add an Advisory Parliamentary Council in September 1946. This advisory panel, which was not approved until after the state elections, was composed of 24 representatives from the elected state parliaments. Thus it indirectly provided some measure of popular support for the work of the *Länderrat*. The powers of the various state governments and legislatures were still circumscribed, but the political evolution of the American sovereign territory clearly showed the importance placed on government by both constitution and legitimation by popular sovereignty.

Both the British and the French authorities had different priorities. In contrast to the American, the British Military Government was slow to recruit German politicians into their policy-making apparatuses,[26] such as the *Zonenbeirat der Britischen Zone* (Advisory Council of the British Zone), or to proceed with elections. Municipal elections in the British occupation zone were not held until September and October 1946; *Landtag* elections took place even later in April 1947. Furthermore, unlike the American federal approach, the British treated their whole zone as an administrative unit and also favoured a central government for Germany. To this end, they set up a Central Economic Office in October 1946. Quite in contrast to the British conception of a centralised German administration, the

French Military Government on the other hand was unwilling to tolerate any German government above the district level, and delayed zonal elections.[27] Thus municipal elections, which formed the basis for consultative assemblies in the various *Länder* of the French sovereign territory, were not held until September and October 1946. The emerging constitutions in the French occupation zone were finally approved by popular referenda with simultaneous *Landtag* elections in May and October 1947.

When US Secretary of State, James F. Byrnes requested the consolidation of the four zones at the second Conference of Allied Ministers of Foreign Affairs in Paris between 15 June and 12 July 1946, precisely these abovementioned differences in approaches to returning post-war West Germany to self-government led to major dissension which, in turn, significantly affected German economic and political reconstruction.[28] As for the time being only Britain and the United States agreed on the amalgamation of their two zones – the French zone of occupation was eventually integrated on 8 April 1949 – the Anglo-American Economic Bizone or *Vereinigtes Wirtschaftsgebiet* (VWG), which included 50 per cent of German territory[29] and 39 million people corresponding to 64 per cent of the total German population at that time,[30] was stipulated. The relevant British–American agreement signed by the Ministers of Foreign Affairs Ernest Bevin and James F. Byrnes in New York on 2 December 1946 formed the legal framework for the Bizone, which finally became effective on 1 January 1947.[31] The aim of the Bevin–Byrnes Agreement was to implement the economic principles of the Potsdam Agreement in order to give Germany economic autonomy by the end of 1949.[32] Initially, however, the bizonal agreement was supposed to foster economic rather than political cooperation in order to cope with Germany's pressing economic needs in 1947. According to the proposals and provisional agreements on the part of the provincial governments in the American and British zone of occupation, five administrative authorities each headed by an Administrative Council were set up soon afterwards.[33] In order to prevent any appearance of political amalgamation, the various 'ministries' were dispersed over the area of the Bizone: the Administration for Food and Agriculture was set up in Stuttgart, the Transportation Unit in Bielefeld, the Head Office of Post and Communications in Frankfurt, the German Council of Finance – the official labelling of the Administration of Finance – in Frankfurt and later in Bad Homburg. The *Verwaltung für Wirtschaft* (VfW) (Administration for Economics) was constituted in Minden so it could organisationally emanate from the already existing Central Office for Economics of the British zone.[34] After the formal economic amalgamation of the American and British occupation zones, the deficiencies of the new structure became apparent, among which were: the spatial separation of central institutions in times of difficult conditions for transport and communications, the absence of both a coordinating authority and parliamentary control of the bizonal institutions, and, finally, the lack of legal competence. The different constitutional circumstances in both zones complicated the legislation procedure with the consequence that not a single act recommended by an administrative council was put into effect.[35] However, the first institutional manifestation of the Bizone failed not only because of its structural shortcomings, but also due to the Anglo-American antagonism regarding centralism versus federalism, aggravated by south German suspicion and a lack of genuine commonality of interest between the zones.[36] Despite obvious deficiencies neither the British nor the Americans wanted to change the institutional structures of the Bizone before the conference of the Foreign Ministers in Moscow between 10 March and 24 April 1947. After no agreement was reached there, the new American Secretary of State George C. Marshall instructed the then American Military Governor in Germany, General Lucius D. Clay, to push for organisational improvements in the Bizone. As early as on 29 May the two Military Governors Lucius D. Clay and Sir Brian Robertson – German negotiating partners were not invited – signed the 'Agreement for Reorganisation of Bizonal Economic Agencies'[37] resulting in the creation of the so-called '*Wirtschaftsrat*' (Economic Council) which became effective on 10 June 1947. In principle, the Economic Council consisted of three organs concentrated in Frankfurt am Main: the *Exekutivrat* (Executive Committee) as a second chamber with representatives of the eight *Länder* in the Bizone, the *Direktoren der Verwaltung* (Executive Directors) as quasi-ministers presiding over the five already existing administrations, and, finally, the actual *Wirtschaftsrat* as first post-war parliament.[38] In particular the latter was granted legislative and budgetary competence to facilitate the solution of pressing economic problems and the reconstruction of economic life.[39] On 25 June 1947, the 52 delegates elected in an indirect ballot of one delegate per 750,000 citizens by the *Landtage* (parliaments) of the eight *Länder* in the Bizone gathered in Frankfurt am Main;[40] on 9 August, the law for the reorganisation of the bizonal economic agencies was passed.[41] Soon afterwards, however, the constructional flaws of the Economic Council as a whole came to the fore requiring the reorganisation of the bizonal administration.[42] On 9 February 1948, the *Frankfurter Statut*[43] defining the changes to the Economic Council came into effect. These were the renaming of the Executive Committee as *Länderrat*, the creation of a *Verwaltungsrat* (Administrative Council) formed by the Executive Directors and supervised by a chairman officially titled

Oberdirektor, and, finally, the doubling of the delegates in the Economic Council, something which did not affect the proportion of political parties in this second economic parliament.[44] While the Economic Council was a decisive platform for the political debate and factual implementation of any emerging economic concept, the parliament's resolutions and acts remained subject to the authorisation by the Allied *Zwei-Zonen-Amt* (Bipartite Board) in Berlin and were controlled by the so-called '*Zweizonenkontrollamt*' (Bipartite Control Office) (BICO) in Frankfurt. Foreign trade and monetary transactions were carried out by the Allied Joint Export-Import Agency (JEIA). Due to the fact that the Economic Council was restricted in its legislative scope and also not a representative assembly elected by the plebiscite, the bizonal institution was often ill-regarded as quasi-parliament. Thus the formation of the Economic Council did not meet with public enthusiasm, and people did not feel themselves to be stepping into a new era. Nevertheless, this first German parliament after the Second World War was a central prerequisite for Germany's political and economic reconstruction and marked an important step towards German political and economic self-determination. Henceforth, German political parties were given the opportunity actively to conduct an economic policy and to affect the definition of an emerging economic model for post-war West Germany.

Due to the focus of this study on the communication of politics, it is essential to examine what options the interest groups and licensed political parties had in addressing the public and in disseminating their ideas and programmes in times of elections. Next to public speeches and those transmitted by radio, party publications, i.e. papers that are either owned by political parties, or are organisationally bound to or ideationally attached to them, and newspapers were seen as a very effective way of addressing the citizenry. In this process of political communication between political elites and the public, the media played indeed a key role because the content of most politically relevant information, as well as of conversations about politics, is generally dependent on information obtained from the media. As Walter Lippmann observed, most citizens do not experience the world of public affairs first-hand and instead are inherently dependent on the media for the 'pictures in our heads of the world outside'.[45] Further, media coverage of politics often stimulates informal discussions that might otherwise not take place. In these ways, the political information flow dynamic may be characterised as a process by which information from the media reaches the public both directly and through the filter of interpersonal discussion – often stimulated by so-called 'opinion leaders'.[46] However, whereas the media serve merely to reinforce preexisting opinions, it is rather the interpersonal context, which is more politically consequential for individual attitudes.[47] Political communication at the person-to-person, or dyadic, level is expected to be very influential precisely because of the homophilic nature of such interaction. This special power of one-to-one influence has received much empirical support, even from the early communication studies, which found that argumentative speech had more influence face-to-face than on individuals in an audience.[48] Nevertheless, whether the process is person-to-person, group-to-person, or opinion climate-to-person, these three levels of influence usually operate simultaneously and dynamically on the individual. In the aftermath of the Second World War and the downfall of the Third Reich, however, the interplay between politics and the media, usually generating publicity and providing platforms for debate,[49] occurred in a different framework.[50]

Already before the ending of the armed hostilities, the American Office of War Information (OWI), which was later replaced by an Assistant Secretary for Public Affairs, and the Anglo-American Psychological Warfare Division of the Supreme Headquarters Allied Expeditionary Force (PWD/SHAEF), which was succeeded by the Information Control Division (ICD) headed by General Robert A. McClure when the SHAEF ceased to exist on 14 May 1945, worked out a plan to establish a new press for occupied Germany. After the Allies agreed on the destruction of the Nazi press which constituted the majority of all newspapers in Germany – in 1944, only 977 newspapers were left in the Reich; of those, 352, with a circulation of 82.5 per cent of all German papers, belonged to the trust of the NSDAP[51] – the divestiture of publishing houses and reeducation of the German mind were envisaged in three systematic stages: initially, all publishing was stopped and editorial departments were dissolved; thereafter, so-called '*Heeresgruppen-Zeitungen*' (overt publications), namely newssheets exclusively edited and initially distributed free of charge, later for 20 *Pfennige* (pennies), by the military authorities, would supply the German people with information. In total, there were thirteen such publications with a total circulation of up to 4.6 million appearing between April and November 1945: *Kölnischer Kurier* (Cologne), *Frankfurter Presse* (Frankfurt am Main), *Hessische Post* (Kassel), *Braunschweiger Bote* (Braunschweig), *Ruhr-Zeitung* (Essen), *Bayerischer Tag* (Bamberg), *Münchener Zeitung* (Munich), *Süddeutsche Mitteilungen* (Heidelberg), *Weser Bote* (Bremen), *Regensburger Post* (Straubing), *Augsburger Anzeiger* (Augsburg), *Stuttgarter Stimme* (Stuttgart), *Allgemeine Zeitung* (Berlin).[52] These military publications, which were gradually replaced by semi-official papers, such as *Die Welt* in the British occupation zone, *Nouvelles de France – Westausgabe* (titled *West Echo* from 1948 onwards) in the French territory, and the *Neue Zeitung – Eine Amerikanische Zeitung für die Deutsche Bevölkerung* and the glossy *Heute* in the American zone, were served by specially set up news agencies: in the American occupation zone, this was the *Deutsche Allgemeine Nachrichtenagentur* (DANA), in the British zone the *Deutscher Pressedienst* (dpd), and the French military authorities established the *Rheinische Nachrichtenagentur* (RHEINA, later renamed *Süddeutsche Nachrichtenagentur*, SÜDENA). In August 1949, these news services formed the *Deutsche Presse-Agentur* (dpa). Subsequently, 'acceptable Germans',[53] i.e. skilled and politically untarnished publishers and journalists, would receive a licence to publish, albeit one subject to censorship commonly and effectively carried out via the rationing of paper. Finally, the press and other media equally affected by the Allied licensing would be transferred back to German information services by Germans under Allied supervision.[54] Thus in regard to the reconstruction of a democratic and non-party press, the Allies initially did not revert to the tradition of a free press in Germany but introduced a system of licensing instead. Although the occupying powers were aware of the fact that a democratic Germany, in which the formation of opinion leads to decision-making, required mediation between politics and the public and thus freedom of speech and its consequent means of publication,[55] the German media had to follow detailed instructions for a transition period, which gave them little scope for the transmission of political content. In contrast to the licensing of political parties, and notwithstanding the declarations in the Potsdam Agreement to foster German political life, newspapers, in particular those attached to political parties, were approved reluctantly. Although the Allies agreed upon German reeducation with 'austerity', there was no coordinated media policy. Directive 1067 of the Joint Chiefs of Staff, issued *inter alia* for this purpose and revised by the Informal Policy Committee on Germany (IPCOG) in April 1945, was adopted and put into practice by the American authorities alone. However, even among the Americans, the issues of collective guilt and how to reconstruct the German media were controversial. This, for instance, was expressed, in the contradictory interpretations of the directive, namely the versions 1067/1 and 1067/2 issued by the PWD on 22 May 1945 and 28 May 1945 respectively. Initially, however, all Allied regulations concerning the media were based on the law No. 191 issued by the PWD/SHAEF on 24 November 1944. According to this directive, the printing, production, publishing, marketing, sales and commercial distribution of newspapers, magazines, periodicals, books, brochures, placards, music supplies and other printed or mechanically duplicated publications, and the activity or operation of any news service or agencies were prohibited.[56] Only a few months later, however, an executive order, i.e. the Information Control Instruction No. 1, granted authorised German political parties the use of press, publications and other publicity media with the provisions of information control regulations, which specified that no person would operate such publicity media except under a licence granted by the Military Government through the District Information Services Control Command (DISCC).[57] The subsequent *Nachrichtenkontrollanweisung* (Information Control Instruction) No. 2, issued on 2 June 1945 pinpointed the use of information media: e.g. three copies of each publication had to be submitted to the local Military Government, the number of handbills was limited to ten per cent, and the number of posters to one per cent of the population, and even the size of these publications was exactly defined.[58] Thus the initially issued regulations were in principle conditional prohibitions varying between the zones of occupation.[59]

Apart from democratic principles, German political parties increasingly demanded an independent press, and equally party organs, in order to publish and legitimise their conduct, but also for revenue.[60] While the first independent German newspaper, the *Aachener Nachrichten*, which appeared once a week with a circulation of 12,000, was established by invading American forces as early as 24 January and eventually licensed by General McClure on 27 June 1945 (though the British authorities confirmed this licence granted to the Social Democrat Heinrich Hollands not before 1 March 1946), the American military authorities were suspicious of the political parties' efforts to establish a party press. Not merely were party organs unknown in the USA, but also the military authorities did not want to create competition to the licensed independent media. According to the Commander-in-Chief in the American zone, General Lucius D. Clay, in a letter to the War Department:

> This office does not believe there is any need for instructions in the US zone of Germany. While newspapers controlled by political parties are not permitted at the present time, this results from the need for the establishment of a strong independent press in the American zone in Germany and our inability to supply at present time sufficient newsprint to make this possible. Political parties are given newsprint to permit circulation to party news and views. However, we doubt the advisability of establishing subsidized party press [...]. Of course, it is our purpose when newsprint conditions permit to remove restrictions in licensing press, which would make it possible for any publisher not banned by denazification who is financially responsible to enter into news publishing field. [...] At present [...] we believe that the real answer to our press problem is the establishment of competitive independent papers in all large cities

> and our problem is directed to this end. We urge that we not be instructed to establish a party press until independent competitive newspapers are on a firm basis and there is sufficient newsprint to warrant allocation to other than an independent press. We do not believe that we can establish a free and independent press in Germany if we deviate from our present policy to attempt to establish with the limited newsprint now available party controlled newspapers, which would reduce the number of independent papers.[61]

Despite this statement, the successor organisation of the Psychological Warfare Division (PWD), the Information Control Division (ICD), abstained from imposing a ban on newspapers controlled by political parties, but rather justified the delay in licensing party papers by paper scarcity. In regard to licensing independent newspapers, it is important to mention that the officers assigned the task to license German media were mostly acquainted neither with German history nor politics; often they could not speak the language. Therefore, they had to rely on advice and translation from the occupied. This deficiency was also not moderated by the Manual for the Control of German Information Services edited and distributed for this purpose to the American staff in May 1945.[62] However, in order to assure a certain independence and 'that newspaper columns be open to all groups',[63] the papers were often edited by panels of people with different political dispositions and backgrounds. For instance, the first such *panel* newspaper was the *Frankfurter Rundschau*, which appeared from 1 August 1945. Its licence for publishing was shared by the Social Democrats Hans Etkorn, Paul Rodemann, and Wilhelm Knote, the former member of the *Zentrum* party, Wilhelm Karl Gerst, the two communists Emil Carlebach and Arno Rudert (though the latter one was not a member of the KPD), and, finally, Otto Grossmann who was not affiliated to any political party. For the licensed media, the military authorities edited general instructions, such as the bilingual *Fair Practice Guide* issued by the Information Control Division of the American Military Government in April 1947, which provided a guideline for journalists on content and form of articles.

Fuelled by frictions between the Allies and with due consideration to the necessity for maintaining military security, the Allied Control Council Directive No. 40 (Policy to be followed by German Politicians and the German Press) issued on 12 October 1946 finally allowed the German democratic parties and the German press to discuss freely German political problems. Furthermore, comments on the policy of the occupying powers in Germany and publications about world events, including informative articles from the foreign press, were allowed. However, members of German political parties and the German press had to refrain from all statements and from the publication or reproduction of articles which contributed towards the spreading of nationalistic, pan-Germanic, militarist, fascist or anti-democratic ideas.[64] While the area of conflict between the Soviet and the western zones of occupation on the one hand gave political parties the welcome opportunity to transmit political messages and programmes, on the other hand by mainly licensing non-party newspapers and clearly distinguishing between information and commentary, the American military authorities limited the development of party organs and the communist press in particular faced controls and restrictions. Despite various directives stating that 'every authorised political party should have the right freely to state its views and to present its candidates to the electorate, and [...] no curtailment of nor hindrance to the exercise of that right [is tolerated]',[65] the Commander-in-Chief in the American zone, General Lucius D. Clay, issued orders to 'combat communism in any form'.[66] Nonetheless, the majority of the German press in the American zone of occupation refused to take part in this anti-communist campaign. Thus very few anti-communist articles appeared in the licensed German press at that time.[67] After many licensees publicly denounced the American counter-propaganda as a return to the *Gleichschaltung* of the press, i.e. the systematic elimination and consolidation of the press, the Information Control Division, headed by Colonel Gordon E. Textor, reacted with the revocation of licences; often the communist press was explicitly forbidden and had its property confiscated. Following a so-called 'carrot-and-stick approach', renouncing communism and resigning from the Communist Party spared the licensee. For instance, while one of the two communist editors of the *Frankfurter Rundschau*, Emil Carlebach, had his licence withdrawn, the other, Arno Rudert, was kept in place after complying with the requests of the US military authorities. While sympathisers of a socialist agenda, such as another editor of the *Frankfurter Rundschau*, Wilhelm Karl Gerst, occasionally also faced the revocation of licence, mainly the communist press and those opposed to anti-communist propaganda were persecuted. By June 1947, only four out of the 92 licensees in the American sovereign territory were members of the KPD; by November 1947 merely one member of the Communist Party, Rudolf Agricola, was in possession of a licence, namely the *Rhein-Neckar-Zeitung* in Heidelberg. Similarly, the statistics of the then chairman of the Bavarian organisation of professional journalists, Walther de Bouché, list only one member of the KPD to possess a licence to edit a newspaper in June 1947; 23 licensees were associated with the SPD, 15 were members of or associated to the CSU, two were members of the FDP and two were without any party affiliation.[68] After publicly criticising the Americans for their undemocratic behaviour, Agricola, who conjointly edited the *Rhein-Neckar-Zeitung* with Hermann Knorr (SPD) and the future President of the Federal Republic of Germany, Theodor Heuss (DVP), finally lost his licence in September 1948. The trend both to counteract the Soviet propaganda, for instance via the so-called 'Operation Talk Back' of the Political Information Branch (PIB) established by General Clay on 28 October 1947 which urged western newspapers to actively attack communism,[69] and to disadvantage the communist press in post-war West Germany continued with the consequence that there were no licensees with a KPD membership left in 1949.[70] While the SPD and CDU/CSU press were not persecuted in a similar manner, control of printed party materials remained severe. General Clay's firm decision to establish a non-party press rested *inter alia* upon a survey on the public opinion regarding the press in which the majority favoured an independent press.[71] Although many agreed with Clay's course of action, others, among them German and American officials alike, such as the diplomat Robert Murphy according to whom the State Department unavailingly tried to convince General Clay to license party papers,[72] were opposed to this view. Consequently, the publicist and editor of the *Frankfurter Hefte*, Eugen Kogon (CDU), criticised the rigid licensing practices and requested more political autonomy and party papers.[73] Especially the SPD, which had operated numerous papers before the *Gleichschaltung* by the National Socialists, felt disadvantaged. However, other parties also complained about the restrictive licensing of newspapers affiliated to political parties.[74] After further interventions by German politicians referring to the approval of party papers in the British zone of occupation, the American Military Government eventually permitted party organs, provided that the respective *Länder* parliaments passed laws ensuring freedom of the press. Although a uniform press law for all zones of occupation initiated by the *Länderrat* in the American occupation zone was rejected by the American Military Government due to a pursued decentralisation on 15 July 1947, more newspapers affiliated to political parties were approved. However, there were no organs owned by political parties among the newspapers, which received a licence in the American zone of occupation.[75]

Quite in contrast to the American licensing practices concerning party papers, the British authorities privileged newspapers with a party affiliation. In the first instance, however, British officials were rather hesitant to license any newspaper in their sovereign territory and followed a procedure similar to the American – in fact, with the exception of the *Aachener Nachrichten*, there was no other German newspaper appearing in the British zone until the licensing of the social democratic-oriented *Braunschweiger Zeitung* on 8 January 1946. After a change of policy in early 1946, licences were increasingly given to so-called '*Gesinnungszeitungen*' or '*Parteirichtungszeitungen*',[76] namely those with a disposition for a particular political party; few independent newspapers were considered. According to a list compiled by Heinz-Dietrich Fischer, out of 42 registered newspapers in the British zone including the corresponding sector in Berlin, 33 can be counted as party papers of which 13 favoured the SPD and 10 the CDU.[77] In doing so, the licence was not issued to the respective party but to an individual person recommended by his/her political organisation. Thus the representation of interests of the political parties was ensured; equally, the influence of interest groups on editorial functions was limited. Nevertheless, in contrast to the prevailing perception in academic and popular literature,[78] the British authorities also licensed political parties and their explicit organs, such as *Der Sozialdemokrat* (later *Berliner Stadtblatt/Berliner Stimme*) issued up to six times per week by the SPD Greater-Berlin or the central organ of the SPD, *Neuer Vorwärts*, which appeared from 11 September 1948 onwards, or the CDU party organ *Union in Deutschland*, *Union im Norden*, or *Union im Wahlkampf: Informations- und Rednerdienst der Arbeitsgemeinschaft der CDU/CSU Deutschlands*. Although there was no clear preference for one particular party, the British authorities initially supported the SPD. This can be explained by the fact that both wanted a centralised government for Germany. However, the American military authorities, General Lucius D. Clay in particular, supported a federal organisation and therefore preferred the CDU/CSU with their federal-democratic accentuation.[79] This imbalance with its preference for SPD publications, however, was changed when the circulation of party papers was coupled with the results of the first elections at the end of 1946. In consequence of this reallocation in a ratio of one exemplar of newspaper per five citizens, the conservative parties generally gained at the expense of the KPD and SPD (CDU +25.8 per cent, FDP +17.6 per cent, Z +2.7 per cent, KPD –49.2 per cent, SPD +0.4 per cent).[80] In spite of this readjustment of newspapers, a particular uncertainty concerning the selection of licensees remained among British officials. Therefore, German parties and organisations were soon called in to participate in the authorisation process. Whereas a decree issued on 1 March declared that the press was exempted from German legislation and purely a matter of the Military Government,[81] Directive No. 108 which became effective on 15 October 1947 marked a decisive step towards an independent German press in the British zone of occupation. Accordingly, consultative committees consisting of publishers, journalists, and representatives of the general public to be nominated by the Prime Ministers, were formed. Interestingly, an annex stated that in this composition agents of political parties were not allowed to be appointed.[82] These institutions in the various *Länder* were consulted on factual issues regarding the issuance but also withdrawal of licences, and furthermore in the limitation of circulations of newspapers and magazines.[83] Despite this commissioning of authorities to German representatives, the British military authorities intervened directly or indirectly via paper rationing if they considered it necessary. This was often the case with the communist press, which was deemed to be in breach of the ban on criticising the occupying powers. Due to this argument, which was frequently a pretence to foster anti-communist political life in Germany, however, the KPD was prosecuted and dispossessed of several licences: after several prohibitions to publish, the *Westdeutsche Volksecho* in Dortmund lost the licence on 4 May 1948, the KPD organ *Freiheit* in Düsseldorf on 8 October 1948. Thus the direction selected matched the American attitude. Nevertheless, the approach to revive political parties and their influence on the electorate in the British zone of occupation was different. Even though more independent newspapers were licensed in the course of time, party papers with a zonal circulation constituted the majority in the British sovereign territory in 1949. Out of 58 newspapers in the British zone of occupation, 47 were party papers and only eleven can be considered as independent.[84] This fact which enabled supra-regional communication provided an explanation for the advanced organisation of political parties in the British occupation zone.

Due to the fact that the French zone of occupation did not come into existence until 30 June 1945, Law No. 191 of the American Military Government issued by the Supreme Headquarters Allied Expeditionary Force was equally in effect here. Although initially following the American licensing practices in mainly approving independent newspapers, the French authorities gradually changed to the British approach by permitting newspapers with party affiliation. Directive no. 40 issued by the French Military Government in October 1946 allowed German parties and the press '*de discuter librement des problemes politiques allemands*' (to discuss freely German political problems).[85] This alteration was mainly due to the increasing awakening of German political life and the wish to discuss freely political and economic problems in the French occupation zone. Although the French Military Government was hesitant in permitting and supporting German political parties, the first communal elections took place in the Saarland on 15 September and in Baden, Rhineland-Palatinate and Wuerttemberg-Hohenzollern on 13 October 1946. The political interaction between parties and electorate during campaigns led to the demand for explicit party organs. Following the wish of the German parties and public for so-called '*Meinungsblätter*', namely newspapers expressing the opinion of a particular political party, the French authorities met these demands by decreasing the number of independent newspapers. After a decision by the *Comité de Direction de la Presse* (Committee for the Direction of the Press) of the French Military Government, taken on 3 February 1947, there remained only few independent papers, such as the *Rhein-Zeitung* (Koblenz), the *Südkurier* (Konstanz), the *Schwäbisches Tagblatt* (Tübingen), the *Allgemeine Zeitung* (Mainz), or the *Badische Zeitung* (Freiburg im Breisgau), to the favour of '*feuilles d'opinion*', notedly party papers. This was mainly carried out by transforming non-party papers into party papers. The aim behind this restructuring of the press was to ensure that every licensed political party disposed of its own organ. In essence, each of the four licensed parties disposed of three newspapers, which were requested to have the party logo in the respective header; for the CDU, those were *Der Westen* (Neuwied), *Südwestdeutsche Volkszeitung* (Freiburg im Breisgau), and the *Schwäbische Zeitung* (Leutkirch). Whereas *Die Freiheit* (Mainz), *Das Volk* (Freiburg im Breisgau), and *Der Württemberger* (Rottweil) were SPD organs, the KPD addressed the public via the *Neues Leben* (Neustadt), *Unser Tag* (Offenburg), and *Unsere Stimme* (Schwenningen). Finally, the *Rheinisch-Pfälzische Rundschau* (Bad Kreuznach), *Das Neue Baden* (Freiburg im Breisgau), and the *Schwabenecho* (Oberndorf) constituted the FDP party papers. The respective issues were allocated according to a quota based on election results similar to the British mode explained above. However, due to limited circulation and frequency of the party papers – whereas independent newspapers appeared up to six times per week and had a share of 68.8 per cent of the overall circulation, the party papers appeared only three times per week at most and had a share of merely 31.2 per cent[86] – the independent newspapers remained dominant in the press. In addition, the non-party papers gave full coverage of political life and a remarkably free expression of German opinion. This competition for readership and limited support from the occupying authorities led to the decline of the party press in the French occupation zone: in 1949, only two of the former twelve party papers still existed, namely the SPD organ *Die Freiheit* and the *Schwäbische Zeitung* of the CDU.

Despite varying licensing procedures in the three zones of occupation, the influence of party papers remained relatively weak with the consequence that German political parties attempted to influence the more widely read independent newspapers. While it is difficult to establish readership numbers for the licensed newspapers in post-war West Germany, it is estimated that each copy had on average four to six readers as papers were not only read in private but also in public where they were, for instance, available in libraries or waiting rooms.[87]

Aside from non-party papers, radio constituted the main source of information for the general public in Germany between 1945 and 1949. Although only two out of seven major broadcasting studios in occupied West Germany, namely the radio stations in Berlin and Hamburg, remained unscathed after the war, radio production increased considerably between 1946 (*c.* 130,000) and 1949 (*c.* 1,200,000).[88] While these radio transmissions were indeed received by an audience that went far beyond the registered radio-receivers (totalling 6,032,331 in 1947)[89] as an average of three people listened to each set at work,[90] with family or friends, they mainly consisted of an educational *Schulfunk*, the *Suchdienst* in order to facilitate the finding of missing people and the broadcasting of the Nuremberg Trials. Furthermore, both the (re)emerging broadcasting corporations and their programmes were almost entirely administered by the Allied authorities: while in the American zone, the ICD controlled the radio stations in Berlin (DIAS = *Drahtfunk im amerikanischen Sektor* which became RIAS = *Radiosender im amerikanischen Sektor* later on), in Bremen (*Radio Bremen*; RB), in Frankfurt (*Radio Frankfurt* which became the *Hessischer Rundfunk*; HR), in Munich (*Bayerischer Rundfunk*; BR), and in Stuttgart (*Süddeutscher Rundfunk*; SDR), in the British occupation zone, *Radio Hamburg* (renamed *Nordwestdeutscher Rundfunk*; NWDR), was organised as a central public corporation along the lines of the BBC and in the French sovereign territory, *Radio Koblenz*, the *SWF* (*Südwestfunk*), and the *Sender Freiburg* were severely monitored.[91] Thus, the radio proved to be less useful than the press in assessing the communication of political content and its public reception.

Other media, such as books, movies or the weekly bizonal news show *Welt im Film*, equally liable to licensing regulations, were not included in this research. This instance is simply due to the fact that they are not considered information media as serving another purpose. In addition to the 148 newspapers, which were eventually licensed in occupied West Germany (60 in the American zone, 58 in the British sovereign territory, and 30 in the French zone),[92] some multi-national newspapers in neighbouring countries, primarily the Swiss liberal-conservative *Neue Zürcher Zeitung* (NZZ), promised to be a fertile ground by which to influence public opinion in Germany.[93] Despite the low circulation of 3,000 of so-called '*Fernausgaben*', i.e. special issues for the northern neighbour,[94] the foreign daily appearing seven times per week since 1947 was one of the most demanded and respected newspapers in West Germany.[95] In particular the ruling classes from industry and politics appreciated the quality paper from Zurich. Indeed, Konrad Adenauer, who obtained the newspaper via the emigrated German-Jewish industrialist Paul Silverberg, considered the NZZ entirely indispensable for his political work.[96] However, due to the fact that international newspapers were too expensive for the ordinary citizen, their influence on the general public was very limited.

During pre-election campaigns, political posters and pamphlets complemented communication via newspapers. While similarly subject to censorship by the Allies, political placards and flyers were the first public communications media after the war. The various political parties tried to distinguish themselves, their programmes and ideas, from their political opponents in striking ways. Moreover, by expressing the political culture, posters and pamphlets are unique and succinct witnesses of history.[97] However, most astonishing is the fact that historical and political research has almost ignored the use, prevalence, and impact of these vitally important means of communication.

In essence, due to the restrictions imposed by the Allied Military Governments, the German political parties had limited options for disseminating information to the general public. The control of German media in the three zones of occupation examined remained in the hands of the Allied military authorities until 1949. On 21 September, in parallel with the Statue of Occupation, the occupying authorities granted the German press and other media the freedom for unlicensed reporting by law.[98]

Apart from these external restraints, the German political parties faced another problem in getting their message across. Due to the consolidation of institutional powers and the media during the Third Reich, the credibility of political parties and confidence in the press were eroded. In the immediate aftermath of the war, certain scepticism towards political elites, the press and the future in general was prevalent among the German population. This crisis of confidence could only be countered by a free press and truthful reporting. Thus it was considered an absurdity that the intellectual gagging by Hitler and his regime be substituted by Allied reprimands and the decreed reading material from the military authorities.[99] The public widely rejected the content of the newspapers as caricaturing the existing circumstances. In spite of these external restrictions and the press's credibility gap, newspapers constituted a major source of information for the citizens in occupied Germany, and the media in general inherited a constitutive and indispensable element for the political and economic reconstruction of post-war West Germany.

In examining how the schools of economic thought and political parties appeared before the public in order to promote their respective agenda, it is important to consider the circumstances and restrictions outlined above.

Furthermore, for this study on political decision-making and the formation of public opinion, it is vital to have fundamental background information on the various socio-political and economic concepts. These provide the framework for political objectives, and influenced the programmes and policies of the existing political parties. The theories were also popularised and instrumentalised for political communication and the manipulation of public opinion. Thus an understanding of these academic and political conceptions served as an approach to the evaluation of the economic and socio-political debate of that particular time. The following chapter is a critical assessment of the principal ideological and economic concepts, which formed the foundation of the emergent economic policy regime in post-war West Germany, and their communication to the public.

1

ACADEMIC CONCEPTS BETWEEN NEO-LIBERALISM AND NEO-SOCIALISM

Liberalism was to all intents and purposes dead in Germany. And it was socialism that had killed it.[1]

(Friedrich August von Hayek, 1943)

In the aftermath of the Second World War, the socio-political and economic reorganisation of Germany was intensely disputed by politicians and public alike. Thus continued the debate and development of economic models, which had their origins in opposition circles to National Socialism, in exile, or even in the Weimar Republic. Certain historical experiences and guiding principles characterised the discussion: the reaction of anarchy and utopia on the one hand, and also of a past which, though repudiated, was necessarily present and ubiquitous, together with an uncertain future to be shaped amid immediately pressing material needs. Furthermore, the framework for the definition of the individual concepts was set by a common starting point and political prerequisites: by Germany's preoccupation with the social question since the late nineteenth century embodied in the both anti-socialist and anti-free-market *Verein für Socialpolitik* (Association for Social Policy),[2] by the criticism of liberal capitalism triggered by the world economic crisis of the early 1930s, by a pronounced anti-totalitarianism as well as anti-collectivism formed by the experiences of the Third Reich, and, finally, by the emphasis on human dignity and personal freedom. Whereas Marxism and Leninism could not be debated due to guidelines issued by the Allied military authorities, the concepts of neo-liberalism, democratic socialism, and Catholic social doctrine provided a third way between the antagonism of capitalism and socialism.

Despite fundamental congruence in the classification of emerging economic models, the prevalent academic literature provides varying interpretations of the respective schools of thought. For instance, Helmut Paul Becker identifies three groups, namely the Freiburg School, the social and the extreme neo-liberalism,[3] Rolf Wenz uses the classification neo-liberalism, democratic socialism and Catholic social doctrine,[4] and according to Otto Schlecht, individuals represent and classify specific schools of thought.[5] Frequently, the contours are blurred and categorisations inadequately reflect the specific conceptions or even neglect academic efforts, such as that of the Freiburg Circles. These shortcomings are balanced by more recent examinations distinguishing between various neo-liberal approaches and giving consideration to the latter group of scholars.[6] Referring to the conceptions of neo-liberalism, ordo-liberalism, and social market liberalism, and, in order to serve the purpose of this research focused on the communication of concepts, this section classifies three separate and coherent groups trying to influence the post-war economic reconstruction of Germany: the Freiburg Circles, the Freiburg School, and the social market economists.

In doing so, the principal theoretical academic approaches which all sought to reconcile nineteenth-century liberalism with the demands of the twentieth-century economy and politics are contrasted and differences examined. Due to a vast amount of academic research and literature on economic conceptions, this book will not add another interpretation of economic theory, but instead make amendments where it deems appropriate and necessary.

1.1

THE FREIBURG CIRCLES AND NEO-LIBERALISM

Neither the command economy nor the free market economy can cope with present demands. Thus one needs to combine the two systems to a market-conform or indirectly controlled economy.[1]

(Adolf Lampe, 1943)

After the collapse of the totalitarian Third Reich with its statist, corporatist economic policy, economists and academics at the University of Freiburg im Breisgau in Germany advocated a new liberal economic order. This 'neo-liberal'[2] conception encompassing economic-political and socio-philosophical ideas was based on classical liberalism and neo-classical theory. In contrast to *laissez-faire*[3] or free market liberalism, however, the neo-liberal concept considered regulatory interference as legitimate provided it was solely to safeguard the functioning of the market. Thus, unlike Keynesianism, which required an active governmental economic policy, neo-liberalism aimed to minimise the influence of the state. Nevertheless, in view of the situation after the war, the state was expected to regulate supply and demand in order to create a market economy without aggravating social distress. On the basis of these considerations, neo-liberals and the Freiburg scholars became the intellectual precursors of the emerging Social Market Economy.

In this context, it is important to distinguish between the Freiburg School and the Freiburg Circles. The prominence of the former, well-known due to its influential publications on post-war economic policy in the late 1940s, contrasted with the relatively secret activities and late publication of the reports of the latter school of economic thought, led to distinctions becoming blurred and the impact of the Freiburg Circles on the concrete shaping of post-war economic policy remaining nebulous even to scholars. Frequently, the two schools of thought were believed to be the same[4] although the first emerged from the latter and among the members of the Freiburg School only the founders Walter Eucken and Franz Böhm belonged to the Freiburg Circles and, conversely, no member of the Freiburg Circles can be attributed to the Freiburg School which partly advocated different economic objectives. It was not until the publications by Christine Blumenberg-Lampe,[5] that the differences in conception and communication became clear. According to recent research,[6] it was precisely the Freiburg Circles subsuming three initially religiously-motivated working groups whose memberships overlapped, namely the *Freiburger Konzil*, the *Bonhoeffer Kreis*, and the *Arbeitsgemeinschaft Erwin von Beckerath* (AG$_{\text{EvB}}$), that provided the platform for the renaissance of liberal political and economic thinking in post-war Germany.

In particular the latter working group, presided over by Erwin von Beckerath, as a private continuation of the former *Arbeitsgemeinschaft Volkswirtschaftslehre* (AG$_{\text{VWL}}$) (Working Committee of Political Economy), which was established within the *Akademie für Deutsches Recht* (AfDR) (Academy for German Law) in 1940 but suspended on 1 March 1943, was concerned with the transformation of a wartime economy into a peacetime one and finding an order to govern it.[7] To the first meeting in Freiburg im Breisgau on 21 March 1943, the eponym of the consortium, Erwin von Beckerath, invited the economists Constantin von Dietze, Walter Eucken, Adolf Lampe, and Clemens Bauer from the University of Freiburg, Jens Jessen and Heinrich von Stackelberg from the University of Berlin, Günter Schmölders and Theodor Wessels from Cologne University, as well as Erich Preiser and the jurist Franz Böhm from the University of Jena.[8] For further meetings, the former chief editor of the *Industrie- und Handelszeitung*, Hans Gestrich, received invitations; unfortunately, he unexpectedly died in November 1943. Additionally, the social policy specialist at the University of Marburg, Gerhard Albrecht, and the editor of the business section of the *Kölnische Zeitung*, Fritz Hauenstein, joined the working group pursuing a new liberal and social economic order.[9] It is in this context of the rehabilitation of classical economics in the face of the Nazis' plans for an autarkic economic system, but even more due to its submitting reports directly to the political leader of the anti-Hitler resistance, Carl Friedrich Goerdeler, that the AG$_{\text{EvB}}$ has predominantly been viewed as an opposition circle to National Socialism. The group's advocacy of a neo-liberal economic policy also accounts for the conceptual development of the Social Market Economy and its eventual acceptance in academia, politics and among the public. In examining the means by which the AG$_{\text{EvB}}$ conveyed its economic and socio-political concept to experts and the general public, this analysis also reveals important conceptual differences between the Freiburg Circles and the Freiburg School.

Principally, a total of 41 reports of the AG_{EvB} and the four preparatory works of the AG_{VWL}, edited in 1986 by the daughter of Adolf Lampe, Christine Blumenberg-Lampe, defined their economic and socio-political position.[10] Furthermore, the economic exposé *Wirtschaftsfibel* presumably written by Adolf Lampe, Constantin von Dietze and Walter Eucken, which amounted to both a socio-political criticism of National Socialism and a clear commitment to market liberalism, was intended to address academics, politicians and the wider public.[11] However, this informative document disappeared soon after its completion until it was retrieved recently. In addition, no coherent final report was published by the AG_{EvB} due to the arrest of Adolf Lampe and Constantin von Dietze in connection with the assassination attempt of 20 July 1944.[12] Moreover, discrepancies and even frictions within the group concerning the method and degree of governmental intervention constituted another potential reason for the failure. Whereas Lampe and Wessels favoured 'productive' governmental intervention, i.e. an economy regulated by a relatively strong state, Eucken and von Dietze believed in self-regulating market forces.[13] Although the majority of the AG_{EvB} sided with Adolf Lampe, ambiguity remained with regard to the mode of interference, i.e. direct or indirect control of the economy.[14] Whereas in the former the state or another central authority instructs the market participant to act in a particular way, in the latter the terms and conditions for the market are defined in order to influence the individual entrepreneur, e.g. via franchising and licensing. Due to such diverging views, Walter Eucken was sceptical about the proceedings of the AG_{EvB} and the consistency of its ideas.[15] Nonetheless, there was agreement among the academics with regard to the eventual return to an economy regulated by the market.[16] According to the economists around Erwin von Beckerath, the economic and socio-political reconstruction of Germany could be achieved only by the reinstatement of a market economy fostering individual freedom and entrepreneurship.[17] However, the predominant thinking was that a certain form of planning was necessary for a transitional period following the war; and so the *Befehlswirtschaft* (Command Economy) of the Third Reich and a free market economy were both excluded from consideration. Consequently, the working group debated a so-called '*Zentralverwaltungswirtschaft*' (Centrally Administered Economy). In contrast to the Command Economy, this model was regarded as neither opposed to personal freedom nor to market principles.[18] Thus the notions of Command Economy and Centrally Administered Economy are not interchangeable – strictly speaking, academia distinguishes two fundamentally different types of economy, i.e. the decentrally organised Market or Competitive Economy and the Centrally Administered Economy; to equate the latter with a Command or Centrally Planned Economy is rather misleading. However, Erwin von Beckerath did not develop the distinction between the two,[19] and also Blumenberg-Lampe frequently uses these terms without differentiation.[20] However, a Centrally Administered Economy required above all an administrative organisation, which would not exist in the aftermath of the war. Additionally, direct control would conflict with the private and corporate initiatives essential for the stimulation of a market economy. Thus a Centrally Administered Economy was not believed to meet the requirements of the time.[21] In rejecting the above-described economic models, the AG$_{EvB}$ sought to combine the two systems in such a way that the respective advantages of each were employed without having to accept either's disadvantages.[22] Taking into account the conflicting claims of personal freedom and social orientation in times of pressing economic needs, the concept of *mittelbare Wirtschaftssteuerung* (indirect economic control) was proposed.[23] This supposed market-compatible government practice, i.e. any stimulation or interference should not eliminate the proper functioning of market forces, was embodied by a so-called '*marktliche Wirtschaftsordnung*' (market economic order). In this connection, the liberal and simultaneously social economic order safeguarded by a strong state not only represented social balance but required the active participation of society. Thus it was essential to address not just elites, but also much more importantly the general public in order to anchor this economic conception.

Immediately after the collapse of National Socialism, the members of the AG$_{EvB}$ endeavoured to submit their reports to the American and the French military authorities. In particular Adolf Lampe made the effort to win over to their ideas the United States' Military Government for Germany situated in Frankfurt-Hoechst. Eventually, the head of the economic section, Colonel Gilchrist, commissioned a study from the AG$_{EvB}$ on inflation control, and announced that cooperation would begin with the working group. Due to spatial separation and the difficulties of travelling in a time of occupation, however, only the Freiburg economists Lampe, von Beckerath, and Eucken were able to convene to formulate their monetary report entitled *Währungssanierung durch Kaufkraftabschöpfung mit anschliessender Geldumlaufsauffüllung* (Reorganisation of Finances by Absorption of Buying Power followed by Increasing the Circulation of Money) in Freiburg on 3 and 11 August 1945 respectively.[24] Although General Clay repeatedly dispatched officers to Freiburg in order to discuss this report,[25] the cooperation between the German economists and the American authorities ended abruptly without explanation in November 1945. Another group of economists in Munich, namely the *Volkswirtschaftliche Arbeitsgemeinschaft für Bayern* (AG$_{VWB}$) (Economic

Working Committee for Bavaria), had had similar experiences: in their case, it was the former Director of the Nuremberg Institute for Economic Studies, Ludwig Erhard, who had submitted his *Entwurf eines Gesetzes zur Neuordnung des deutschen Geldwesens* (Draft Law on the Reorganisation of German Finance) to OMGUS in July 1945; this market-researcher, who had previously studied long-term economic problems of the city of Nuremberg and thus had demonstrable experience in dealing with problems of war debt and economic policy in a defeated country, was soon to occupy the attention of the domestic political audience.

Initially more promising, however, was the contact between the AG$_{\mathrm{EvB}}$ and the French Military Government, i.e. the *Gouvernement Militaire en Allemagne*. In August 1945, the latter's economic and planning divisions, i.e. the *Section Economie Générale* (Economic Office) and the *Section de Documentation à la direction de l'Economie Générale* (Documentation Office for Economic Policy) in Freiburg/Baden, proposed a cooperative venture by asking the Freiburg economists to be available as experts; this initiative for cooperation presumably emanated from an order issued on 13 June 1945, which requested the military authorities to establish a *Service de Statistique et d'Etudes Economiques* (Service for Statistics and Economic Studies) for the French occupying power. In the hope of revitalising the AG$_{\mathrm{EvB}}$,[26] the reduced working group, operating under the name *Comité d'Etudes Economiques* (Committee for Economic Studies), elaborated around 20 reports for the French military authorities until spring 1946.[27] When the German economists criticised the French economic policy, namely *l'économie dirigée* (Directed Economy), cooperation was jeopardised.[28] Finally, the detention of Adolf Lampe, who was accused of supporting the former Nazi wartime economy by his book *Allgemeine Wehrwirtschaftslehre* (General Wartime Economics) published in 1938, brought cooperation between the Freiburg economists and the Allies to an end in March 1946.

Although the theoretical developments of the AG$_{\mathrm{EvB}}$ attracted interest, the Allies in their actual economic policy did not apply them. Nevertheless, Erwin von Beckerath considered the reports to be important for the economic reconstruction of Germany and so encouraged their publication.[29] Although a publisher, namely the *Bondi-Verlag* in Bonn-Bad Godesberg, was found and other members of the working group agreed, this project was never realised. This could be attributed to the scepticism and objection of Adolf Lampe who considered the reports to be only half-finished, potentially risking public misconceptions.[30] The reports by the AG$_{\mathrm{EvB}}$ merely formed the basis for various articles mainly published in the fortnightly periodical *Die Gegenwart*.[31]

Another opportunity to present the conceptions of the Freiburg economists to a broader audience was the symposium for professors in Rothenburg ob der Tauber between 27 and 29 September 1947. Here, Adolf Lampe and the initiator of the conference, Gerhard Albrecht, who aimed to revive the *Verein für Socialpolitik*, planned to formulate a common experts' report, the *Rothenburger Thesen*, intended to stimulate and to influence the political discussion. When no agreement among the 60 conferees was achieved and no result presented, the four attendant members of the AG_{EvB}, Albrecht, Lampe, Weiser, Wessels, were disappointed. So they decided to discuss their ideas further in order to present them to the institutions responsible for economic policy. Finally, in December 1947, the *Rothenburger Thesen*, signed by 48 professors, among them Walter Eucken, Leonhard Miksch and Alfred Müller-Armack, were submitted to the then Chairman of the *Sonderstelle Geld und Kredit* (SGK) (Special Bureau for Money and Credit) within the Administration for Finance, i.e. an expert commission preparing the currency reform in the Anglo-American Bizone, Ludwig Erhard. The recapitulatory reports of the symposium were published by the *Verein für Socialpolitik* in 1948.[32]

The successful transmission of their economic and socio-political ideas raised the hopes of the working group that they would be able to have an active influence on political decision-making. Although the former AG_{EvB} was not reactivated, the Freiburg economists considered the *Wissenschaftliche Beirat bei der Verwaltung für Wirtschaft* (WB_{VfW}), i.e. the Advisory Council on Economic Affairs within the Administration for Economics formed on 23/24 January 1948 in Königstein im Taunus, the appropriate platform to express their views. Among the 17 participants nominated by the then State Secretary in the bizonal Administration for Economics, Walter Strauß, who had been informed about the activities of the working group by Franz Böhm, were the following members of the AG_{EvB}: Lampe, Böhm, Eucken, Preiser, Wessels and von Beckerath.[33] When Böhm became chairman and von Beckerath his deputy, the Freiburg economists saw their hopes reaffirmed. Indeed, this progenitor of today's Council of Economic Advisors at the Federal Ministry of Economics and Labour became the first independent panel of academics to advise policy-makers. Furthermore, the then Director of the Administration for Economics in the Bizonal Economic Council, Johannes Semler, encouraged the members of the WB_{VfW} to criticise policies freely and comment publicly.[34] This invitation, and the fact that the reports were published, provided the Freiburg economists with the opportunity to address both political elites and the general public. Conversely, however, this also meant that the experts were subject to political and public criticism. This prominent position of the WB_{VfW}

created not only transparency but also credibility. Consequently, the first report submitted on 18 April 1948 received a remarkable response in political and public circles. Following the publication of the report, Ludwig Erhard in particular recognised the ability of the independent advisory council to offer influential support for his economic policy. Thus the AG$_{\text{EvB}}$ had access to the most influential political actor at that time. Beyond dispute, by presenting its neo-liberal views via the Advisory Council on Economic Affairs as its genuine successor, the AG$_{\text{EvB}}$, according to the published reports of the council, successfully influenced the future economic reorganisation of Germany.[35]

It was not only because of the beneficial cooperation between the AG$_{\text{EvB}}$ and the WB$_{\text{VfW}}$ that the Freiburg economists attached great importance to their contacts with policy-makers.[36] Initially, they made formal approaches to the Allied Military Governments and Ludwig Erhard as head of the SGK and successor of Johannes Semler as Director of the Administration for Economics. However, there followed further unofficial or private contacts, which may have had an impact on the shaping of the economic policy. In fact, many of Erhard's proposals, such as the report on the reorganisation of German finances, were based on the ideas of the economist Adolf Weber. After all, both were professors at the Ludwig-Maximilians University in Munich, who had worked together in the AG$_{\text{VWB}}$ as early as 1945.[37] In turn, Adolf Weber was the doctoral supervisor for Adolf Lampe and also for Constantin von Dietze and Fritz Hauenstein. Like the AG$_{\text{EvB}}$, Weber advocated a major currency reform in order to enable the economic reconstruction of Germany, and so Adolf Lampe contacted his former supervisor in preparation of his own studies.[38] This interchange of ideas may have reached Erhard as well. There existed yet another connection between the AG$_{\text{EvB}}$ and the Director of the Administration for Economics in the Bizonal Economic Council: research for this chapter has revealed that Erich Preiser wrote his doctoral thesis with Franz Oppenheimer in Frankfurt in 1923 – at the same time as Ludwig Erhard. Furthermore, directly contrary to the assumption by Blumenberg-Lampe that no personal contacts with Konrad Adenauer had been established before 1947,[39] one must consider this as probable since the preliminary meeting of the AG$_{\text{EvB}}$ took place in the Hotel Wolkenburg in Rhöndorf, in immediate proximity to Adenauer's home. Although no concrete proof exists of an unofficial and influential connection between the AG$_{\text{EvB}}$ and Ludwig Erhard or Konrad Adenauer before 1947, the work of the academics in Freiburg indirectly affected the politicians' economic policy. However, at least their views arrived on a political level and from there were brought before the public.

Beyond dispute, what had been started as an underground movement by resolute opponents of National Socialism went on to shape the formation and implementation of the emerging Social Market Economy. Furthermore, by writing reports for Carl Goerdeler, the Allied Military Governments and finally Ludwig Erhard, the *Arbeitsgemeinschaft Erwin von Beckerath* introduced and anchored liberal economic thinking in post-war Germany. Admittedly, by mainly addressing academic and political classes, the AG_{EvB} hardly affected the general public, and so the economic and socio-political conceptions of the Freiburg economists were debated almost exclusively at elite rather than popular levels.[40]

1.2

THE FREIBURG SCHOOL AND ORDO-LIBERALISM

The real challenge in the political realm no less than in that of the economy is to establish a framework that induces ordinary self-interested people to pursue in their own interest what is in the common interest of all.[1]

(Walter Eucken, 1940)

The destruction of the democratic system from the inside by the National Socialists and the dire economic situation after the collapse of the Third Reich meant that the immediate post-war years were widely characterised by prevalent disenchantment with politics and the struggle for existence. Nevertheless, due to the inadequate supply of food and basic goods, there was increasing public interest in economic affairs and a corresponding demand for information.[2] In this context, the so-called 'ordo-liberal Freiburg School', or 'Freiburg School of Law and Economics', aimed not only to provide an economic concept adequate to deal with the prevailing situation but also directly informed the public about its concept and approach. Thus, quite in contrast to the Freiburg Circles, the Freiburg School targeted its ideas at the general public. Significantly, a progressive publication entitled *Ordnung der Wirtschaft* published in 1937 had marked the birth of the Freiburg School and also ordo-liberalism's first public appearance as a new variant of neo-liberalism.

With regard to the communication of a particular concept, however, the commonly used expression 'Freiburg School' for ordo-liberalism is correct but imprecise: the two must be distinguished. The first usually refers to the research and teaching community with Walter Eucken, Franz Böhm, and Hans Großmann-Doerth as its pivotal members at the University of Freiburg im Breisgau in the 1930s and 1940s. Furthermore, Walter Eucken's disciples Friedrich A. Lutz, Karl Friedrich Maier, Fritz Walter Meyer and Leonhard Miksch can be included in the Freiburg School.

Ordo-liberalism in a broader sense includes other liberal currents and their representatives, for instance, Alexander Rüstow and Wilhelm Röpke.[3] Whereas the latter predominantly expressed their views in monographs and articles, the Freiburg School presented its economic concept *inter alia* in the co-edited publication series *Ordnung der Wirtschaft* which passed into the annual *ORDO, Jahrbuch für die Ordnung von Wirtschaft und Gesellschaft*, founded by Böhm and Eucken in 1948. In the first volume of their joint publication, the editors Franz Böhm, Walter Eucken and Hans Großmann-Doerth included a co-authored programmatic preface in which they stressed the importance of an 'Economic Constitution' as a formal legal institutional order[4] within which economic activities take place.[5] Accordingly, the state must create a proper legal environment for the economy and maintain a healthy level of competition through measures that follow market principles. Thus the paramount means by which economic policy can seek to improve the economy is by improving the institutional framework. Precisely this interdependence of the economic and the legal orders, which was further elaborated by Franz Böhm in the first essay of the publication series,[6] was both fundamental to the development of ordo-liberalism and in opposition to the relativism of the German Historical School of Economics.[7] While the latter school of economic thought used the empirical method in examining society as a whole, Eucken, whose procedure was reportedly rooted in the philosophical anti-relativistic perspective of his father, the Nobel prize laureate Rudolf Eucken, and the ontological paradigm as 'absolutism in transition' by the philosopher Edmund Husserl,[8] preferred a methodological approach based on phenomenological methods combined with the programme of a so-called 'isolating abstraction'.[9] In particular Walter Eucken aimed to overcome the antinomy of historical and theoretical examination in order to cope with the interdependence of orders, as economic and political tasks cannot be approached in isolation. He considered joint efforts indispensable, and aspired to bring scientific reasoning, as displayed in jurisprudence and political economy, into play in order to create conditions under which economic actors while pursuing their own interests promoted the common interest too.[10] This pursuit finally became the foundation subject matter of Walter Eucken's *Ordnungsökonomik* (Constitutional Economics); whereas classical economics is concerned with individual behaviour in the context of an economic order, constitutional economics focuses on analysing alternative regulatory policies in order to achieve shared commitment leading to shared gains.[11]

Eucken's thinking in terms of economic orders, or styles, which also gave its name to the school, owes much to the historical and sociological studies of Werner Sombart and Max Weber. Sombart's *Modern Capitalism*,[12] is an overview of the historical path of European economic life. It deals in great detail with the phenomena, which created the unique history of capitalism, its cultural, psychological, religious and technical background. Furthermore, Weber's immense sociological and historical studies linked the world religions with their economic manifestations.[13] His basic tenet that in the social sciences understanding of economic relations requires the understanding of all cultural contents and their meaning was applied to a vast conspectus of historical facts from which he abstracted his famous ideal type. These thoughts led Eucken to derive from the various economic models the two main types: the Centrally Directed Command Economy and the Free Market Economy. While the members of the Freiburg School placed themselves firmly in the tradition of classical liberalism, they distanced themselves from a *laissez-faire* liberalism that failed to appreciate the essential positive, or functional, role government has to play in creating and maintaining an appropriate framework of rules and institutions which allows market competition to work effectively.[14] Equally, they rejected the Controlled or Command Economy as it limited the freedom of the individual.[15] Thus, they addressed the question of how to prevent economic freedom from being destroyed by economic concentration, such as cartels and monopolies. In contrast to the AG_{EvB}, the Freiburg School advocated unadulterated competition as the prime means to counter the accumulation of market power, as well as to achieve freedom and social justice.[16] In their constitutional approach to market competition, the ordo-liberals emphasised that the competitive order must be seen as a public good in the sense that the constitutional framework induces self-interested individuals while pursuing their own interest to do what is in the public good.[17] It was in the common interest of all citizens that legislature and government act in accordance with their constitutionally determined mandate to create, preserve and manage the regulatory framework that guarantees the functioning of the market.[18] As the ordo-liberal competitive order depended on a person's interest both in enjoying the benefits of a public good and in contributing to its production, the active individual was at the centre of the economic concept. This required an informed public and thus their incorporation in economic policy.

Although the conceptual framework was presented to academia and the public, the Freiburg School's economic model remained virtually nameless, and so it ran the risk of being widely perceived as abstract and intangible; furthermore, conceptual complexity impaired its communication. Eucken recognised this deficiency but found fault only in the absence of a ruling class which understood the competitive order not only as an economic one but also as indispensable for a social order opposed to totalitarianism.[19] In view of the fact that the Freiburg School aimed to address the general public, his explanation is hardly satisfactory. Nevertheless, there were numerous attempts by members of the Freiburg School and supporters of ordo-liberalism to describe their concept and bring it closer to the people. For example, Franz Böhm characterised it as a 'synthesis between socialism and liberalism'.[20] Similarly, the liberal economist Alexander Rüstow located it as lying between capitalism and communism.[21] Finally and decisively, it was Wilhelm Röpke who introduced the notion 'Third Way' or 'Economic Humanism'.[22] However, besides these efforts to argue for the implementation of complex economic ideas, there were obstacles impeding the communication to the public.

Due to their theoretical and conceptual works, the Freiburg School and ordo-liberalism are viewed as the intellectual precursors and Walter Eucken as the progenitor of the emerging Social Market Economy.[23] Such paternity, however, is debatable, as Walter Eucken dissociated himself both from that notion and from the idea of the Social Market Economy, which he considered a drifting policy of *Sichtreibenlassen*.[24] In contrast, Eucken favoured a strictly procedural or rule-oriented liberalism in which the state solely sets the institutional framework and abstains generally from interference in the market. Wilhelm Röpke, who labelled this *Rahmenpolitik* (framework policy) as opposed to *Marktpolitik* (market policy), however, preferred a slightly more interventionist economic policy, as did Alexander Rüstow.[25] These different positions between the liberal economists who had previously involved themselves in the *Deutscher Bund für freie Wirtschaftspolitik* (German League for the Free Market), a group of businessmen and economists supporting the free market system in the early 1930s, led to an irreconcilable conflict which recurrently revealed itself,[26] and thereby prevented a coordinated effort in the communication of an ordo-liberal economic concept. Moreover, even within the Freiburg School frictions are identifiable and the notion 'school' suggests a unity, which had already disappeared in 1943 when Eucken ended cooperation with Großmann-Doerth, who had placed his work in the service of the National Socialist regime; Hans Großmann-Doerth was killed in action in Russia 1944.[27] Consequently, these discrepancies produced individual and uncoordinated efforts in communicating a common economic and socio-political concept.

Immediately after the war, the most prominent member of the Freiburg School, Walter Eucken, sought contact with the occupying powers in order to promote his economic ideas. Due to the efforts of Adolf Lampe and the AGEvB, to which he too belonged, Eucken co-authored a study on inflation control for the Office of Military Government for Germany.[28] After contacts between the working group and the American authorities ended in November 1945, Walter Eucken alone remained in touch with them. Owing to Eucken's participation in meetings with the then Director of the Finance Division, Joseph M. Dodge, and the German public finance economist and advisor to the US Government, Gerhard Colm, some have assumed that he had an influence on the Colm–Dodge–Goldsmith Plan to reform the German finances and currency.[29] Eucken, however, stated that his proposals had hardly affected it.[30] Nevertheless, the Freiburg ordo-liberal's scholarly works attracted the interest of the Allies and were praised by the French *Gouvernement Militaire en Allemagne*, for which Eucken and the AG_{EvB} elaborated reports until spring 1946.[31] Appreciation of Walter Eucken's expertise is also shown by his appointment to the *Sachverständigenrat* (Council of Economic Advisors) to the *Länderrat* in the American zone of occupation and later in the Bizone. Within this commission, responsible for preparing a German anti-trust law, Eucken and Böhm successfully promoted their competition order.[32]

In January 1948, the ordo-liberals were given another influential body in which to promote their economic and socio-political conception: the Advisory Council on Economic Affairs within the Administration for Economics. By advocating free price setting and the prevention of economic concentration by competition, the council's first report published on 1 April 1948 reveals an ordo-liberal influence.[33] There was a consensus that the introduction of a new and stable currency could put an end to structural inflation and so make the macroeconomic reason for comprehensive control of prices and production obsolete. Hence, the return to sound money was coupled with a reform of the economic system in general. The majority pleaded for a genuine market economy, albeit with fixed prices for some goods during a transition period. A minority, however, made a case for a mixed economy, i.e. for the parallel existence of markets and central planning. The experts' eventual proposal contained integral parts of the later *Gesetz über Leitsätze für die Bewirtschaftung und Preispolitik nach der Geldreform*, the so-called '*Leitsätze-Gesetz*' (Guiding Principle Law),[34] by which Ludwig Erhard as Director of the bizonal Administration for Economics initiated price decontrol simultaneously with currency reform. Similarly with regard to other legal and economic initiatives, such as monetary and credit policies,[35] Ludwig Erhard consulted the WB_{VfW} regularly and maintained close ties with the panel chaired by Franz Böhm.

The controversial Guiding Principle Law, which finally enabled the currency reform, was primarily authored by Walter Eucken's disciple Leonhard Miksch, who later assumed a position within the Administration for Economics as Director of the Central Department for Pricing and Wages. However, Miksch was not only an architect of regulatory policy but also a close advisor to Erhard, who referred to the ordo-liberal economist as the main advocate of returning to a free market economy.[36] Surprisingly, Miksch was a member of the German Social Democratic Party, which favoured a controlled economy; some argue that the ordo-liberal economist hoped to 'teach Social Democrats some sensible economics.'[37] Indeed, Leonhard Miksch advocated the reactivation of the market economy in numerous academic essays addressing mainly experts and politicians.[38] However, the former publicist[39] – beginning in 1929, Miksch worked for 15 years as a journalist at the *Frankfurter Zeitung* (FZ), where he managed the economic policy section – also appealed to the general public with various journalistic essays.[40]

In contrast to Leonhard Miksch, Walter Eucken, who considered himself first and foremost a scholar, rarely addressed the general public. Although Eucken aimed to promote his neo-liberal views to the populace,[41] his academic monographs and the Freiburg School's own publication series were received by a mainly academic audience.[42] In order to communicate between academia and a wider readership, the advocate of ordo-liberalism and influential journalist, Erich Welter,[43] encouraged Eucken to contribute journalistic essays.[44] Although Eucken published few newspaper articles,[45] when Welter became editor of the *Frankfurter Allgemeine Zeitung* (FAZ) in 1949, ordo-liberalism determined the approach of that national newspaper to political economy. Thus Eucken's own ideas finally reached the wider public. Unfortunately, Walter Eucken's death in 1950 ended cooperation with the FAZ and newspapers in general.

While the social scientist and economist Alexander Rüstow formulated his neo-liberal maxims in exile in Istanbul, and proclaimed his views mainly to an academic readership,[46] the credit for having promoted and established ordo-liberal ideas in the German general public is primarily due to Wilhelm Röpke. In times when many academics considered it beneath their dignity to approach the general public, the German economist addressed a readership outside academia in more than half of his roughly 800 newspaper and journal articles. After accepting a professorship at the renowned *Institut Universitaire de Hautes Études Internationales* (IUHEI) (Graduate Institute of International Studies) in Geneva in 1937, the exiled German economist used the Swiss media and in particular the liberal-conservative international daily *Neue Zürcher Zeitung*, which appeared in occupied West Germany by special editions seven times a week, in order to publish his socio-economic views and recensions of other German economists' scripts, such as Walter Eucken's acclaimed *Grundlagen der Nationalökonomie* (Principles of National

Economy).[47] More important, however, due to the consolidation of institutional powers and the media in the German Third Reich, Röpke aimed to raise awareness of Germany's economic and social situation abroad[48] and hoped to stimulate and influence public discussion in Germany from abroad about a German and European post-war economic model.[49] An analysis of Wilhelm Röpke's voluminous bequest at the IUHEI, containing substantial correspondence and numerous newspaper articles, documents that due to his preoccupation with the German economy and society he succeeded in both achieving publicity and initiating a public debate on economic policy issues in neighbouring Switzerland and other European countries.[50] Furthermore, by his eagerness to contribute to the rebuilding of the German economy[51] and his scholarly works advocating a humane order for society and economy, in particular his acclaimed sociocritical trilogy,[52] Wilhelm Röpke gained national prominence[53] and some considered him *the* intellectual figure *par excellence* in the establishment of economic liberalism in post-war Germany.[54] However, as few Germans could then afford international newspapers, Röpke also became one of the most frequent and prominent authors in German newspapers, such as the *Stuttgarter Zeitung* and later the liberal-conservative *Frankfurter Allgemeine Zeitung*.[55] By inviting various representatives of ordo-liberalism to explain their economic ideas in his paper,[56] the editor of the FAZ, Erich Welter, hoped to influence the German public.[57] Wilhelm Röpke appreciated the invitation to publish in a German national paper, which he considered an ample platform to communicate his economic and socio-political views to the German people.[58]

Finally, his equally elaborate and numerous articles in various national and international newspapers not only earned him a wide reputation – for instance, Röpke's articles reportedly attracted the attention of the *Reichsbankleitstelle* in Hamburg, i.e. the Central Bank of the British occupation zone which also informed the Zonal Executive Offices' Finance Division of the Banking Branch[59] – but also contact with Konrad Adenauer.[60] The then leader of the CDU in the British zone of occupation was familiar with the best known works of Röpke,[61] and frequently referred to the economist's ideas.[62] Equally, Wilhelm Röpke's journalistic essays and monographs left a mark on Ludwig Erhard,[63] who, as Director of the Administration for Economics in the Bizonal Economic Council, often used the economist's terminology when expounding his own economic and political convictions; both, for instance, referred to '*Kapitalistisches Freibeutertum*' (capitalist exploitation) or '*Kollektivismus*' (collectivism).[64] In the course of time, a mutual relationship of trust and respect developed and the two economists frequently met either in

Geneva or at the annual conferences of the Mont Pèlerin Society (MPS)[65] near Montreux in Switzerland. However, it was Walter Eucken who put Erhard in touch with this leading think tank of neo-liberalism, founded by Friedrich August von Hayek in 1947.[66] In annual international meetings, the society's members, mostly economists, historians and philosophers, aimed at reviving and redefining classical economic liberalism and at anchoring neo-liberal thinking in post-war Europe. The scholars, among them Wilhelm Röpke, Alexander Rüstow, Ludwig von Mises, Karl Popper and Milton Friedman, however, did not act as a coherent group; instead individual efforts characterised the MPS's advocacy of economic liberalism.[67]

Since the members of the Mont Pèlerin Society, in line with liberal tradition, deliberately wished to avoid collective resolutions, let alone a programme, both ordo-liberalism as a school of economic thought and the Freiburg School appeared unintentionally divided. In contrast to the AG_{EvB}, the devotees of ordo-liberal economic and socio-political ideas did not act as a unified group although Röpke frequently referred to common action and consensus.[68] Due to diverging views neither a tangible concept nor a coordinated effort in communicating the economic framework developed. Nonetheless, whereas the Freiburg Circles mainly influenced the academic discussion, the Freiburg School stimulated the national debate beyond that, and finally anchored socio-economic conceptions in the general public.

1.3

THE COLOGNE SCHOOL AND SOCIAL MARKET ECONOMICS

The Social Market Economy as a regulative policy aims to combine, on the basis of a competitive economy, free initiative and social progress.[1]

(Alfred Müller-Armack, 1956)

In order to return to economic liberalism after more than a decade of a controlled economy, and in view of the absence of functioning market principles in the immediate post-war years, the ordo-liberal competitive order was further developed by the Cologne School around the economist and anthropologist Alfred Müller-Armack who therefore coined the term '*Soziale Marktwirtschaft*' (Social Market Economy) in a publication in December 1946.[2] Although it evolved from ordo-liberalism, this concept was not identical with the conception of the Freiburg School as it emphasised the state's responsibility actively to improve the market condition and simultaneously to pursue a social balance.[3] In contrast to Eucken, who sought an answer to the social question by establishing a functioning competitive order within a constitutional framework, Müller-Armack conceived the Social Market Economy as a regulatory policy idea aiming to combine free enterprise with a social programme that is underpinned by market economic performance.[4] In putting social policy on a par with economic policy, Müller-Armack's concept was more emphatic regarding socio-political aims than the ordo-liberal economic concept. This dual principle was also to be found in the name of the model. Although the adjective 'social' was often criticised as a decorative fig leaf or conversely, a gateway for anti-liberal interventionism,[5] it meant more than simply distinguishing the concept from that of *laissez-faire* capitalism on the one side and of ordo-liberal conceptions on the other.[6] In drawing on Röpke's anthropo-sociological approach of an economic humanism leading to a 'Civitas Humana',[7] Müller-Armack pursued a

'Social Humanism' or 'Social Irenics'[8] – the notion 'irenics' is derived from the Greek word *ειρηνη* (eirēnē) which means being conducive to or working toward peace, moderation or conciliation – to overcome existing differences in society. Therefore, the Social Market Economy as an extension of neo-liberal thought was not a defined economic order but a holistic conception pursuing a complete humanistic societal order as a synthesis of seemingly conflicting objectives, namely economic freedom and social security.[9] This socio-economic imperative actively managed by a strong state – in contrast to the ordo-liberal minimal state solely safeguarding the economic order[10] – is often labelled by the ambiguous but historical term '*Der Dritte Weg*' (Third Way).[11]

The concept of the Social Market Economy received fundamental impulses from reflection and critique of historical economic and social orders, namely Smithian *laissez-faire* liberalism on the one hand and Marxian socialism on the other. Furthermore, various 'Third Way' conceptions prepared the ground for the socio-economic concept. Already in the late nineteenth century, the *Kathedersozialisten* (lectern socialists), engaged in social reforms in the *Verein für Socialpolitik*, turned away from pure liberalism to demand a purposive state policy designed to regulate economic life and advocated a middle course between anarchic individualism, traditionalistic corporatism and bureaucratic etatism.[12] In the early twentieth century, the Frankfurt sociologist and economist Franz Oppenheimer postulated a so-called 'Liberal Socialism', i.e. socialism achieved via liberalism, as the pursuit of a societal order, in which economic self-interest preserves its power and persists in free competition.[13] This desirable order of freedom and equality was labelled by a later programmatic publication entitled *Weder so – noch so. Der dritte Weg*.[14]

This position was widely shared by Oppenheimer's doctoral student and friend, Ludwig Erhard;[15] although the latter displaced adjective and subject by promoting a 'Social Liberalism'[16] and never liked the expression 'Third Way'.[17] In his opinion the term was tainted, reminding him too much about ideas of a mixed economy, somewhere between a market economy and central planning. He vehemently and consistently argued against the view that models were converging.[18] Further, in contrast to Müller-Armack who emphasised the social aspect, for Erhard the Social Market Economy was always first and foremost a market economic system.[19] By proclaiming 'the freer an economy is, the more social it is,'[20] Ludwig Erhard was rather inclined to Walter Eucken's ordo-liberal competitive market order.[21] Although he even considered himself an ordo-liberal,[22] Erhard based his economic conception neither on Eucken nor on Müller-Armack. In fact, his doctoral supervisor Franz

Oppenheimer and especially Wilhelm Röpke, like Erhard a student of Oppenheimer, was his source of inspiration.[23] Erhard perceived Röpke's books as works of revelation[24] and considered the economist a brother in spirit.[25] On 17 August 1948, however, Erhard referred to Müller-Armack, whom he met after some contact for the first time at the latter's residence in Vreden (Münsterland) in 1940 and by whom he was strongly impressed most of all not as a theorist, but instead as one who wanted to transfer theory into practice,[26] and his concept of the Social Market Economy.[27] Soon after, at the second party congress of the CDU in the British zone in Recklinghausen on 28 August 1948, Erhard circumscribed the concept as a 'socially committed market economy'.[28] Whereas most neo-liberal economists viewed the concept not only as an economic path between the Scylla of an untamed pure *laissez-faire* capitalism and the Charybdis of a collectivist planned economy, but also as a holistic and democratic social order, Erhard and in particular Müller-Armack, however, emphasised public acceptance and civic engagement as prerequisites for the success of the socio-economic model.[29] For instance, Müller-Armack stressed that by 'more socialism' he meant the social engagement *for* and *with* the people.[30] Equally, Ludwig Erhard pointed out that the principles of the Social Market Economy could only be achieved if the public was determined to give them priority.[31] This conceptual imperative had in turn an effect on the communication of the socio-economic concept.

Given that the Social Market Economy required public debate, for its acceptance or rejection, its discussion went beyond an academic and political audience, e.g. within the Mont Pèlerin Society, the *Verein für Socialpolitik*, or at conventions of political parties. Even the academic publications by Alfred Müller-Armack and Ludwig Erhard evidently addressing so-called 'opinion leaders', i.e. academics, the Allied military authorities, journalists, politicians and representatives of various associations and industry, ultimately aimed to influence and direct public opinion. Alfred Müller-Armack noted that

> if it is said that only 30 per cent of the electorate understands the sense of the Social Market Economy, then I reply 'How is it with the socialist theories? Are they better comprehended?' In my opinion 30 per cent of a population is quite a lot [...]. This world is ruled by a minority.[32]

Although appealing to an opinion-leading minority, the general public was the final addressee and Müller-Armack and Erhard applied various methods and media in order to inform and gain credibility in their socio-economic programme.[33] In doing so, despite the potential inwardness of persuasion carried out by communication media as such distinct from their content, the two economists did not attach great importance to the individual communication medium, as long as the message directly reached the audience which was eased by the supportive slogan 'Social Market Economy'. In fact, a former advertising manager for consumer goods, Ludwig Erhard, applied the same strategies as for any other product as far as it was good merchandise.[34] And thereof, the great communicator who passionately fought for his doctrine was entirely convinced. According to Erhard, who made use of the media in order to convey his economic views, as when he founded the periodical *Der Markt der Fertigware* in 1929 which appeared as *Die deutsche Fertigware* in 1933 and when he expressed his economic views in Leopold Schwarzschild's liberal paper *Das Tage-Buch* in 1931,[35] economic policy and publicity were inseparable; the more publicity the better for the economy.[36]

However, Alfred Müller-Armack noted the danger of a public debate on economic policy and advocated a cautious discussion. According to the economist, the public spirit could not yet cope with the tasks demanded of it.[37] Similarly Ludwig Erhard cautioned against a broad and public discussion:

> What makes the attempt to debate the question of an economic constitution [...] complicated is on the one side the electorate's overreliance [...] to accept political doctrines enunciated by single personalities [...]; on the other side the [...] inability to comprehend these complex economic and sociological issues.[38]

Nonetheless, in order to counteract falsification but mainly to promote their socio-economic model, Ludwig Erhard and Alfred Müller-Armack wrote newspaper articles[39] and unremittingly toured through West Germany. The latter stated:

> I practised the business of itinerancy and held presentations. It was the time [...] where even a business card [...] needed the licence number of the [...] military authorities. The officers [...] would have probably not given the licence for [...] a book. Also I did not request it but rather disseminated my thoughts via […] exposés to the German public. [...]. A circulation of 10,000 or 100,000 was not necessary; 200 were sufficient to address the essential receivers.[40]

This source reveals both the effort and the approach with which Müller-Armack campaigned for the common goal, namely to implement the Social Market Economy. In comparison, Ludwig Erhard considered an informed influential minority as necessary but insufficient and rather aimed to mobilise the information media in order to address the German people as a whole. In essence, while Müller-Armack can predominantly claim credit for the conceptualisation and preparatory implementation of the Social Market Economy,[41] it became the mission and merit of Ludwig Erhard to publicly communicate and politically implement the socio-economic programme.[42]

According to Erhard, the realisation of the Social Market Economy could not only be achieved by direct contact to both the public and policy-makers, but also by becoming a decision-maker himself. Thus, the former Director of the *Institut für Industrieforschung* (Institute for Economic Studies) in Nuremberg offered his services to the German *Regierungswirtschaftsamt* (Governmental Economic Office) for Upper and Lower Franconia and shortly afterwards to the American district administration. The US Military Government, familiar with Erhard's detailed memorandum on war finance and debt consolidation[43] in which he advocated a market economy, hired him as economic expert. On 3 October 1945, Erhard was made Bavarian Minister for Economic Affairs in the cabinet of Prime Minister Wilhelm Hoegner (SPD).[44] Apart from some articles in the semi-official paper of the American occupying force *Die Neue Zeitung*, in which he echoed the ideas of the neo-liberals and stressed the idea that the government was responsible for stepping into the economy in order to preserve free competition as a form of the economy that was social because it benefited all consumers within society,[45] the ambitious minister failed to organise the post-war economy in Bavaria and was laid off by the American military authorities on 16 December 1946. Due to his contacts to the liberal economist Adolf Weber, however, the Faculty of Economics at the University of Munich requested a professorship for the dismissed minister. The contact to Weber, who was the doctoral advisor of Adolf Lampe, Constantin von Dietze and Fritz Hauenstein, not only earned him an honorary professorship conferred on 7 November 1947, but also the contact to the Freiburg economists. Furthermore, due to Adolf Weber's advocacy of a major currency reform, Erhard acquired decisive ideas and knowledge about how to enable the financial and economic reconstruction of Germany. This in turn helped him to be nominated Chairman of the bizonal Special Bureau for Money and Credit, which convened in Bad Homburg on 10 October 1947. This panel finally enabled Erhard to attain the most decisive post in the reorganisation of the German economy: on 2 March 1948, Ludwig Erhard succeeded Johannes Semler as Director of the Administration for Economics in the Bizonal Economic Council. Thus the Social Market Economy entered the political sphere and, as noted by Anthony Nicholls, 'Erhard entered into his kingdom. [...] He now had the opportunity to put his theories into practice.'[46]

Although the political implementation was still far from being assured, Erhard now had at his disposal a so-called 'information office' within the Administration for Economics.[47] Indeed, virtually all public relations were incumbent on the Administrative Council's *Oberdirektor* Hermann Pünder (CDU),[48] or rather his *Direktorialkanzlei* (Directorial Office) headed by Carl Krautwig, however, Erhard managed to maintain an effective press office for his administration.[49] This did not even change after Pünder aimed to gradually deprive the independent press offices of their competencies and assigned the coordination of press releases to a centralised press office headed by Karl Heinrich Knappstein[50] due to increasing criticism on the part of members of the Economic Council regarding inconsistencies in the dissemination of information.[51] In charge of Erhard's so-called 'Secretariat II' for information affairs, which was later renamed Department I for press and information, was Kuno Ockhardt. By means of this secretariat, Erhard was able to conduct an active public relations campaign for the Social Market Economy. Using the Administration for Economics and its information journals, namely the *Informationsdienst der Verwaltung für Wirtschaft* and the *Wirtschaftsverwaltung* which both had a respective circulation of 30,000 issues twice per month, he was able to address journalists in press conferences held at regular intervals and launched newspaper articles in order to inform the public about his economic programme and policy.[52] However, although all actions of the administration had to be concerted and virtually all publications were coordinated,[53] the information by the Administration for Economics barely reached the general public.

Thus Erhard aimed to win the public media as multiplicator over to his socio-economic conception. According to the former advertising manager, great ideas require interpretation by the press;[54] a permanent discussion in the media was necessary in order to create awareness and anchor the Social Market Economy in the general public. Thus economic journalism became for him both a functional instrument and an appreciated partner. Ludwig Erhard, constantly concerned about public opinion,[55] attached great importance to the cooperation with the media[56] as he unambiguously revealed: 'it is essential that all cooperate in order to restore the faith and hope of the German people [...] to reverse our destiny. [...] Therefore, I request your support. […] In your function rests an immense responsibility.[57] In addition to the collaboration between official authority and the media for which he was very grateful,[58] Erhard aimed to establish a relationship of mutual trust between him and selected journalists in order to receive support for his economic policy. The Director of the

Administration for Economics was aware of the fact that the public communication and political implementation of the Social Market Economy required influential proponents. A small group of market-oriented journalists, politicians and civil servants formed. Among the members of this so-called '*Brigade Erhard*' or '*Neuhauser Kreis*'[59] were the journalists Hans-Henning Zencke, Gerd Hassenkamp, Hans Herbert Götz, Ferdinand Himpele, Kurt Steves, Antonius John, Klaus Emmerich, Fritz Ullrich Fack, the politician August Dresbach, Erhard's members of staff Dankmar Seibt, Kuno Ockhardt and Karl Hohmann, as well as the economists Karl-Otto Pöhl and Franz Böhm.[60]

In addition, Ludwig Erhard carefully maintained close contacts with both the top leadership of the labour union and the (re)established trade associations, such as the *Wirtschaftsverband Eisen-, Blech- und Metallwarenindustrie* (Trade Federation of Iron, Steel and Metalware Industry), the *Wirtschaftsvereinigung Eisen- und Stahlindustrie* (Trade Association of Iron and Steel Industry), the *Arbeitsgemeinschaft Eisen und Metall* (Consortium of Iron and Metal), or the *Arbeitsgemeinschaft der Bauindustrie in den Vereinigten Westzonen* (Syndicate of the Construction Industry in the Bizone).[61] Consultations with labour were quasi-institutionalised through a labour union liaison office in his administration headed by Eberhard Bömke who as an old confidant of the labour union's leading economic expert and later president, Ludwig Rosenberg, had also been instrumental in drawing up the June 1947 labour union draft bill for economic chambers. Equally, Erhard aimed to influence the employers and industrial associations, such as the *Industrie- und Handelskammern* (IHK) (Chambers of Industry and Commerce). The particular nature of the post-war German situation gave both the representative institutions of self-government with extensive public functions and the long national tradition of corporatism a new importance. After the collapse of the German state administration, the IHK were, in fact, the only surviving agencies of economic administration. For in contrast to government offices, which had been directly integrated into the Nazi state, the chambers had maintained a degree of autonomy even under Hitler and were therefore able to reconstitute themselves in their pre-Nazi form immediately upon the arrival of the occupying forces.[62] Since their technical personnel had an intimate knowledge of the regional economies and had, in fact, in their Nazi incarnation of *Gauwirtschaftskammern* (District Chambers of Commerce), handled much of the wartime raw materials distribution, they were indispensable to both the early occupation governments, who were unfamiliar with the details of the German economy, and the post-war Administration for Economics. Thus the chambers were a natural early focus of Ludwig Erhard's reform efforts.[63]

However, the bizonal *Industrie- und Handelskammern* lobbied for a free market economy and supported Erhard's economic liberalisation in politics, by mainly appealing to the Economic Council via the liberal and conservative parties, and in public expressed by a resolution published in the domestic and foreign press in April 1948:

> The committee of the consortium of the chamber of industry and commerce in the conjoined economic area sees in the adherence to a controlled economy a significant causation for the gradual decline of the German economy. Therefore, [the committee] argues for a return to a market economy [...]. Only in conjunction with a free economy, the Marshall-Plan can release the essential initiative for improved German and therewith European economic conditions. Thus the consortium of the chamber of industry and commerce considers the accelerating gradual reduction of the controlled economy as paramount [...].[64]

Another vital ingredient to implement the Social Market Economy on the policy level was arguably the informal and intimate contact Erhard kept with numerous industrialists, such as the Managing Directors of *Salamander* and *Degussa*, Theo Hieronimi and Felix Prentzel, the Director of *Reemtsma*, Rudolf Schlenker, Otto Seeling of the *Deutsche Tafelglas AG* and Karl Neuenhofer of *Brown, Boveri & Cie.*[65] Amongst those Erhard frequently invited to a so-called 'round table'[66] were the members of the *Wirtschaftspolitische Gesellschaft von 1947 e.V.* (WipoG) (Politico-Economic Society of 1947) founded in Frankfurt on 1 November 1947.[67] This neo-liberal lobbying organisation which aimed to arouse public interest in economic issues and to promote the Social Market Economy[68] listed amongst others the following members: the Executive Chairman of the *Metallgesellschaft* in Frankfurt, Alfred Petersen, the President of the Chamber of Commerce and Industry in Augsburg, Otto A. H. Vogel, the private banker Robert Pferdmenges, the journalists Hans-Christoph Seebohm and Volkmar Muthesius, the former Chairman of the bizonal Department for Economics in Minden, Rudolf Mueller, then State Secretary in the bizonal Administration for Economics, Walter Strauß, the former Prussian Minister of Finance, Otto Klepper, the Senator for Economic Research and Foreign Trade in Bremen, Gustav W. Harmssen, and the future Federal President, Theodor Heuss.[69] According to other sources, the latter's successor in office, Heinrich Lübke, the Executive Chairman of the *Salamander AG*, Alex Haffner, and the journalist Erich Welter also attended the foundation of the WipoG.[70] Unquestionably and interestingly, however, Alfred Müller-Armack was an associate member and Ludwig Erhard was even a charter member of the influential lobbying union comprised of industrialists, self-employed professionals, journalists, bureaucrats and politicians which attempted to influence the economic reconstruction of post-war Germany.[71] Thus, via the proposals and petitions sent by the WipoG to the parliament, i.e. the Economic Council, Erhard not only lobbied politically for his economic programme but also acted on his own administration.[72] Furthermore, the WipoG served as a platform to perform preparatory promotion and anchor the conception of the Social Market Economy in the wider public.[73] Therefore, the association hosted numerous conferences, published newspaper articles[74] and even edited specific newsletters and information bulletins, such as the *Beratungsbriefe* or the *Rundschreiben*.[75] The professional organisation and distribution of these promotional documents was managed by the *Wirtschaftsberichte GmbH* (Economic Reports Ltd) founded by Mueller, Klepper, Petersen and Erhard on 5 December 1947.[76]

In this environment, the first consideration of a national liberal newspaper took place. Especially Ludwig Erhard desired to give the WipoG and his conception a broader platform by which to reach the general public. Furthermore, in order to confront the media opposed to his socio-economic concept and policy, he inspired friendly industrialists and journalists to establish an independent but market-oriented liberal newspaper.[77] The WipoG was to provide the essential contacts and financial funds for this endeavour. On 11 August 1949, around forty entrepreneurs met in Kornwestheim and made 51 per cent of the seed capital available to establish a German national liberal quality newspaper.[78] The other 49 per cent of the share capital were provided by the *Mainzer Zeitungsverlags-GmbH*.[79] Erich Welter, a member of the WipoG and journalist at the *Allgemeine Zeitung* (AZ) in Mainz, acted as a facilitator. It was the editor's ambition to revive the former liberal daily *Frankfurter Zeitung*, which was closed by the National Socialists in 1943.[80] When the obligatory licensing by the Allied authorities was abolished in September 1949, the appearance of the first national daily newspaper in post-war West Germany was enabled, and, finally, on 1 November 1949, the *Frankfurter Allgemeine Zeitung* appeared. Its first issue contained a clear commitment to quality and independence.[81] However, the eminently respectable newspaper[82] could not disengage from its investors and founders. Next to the industrialists, who favoured a market-oriented economy,[83] the editor of the FAZ and devotee of Walter Eucken's ordo-liberalism, Erich Welter,[84] influenced the orientation of the liberal-conservative newspaper. In turn, the FAZ, in which Leonhard Miksch and Alexander Rüstow also published articles,[85] not only prepared the grounds for neo-liberal thinking but also became one of the most important organs and proponents of the Social Market Economy.[86] The organ with the subtitle *Zeitung für Deutschland* (Newspaper for Germany) gave Erhard and the social market economists a voice and nationwide audience. In realising and using this opportunity, Ludwig Erhard not only wrote for the *Frankfurter Allgemeine Zeitung*,[87] but was also the object of reporting and advertisement after Erich Welter suggested that the paper write more about the 'Erhard Era'.[88]

Similarly other private initiatives, such as the *Bund Katholischer Unternehmer* (BKU) (Organisation of Catholic Entrepreneurs) founded in Königswinter in March 1949, *Die Waage – Gemeinschaft zur Förderung des sozialen Ausgleichs e.V.* (The Weigh Scales – The Society for the Promotion of Social Compromise) founded by the economist Götz Briefs, the entrepreneurs Curt Becker and Philipp F. Reemtsma, the Managing Director of *Glashütte J. Weck*, Alphons Horten, the President of the Chamber of Commerce and Industry in Cologne, Franz Greiss, and the Chief Executive of *Bayer Leverkusen*, Fritz Jacobi, in Cologne in 1952, or the *Aktionsgemeinschaft Soziale Marktwirtschaft* (ASM) (Action Group for the Social Market Economy), established in Heidelberg in May 1953, not only endorsed Erhard's economic policy but also informed people about the Social Market Economy's distinctive exponent.[89] Thus, soon after his assumption of office as Director for Economics in the bizonal administration in March 1948, Erhard and his imperturbable conviction and passion to campaign for his conception were already well-known though the German public considered Kurt Schumacher to be the most competent politician at this time.[90] In essence, the publicity organised and financed by the private sector proved to be extremely successful and conducive to Erhard's image as a competent economist and politician.[91]

This public perception was affirmed and amplified by Ludwig Erhard's charismatic appearance in pre-parliamentary lectures and debates. The unpretentious rosy-cheeked man with the round face and the big cigar along with his polemic and metaphoric speeches radiated optimism and inspired confidence.[92] Moreover, his strong conviction embodied by an altruistic and authentic leading official became 'the power of a message' as the historian Klaus Hildebrand termed it.[93] Hardly anyone in the audience was immune to his charisma and power of persuasion; often the bearer of the message on the marketplaces became more important to the people than the message itself. This gift to appear convincing and to convey his own conviction to the masses inevitably aroused the interest of political parties.[94]

Overall, three parties, namely the FDP, the CDU and the CSU aimed to win over the unaligned Erhard.[95] The advocate of the Social Market Economy rejected all proposals, however, he was aware of the fact that the implementation of his economic policy required a majority in the Economic Council. Precisely here, on 21 April 1948, Erhard delivered a kind of a government economic policy statement by which he informed the parliament about his economic policy and forthcoming measures. After this rhetorically brilliant speech[96] that he concluded by picking up Walther Rathenau's famous words 'the economy is our fate,'[97] the delegates were familiar with the Social Market Economy and its prophet. Although there was no unanimous applause, the Liberal Democrats and the conservatives widely welcomed the transition to a more market-oriented economy.[98] Thereupon, the chairman of the CDU in the British occupation zone, Konrad Adenauer, invited Erhard to introduce and to explain his socio-economic conception to the party members during the party convention in Recklinghausen on 28 August 1948. In a visionary and stirring speech, entitled *Marktwirtschaft im Streit der Meinungen* (Market Economy in Dispute),[99] Ludwig Erhard defended his concept of the Social Market Economy alluding to the dualism between a controlled economy and a market economy.[100] In view of the upcoming elections, Adenauer, who was initially sceptical about Erhard,[101] was not only impressed by the polarising slogan, i.e. 'Controlled or Market Economy', but also by the efficacy of Erhard and his programme.[102] The foundation for a successful political alliance was laid.[103]

The Director for Economics also proved the ability to assert himself in parliament, i.e. the Economic Council, and in politics in general. After Erhard's *Leitsätze-Gesetz* was passed by the economic parliament on 17/18 June, he summarily enforced the law that abolished virtually all rationing and lifted price controls. It was an astonishingly bold manoeuvre, the more so given that a great deal of it had been done without the prior consultation and agreement of the military governors. The French and the British officials were aghast and furious. The Americans were nervous. The following day, the United States' Military Governor, General Lucius D. Clay, who was rather an administrator than a soldier which certainly influenced his approaches that generally proved to be beneficial for Germany, confronted Erhard on his decision to alter the rationing regulations in view of the fact that all his advisors were opposed to this move which they considered a terrible mistake. To Clay's surprise, the Director of the Administration for Economics responded without hesitation: '*Herr General*, I did not alter the rationing regulations, I abolished them! [...] Pay no attention to your advisors, mine tell me the same thing.'[104] Clay seemed impressed by this attitude and realised that stopping the dynamic won by Erhard's decision would have been the wrong move.[105] Hence, a dismissal of the head of the Administration for Economics was out of question.[106] Eventually, the Allied military authorities tolerated Erhard's behaviour and approved the *Leitsätze-Gesetz* on 30 June 1948.

One of the main principles of Ludwig Erhard's liberal economic policy was a financial reorganisation. Without a reform of the German currency, the successful integration of the Bizone into the European Recovery Programme (ERP) was challenged. Furthermore, it was essential to remove a domestic inflationary glut of money of estimated 300 billion *Reichsmark* (RM); at the same time there was a scarcity of food and goods. German officials and Allies alike agreed that a new currency should replace the then barter trade and cigarette valuta. However, in view of incalculable economic, financial and political consequences, mainly the American authorities took charge of a necessary currency reform. The German experts, who initially believed themselves able to contribute their own approach,[107] were merely given the subordinate task of drafting the laws and regulations. Thus, they insisted on a public Allied proclamation stating that the three occupying powers carry sole responsibility for the currency reform.[108] Eventually, the Chairman of the Executive Committee, Hermann Pünder, and the president of the Economic Council, Erich Köhler (CDU), publicly announced the currency reform on 18/19 June 1948.[109] By this first concrete step of the Social Market Economy, Erhard's socio-economic programme became concrete and noticeable to everyone. Indeed, like other important messages at the time, the monetary reform was proclaimed via radio transmission commenced by a well-known signature tune that guaranteed a big audience, however, just the implementation of the tangible concept itself which Ludwig Erhard considered to be very popular[110] was simultaneously the most effective form of communication. In equal measure, Erhard justified his action to both the general public[111] and the parliament.[112] Furthermore, in front of an auditorium of more than 3,000 people in Frankfurt on 14 November 1948, Erhard defended his economic concept in a public debate with the Minister for Economic Affairs of North Rhine-Westphalia, Erik Nölting (SPD).[113]

Indeed, Erhard proved himself in the pre-parliamentary as well as in the parliamentary arena. Now, Adenauer invited him to present his concept to the *Zonenausschuss*, namely the executive committee of the CDU in the British zone of occupation, in Königswinter on 24 February 1949. Although Adenauer introduced him as a liberal democrat, Erhard commenced his speech with a clear commitment to the CDU and offered his services: 'for my part, you can deploy me in your campaign twice or three times a day. [...] Then we will not only win the elections, and thus make the history of Germany, but shape the vision of Europe.'[114] Overall, Erhard not only aimed to mediate between an academic, political and professional elite on the one side and the general public on the other, but also finally wanted to implement his socio-economic conception. For him, the CDU was the means to an end. Although without party affiliation,[115] Erhard affirmed that he would 'go into the upcoming political party clashes with particular energy for the CDU'[116] and campaigned for the conservative party that finally adopted the Social Market Economy in its party platform, the *Düsseldorfer Leitsätze* on 15 July 1949.[117]

During the election campaign, which was dominated by the economic agenda, Erhard held presentations in more than ninety locations all over West Germany. Up to ten times a day in six weeks, the untiring communicator of an economic and socio-political programme was on stage.[118] Additionally, the agent of the Social Market Economy addressed and informed the public in audio transmissions.[119] Wherever the eloquent proponent of a market liberal course and opponent of a controlled economy, which he saw represented in the tenets of the SPD's economic programme,[120] went during the campaign, places were packed and a wide audience was guaranteed,[121] to the benefit of both himself and the CDU. While Erhard was offered a candidateship in the constituency Ulm-Heidenheim in North-Wuerttemberg-Baden and the prospect to become Minister for Economic Affairs in the event of an election victory,[122] the political party disposed of a powerful manifesto. This both unified its members and provided the opportunity to employ the dichotomy of 'Market or Planned Economy' to act as a wedge issue against the political opponent in the upcoming campaign for the federal elections.

Irrespective of the outcome of the elections on 14 August 1949, it was Ludwig Erhard who succeeded in transferring the abstract, theoretical ideas of the Social Market Economy as an economic and social order into both the political and public realm.[123] In particular the citizenry was *the* constitutive element in the socio-economic conception of Alfred Müller-Armack and Ludwig Erhard. Thus the concept itself was as important as its communication. While both economists attached great importance to public relations, the contact to the public became Erhard's elixir.[124] Ludwig Erhard was the Social Market Economy's most passionate proponent if not the concept itself.[125] Hence, whereas the ordo-liberal Freiburg School had neither a tangible concept nor a coordinated effort in communicating its economic conception, the Cologne School disposed of both. Although the Social Market Economy is often viewed as a mélange of socio-political ideas rather than a precisely outlined theoretical order,[126] the conception possessed an effective slogan that enabled and supported its communication to the populace. And this was exactly what Müller-Armack and Erhard were concerned about. In contrast to the AG_{EvB} that mainly addressed academic and political classes, the social market economists addressed the entire population and thus arguably stimulated the public debate. Fundamentally, this was achieved by Müller-Armack's and Erhard's sedulous advocacy for the Social Market Economy. However, finally by Erhard's assumption of office as Director in the bizonal Administration for Economics, the economic concept entered the public and political sphere. This post enabled Erhard to mediate between an academic, political and professional elite on the one side and the general public on the other. Furthermore, this function equipped the economist not only with the necessary political influence but also with an effective press apparatus. Although Erhard did not attach great importance to the individual medium as such in promoting his economic view, the media in general became both an appreciated partner and an indispensable vehicle for him. Not least, the press helped to make political decisions transparent and it is arguable whether Erhard would have politically survived without the support of the media given that his economic measures, i.e. the ending of price control and government control of the economy, were very unpopular.[127] In order to ensure that the media were also conducive in presenting him as a competent economist and politician, Erhard cultivated the company of selected journalists and influential personages.[128] These contacts proved also beneficial in establishing private initiatives in order to promote his economic programme and policy. The eventual implementation, however, required not only communication but also political backup. Here, the socio-economic concept met the economic conceptions of the conservative parties, in particular the CDU and his leader, Konrad Adenauer.

2

POLITICAL CONSIDERATIONS BETWEEN PROGRAMMATIC INTENTION AND PRAGMATIC IMPERATIVE

What has always made the state a hell on earth
has been precisely that man has tried to make it his heaven.[1]

(Friedrich Hölderlin, 1798)

After the collapse of the Third Reich and the war with its terrible consequences, namely the disintegration of the state and the dire economic situation, academics were not the only group aiming to find an answer to the pressing political and economic needs. Established and emerging political parties were also concerned about the situation and developed concepts between programmatic progression and pragmatic practicability. After twelve years of an anti-democratic Nazi despotism, however, political associations and organisations were confronted with a credibility gap in the general public. Furthermore, the collapse of the centralised regime entailed a regionalisation of public political identification. As Theodor Heuss (FDP), the first President of the Federal Republic of Germany, was to put it: 'world catastrophes, which vehemently shake a nation, have at first the strange effect of decentralising the emotions. [...] People attempt to escape to fields where the [...] great political world is not felt so directly.'[2] Notwithstanding the fact that such a mood was at best a transient phenomenon, political parties initially had to fight both a credibility gap and political disenchantment.

At the same time, however, the German people welcomed the resurrection of a democratic consciousness and appreciated the opportunity to express themselves via representative bodies. In particular the regained democracy in post-war West Germany was not taken for granted. The German people were aware of the fact that the perpetuation of democracy ultimately required the active participation of the citizenry as the actual sovereign. Thus political parties committed to common welfare were important for the integration and representation of individual interests. Furthermore, in order to facilitate the formation of opinion, democracy entailed transparency. These preconditions influenced political objectives, party platforms, and not least the communication of political and economic programmes.

While the academic schools had to fight for publicity, the political parties fought for credibility. Ultimately, both were dependent on public acceptance and the latter on voter preferences. The representative character and exposed nature of political parties, however, not only involved the opportunity to fight for majorities in parliament, but also entailed more public attention and, thus, media coverage. Additionally, the parties had more opportunities and facilities to address the general public with their party platforms. Programmatic conceptions were not only publicised by newspaper articles, posters and pamphlets, but also enunciated at presentations and stagings during election campaigns. For this purpose, the complex political programmes were simplified and popularised.

This chapter is a critical assessment of the programmatic developments regarding economic and socio-political conceptions of the major political parties in the three western zones of occupation, i.e. the SPD, the CDU/CSU, and finally the FDP, and the communication of their respective party platform.

2.1

THE SOCIAL DEMOCRATIC PARTY AND LIBERAL SOCIALISM

We need pragmatic solutions not programmatic declarations.
There is no particular theoretical economic concept
that can tell us how to cope with the problems in times of need.[1]

(Kurt Schumacher, 1946)

Of all the political parties in post-war Germany, the *Sozialdemokratische Partei Deutschlands* (SPD) was best positioned to legitimately assume leadership in German political and economic reconstruction.[2] In comparison with most other parties at the time, the Social Democrats could draw on an extensive organisation and party history dating back to pre-war times.[3] Furthermore, due to the party's resolute anti-fascist and oppositional role during the Third Reich, the former SPD delegate in the German *Reichstag* and opponent of National Socialism, Kurt Schumacher, aimed to revive the Social Democratic Party[4] and derived a claim for leadership for his party in a period of political and economic reorganisation.[5]

Marked by a decade in concentration camps, the antagonist of totalitarianism and advocate of a parliamentary democracy soon became both a symbol of a renewed social democratic self-confidence and hope for liberation from isolation and depression.[6] Schumacher's physical appearance – aged 19, in December 1914, the combatant in the First World War lost his right arm and, furthermore, the imprisonment for a decade in various concentration camps affected his physical health resulting in the amputation of his left leg – symbolised the victims of Nazi dictatorship and provided his already brilliant rhetoric with additional credibility.[7] Through his patriotism and optimism,[8] the charismatic democrat won both personal devotees and party members – already one year after the legalisation of political parties in West Germany, the SPD had 700,000 members. Thus the, at that time, relatively unknown Kurt Schumacher soon became the dominant figure within the SPD.[9] Having already been elected authorised party representative for the western zones of occupation in October 1945, Schumacher became party chairman at the first party convention taking place in Hanover between 9 and 11 May 1946.[10] There he explicitly emphasised the significance and mandate of the SPD in post-war Germany:

> Germany must never again be object of capitalist exploitation but be subject of socialist organisation; [...] either the Social Democratic Party will be the decisive and formative factor in the political and economic reorganisation of post-war Germany, or it will refuse to cooperate.[11]

Accordingly, the political principles adopted at the party congress reflected this demand for political leadership:

> Social Democracy is not content with the historical legitimation given by its great history in the struggle for freedom. It wants to perennially justify its claim as a guiding political force in German politics by its positive achievements for state and people, by its honesty, sincerity, and practicality of its policy.[12]

Furthermore, this statement provides an indication of Schumacher's intended socio-political and economic direction of the post-war SPD. By referring to the labour party's glorious past and previous achievements, the party chairman aimed to establish a link with the pre-war SPD and to revive the old reform-oriented labour movement. Furthermore, Schumacher also aspired to the pluralistic opening of the SPD. By 'winning the middle classes as historical mission'[13] the party leader hoped to enlarge the party's social basis without losing cohesion and conviction.[14] Thus one can observe both reconstruction of the old labour party and rebirth of a socialist *Volkspartei*; even though academic literature provides numerous and different interpretations of the SPD's political restart in 1945.[15] However, Schumacher's intention to form a uniform democratic socialist mass party[16] was based on a historical continuity but emerged from the social and political context of the immediate post-war years. Through his politically motivated programmatic speeches, the party chairman aimed to gain political influence and public support.[17] In order to form a social democratic *Volkspartei*, the pragmatic Marxist was prepared to abandon Marxism as dogma whereas Marxism as applicable method remained incontestable.[18] For Kurt Schumacher, who clearly differentiated between Marxism and communism, which he rejected as a degenerate form of Marxism, the German post-war democracy had to be socialist and anti-capitalist. According to the party chairman 'there is no socialism without democracy. [...] Conversely, in capitalism democracy is in permanent danger [...], thus the German democracy must be socialist.'[19] This view was founded on a socio-political, economic and psychologically-oriented analysis of totalitarian fascism, Leninism and Stalinism: while fascism and Bolshevism were characterised by an undemocratic structure of society, capitalism was characterised by an undemocratic structure of the economy; thus the way of Germany could only be a 'third' one.[20] Political and economic democracy were supposed to complement each other leading to the conception of a 'Third Way' which Schumacher explicitly formulated in June 1947: 'we must differentiate ourselves from the Russians in that Europe must be democratic [...]; and we must differentiate from the United States in that Europe must be socialist.'[21] With regard to the German political and economic structure, Schumacher outlined the alternative: 'either we succeed in forming Germany's economy socialist and its policy democratic, or we will cease to exist to be a German people.'[22] Adopting the terminology of Marxist criticism of capitalism and combining anti-fascist views with anti-capitalist points, the chairman of the SPD derived the *Sozialistische Demokratie* (Socialist Democracy) located between Bolshevism and capitalism.[23]

The economic foundation of this social democratic Third Way was based on the concept of a mixed economy labelled *Wirtschaftsdemokratie* (Economic Democracy), which combined elements of socialism with aspects of capitalism. According to Kurt Schumacher, the socialist reform of society and the anchor of democracy could only be achieved by the non-profit orientation of the economy and the nationalisation of basic industries.[24] Primarily, the devotee of labour leader Ferdinand Lassalle[25] aimed at limiting the power and influence of large-scale industry and requested a shift away from market capitalism towards socialist planning. Thus, in contrast to the British and French post-war nationalisations, socialisation and planning in Germany were primarily concerned with wresting the power to abuse economic and ultimately political influence from cartels and industrialists without returning it to the hands of an all-powerful government or state bureaucracy. However, especially in the light of the severe economic situation in the aftermath of the war, Schumacher considered the capitalist system as economically, politically and ethically inadequate and unjustifiable. For a period of transition with its exceptional circumstances, such as the absence of a dependable, or rather morally and politically acceptable, market mechanism, the party chairman requested some kind of economic planning and the practicality in terms of applicability of policies and stipulated the postulate 'socialism as day-to-day task'.[26] By a gradualistic economic policy, Schumacher gave priority to pragmatic solutions carried out by a centralised administration in order to help the people and deferred programmatic developments of overall political and economic concepts: 'we need concrete programmes for assistance in day-to-day life [...]; there is no programme that can tell us how an acute emergency can be solved under certain conditions.'[27] Thus, despite the early appeals of various economic theorists, such as Gustav Klingelhöfer, to search for a new economic structure,[28] the SPD's economic direction and definition of Economic Democracy remained to a large extent undecided. Although according to the party there was neither uncertainty nor dissension about the social democratic economic policy,[29] diverse concepts collided at different meetings and party conventions and are evidence of an unfinished debate and a conflict of interests.[30] It is not the intention of this chapter to present these economic concepts in detail as done in other academic publications,[31] but to show the broad spectrum of social democratic ideas which may have complicated a consistent appearance and coherent communication of ideas.

At the first party congress in Hanover in May 1946, for instance, traditional socialist views met liberal market-oriented agendas. In his position paper, the confidant of Kurt Schumacher and Director of the bizonal Department of Economics in Minden, Viktor Agartz, proclaimed a socialist planned economy characterised by central governmental control and extensive nationalisation.[32] Although most Social Democrats favoured nationalisation and a certain form of economic control to cope with the economic situation at this time,[33] some party members, such as the academic Fritz Naphtali and the Secretary General of the *Zonenbeirat der Britischen Zone*, the Advisory Council of the British Zone, Gerhard Weisser, endorsed a limitation of governmental interference in the market and private initiative.[34] Eventually, Weisser succeeded in influencing the party members and the party executive by his liberal socialism, which was reflected in the economic principles adopted at the party conference.[35] Whilst the principles of the SPD for the formation of a socialist German economic constitution also considered nationalisation and state control as essential,[36] the supporters of an indirect control of the economy, namely a more liberal economic policy, increasingly won recognition.

Whereas Viktor Agartz was the keynote speaker at the party conference in Hanover, Gerhard Weisser was given the opportunity to present his views at the meeting of the *Wirtschaftspolitischer Ausschuss beim Parteivorstand*, the intra-party commission for the formulation of a socialist economic programme, which was chaired by Kurt Schumacher. Weisser also represented the liberal social wing of the SPD at the convention of economic experts and politicians from all four zones in Hamburg on 21/22 June 1946.[37] This conference showed how close some social democratic political positions were to market-oriented ideas at that time. According to the minutes of that meeting, even the liberal economist Alfred Müller-Armack was only willing to act as *advocatus diaboli* as his arguments were comparable with the conception of Gerhard Weisser arguing for a Third Way described by 'optimum instead of maximum'.[38] Accordingly, the objective of the economy was not to achieve a maximum of private profit but an optimum for the people. Indeed, in order to supply the population with food and basic goods in times of need, the liberal socialists agreed with most of the conferees and the public who considered central governmental economic planning and the nationalisation of core industries as essential.[39] In contrast to Agartz and some representatives of neo-Marxist agendas, Weisser and several other Social Democrats, however, advocated the limitation of state control to large-scale industry and the retention of private entrepreneurial initiative.

This opinion was shared by the Minister for Economic Affairs of North Rhine-Westphalia, Erik Nölting. The professor for economics and former student of Franz Oppenheimer was the designated speaker at the SPD party congress in Nuremberg between 29 June and 2 July 1947. Here, the spokesman of the consultative committee for economic affairs appointed by the party executive reported on the panel's outcomes and he used the opportunity to present his economic ideas. Nölting aimed at restructuring the German economy in a socialist sense, namely by socialisation and a directed economy.[40] However, nationalisation was confined to basic industries and state control was reduced to a minimum.[41] Nölting who distinguished between direct and indirect control, e.g. via fiscal policies, requested free enterprise, competition and worker participation.[42] Particularly with regard to the Nazi dictatorship, the German economy ought to be democratic and Nölting resisted any allegation the SPD wanted to maintain the controlled economy of the Third Reich. Despite Agartz's still dominant position in the intra-party commission for the formulation of a socialist economic programme, the more market-oriented members of the intra-party commission for economic affairs, such as Gerhard Weisser, Erik Nölting or Gert von Eynern,[43] increasingly prevailed. This influence is reflected in the resolution for a social democratic economic policy passed at the party convention in 1947.[44]

The concept of a Liberal Socialism characterised by a regulated form of market economy was pushed further in the presentations by the Minister for Economic Affairs of Wuerttemberg-Baden, Hermann Veit, and the Bavarian Minister for Economic Affairs, Rudolf Zorn, during the SPD party conference in Düsseldorf in September 1948. Here, the speakers campaigned for a combination of organised supply and free demand labelled *Regulierte Marktwirtschaft* (Regulated Market Economy).[45] In contrast to Agartz's planned economy, Weisser's conception of a Third Way and Nölting's directed economy, the advocates of such a regulated market economy who also included the Senator for Economic Affairs in Hamburg, Karl Schiller, the Secretary General of the *Länderrat*, Heinrich Troeger, and the SPD's spokesman for financial affairs in the Economic Council, Walter Seuffert, did not demand the nationalisation of production facilities and governmental control of the economy. Instead, they requested the democratisation of the economy via worker participation and the abandonment of direct governmental interference; only indirect measures were accepted to regulate the market.[46] While an opinion poll among party members at the party convention signified that the majority of the SPD supported this change of direction in economic policy from a Planned to a Regulated Market Economy, the party executive was hesitant to pass any declaration or manifesto as an outcome of the convention in 1948, but further on supported production control and nationalisation in particular cases.[47]

In essence, two opposing parliamentary groups had emerged within the SPD: the followers of Viktor Agartz and a planned economy on the one side, and the supporters of a regulated market economy on the other. This inconsistency was both a sign of the continuing internal party debate on the programmatic development of economic policy, as well as of the insecurity triggered by the unexpected success of Erhard's liberal economic policy. Various members of the SPD, such as the chairman of the SPD parliamentary group in the Economic Council, Erwin Schoettle, cautioned against an uncoordinated appearance and its consequences for public elections: 'it is not so much the fact that we Social Democrats did not have clear concepts, it is rather that our concepts are not yet coordinated.'[48] Even Erich Ollenhauer, representing Kurt Schumacher on the party board due to the latter's illness, criticised the SPD:

> We neither had the time, nor the energy, nor the people to develop [...] a programme in which it is in concrete terms stated, what practical politics and economic policy Social Democracy would conduct in Germany in the near future. [...] The question whether we can achieve this task in the coming years will be decisive for the political future of German Social Democracy.[49]

Even during the campaign for the upcoming first federal elections in August 1949 the criticism levelled at the disunity regarding a coordinated social democratic economic policy did not cease. Although the party brochure for the election to the first *Bundestag* expressed a universal commitment to a socialist planned economy,[50] it could not conceal the general dissension among the Social Democrats. This party inconsistency and programmatic deficiency which was due mainly to Kurt Schumacher, who never put emphasis on the development of a specific theoretical programme of economic policy but considered a pragmatic socialism as expedient and essential, was possibly detrimental to the reputation of the SPD and its success at elections. At the same time, the democrat and former political editor of the social democratic daily *Schwäbische Tagwacht* in Stuttgart recognised both the importance of integrating the public in the political course of action and of the risk of deficient or inconsistent public relations. Finally, not only the academic schools but also any political party required the public in the formation and implementation of a democratic economic model. Thus it is important to examine what social democratic economic concepts were communicated to the general public and how this was achieved.

Immediately after the end of the Second World War, Kurt Schumacher, fought for the reconstruction of the SPD and a socialist democracy in Germany.[51] In doing so, however, he mainly addressed a political audience, i.e. the occupying forces, the political opposition or his own party. Rarely did his campaign for an Economic Democracy and economic planning move beyond the political sphere and the party media, such as the *Sozialdemokratischer Pressedienst* (spd), *Der Sozialdemokrat*, *Volks-Wirtschaft*, the *Feuilleton*, or the *Neuer Vorwärts*.[52] Although the SPD press service, the *Sozialdemokratischer Pressedienst*, supplied numerous independent newspapers with articles,[53] social democratic economic conceptions were rather publicised by other Social Democrats, such as Otto Schäfer, Viktor Agartz, Friedrich Stampfer, Alfons Montag, Paulus Skopp, Ulrich Grothe-Mißmahl, Rudolf Zorn, Gerhard Weisser, Herbert Kriedemann or the Secretary of the Trade Union for Banking and Insurances, Paul Kronberger.[54] Furthermore, an analysis of newspapers and publications of that time revealed that neither the social democratic economic conceptions nor their communication to the public via newspapers were coordinated.

However, the upcoming elections – in 1946, communal and local elections took place in all *Länder* of the western occupation zones; additionally, *Landtag* elections indicating the relative strength of the various political parties on a national level were scheduled in Bavaria, Hesse and Wuerttemberg-Baden[55] – required both a coordinated public appearance and a coherent concept. Whereas all members of the SPD were linked by the advocacy of Christian-humanistic values due to the past experiences with National Socialism and the present economic situation in post-war Germany,[56] there was no specific economic concept communicated via election posters and pamphlets. The ideological campaign for the communal and *Landtag* elections in 1946/47 merely opposed capitalism as antagonist of democracy[57] and presented the SPD as the party for the poor and helpless.[58] In order to overcome the economic and social misery in these years, the SPD advocated extensive central planning and the nationalisation of large-scale core industry in line with the example set by the British Labour Party in the United Kingdom.[59] However, on its placards, the party seldom made a statement about a concrete economic model, for instance the pun with its initials: Socialism, Planned economy, Democracy.[60]

Precisely this insufficient and imprecise information about the social democratic economic conception gave the political opposition an opportunity to distort facts and terminology. For tactical political considerations, the opposition reduced the campaign to the polarising slogan 'Controlled Economy versus Social Economy'.[61] Thus the SPD was repeatedly forced to emphasise that its objective was a short-term planned economy, not a long-term controlled economy.[62] Kurt Schumacher tried to disengage from the dilemma by appealing to the socialists 'to make another effort to [...] turn a controlled economy into a planned economy, [...] because, it is easy for the opposition to appeal to the stupidity of those who cannot distinguish a prison from a free athletics club.'[63] Consequently, the SPD not only resisted the demagogy to equate a controlled with a planned economy but also attacked the political opposition by denouncing capitalism.[64] However, it was difficult for the Social Democrats to confront the political opponent campaigning with its economic programme of a so-called '*Gemeinwirtschaft*'[65] (Social Economy) with its own concrete economic programme. Especially in times of campaign where the complex political programmes were simplified and popularised, the SPD lacked an effective slogan.

It would appear that the Social Democrats assumed that the majority of the German people wished for collectivisation of core industries.[66] In order to affirm this position and to gain political ground, the SPD tried to integrate the will of the people by requesting a referendum on the socialisation debate to be held in conjunction with the *Landtag* elections in the British occupation zone on 20 April 1947.[67] Although the SPD was confident about the outcome, the unionists within the CDU in North Rhine-Westphalia headed by the Deputy Prime Minister, Karl Arnold, dismissed the application and with this the public opinion poll. However, achieving relatively good results in the *Landtag* elections,[68] the SPD won the post of Prime Minister in five out of eleven *Länder* parliaments.[69]

Additionally, the Social Democrats occupied eight ministries of economics. Hence, the CDU/CSU demanded the post of the Director of the Administration for Economics in the Economic Council.[70] After an increasing political conflict culminating in a crucial and historical confrontation between the two parliamentary groups regarding the key position in the administration of the bizonal economic area, the SPD virtually abandoned its claim for cooperation under social democratic leadership and decided to form the opposition as Erwin Schoettle declared on 24 July 1947:

> The Social Democrat parliamentary group will not refuse to cooperate in [the Economic Council]. Yet our cooperation will be of a different character [...]. It will not have the form of an unrestrained opposition. It will have the form of a practical, constructive opposition against measures we consider to be harmful to the German people.[71]

This decision can be ascribed to Kurt Schumacher,[72] who considered the Economic Council and its Administration for Economics in Frankfurt to be merely provisional institutions[73] and not decisive political instruments in the implementation and communication of economic ideas and policies. While some Social Democrats, such as Georg Berger, shared Schumacher's opinion that it was therefore not important whether Viktor Agartz or Johannes Semler (CSU) became Director of the Administration for Economics, the disappointment among many members of the SPD was noticeable;[74] after all, the Administration for Economics and its Director were given both increasing room for manoeuvre regarding the implementation of economic policies[75] and, importantly, a media apparatus with its own publications facilitating the communication of these policies. While the German legislature and its administration remained subject to Allied supervision, several Social Democrats, such as the economic experts Gerhard Weisser and Rudolf Zorn, realised that important opportunities existed to develop and implement their own economic and socio-political ideas.[76] Nevertheless, when Johannes Semler assumed his office, Kurt Schumacher merely pledged an intransigent opposition to capitalist interests in the Economic Council[77] and a determined advocacy of the needy in the wider public[78] without further contemplating the enhanced political opportunities to implement and communicate social democratic economic ideas. While the stance of the SPD and its parliamentary group in the following parliamentary debates on the formulation and implementation of an economic model for post-war West Germany has been extensively examined and documented in other research,[79] the purpose here is to analyse the public stance of the *Volkspartei* and the communication of its conception of economic policy.

After the Administration for Economics under the direction of Johannes Semler started operation at the end of July 1947, the power struggle and conflict of competence between the two major political parties continued in parliamentary committees and in public, and, for the time being, the bizonal administration did not reach a *modus vivendi* to confront the then prevalent economic difficulties. In anticipating negative headlines and public hostility,[80] the members of the Social Democrat parliamentary group in the Economic Council recalled that they had committed themselves to constructive opposition and so collaborated in the legislation for the reorganisation of economic planning and rationing. Already in August of that year, the Bizonal Executive Committee dominated by a Social Democratic majority called on the Administration for Economics to complete the drafting of new regulations on rationing.[81] Thereupon, the administrative agency submitted the draft for the *Warenverkehrsgesetz* (Draft Law for the Movement of Goods in the Bizone) to the Economic Council on 28 August 1947. This document revealed the conceptual differences regarding the future economic order: whereas the CDU and the CSU were interested in limiting the law as an emergency law to be restricted to essential goods and valid only until 31 December 1949, the SPD aimed to broaden the scope and attached importance to the wording 'planning and control' in the text of the law in order to form the foundation for an enduring economic policy aligned with planning and control.[82] Eventually, however, after heated debates in the quasi-parliament, the law was not only renamed *Gesetz über Notmassnahmen auf dem Gebiet der Wirtschaft, der Ernährung und des Verkehrs* or simply *Bewirtschaftungsnotgesetz* (Rationing Emergency Law) but was also passed by a close vote on the back of CDU/CSU and FDP support (24 votes to 18) in the Economic Council on 30 October 1947.[83] Having refused to endorse the overall law because of an explicit or *demonstrative opposition*,[84] the Social Democrats thereupon approved the executive orders, which determined the actual application and interpretation of the law by the Administration of Economics, on the basis of their commitment to *constructive opposition* and their opinion that government control of the economy was inevitable at the time.[85]

In order to emphasise the polar dichotomy between the Social Democrats and the more capitalist-oriented parties in the public debate, several party members, such as Emil Groß and Friedrich Caspary, both cautioned against underestimations of the conservative parties' potential with regard to elections, and urged the party executive to confront the political opponent with a practical and concrete economic programme.[86]

Despite these warnings, and the CDU's relatively high percentage of votes in the first state legislature elections in April and May 1947,[87] Kurt Schumacher still assumed that the Christian Democrats would fall apart as soon as the public identified them as reactionary Catholics and bourgeois capitalists.[88] Nevertheless, the party chairman sought to coordinate the activities between the party and its parliamentary group to publicise its position;[89] finally, the upcoming *Landtag*, local and communal elections in the Saarland, Bremen and Wuerttemberg-Baden (October and December 1947[90]) required harmonious appearances and concerted action.

When the more market-oriented Ludwig Erhard succeeded Johannes Semler as Director of the Administration for Economics in the Bizonal Economic Council on 2 March 1948, the SPD had an enemy who promised to facilitate parliamentary and public campaigning. The following day, a report presenting Erhard as a protégé of the American occupying power appeared in the popular news magazine *Der Spiegel*[91] in which leading Social Democrat circles who had planted the story hoped to discredit the newly appointed director. Similarly, in parliament, the chairman of the SPD parliamentary group, Erwin Schoettle, attempted to exert pressure on the politically still relatively inexperienced Ludwig Erhard by unambiguously warning him against any intended measures that were not consistent with the Social Democrats' viewpoint.[92] Erhard, however, was not at all intimidated by their actions; on the contrary, he self-confidently introduced a bill that extended the scope of his responsibilities. According to the wording of this *Übergangsgesetz über Preisbildung und Preisüberwachung*, the so-called '*Preisgesetz*' (Pricing Law), henceforth, the Administration for Economics and its director were in charge not just of macroeconomic policy but also price policy.[93] While the Social Democrats agreed with the idea that a single authority be responsible for pricing, they pushed for an independent agency. Although even some Christian Democrats, such as Andreas Hermes, shared their opinion,[94] Erhard eventually prevailed and the Economic Council passed the Pricing Law on 10 April 1948; the SPD merely succeeded in limiting its period of validity to the end of the year.[95]

After Ludwig Erhard introduced his concept of a Social Market Economy to the Economic Council at its fourteenth plenary meeting on 21 April 1948,[96] not just Social Democrats but also Christian Democrats, such as the Director of the Administration for Alimentation, Agriculture and Forestry, Hans Schlange-Schöningen, had second thoughts about the Director of the Administration for Economics and his audacious project. In view of the nationwide demonstrations against food shortages in spring 1948, Schlange-Schöningen endorsed planning and government control of the economy.[97] Seeing no remaining political scope for liberal experiments, this amounted to a fundamental attack on Ludwig Erhard's economic policy. Erhard's position came under increasing strain within his own party; in addition, he was confronted by a commission of enquiry of the Bavarian *Landtag* that reprimanded him for his administrative and political conduct as former Bavarian Minister for Economic Affairs.[98] The SPD therefore aimed to capitalise on the dissent within the coalition of conservative parties by publicising it.[99] Supported by leading conservatives, Erhard resolutely responded and warned the SPD against disrupting the relationships within the bourgeois coalition and employing the public for cynical political purposes.[100] Eventually, however, the SPD did not succeed in challenging the coalition over this topic, nor was the debate made public, though the populace had once more played a decisive, albeit indirect, role in influencing the political debate.

For the time being, it remained difficult for the Social Democrats to form political alliances and publicly to criticise Erhard and his concept of a Social Market Economy without providing a viable alternative. Despite the scepticism and the declared political resistance on the part of the SPD, as expressed by its economic spokesman, Gerhard Kreyssig,[101] surprisingly no further discussion of Erhard's theses followed within the Social Democrat parliamentary group. Ironically, however, it was the Social Democrat and then Director of the Central Department for Pricing and Wages within the Administration for Economics, Leonhard Miksch, who in cooperation with Ludwig Erhard conceptualised the gradual liberalisation of the economy. Their co-authored *Gesetz über Leitsätze für die Bewirtschaftung und Preispolitik nach der Geldreform* marked the principles for the rationing and price policy after currency reform.[102] This law – aimed at initiating economic liberalisation for a gradual transition to the Social Market Economy – provided the Director of the Administration for Economics, Ludwig Erhard, with such extensive political powers that some termed these principles 'the authorisation to the greatest possible extent ever issued in Germany, apart from the [...] Enabling Act of 1933.'[103] Nevertheless, the draft law was not only adopted by the Administrative Council and the Economic Committee of the Economic Council as expected but also widely approved by the Economic Committee of the *Länderrat* and even by the Social Democrat Ministers of Economic Affairs.[104] In order to become legally effective, however, the so-called '*Leitsätze-Gesetz*' ultimately required parliamentary assent. During the first reading of the law in the eighteenth plenary meeting of the Economic Council on 17 June 1948, Erhard used the debate to present his overall economic ideology and to reaffirm his determination to pursue it.[105] Thereupon, the economic spokesman of the SPD, Gerhard Kreyssig, criticised Erhard's intention to liberalise rationing and pricing by retorting that his party agreed wholeheartedly with the principle of liberalising prices in a sound economy, but not in one of scarcity.[106] According to the SPD leadership and the trade unions, a transition to normal economic conditions was only possible via systematic economic planning[107] – a perception they understandably believed was shared by the public.[108] Thus, the SPD vehemently opposed Erhard's approach and ideology as appearing too utopian for the needs of the population at that time. Yet, the opposition in the Economic Council could not offer an alternative concept and tried not to be pushed into identification with a controlled economy:

> [We] once more want to destroy the consistently appearing misconception [...] the Social Democrats have been advocates of the existing controlled economy. The Social Democracy detests what we have come to know as controlled economy as a legacy of National Socialism in Germany [...] as much as anybody else in this hall. We just have a different opinion regarding the means and the timing to get away from this controlled economy.[109]

The Social Democrats' dilemma was intensified by their shared interest in the success of the currency reform to be initiated by the Guiding Principle Law under discussion. While the delegates of the SPD in the Economic Council widely agreed with Miksch's and Erhard's bill, which granted the Administration for Economics more room for manoeuvre, they refused to assign the director of the administration 'dictatorial authority'.[110] Thus, the SPD parliamentary group submitted a counterdraft suggesting an independent consultative board of trustees.[111] After the original draft law was modified accordingly, the so-called '*Leitsätze-Gesetz*' was eventually passed by 50 votes to 37 in the eighteenth plenary session of the Economic Council on Friday 18 June 1948.[112]

In view of the fact that the Guiding Principle Law – enabled not least by the disunity of the Social Democrats, their members in the Economic Council opposing it, but their delegates in the *Länderrat* unanimously approving it (21 June)[113] – assigned decisive legislative competence across the range of economic and price policy to the Director of the Administration for Economics, Ludwig Erhard, it constituted a turning point in favour of economic liberalisation, and so came to be perceived as 'the most significant parliamentary decision of post-war German history.'[114] In spite of such importance, the *Leitsätze-Gesetz* thereafter received relatively little attention in both political and public debate; the latter instead focused on the imminent currency reform.

With regard to that reform, however, the German authorities enjoyed little potential for influence. Although the Economic Council had even appointed a separate committee to prepare a monetary reform, namely the *Sonderstelle Geld und Kredit* within the Administration for Finance, in October 1947, and even though this panel of experts – once chaired by Ludwig Erhard, now by Erwin Hielscher – submitted a Draft Law on the Reorganisation of German Finance to the Allied Bipartite Control Office in February 1948,[115] the German proposal was eventually not considered.[116] Nevertheless, the currency reform and the subsequent amelioration of the general economic situation were widely associated with the Director of the Administration for Economics, Ludwig Erhard, who had announced the reform together with its far-reaching implications for regulatory policy to the general public in a broadcast on 21 June 1948.[117]

However, once the general euphoria about the new currency gave way to disillusion and disappointment due to rising prices forced up by the enormous demand and relatively low production, strikes and even affrays took place all over Germany in the following months, and the SPD as the advocate of the poor felt justified in presenting a motion of no confidence against Erhard in the Economic Council on 17 August 1948.[118] This attracted considerable media attention upon which the Social Democrats hoped to capitalise; yet, in the event, the endeavour was to fail by 47 votes to 35 *inter alia* due to the absence of eight SPD members.[119] After the press reported about the behaviour of the delegates which in other respects followed the whip in all caucuses and accepted the command of Kurt Schumacher without a word of protest even if they were of another opinion,[120] various leading Social Democrats feared for the public image of the SPD as a whole.[121] In view of these negative headlines, the party executive suggested publicising the positive activities and achievements of the social democratic party representation in the Economic Council.[122] While the SPD recognised the importance – if not necessity –integrating the public by informing about its course of action, the absence of concrete party directives based on an overall economic programme constituted a handicap for the SPD parliamentary group. The lack of coordination between party and its parliamentary representation was detrimental to the reputation of the SPD as a whole.[123] Despite various complaints sent to the party executive, for instance by the SPD in Hesse-Kassel that 'in all reports on the activity of the Economic Council the opinion [about the SPD] was not favourable'[124] and the perception of Herbert Kriedemann that 'the reporting on the social democratic activity in the Economic Council is [...] actually in disorder,'[125] the party leadership did not react to amend this situation. This inactivity confirmed the fact that Schumacher underestimated the competence of the Economic Council and thus the consequences of an inadequate communication of the SPD's achievements in this quasi-parliament to the public. Although the whip and the voting behaviour improved when the SPD presented a second motion of no confidence against Ludwig Erhard and Hermann Pünder on 10 November 1948, the motion for dismissal was rejected by 52 to 43 votes[126] and the labour party failed to use the potential of the Economic Council which was increasingly the focus of the press and the public since its inception on 10 June 1947.[127]

The social democratic electoral campaign for the local and communal elections in the second half of the year 1948[128] was confined to criticism of the economic policy implemented by the Administration for Economics.[129] The political leaflets and election posters denounced the Social Market Economy and its direct tangible accompaniments, such as the increase in prices[130] and rising unemployment.[131] Equally in political and public speeches and newspaper articles, Social Democrats merely criticised Erhard's political procedure and remained vague about their own economic concept.[132] While no viable and concrete economic alternative was presented to politics and the public at that time, there were indeed some social democratic options, such as a regulated market economy discussed at the party conference in Düsseldorf in September 1948. However, according to the party chairman, Kurt Schumacher, who attacked Erhard's ideas as absurd and concluded the early ending of the Social Market Economy and of its proponent,[133] a transition to normal economic conditions was only possible via a controlled economy – a perception he believed he shared with the public.[134] After the Bavarian unions called for a mass rally in August at which around 100,000 workers protested against rising prices,[135] and later when the trade unions, headed by the Social Democrat and union official Hans Böckler, led a general strike on 12 November 1948 in which the men on the picket line demanded socialisation, planning and control of the economy,[136] the representative chairman of the SPD, Erich Ollenhauer, considered Schumacher's perception affirmed.[137] The SPD hoped to benefit from this public criticism on the present governance and immediately tried to integrate the dissatisfaction among the workforce in its strategies and campaigns. Hence, it supported this 'understandable reaction of the organised workforce against the economic policies of Erhard'.[138] This climax of public resentment provided ammunition for the social democratic Minister for Economic Affairs of North Rhine-Westphalia, Erik Nölting, who attacked Ludwig Erhard and the Social Market Economy in the so-called *Frankfurter Streitgespräch*, a public dispute between the two contestants, taking place in Frankfurt on 14 November 1948. There, however, Nölting's statement did not go beyond criticism and no conclusive social democratic economic alternative was presented to the public.[139] Thus, when the price development stagnated noticeably in December 1948, Erhard and the coalition of CDU/CSU, FDP and DP had good reason to be optimistic regarding the first *Bundestag* or federal elections in the subsequent year.

While the success of the Social Market Economy became increasingly noticeable to the general public in the first few months of 1949, Schumacher and the recently established central *Wahlkampfprogramm-kommission* (election campaign programme commission) in Hanover, on which the leading figures of the party were represented under the guidance of Fritz Heine, who had coordinated SPD campaigns in the late Weimar period,[140] continued to believe in the public interest in socialisation[141] and the failure of Ludwig Erhard and his economic policy.[142] According to most political leaflets distributed by the Social Democrats, the capitalist system did not give consideration to economic and social needs but was responsible for the widening of economic and social disparities in German society.[143] Schumacher, who endorsed this position in his speeches throughout the campaign, reminded West Germans that circumstances for many continued to be desperate by pointing out the squalid living conditions, unemployment, high prices, and dislocation that beset many at that time. In addition, he asserted that the bourgeois parties had nothing to do with the economic upswing that West Germany had enjoyed since the currency reform. Instead, the economic improvement was rather the result of factors, such as a milder winter, a good harvest, and the funds provided by the European Recovery Programme.[144] While other leading Social Democrats also merely criticised Erhard's economic policy,[145] the SPD did not provide any concrete economic programme but rather extended the election campaign to class struggle.[146] Consequently, in order to underline the support of the unemployed and blue-collar workers, the Social Democrats opened their campaign in Gelsenkirchen in the *Ruhrgebiet* on 19 June 1949 while Konrad Adenauer and Ludwig Erhard started in middle-class Heidelberg. In his numerous election speeches, Kurt Schumacher polemicised with aggressive rhetoric that due to Erhard's economic policy an upper class was living in luxury compared to ordinary Germans who suffered from economic deprivation and unemployment.[147] Similarly, the SPD election appeal accused the Administration for Economics in Frankfurt as an instrument of *Klassenkampf von oben* (class conflict from above) which solely made the poor needier and the wealthy richer.[148] In order to avoid social frictions but mainly to cope with the economic situation of post-war Germany, the party brochure *Wahlaufruf* of the SPD advocated economic planning and socialisation of certain key industries, such as raw material sectors.[149]

Thus, on election day on 14 August 1949, two fundamentally different economic concepts confronted each other and the voter was called to cast a ballot either for the socialist planned economy or the Social Market Economy.

This clear alternative, however, could not disguise the fact that the SPD lacked a concrete economic concept and thus an effective slogan and communication of party objectives in times of campaign. While it is arguable whether Erhard's economic concept led the SPD to a more confrontational line away from its previous course, however, the programmatic deficiency was predominantly due to party inconsistency. Furthermore, the socialist planned economy confronted the primacy of economics with the primacy of politics despite the wide absence of governmental institutions, viz the economic concept of the SPD rested upon unrealistic premises, such as a strong parliamentary government. However, by performing effectively a constructive opposition in the Economic Council, the Social Democrats contributed considerably to the legislation and the formation of economic policies and to the establishment and stabilisation of a new German parliamentary democracy, an accomplishment Kurt Schumacher unfortunately relativised in a public speech by stating that 'in Frankfurt, all action emanated from the occupying powers and not from the German parties.'[150] This imprudent presentation of the political parties in post-war West Germany was arguably detrimental to the appearance of the SPD and the communication of its political objectives. In essence, the SPD did not use the potential to communicate either its achievements in the Economic Council or its economic conceptions to the general public.

2.2

THE CHRISTIAN DEMOCRATIC UNION/CHRISTIAN SOCIAL UNION AND SOCIAL LIBERALISM

Economic policy
ensured by the concept of the Social Market Economy
is the best social policy.[1]

(Konrad Adenauer, 1949)

In contrast to the Social Democrats, the Christian Democrats in post-war Germany were initially not organised as a national political party but existed solely in the form of various parliamentary groups and former parties, such as the *Deutsche Demokratische Partei* (DDP). In order to absorb civic and liberal groupings and to include Catholic and Protestant democrats in a common conservative and cross-confessional party, in all four zones of occupation Christian-based communities of interest formed on a regional level. The numerous newly founded parties, such as the *Christlich-Demokratische Union Deutschlands* (CDU), the *Christlich-Demokratische Partei* (CDP), the *Christlich-Soziale Union* (CSU), the *Christliche Union* (CU), the *Christlich-Soziale Volkspartei* (CSVP), the *Christliche Volkspartei des Saarlandes* (CVP), the *Christlich-Soziale Unionspartei* (CSUP), the *Christlich-Nationale Union* (CNU), the *Christlich-Demokratische Volksbund* (CDV) or the *Christlich-Demokratische Block* (CDB), were unified by a commitment to Christian social responsibility in order to cope with the prevailing social and economic situation in the aftermath of the Third Reich and the Second World War.[2] Thus the early programmatic discussions of the Christian Democrats were concerned with the reestablishment of a liberal, democratic and humane social and economic order. Based on Thomas Aquinas' teaching and the *Katholische Soziallehre* (Catholic social doctrine), the conviction that neither an evidently inadequate pre-war liberal capitalism nor an equally antisocial doctrinaire communism but only an economic and social model oriented entirely toward common welfare would serve society, became manifest in so-called 'Christian Socialism'.[3] While in the first post-war years socialism became *the* socio-political slogan and socialist planning was at the centre of both the political and the public debate,[4] the economic conception and the programmatic definition of Christian Socialism remained subject to interpretation and even criticism.

According to the so-called '*Walberberger*' or '*Kölner Kreis*'[5] around the Dominicans P. Eberhard Welty and P. Laurentius Siemer, as well as the trade unionists Johannes Albers, Karl Arnold and Michael Rott, Christian Socialism was derived from Thomas Aquinas' holistic anti-capitalist social doctrine.[6] Thus the economy's foremost objective was the fulfilment of public demand via macroeconomic planning and control rather than the free market and competition. While the socialisation of core industries was pursued, private initiatives and personal responsibility remained unaffected. These socio-ethical and economic principles finally formed an integral part of the so-called '*Kölner Leitsätze*' (Cologne Principles), which were brought forward by the Christian Democrats in Cologne as a party platform for an emerging national CDU in June 1945.[7] Thus Christian Socialism was meant to be the socio-political and economic model for a new political party formed by the Catholic working class.[8]

Similarly and simultaneously, the CDU in Berlin around Jakob Kaiser, Andreas Hermes and Ernst Lemmer considered the pre-war social and economic order characterised by the bourgeoisie and liberal capitalism as obsolete and propagated a new socialist era of the working class.[9] With their public appeal *Deutsches Volk!* in which they argued for a planned economic and social reorganisation with private interests subservient to collective responsibility, and advocated the nationalisation of core industries while maintaining private property, they appealed for the assembling of Christian, social and democratic forces in order to establish the *Christlich-Demokratische Union Deutschlands* (CDUD) as the political representation of all workers and employees.[10]

These corporate and socialist principles embodied in Christian Socialism also formed the basis of the Christian Democratic founding circles in Wuerttemberg-Hohenzollern, North Baden and Hesse.[11] While here the radical Christian revolution was considered equally essential in order to overcome capitalism and to establish a new Christian Socialist Democratic order, in particular the *Frankfurter Kreis* with its editors of the *Frankfurter Hefte*, Eugen Kogon and Walter Dirks, interpreted Christian Socialism more individualistically and less oriented towards common welfare.[12] Thus in their publications they argued for a liberal rather than state-controlled

Sozialismus aus christlicher Verantwortung (Socialism in Christian responsibility), a *Sozialismus der Freiheit* (Liberal Socialism), or a *Wirtschaftlicher Sozialismus* (Economic Socialism).[13] According to Kogon, such a liberal or economic socialism was best achieved by a mixed economy labelled *Sozialisierte Wirtschaft* (Socialist Economy) combining governmental macroeconomic planning and limited nationalisation with private ownership and economic competition.[14] On 15 September, these economic and socio-political ideas expanded into the so-called '*Frankfurter Leitsätze*' (Frankfurt Principles) which served as party platform for the newly founded Hessian *Christlich-Demokratische Partei* (CDP), later to be renamed the *Christlich-Demokratische Union* (CDU) in November 1945. Moreover, these principles were supposed to be a programmatic directive for a projected national *Volkspartei.* Thus, in their effort to establish a supra-zonal *Partei der Arbeit* (workers' party), the Christian Democrats in Berlin were supported by the Frankfurt Circles and by founding members of the Hessian CDU; to these groups belonged the left-wing Catholics Walter Dirks and Eugen Kogon, the former chairman of the *Deutsche Zentrumspartei* (Z) (Centre Party) in Frankfurt and henceforth chairman of the CDP, Jakob Husch, the Deputy Prime Minister of Hesse, Werner Hilpert, the politician Bruno Dörpinghaus, the economist Karl-Heinrich Knappstein, later editor in chief of the *Frankfurter Neue Presse*, Marcel Schulte, the journalist and co-founder of the later *Frankfurter Allgemeine Zeitung*, Erich Dombrowski, the writer August Kober, the medic Hermann Frühauf, the Catholic priests Alois Eckert and Jakob Herr, the jurists Wilhelm Fay and Hans Wilhelmi, the fabricant Ludwig Jost, and, finally, the Christian trade unionists Josef Arndgen and Adolf Leweke.[15]

The aim to form a national Christian Democratic political party guided by a personal-liberal Christian Socialism was also shared by the influential former Lord Mayor of Cologne, Konrad Adenauer, who defined his position at a meeting of the recently founded Rhenish-Westphalian CDP on 4 October 1945.[16] Arguing for a Christian and social orientation without socialisation, he objected to both the socio-ethical anti-liberal agenda of the *Kölner Kreis* and the socialisation attempts by the trade unionist and former deputy chairman of the Centre Party in Düsseldorf, Karl Arnold. According to Adenauer's pragmatic argumentation, socialisation and central governmental planning spawned an extensive bureaucracy and jeopardised badly needed foreign direct investments. Only private initiatives and entrepreneurship enabled the economic reconstruction of post-war West Germany.[17] Finally, he managed to convince Arnold and other charter members of the CDP to abstain from a general nationalisation and extensive governmental interference in the economy.[18] While Adenauer's exertion of influence and contribution to the programmatic development in 1945 are still controversial,[19] for the time being, the commission of the CDP for the formulation of a party platform did not make a statement regarding socialisation and state control.[20] Furthermore, the final party programme of the Rhenish-Westphalian CDP, which widely adopted the *Kölner Leitsätze*, abandoned the term 'Christian Socialism'.[21] Not until the so-called '*Reichstreffen*', the first official meeting of the various founding circles in Bad Godesberg between 14 and 16 December 1945, did the Christian Democrats in the British zone of occupation commit themselves to the Christian Socialism of the *Walberberger Kreis*, and decide to follow the Berlin proposal by taking on the name *Christlich-Demokratische Union Deutschlands* (CDU). However, they agreed upon the formulation *Sozialismus aus christlicher Verantwortung* (Socialism in Christian responsibility).[22]

Solely the Bavarian Christian Democrats held on to their name *Christlich-Soziale Union* (CSU),[23] while deliberately abandoning the term *and* concept of Christian Socialism. According to the party chairman, Josef Müller, the notion 'socialism' put off the middle classes, the bourgeoisie and entrepreneurs.[24] Due to this consideration, the party's foundation charter instead referred to a so-called '*soziale Wirtschaftsordnung*' (social economic order) rejecting general socialisation and valuing free enterprise.[25] Equally, the fundamentals of the CSU published on 31 December 1945 did not correspond to an anti-liberal Christian Socialism but emphasised personal responsibility and private initiatives.[26] However, Müller and the party's internal commission for economic policy, which was established immediately after the CSU received provisional permission by the Office of Military Government for Bavaria on 8 January 1946, avoided an early programmatic commitment to any particular economic order.[27] For the time being, in its policy statements as well as in the campaign for the first communal and local elections in Bavaria on 27 January, 28 April and 26 May 1946, the CSU merely distanced itself from both economic liberalism and a collective economy.[28] While the party further defined its economic and socio-political objectives in the resolution *Die fünf Punkte der Union* (Five Articles of the Union), adopted at the first party convention in Munich on 17 May 1946,[29] and circumscribed its perception of a liberal socio-economic order in the first post-war constitution, namely the constitution of the Free State of Bavaria coming into effect on 8 December 1946,[30] the CSU did not determine a specific economic model at this stage. Not until the guiding principles *Dreissig Punkte der Union* (Thirty Articles of the Union) based on the policy statements of the *Christlich-Soziale Union*, agreed upon at the second party conference in Eichstätt on 14/15 December 1946, did the CSU identify an economic order between doctrinaire liberalism and socialism labelled the so-called '*Mittlerer Weg*' (Middle Way).[31] This third path rejected a planned economy and economic liberalism in equal measure. Further, the CSU argued against collectivisation and general socialisation and advocated personal responsibility as part of common welfare.[32] Although this economic conception was not part of the first post-war *Landtag* elections on 1 December 1946, the CSU wholeheartedly and eventually successfully campaigned for economic reconstruction and political reliance in times of disenchantment with politics, occupation and a destroyed infrastructure.[33] Furthermore, in order to anchor the CSU's economic and socio-political ideas in both political and general public opinion, the CSU party chairman Josef Müller applied to the American military authorities for a permit to edit the party's own newspaper.[34] Although the weekly journal in the style of the economic concept *der Gerade Weg* (the Direct Way)[35] only appeared for a few months, the party's efforts for publicity and public relations were noticeable. Thus the CSU set going a decisive impulse for both the conception and communication of an economic and socio-political model for post-war Germany.

While more recent academic research on the economic and political reorganisation of Germany generally subsumed the various Christian Democratic and Christian Socialist approaches in defining and communicating an economic and socio-political model in the immediate post-war years,[36] this study of the communication of politics essentially provides a differentiated account considering the activities of the Bavarian Christian Socialists and the federal state under American occupation which saw the first post-war government with the much lauded 'founding father of the Social Market Economy' Ludwig Erhard as Bavarian Minister for Economic Affairs, the first political campaigns and the first democratically elected cabinet. Indeed, while particularly the Rhenish CDU in the British zone of occupation obtained a more effective organisational structure and uniform appearance, and thus arguably disposed of greater political influence in the economic and political reorganisation of Germany,[37] however, in contrast to the CSU, the CDU in general initially did not possess a coherent manifesto defining economic and socio-political objectives and thus was not representative of the Union as a whole.[38]

This deficiency was predominantly due to Konrad Adenauer's political calculations aimed at including the several fractions within the party, and the power struggle between the chairman of the Rhenish CDU and the chairman of the CDU in Berlin, Jakob Kaiser.[39] In order both to anchor his economic ideas and to strengthen his position, Adenauer submitted a well-structured concept for a party platform, which was widely adopted at the second party conference in Neheim-Hüsten on 1 March 1946, and, which finally gained him the party chair of the CDU in the British zone of occupation.[40] Only a few days later, Konrad Adenauer began general public campaigning for his Christian-oriented economic and social order following the principle that the economy serves the human being, not the human being the economy.[41] Furthermore, he appealed to all political parties to present their respective concrete party platforms to enable the electorate to make a decision in the upcoming elections. Still, Adenauer did not commit himself to a particular economic model instead merely stated that the materialistic *Weltanschauung* (ideology) had to be replaced by a Christian philosophy; he deferred the debate about nationalisation of core industries to a later stage.[42] However, by making sure that the formulation of the CDU party platform permitted room for interpretation,[43] the abstract resolutions also gave rise to internal debate and public speculation complicating the communication of a conclusive economic and socio-political concept: for instance, when Jakob Kaiser proclaimed socialisation and Christian Socialism as the intention of the CDU and the content of the official party platform in Essen on 31 March 1946.[44] In order to defuse the intra-party conflict about the economic conception, and mainly to control the claims to the leadership, which threatened to split the CDU, Adenauer set up the *Wirtschafts- und Sozialausschuss* (Economic and Social Committee) of the Rhenish CDU. The politically instrumental committee with its 17 members chaired by the banker Robert Pferdmenges and the chairman of the Catholic workers association Josef Gockeln was assigned the task of determining the fundamental principles of the party's future economic and social policy on 10 April.[45] Due to tactical political considerations, the party chairman in the British zone compromised both in his public speeches announcing the indispensability of economic planning and control,[46] and in the resolution of the economic and social committee submitted by him to the Rhenish party committee on 24 July. Here, Adenauer departed from his individualistic-liberal interpretation of Christian Socialism, and emphasised a collective and cooperative economy by simultaneously excluding the term and concept of socialisation.[47] This formulation of a so-called '*Gemischtwirtschaft*' (Mixed Economy) that allocated economic power to both the private and public sectors as a compromise and alternative to general socialisation became central to the CDU's principles for economic and social policy proclaimed by Adenauer in Essen on 24 August 1946.[48] According to the party chairman of the Rhenish CDU, these economic and social guidelines were meant to form the basis for a comprehensive party platform for the Christian Union on a national level.[49] Adenauer's pragmatic efforts to integrate the political wings of the CDU and to consolidate the party on a supra-zonal level aimed at providing an alternative economic concept to the socialisation plans of the Social Democrats for both the upcoming parliamentary debates and the communal elections taking place in September and October 1946.[50] Thus, Adenauer was at that time a double focal point, namely in formulating as well as communicating a unifying and attractive party platform based on a so-called '*Wirtschaftsdemokratie*' (Economic Democracy).[51]

According to previous academic research, Adenauer succeeded in convincing the respective regional associations of the Union in the British and American zones of occupation to abandon the 'unsubstantial' term 'Christian Socialism' and to abstain from general socialisation at the conference in Stuttgart on 3 April 1946.[52] This research on the communication of economic and socio-political conceptions, however, has revealed that not only the return to Christian-humanistic values[53] and the intention for a restart of a democratic, liberal and social Germany,[54] but also Christian Socialism or Socialism in Christian responsibility and socialisation played a distinctive role in the campaign for the first local elections in 1946 – in particular though within the East-CDU under Jakob Kaiser.[55] When the latter even promoted Christian Socialism in Dortmund in the Ruhr area,[56] and furthermore in the run-up to the local elections in September and October the CDU in North-Rhine Westphalia argued for a controlled economy in order to overcome the contemporary economic and social misery,[57] the CDU appeared to be far from a united and consolidated political party. Fundamentally, at that time the Union was still fragmented and did not possess a supra-zonal party platform defining uniform and universal economic and socio-political objectives.

In order to overcome the party's internal fragmentation and to consolidate the CDU organisationally and programmatically, Adenauer pushed for consultations in order to produce an attractive manifesto based on an equally liberal and social party platform at the first party convention of the Rhenish CDU in Düsseldorf on 10 December 1946. In view of the forthcoming *Landtag* elections in Baden, Lower Saxony, North Rhine-Westphalia, Rhineland-Palatinate, Schleswig-Holstein and Wuerttemberg-Hohenzollern in spring 1947,[58] the party chairman in the British zone thereupon presented an agenda which both emphasised personal liberty, which he perceived to be fundamental to political, economic and cultural life, and rejected socialism – considered to be opposed to freedom – at the convention of the zonal CDU in Lippstadt on 17/18 December 1946.[59] While the CSU identified an economic concept between both liberalism and socialism termed *Mittlerer Weg* (Middle Way) and successfully campaigned against general socialisation and for economic autonomy in the regional elections already taking place in Bavaria on 1 December 1946,[60] the CDU in the British and French zones of occupation still did not have a convincing manifesto mentioning a concrete economic model by which it could appeal to the electorate – that was in contrast with the CDU in Berlin which advocated general socialisation.[61]

Within a few weeks, however, Adenauer submitted his economic concept for the reorganisation of the economy entitled *Die CDU zur Neuordnung der Wirtschaft* (The CDU's Position on the Reform of the Economy), which enabled and finally constituted a compromise between the intra-party parliamentary groups by pursuing a third path between capitalism and socialism. The programme advocating a *Gemeinwirtschaft* or collective-oriented economy instead of general socialisation achieved mutual consent when it was adopted as provisional party platform and manifesto on 7 January 1947.[62] After the economic and social committee of the CDU in the British occupation zone commented on Adenauer's concept in Cologne on 24/25 January,[63] the decisive agreement[64] supporting socialisation of heavy industry and certain financial institutions was finally adopted as party platform at the third party convention of the CDU in the Westphalian town of Ahlen on 3 February 1947. This programme was binding on the party, but was soon superseded thanks to Adenauer's intense efforts, in collaboration with private industry, to move the CDU leaders away from their infatuation with Christian Socialism. While the *Ahlener Programm* provided an advertising slogan for the upcoming election campaign for the *Landtag* elections, namely '*Gemeinwirtschaft*', it deliberately remained vague in further defining a particular economic model, merely stating that:

> The capitalist economic system has not done justice to the national and social interests of the German people. [...] The German people shall obtain an economic and social constitution that complies with the right and the dignity of the human that serves the spiritual and material composition of our people and secures internal and external peace. [...] The new structure of the German economy must proceed from the assumption that the time of unlimited power of private capitalism is over. But we must also avoid replacing private capitalism with state capitalism, which would be even more dangerous for the political and economic freedom of the individual. A new economic structure must be sought which avoids the mistakes of the past and which allows the possibility of technical progress and creative initiative of the individual.[65]

This formulation enabled the integration of socialist-oriented party members while simultaneously distancing the CDU from its political opponent, namely the SPD and its socialist agendas. Nonetheless, the programme set clear boundaries regarding nationalisation limited to basic industries and governmental control of the economy by maintaining private entrepreneurship.[66] Hence, the far-reaching party platform adopted in Ahlen was to a large extent in line with Adenauer's economic conception[67] and can therefore not be regarded as a document of Christian Socialism[68] or as 'clearly a programme of the left'.[69] In fact, the *Ahlener Programm* was significant because what appeared to be Adenauer's compromise with leftist elements within his own party was actually a clever tactical ploy. Unlike Kaiser, Adenauer believed that 'with the word 'socialism' we will win over five people and twenty will be driven away.'[70] He and his allies succeeded in reducing the programme of Ahlen to little more than a statement of ideals. As far as Adenauer was concerned, the real significance of the programme's more liberal economic elements lay in the function they served within the CDU itself. The reason for the programme's adoption was to provide the party with an economic programme which, as a compromise, would minimise internal party argument, and allow the CDU under Adenauer's direction, to continue to concentrate on developing its political programme as a whole. Adenauer recognised that at some point in the future West Germans would have to make a choice at the ballot box between a planned economy and a market economy. In 1947, however, the time for this choice had not yet come, and Adenauer and Erhard were still laying the foundation on which it would be made. Moreover, the *Ahlener Programm* is significant with regard to the fact that economic principles were anchored in a party platform for the first time; so far the programmatic declarations by the CDU for a political and economic reconstruction of Germany were characterised mainly by socio-political postulates rather than by economic-political ideas.[71] Predominantly due to the severe economic situation after the cold winter of 1946/47, and further the challenge to integrate the refugees and expellees coming to Germany in the aftermath of the Second World War, economic and social concerns dominated both the political and public debate in spring 1947.[72]

Therefore, comparable to the party platform, the concepts of social and economic policy increasingly came to the fore in the run-up to the *Landtag* elections in North Rhine-Westphalia, Schleswig-Holstein and Lower Saxony on 20 April, and in Baden, Rhineland-Palatinate and Wuerttemberg-Hohenzollern on 18 May 1947. Whereas mainly socio-political issues had dominated election campaigns in the previous year, henceforth, these were widely displaced by socio-economic affairs.[73] Nonetheless, comparable to the SPD's campaign, the emphasis of Christian-humanistic values and the intention for a restart of a democratic, liberal and social Germany were still central themes in the campaigns in spring 1947.[74] In contrast to the Social Democrats solely advocating the nationalisation of basic industry in order to overcome the economic and social misery of that time, the Christian Democrats possessed an actual economic programme with an attractive slogan, i.e. '*Gemeinwirtschaft*'.[75] Even though the concept remained vaguely defined, this advantaged the CDU in times of campaign where the partially complex political programmes were commonly simplified and popularised.

Although the *Ahlener Programm* as party platform and manifesto only applied to the CDU in the British zone of occupation – the CDU in the French zone of occupation did not know about it and the CSU refused to accept it as party platform – essentially both the north-western CDU and the Bavarian CSU at that time had reached a relatively homogeneous programmatic conclusion, an economic system between liberalism and socialism, i.e. the *Ahlener Programm* suggesting a *Gemeinwirtschaft* and the *Dreissig Punkte der Union* advocating a *Mittlerer Weg*. In order to coordinate both future campaigns and the programmatic developments of the two political parties commonly referred to as the '*Union*', the *Arbeitsgemeinschaft der Christlich-Demokratischen und Christlich-Sozialen Union Deutschlands* (AG CDU/CSU) (Working Committee of the CDU/CSU), with its General Secretariat headed by Bruno Dörpinghaus (CDU) as liaison body and information centre editing the bulletin *Deutschland-Union-Dienst*, was constituted in Königstein im Taunus on 5/6 February 1947.[76] When the first post-war parliament, i.e. the *Wirtschaftsrat*, became effective in June 1947, the cooperation between both Union parties led to the formation of a common parliamentary group in the economic parliament, which continued later in the *Bundestag* of the Federal Republic. In order to overcome the fragmentation of confessional and middle-class parties, and to offer a broad political spectrum as *Volkspartei*, however, the grouping required a common programme of political action. In addition, it entailed a whip that committed the two political parties to each other regarding both the implementation and communication of a particular socio-economic model. Although the grouping was not without controversy,[77] the designated chairman of the CDU/CSU parliamentary group, Friedrich Holzapfel (CDU), expressed the parties' commitment to the *Ahlener Programm* at the constituent meeting of the Economic Council on 25 June 1947.[78] Hence, when the 52 delegates elected by the *Landtage* of the eight *Länder* in the Bizone gathered in Frankfurt and the 20 representatives of the CDU/CSU parliamentary group faced 20 delegates of the SPD,[79] for the first time in post-war West Germany two opposed economic agendas, i.e. the socialist state-run economy and the more market-oriented *Gemeinwirtschaft*, competed in an official and decision-making political body.

Concerning the implementation and communication of any future economic model, both parliamentary party groups attached great importance to the Administration for Economics; after all, the administration and its director were given both a media apparatus, with its own publications, such as *Wirtschaftsverwaltung*, and an exposed position due to the influence on economic policy. Thus, when the Executive Directors – among them the key position of the Director of the Administration for Economics – nominated for election by the Executive Committee were due for approval by the Economic Council, it came to a decisive confrontation between the two parliamentary groups on 22/24 July 1947.[80] In view of the fact that the SPD had already obtained the post of Prime Minister in five out of eleven *Länder* parliaments and further occupied eight ministries of economics, the CDU/CSU parliamentary group claimed the position of the Director of the Administration for Economics in the Economic Council.[81] Having agreed on a candidate who was supposed to be one hundred per cent in line with the *Ahlener Programm*,[82] Adenauer called for closeness within the parliamentary group when it came to the final ballot.[83] There, supported by the votes of the delegates of the DP and the FDP, the Union obtained the majority and Johannes Semler (CSU), nominated by CSU party chairman Josef Müller,[84] became Director of the Administration for Economics on 24 July 1947.[85]

With regard to regulatory policy, the newly elected chairman represented the party platform adopted in Ahlen.[86] Therefore, Semler not only received support from the CDU/CSU parliamentary group[87] but also from Konrad Adenauer, who wished to reduce government control of the economy,[88] and so welcomed the director's advocacy for entrepreneurial initiative.[89] In his inaugural address to the first party convention of the CDU in the British zone of occupation in Recklinghausen on 14 August 1947, the party chairman affirmed this concept of an increasingly autonomous economy.[90] In order to ensure the corresponding implementation of his socio-economic agenda, Adenauer asked the chairman of the CDU/CSU parliamentary group, Friedrich Holzapfel, for invitations to the caucuses, and there pleaded for cooperation between the directors, parliamentary group and party.[91] In fact, however, with the exception of Josef Müller, the party chairmen of the Union parties in the individual zones of occupation – including Konrad Adenauer who instead met with his informants and confidants Friedrich Holzapfel, the banker Robert Pferdmenges and the delegate of the Economic Council Theodor Blank, although the historian Rudolf Morsey assumed Adenauer's frequent presence in Frankfurt[92] – seldom attended the meetings of the parliamentary party group in the Economic Council.[93] Furthermore, the collaboration between parliamentary group and parties in 1947 was unsatisfactory despite numerous attempts and proposals on the part of various party members, regional party organisations and even the sister party CSU.[94] Although Adenauer realised the potential of the Economic Council and its Administration for Economics as a decisive political instrument in the implementation of his socio-economic agenda,[95] he was arguably more concerned with personnel policy rather than detailed issues regarding economic policy and the latter's communication.

By contrast, the then newly-elected Bavarian Minister for Economic Affairs Hanns Seidel,[96] whose liberal economic and social views based on neo- and ordo-liberal ideas[97] influenced the economic and welfare programme of the CSU adopted at the emergency party conference in Eichstätt on 31 August 1947,[98] aimed at bringing economic policy and the question of the future economic model for post-war West Germany to the fore in the public debate.[99] According to Seidel, the public and its opinion played a crucial role in the implementation of any future economic model as the economy relied on the people.[100] Hence it was essential to centre the individual and to anchor the principle of freedom not only in the economic and political course of action but firmly in people's minds.[101] In doing so, he criticised previous parliamentary and governmental public relations efforts, which had failed to inform the general public about economic policy.[102] Thus, the appointment of Hanns Seidel to Bavarian Minister for Economic Affairs was of particular importance for both the implementation – all other ministries of economics in the western zones of occupation were occupied by the Social Democrats – and the communication of the CDU/CSU's socio-political and economic agenda.[103] Already at the beginning of his term of office, Hanns Seidel used the opportunity in the budget debate in the Bavarian parliament, which was also attended by his fellow party member Johannes Semler, to outline his liberal as well as social economic concept. Referring to the interrelation and interdependence of the economy and the state, Seidel argued for a market economy with regulatory governmental interference in order to safeguard a social balance; economic liberalism had to be combined and balanced with social commitment.[104] In such a *sozial verpflichtete Leistungswirtschaft* (Socially Committed Market Economy),[105] the state's influence in the market was rather limited and contingent on the economic and social circumstances.[106] Thus, this economic order was not dogmatic but pragmatic, as it had to be adjusted to the particular economic realities. Indeed, the dire situation in 1947 which many considered to be the eighth year of the war required a more directed economy, yet, Seidel aimed at reducing governmental control of the economy as soon as possible and pleaded for a currency reform.[107] In doing so, the Bavarian Minister for Economic Affairs who understood well how to communicate the economic challenges at that time and the necessary provisional measures to both the party at grass-roots level and the general public, benefited from the fact that in the second half of 1947 economic liberalism was increasingly standing up to the socialist *Zeitgeist* of the immediate post-war period; numerous publications in both the media and academia document the intensity and the extent of this controversy and trend.[108] Due to his economic views and the competence to communicate these, the nomination of Hanns Seidel as successor of Johannes Semler, who had been dismissed as Director of the Administration for Economics due to his critical utterances concerning the American food supply by the military authorities on 24 January, was discussed at the fourth party convention of the CSU in Marktredwitz the following day as well as in the caucus on 23 February 1948.[109] However, Seidel rejected a candidacy the very next day.[110] After the CDU/CSU parliamentary group could not agree upon another nominee at this stage, for the time being the then State Secretary in the bizonal Administration for Economics, Walter Strauß, presided over the directorate. Finally, after heated negotiations with the FDP and the CSU which both supported the candidacy of Ludwig Erhard, the Christian Democrats abstained from approving the nomination of Hans-Christoph Seebohm (DP) for the sake of the political cooperation. As the SPD also did not nominate its own candidate, the bourgeois coalition of CDU/CSU, FDP and DP came to a mutual agreement and elected Erhard as Director of the Administration for Economics in the subsequent plenary meeting of the Economic Council on 2 March 1948.[111]

The Union's decision to approve the nomination of the then relatively unknown Ludwig Erhard for this decisive post was arguably more influenced by party political considerations rather than by the preference for a particular regulatory policy. The parliamentary group had unanimously and repeatedly committed itself to the *Ahlener Programm* and initially did not intend to move from its part-liberal part-interventionist economic policy to Erhard's consequent liberalisation of the economy.[112] However, due to some doubts about the effectiveness of government control of the economy, the lack of alternatives,[113] the need to coalesce with the Liberal Democrats, which strengthened the liberal economic forces within the parliamentary group leading to the nomination of the managing director Alex Haffner (CDU) to head the committee on industry and trade within the Administration for Economics,[114] and not least by virtue of the persuasiveness of the former advertising manager Ludwig Erhard, the parliamentary group of the CDU/CSU finally supported Erhard's enterprise to liberalise the economy.[115] After delivering his convincing economic policy statement at the fourteenth plenary meeting of the Economic Council on 21 April 1948 by which he informed the delegates about his economic concept labelled *Soziale Marktwirtschaft* (Social Market Economy),[116] Ludwig Erhard also won the majority of party members of the CDU in the British zone of occupation over to his socio-economic conception. This is reflected in the party's principles of economic policy elaborated by the zonal committee on industry and trade headed by Franz Etzel and the department for economic policy presided by Adolph Reifferscheidt which were widely in line with Erhard's concept of regulatory policy.[117] After Erhard also succeeded in convincing the Christian Socialists and worker representatives of his both market and social economic model,[118] the CDU's change of policy from the ideological, Christian anti-materialism reflected in the *Ahlener Programm* with its *Gemeinwirtschaft* to a more pragmatic materialism based on the Social Market Economy finally became noticeable to everyone by the currency reform on 20 June 1948 and official at the party convention in Recklinghausen on 28 August 1948.[119] Indeed, the Director for Economics proved the ability to assert himself in both the parliament and the party, but, given that the Social Market Economy required public debate, for its acceptance or rejection, its discussion had to go beyond a political audience, and Erhard – and the CDU/CSU – had to convince the sovereign, i.e. the people.

This intention, however, increasingly posed a challenge due to the rise of prices and unemployment immediately following the currency reform. The general public euphoria soon gave way to disillusion and disappointment. Erhard's economic policy met with severe criticism and strikes and even disturbances took place in various parts of the Bizone in the following months. In this situation, the Bavarian Minister for Economic Affairs, Hanns Seidel, defended Erhard's course of action against demands to reverse the liberalisation of the economy by the public, trade unions, political opponents and even his own party.[120] However, he also appealed to the trade associations and the Administration for Economics to abstain from further price increases in order not to sap the public's confidence in the new currency.[121] Equally, Konrad Adenauer, who was initially sceptical about Erhard and his concept,[122] backed the new Director of the Administration for Economics and his procedure, both of which were also controversial within the CDU,[123] and praised the Social Market Economy as a turn away from collectivism to the valuation of the individual and the person.[124] At the same time, he urged Erhard and leading party members in the Economic Council to take action against unpopular price rises and unemployment.[125] Thereupon, the Administration for Economics issued periodical price comparison lists in order to inform consumers and started the so-called '*Jedermann-Programm*' that provided reasonably priced and specifically marked goods to the people. Additionally, a law to prosecute the forcing up of prices was passed by the Economic Council on 7 October 1948.[126] However, all these measures had mixed success because they were limited in range and merely aimed at appeasing the public. Thus criticism of Erhard's economic policy regarding the timing of liberalisation of the economy continued. Finally, the trade unions headed by the labour union official Hans Böckler called for a general strike against Erhard's economic policy. Although Ludwig Erhard publicly condemned this procedure[127] and despite scepticism even among unionists, 9.2 million out of 11.7 million workers and employees in the Bizone observed the work stoppage on 12 November 1948. However, the unions remained moderate in both their requests and approach as the strike was deliberately called for a Friday in order to avoid a spontaneous continuation that would interrupt work – this overly cautious attitude on the part of the unions was often criticised at a later stage as some saw a second fateful position of points and the reason for victory of Erhard's economic policy.[128]

In view of the worsened public sentiment and the imminent communal and local elections in North Rhine-Westphalia, Schleswig-Holstein, Baden, Rhineland-Palatinate, Wuerttemberg-Hohenzollern, Lower Saxony and Berlin in autumn 1948,[129] Konrad Adenauer in particular was concerned with the implications of the actions taken by the Administration for Economics for election results, and so criticised the insensitivity of the parliamentary group and its economic policy which triggered the drastic rise in prices immediately prior to the elections.[130] Anticipating the election campaign of the SPD to attack Erhard's economic policy, Adenauer prompted the party and parliamentary group to point out the achievements of the latter which consequently became subject to political communication.[131] However, the CDU did not yet apply the notion '*Soziale Marktwirtschaft*' to its election campaign. Instead and contrary to Erhard's view who tried to avoid the dualism of control versus market economy by arguing that such an antithesis was obsolete and a synthesis provided the better option, the party campaigned with the polarising slogan of 'Free Market Economy versus Controlled Economy'[132] which had the effect of contrasting freedom with control, alluding to the inglorious years of NS dictatorship. However, it also meant that the CDU continuously had to clarify it did not opt for free capitalism but a socially oriented, regulated market economy. Thus the election campaign required a coordinated cooperation between parliamentary group and party as well as a coherent communication to the press and the public. Although Adenauer was committed in this regard[133] and affirmed Erhard's earlier appeal to the parliamentary group to cooperate with the press in order to ensure adequate reporting about the Union's economic programme and policy, for instance by hosting frequent press conferences,[134] both the collaboration within the party and with the media remained unsatisfactory.[135] Numerous petitions and complaints on the part of various politicians, newspapers – including papers associated with the Union – and interest groups document this state of affairs which Konrad Adenauer could also be blamed for.[136] Despite his constant concern with public relations[137] and the great importance he attached to the campaign for the local elections in 1948, which he considered to be an indicator of public opinion regarding economic policy and a prelude to the *Bundestag* elections in the subsequent year,[138] the party chairman kept a reserved attitude towards journalists after the harmful negative press that he received when he was mayor of Cologne in 1933.[139] Although this attitude slightly changed in 1946 when the party chairman cultivated close contacts with various journalists, editors and correspondents, the relations to some papers and their publishers, such as the *Rheinische Post* edited by Anton Betz and the *Kölnische Rundschau* edited by Reinhold Heinen, remained poor due to Adenauer's criticism of their reporting. Furthermore, he continually hesitated to accept public opinion surveys. Upon receiving the first polling results, he reportedly commented: 'this public opinion polling is the devil's work! How can it be possible to find out so precisely what people think politically, or what they think about the political parties and how they will vote. I distrust clairvoyants and people who claim they can read the future.'[140] While Adenauer eventually came to embrace public opinion polling, the concept of public relations did not yet fully pervade his political acting.[141] Nevertheless, the percentage of votes for the CDU increased in comparison to the *Landtag* elections in 1947.[142]

In order to attain more cohesion within the party and thus a more coherent communication in the federal elections in August 1949, which in turn required a national consistent manifesto of CDU and CSU, both party chairmen, Konrad Adenauer and Josef Müller, supported the establishment of a coordinating committee in October 1948.[143] This panel of representatives from party and Administrative Council, headed by the Christian Democrat Franz Etzel, was assigned the task to formulate a common socio-political and economic concept for all three zones of occupation. Moreover, this programmatic statement by the Union parties was also meant to serve as guiding principle for the party representation in the Economic Council and the delegates in the Administration for Economics as well as manifesto for the election campaign; ultimately, it was the party which had to direct and represent the economic policy in politics and to the public while the administration in Frankfurt was solely responsible for its implementation – however, both were accountable for the communication of economic policy.

In this context and in order to convince the party of the concept of the Social Market Economy, Adenauer invited the independently aligned Erhard to present his views to the executive committee of the CDU in the British zone of occupation in Königswinter on 24/25 February 1949.[144] Erhard's speech supposedly resonated a great deal among the zonal committee, which reaffirmed Adenauer's belief that the CDU should build its economic policies upon Erhard's principles.[145] Only a month later, the zonal economic committee, which at Erhard's suggestion was complemented by a supra-zonal committee with the members Franz Etzel, Hugo Scharnberg, Friedrich Holzapfel, Karl Müller, Andreas Hermes, Johannes Albers and Hanns Seidel to formulate principles for the upcoming federal elections,[146] submitted a concept which was not only based on the Director for Economics' neo-liberal and social agenda, but explicitly advocated the Social Market Economy.[147] In view of the stagnating prices and the necessity to use a convincing economic manifesto, which emphasised the distinctions between the Union and its political opponent, the concept of the Social Market Economy prevailed within the CDU albeit with objections from the Christian Socialists and worker representatives who adhered to the *Ahlener Programm*.[148] After the CSU also expressed its commitment to a market economy with social balance, and Hanns Seidel advocated Erhard's liberal and social economic model at the CSU's party convention in Straubing in May 1949,[149] the economic principles elaborated by the CDU/CSU's Working Committee centred the Social Market Economy.[150] Finally, these principles were adopted as party platform and manifesto for the upcoming federal elections at the CDU's party conference in Düsseldorf on 15 July 1949.[151]

In contrast to the *Ahlener Programm*, these so-called '*Düsseldorfer Leitsätze*' not only provided an attractive slogan to reach consensus within the party and to win public consent, but the principles also precisely defined the underlying economic concept:

> The 'Social Market Economy' was taken as a basis for the German economic policy. [... It] is the socially limited constitution of the commercial economy in which the effort of free and proficient people is accommodated by an order generating a maximum of economic benefit and social justice for all. This order is achieved by freedom and commitment expressed [...] by real competition in performance [...]. The Social Market Economy is in sharp contrast to the system of the command economy [...] but also in opposition to the so-called 'free market economy' of liberal coinage.[152]

Accordingly, the Social Market Economy was not an alternative to the *Gemeinwirtschaft* of the *Ahlener Programm* but rather an advancement on it: on the basis of the Christian-humanistic values of solidarity and equality in a mutually supportive society, henceforth a liberal meritocracy and an economic democracy were pursued.[153] The realisation and success of these, however, were considered to be contingent on the confidence and active participation of all tiers of society. Only if the Social Market Economy were borne by the political will of the entire citizenry, would it be possible to construct an economy that was both free and simultaneously social.[154] Thus the election campaign for the federal elections on 14 August 1949 was not only about canvassing in order to ensure the continuance of the CDU/CSU as constitutive government, but also about promoting the Social Market Economy in order to realise a new economic and social system.

To this end, and to coordinate propaganda throughout West Germany, a special central propaganda committee was established, similar to the SPD campaign organisation, and alongside it also a number of subcommittees, such as the *Wahlrechtsausschuss* (electoral law committee), or the so-called *Arithmetiker Ausschuss* (Arithmetic Committee), entrusted with providing demographic statistics and compiling data on previous state and local elections, were created. This election campaign committee, to which belonged – alongside Dörpinghaus, Etzel, Albers and Scharnberg – the editor of the *Kölnische Rundschau*, Reinhold Heinen, and representatives from the various regional organisations and the Economic and the Parliamentary Council, was assigned the task to 'initiate the measures which prove necessary in light of the election for the coordination of the party interests, including the inter-connected organisation, propaganda, and press duties.'[155] On 5 March 1949, this central committee which planned the party's overall campaign strategy and scheduled nationwide speakers was complemented by a press and propaganda committee which supplied posters, leaflets, brochures, and other campaign material to regional and district party organisations, including the Bavarian CSU, for which it often simply replaced 'CDU' with 'CSU' on the display.[156]

Perhaps the most important source of information provided by the central party leadership was its internal party handout *Union im Wahlkampf* (Union in the Election Campaign) with a circulation of up to 25,000. These papers detailed election information and speaker notes for the party organisers at the regional and district level.[157] Central to this national campaign, driven mainly by Konrad Adenauer and the CDU of the British zone, were Ludwig Erhard and his economic policy.[158] In transforming that policy into effective propaganda, Adenauer urged the press and propaganda committee to avoid any technical jargon regarding the intricacies of economics, stressing, 'one must speak simply to the public, not too much, with a few thoughts and large ideas simply represented.'[159] Thus the polarising slogan 'Social Market Economy or Socialisation and Controlled Economy?' was to become the all-dominant question in the election campaign of summer 1949.[160] While the CDU/CSU had chosen a number of different and contrasting central themes in the immediately preceding years – Christian Socialism had been central to the campaigns in 1946, the concept of a *Gemeinwirtschaft* for the *Landtag* elections in 1947, and free enterprise and a market economy in 1948 – henceforth, they centred the Social Market Economy and referred to Ludwig Erhard's success record.

Along with the *Union im Wahlkampf* that introduced Erhard as an economic expert and stressed his instrumental role in the rebirth of Germany to rank-and-file party activists,[161] political posters and leaflets were the chosen means to disseminate the ideas of the Social Market Economy to the electorate. Although these publications indeed addressed a variety of issues such as culture, refugees or the restoration of German unity,[162] most of the propaganda committee's posters and pamphlets concentrated on economic issues. These mass communication media – for the 1949 election campaign the central committee produced around 1.7 million posters, and several hundred thousand broadsheets were reproduced by the regional organisations – were also seen as the most uniform sort of propaganda that the party employed, with the press and propaganda committee producing the same posters and leaflets for use throughout West Germany, thereby creating a unified and coherent party image that transcended local interests.[163] In presenting themselves as a political union with a determination to construct a social and equally free German economy and community, the CDU/CSU encouraged the notion that it was the more competent and responsible party to safeguard West Germans from the threats from within, such as economic hardship, as well as from outside, namely the ever present Asiatic, Bolshevik threat. This image of a politically strong and economically successful Union was cultivated by a variety of political posters and leaflets; most emphatically perhaps in the poster series *1947-1949* which sharply contrasted the dire conditions from the immediate post-war years to the improved situation of 1949.[164]

While the CDU/CSU propaganda did not appeal to potential voters in terms of their class or profession but instead played on widely held perceptions that all in society had suffered equally in the post-1945 rubble economy and secondly that the monetary reform had alleviated class differences, it was nonetheless deliberately directed towards refugees and women. By evoking an anti-materialist, social and humanist West German society achieved through economic reconstruction, the CDU/CSU attempted to attract these specific groups which the party leadership sensed to be crucial for electoral success simply because of their proportions in society at that time – whereas newly-arrived refugees made up nearly 40 per cent of the population in some *Länder* such as Bavaria, Lower Saxony and Schleswig-Holstein, 55 per cent of all eligible voters in post-war West Germany were women.[165]

As Ludwig Erhard's programme of a Social Market Economy together with his personal powers of mass advocacy brought the CDU/CSU great political credit, over time there was not only a fundamental change within the party's economic thinking but also – often overlooked – a shift in principal actor, namely from Adenauer to Erhard. After defending his concept of the Social Market Economy during the second party convention of the CDU in the British zone of occupation in Recklinghausen on 28/29 August 1948, Ludwig Erhard gradually became the dominant figure in the debate on economic policy. In fact, the party chairman, Konrad Adenauer, seldom participated in the meetings of the CDU/CSU caucuses in the Economic Council and left the economic field mainly wide open to his Director of the Administration for Economics in the Economic Council. In the light of their increased public prominence, on federal polling day in the entire Trizone on 14 August 1949 the electorate was called to cast a vote not only between a controlled economy and a Social Market Economy but also between Kurt Schumacher and Ludwig Erhard.[166]

While Erhard, who considered it necessary to directly address the German people in these years of economic uncertainty,[167] unremittingly popularised his economic concept and gradually prepared and implemented the liberalisation of the economy in the Economic Council, Adenauer rather aimed to exert influence on the reorganisation of the German post-war economy via the Parliamentary Council. Since September 1948, Konrad Adenauer presided over this constituent panel of 65 delegates elected by the eleven *Länder* parliaments in the three western zones of occupation to formulate the Basic Law, which became the provisional Constitution of the Federal Republic of Germany promulgated on 23 May 1949. Although the wording of the Basic Law neither mentioned *expressis verbis* the Social Market Economy nor defined another particular economic system, however, some of the central terms within the framework of basic rights, such as the right to the free development of one's personality or the rights of ownership and inheritance, suggested or even predetermined a liberal economic policy.[168] Indeed, the socialisation of private property for the collective good remained possible mainly due to the insistence of the Social Democrats.[169] Nonetheless, the Social Market Economy received constitutional assistance. According to the ordo-liberal economists Wilhelm Röpke and Franz Böhm who were among the first to point out and examine the correlation between *Rechtsordnung* (legal order) and *Wirtschaftsordnung* (economic order), the democratic liberal political system necessitated for its completion the market economy.[170] The political system ultimately geared toward the preferences of the individual required a corresponding institutional mechanism by which the individual could voice his preferences, i.e. the market or set of markets. In recognising and considering precisely this interdependence of constitutional and economic order, Konrad Adenauer and Ludwig Erhard paved the way for the Social Market Economy not only in political bodies but also in the general public.[171] Acting on the assumption that in view of the recent National Socialist dictatorship, the German people wished for political democracy, they continually emphasised the correlation between political and economic freedom.[172] Decisive influences on the communication and finally the implementation of the Social Market Economy were the legislative Administration for Economics of the Economic Council and the constituent Parliamentary Council, and most importantly of all the interplay between both bodies and their chairmen, namely Ludwig Erhard and Konrad Adenauer.[173]

Whereas Konrad Adenauer and Ludwig Erhard saw the councils in Frankfurt and Bonn as decisive political instruments, Kurt Schumacher and the majority of the SPD instead considered the Basic Law to be a temporary solution until a constitution for a united Germany was formulated, and regarded the Economic Council and its Administration for Economics as mere provisional institutions with limited room for manoeuvre, hence unable to solve the immense problems of the immediate post-war years. Indeed, all laws of the German institutions required the approval of the Allied Bipartite Board, and furthermore, parts of the CSU deemed the bizonal administrations in Frankfurt to be incompetent;[174] however, this sentiment was mainly due to conflicts of spheres of interests and influence between Bavarian federalism and German centralism. In retrospect, however, while the Union parties, and Ludwig Erhard in particular, effectively seized the increased political opportunities to implement and communicate their economic ideas, the leadership of the SPD both underestimated the decision-making power of the bizonal administration and the opportunity therein to communicate a socialist economic programme. While initially the Economic Council and the Administration for Economics generally followed guidelines issued by the occupying powers and, furthermore, were preoccupied with administrative matters to the detriment of questions of regulatory policy,

German political parties and officials increasingly not only interfered in the day-to-day administration, but began to make the fundamental choices determining the evolving economic and socio-political order. Although the purpose of the majority of the 131 laws passed in the legislative Economic Council in Frankfurt between 1947 and 1949 was to administer and improve the then prevalent scarcity, few aimed at the implementation of the Social Market Economy as the socio-political and economic model for post-war Germany; for instance, the so-called '*Bewirtschaftungsnotgesetz*' and its far-reaching executive orders adopted in parliament on 30 October 1947. Although these legal documents neither entirely dismissed planning and control of the economy nor specified any particular economic system, they assigned the Director of the Administration for Economics extensive authority and freedom in the application and interpretation of economic planning and rationing. The so-called '*Preisgesetz*' passed by the Economic Council on 10 April 1948 increased this influence on economic policy even further. Henceforth, the new Director of the Administration for Economics, Ludwig Erhard, was not only in charge of macroeconomic policy but also of price policy. Arguably the most significant decision of the legislative quasi-parliament, however, was the adoption of the so-called '*Leitsätze-Gesetz*' on Friday 18 June 1948 which eventually enabled Erhard to initiate economic liberalisation following a currency reform and, importantly, to communicate the success of these policies later on. All these legal measures not only increased Erhard's and thus the conservative parties' influence on economic and financial policy, but, at the same time, they also reduced the political opposition's opportunities for intervention. Thus, the Economic Council and the Administration for Economics both being under the direction of the CDU/CSU throughout proved to be decisive in the implementation and communication of the Social Market Economy as the principal socio-political and economic model for the emerging Federal Republic of Germany. Moreover, many leading Social Democrats not only misjudged the decision-making powers of the bizonal administration but also the feasibility of the market-oriented model in times of prevalent destitution and the initial absence of market mechanisms.

Regarding the concept of the Social Market Economy, not only the opposition but also even some Liberal Democrats of the coalition had second thoughts. For instance the delegate of the FDP in the Economic Council, Everhard Bungartz, laconically commented on Ludwig Erhard's presentation of the Social Market Economy in the Economic Council on 21 April 1948: '*Die Worte hör' ich – allein es fehlt der Glaube mir!*' (While I listen, I do not believe a word of it).[175] The majority of the FDP led by the chairman Theodor Heuss and its parliamentary group in the

Economic Council headed by Franz Blücher, however, supported the economic liberalisation – Ludwig Erhard finally became Director of the Administration for Economics upon the recommendation if not insistence of the FDP.[176] Indeed, the Liberal Democrats believed Erhard to be their candidate to realise a free and competitive economy.[177] While the SPD and initially also the CDU with its *Ahlener Programm* advocated socialisation and economic planning, the liberal, democratic, and federal FDP in the three western zones of occupation consistently and consequently sided with private initiative and the reduction of governmental interference in the economy.[178] Thus, committed to implement its social and economic liberalism which was in many respects based on the writings of Alfred Müller-Armack and Wilhelm Röpke,[179] the FDP largely strove to support Ludwig Erhard's economic policy although cooperation between the parliamentary groups of the Liberal Democrats and the Union proved to be disturbed at times due to different views regarding economic liberalisation. In December 1948, for instance, the liberals parted company with the CDU/CSU over the first law passed by the Economic Council as quasi-parliament compensating German victims of the war (*Lasten-ausgleichsgesetz*) because they felt that the bill favoured collective property owners over individuals thus introducing a disguised collectivisation of the economy.[180] Nevertheless, the Liberal Democrats devoted their campaigns to promoting the Social Market Economy in parliament[181] and in public where they either conjointly campaigned with the Union or indirectly canvassed for Erhard's economic policy by opposing socialisation and controlled economy.[182] In this connection, it is not surprising that the election campaigns of the CDU/CSU and the FDP as well as the DP were widely financed by a consortium of industrialists and businessmen led by the banker and confidant of Konrad Adenauer, Robert Pferdmenges.[183] Although Adenauer did not want the CDU/CSU to become too close to industrial interests, he urged the regional and district party organisations to raise money from all levels of society, including commerce and industry, due to insufficient funds to conduct the campaign fully.[184] While industry's contributions to the respective political parties are difficult to quantify and the system was still in its infancy as of 1949, the practice of industry contributing funds mainly to the bourgeois parties was already forming. For the time being, the difference in funding between the bourgeois parties and the SPD was insignificant, but a pattern had been set nevertheless.[185] However, the CDU/CSU undoubtedly spent more on its election campaign, estimated DM 575,000,[186] than its SPD rivals did.

Just as clearly as the FDP – and incidentally also the NLP and DP[187] – advocated a liberal market economy, the communist KPD rejected the economic liberalisation and rather campaigned for wholesale nationalisation.[188] Thus the Communist Party represented an economic conception similar to the one of the Social Democrats though less evolutionary-socialist, but more pronounced in its anti-fascist, democratic and revolutionary rhetoric.[189] However, the virulent anti-communist Kurt Schumacher opposed any amalgamation of SPD and KPD, which he considered to be in the sphere of influence of the Soviet Union[190] – indeed, by now accessible archival sources confirm the direct control of the communist leadership in the Soviet zone of occupation by Moscow and the on-site Russian Military Administration. As the western occupying powers also prohibited a bipartisan union across the east–west divide, the two parties merged to a single political party forming the *Sozialistische Einheitspartei Deutschlands* (SED) headed by Otto Grotewohl (SPD) und Wilhelm Pieck (KPD) solely in the eastern zone in April 1946. Moreover, the Communist Party in the western zones of occupation faced discrimination and even persecution. While the KPD was initially licensed and allowed to participate in the political and governmental reorganisation of post-war West Germany, it was increasingly restricted in its representation, excluded from inter-party proceedings; furthermore, its ministers, such as the Minister for Reconstruction in Rhineland-Palatinate, Willy Feller, the Ministers for Transport and Reconstruction in North Rhine-Westphalia, Heinz Renner and Hugo Paul, or Minister in Lower Saxony, Karl Abel, were actually dismissed by the Allied military authorities by 1948. In particular in the Anglo-American Bizone, the occupying powers aimed to foster anti-communist political life, and therefore banned the communist press; after several prohibitions to publish, the *Westdeutsche Volksecho* (Dortmund) lost the licence on 4 May 1948, the KPD-organ *Freiheit* (Düsseldorf) on 8 October 1948. In essence, being discredited and limited in its course of political action and communication, the KPD's influence in politics remained marginal even though the results of the elections between 1946 and 1949 prove that the communist electorate cannot be considered *quantité négligeable.*[191] However, despite the shared goal to fight capitalism and economic liberalism, there was no concerted action on the part of the SPD and KPD to the benefit of the bourgeois coalition of CDU, CSU, FDP and DP.

In addition to the disunity of the political left, the social composition of the Economic Council was in favour of conservative and liberal forces.[192] Furthermore, the Christian Democratic Union and Christian Social Union benefited from the Catholic Church's influence. In many dioceses throughout West Germany, the Catholic Church mobilised their flocks for the parties and Church officials led numerous rallies, sent tens of thousands of speech outlines to Church and lay leaders, and distributed

650,000 leaflets prior to the election in order to urge voters to cast their ballots only for 'Christian candidates'.[193] After all, the proponents of a liberal economic policy or the Social Market Economy received backing and even promotion from leading economists and academic schools of economic thought. Already during the Third Reich, the committed opponents of the totalitarian National Socialism and advocates of neo-liberal economic policy, the members of the *Arbeitsgemeinschaft Erwin von Beckerath* within the Freiburg Circles, aimed at introducing liberal economic thinking in post-war Germany. Although limited in their room for manoeuvre in times of political persecution and later Allied occupation, Erwin von Beckerath, Adolf Lampe, Constantin von Dietze, Franz Böhm, Walter Eucken, Jens Jessen, Erich Preiser, Günter Schmölders, Heinrich von Stackelberg, Theodor Wessels, Clemens Bauer, Gerhard Albrecht and Fritz Hauenstein considerably contributed to the conceptual development of a socially-oriented market economy, and its eventual acceptance in academia, politics and among the public. Whereas the Freiburg Circles mainly influenced the academic discussion, the Freiburg School, with its pivotal members Walter Eucken, Franz Böhm, Hans Großmann-Doerth, Friedrich A. Lutz, Karl Friedrich Maier, Fritz Walter Meyer and Leonhard Miksch, additionally stimulated the public debate on liberal socio-economic ideas. The credit for having promoted and established ordo-liberal ideas in the German general public, however, is primarily due to Wilhelm Röpke. The German economist, intent on contributing to the cure of the German post-war economy, addressed the readership outside academia in the majority of his roughly eight hundred publications. Thereby he arguably became *the* intellectual figure in the establishment of economic liberalism in post-war Germany, and stimulated and influenced the public and political debate in equal measure. In drawing on Eucken's ordo-liberal competitive order and Röpke's economic humanist approach, the social-liberal Cologne School around the economist and anthropologist Alfred Müller-Armack pursued an economic order providing a synthesis of seemingly conflicting objectives, namely economic freedom and social security. Although this holistic concept labelled Social Market Economy is often viewed as a mélange of socio-political ideas rather than a precisely outlined theoretical order, the conception possessed an effective slogan, which facilitated its communication to the populace. The eventual implementation, however, required not only communication but also political backup. Here, the socio-economic concept received considerable support from the *Wissenschaftliche Beirat bei der Verwaltung für Wirtschaft* as an official panel of economic experts and the *Industrie- und Handelskammern* as representative corporate institutions with extensive public functions. Both organisations accorded the Social Market Economy political credibility and thus facilitated its communication and implementation in times characterised by a prevalent disenchantment with politics. Above all, however, the Social Market Economy was the economic thinking of Ludwig Erhard and Konrad Adenauer.

While eventually the union of the two recently established political parties, i.e. the CDU and the CSU, possessed a coherent and unifying economic programme – due to the political and economic developments in 1948/49 and the seeming compatibility of the Social Market Economy and Christian social doctrine, with the devotees of Christian Socialism following the official party line – enabling a more consistent public front, the Schumacher SPD did not introduce its own economic concept but merely criticised the negative developments of Erhard's economic policy, such as the widening of economic and social disparities in German society, despite the generally improving conditions. This, in turn, not only complicated the parliamentary work of the party in the Economic Council but also limited the public relations of the party as a whole. Whereas the SPD's message could appeal to mainly its traditional base of electoral support, i.e. the working class, the CDU/CSU's approach of creating multi-dimensional propaganda had broader appeal. In addition, the lack of an effective slogan hindered the SPD propaganda especially in times of campaigning where the partially complex political programmes were simplified and popularised. Thus the political posters and leaflets distributed by the Social Democrats were less visually striking than those of the CDU/CSU and much of the propaganda was based upon lengthy but rather abstract programme statements about economic planning and socialisation.

Precisely this instance of insufficient and imprecise information about the Social Democrats' economic ideas gave their opponents an opportunity both to occupy the field of a socially-oriented economic competence – many Social Democrats, such as the sociologist Alfred Weber, regretted the SPD's inability in this respect[194] – and to distort facts so as to present the Social Democrats as pursuing a command economy. In view of the fact that the public mainly associated planning and control with the tyranny and alienation of the totalitarian NS regime, this was a clever move by the strategists Adenauer and Erhard. Indeed, while the public's vehement indictment of the great industrialists appeared to favour a radical socialisation of the economy and society and led to the widespread anti-capitalist and pro-socialist rhetoric of the period, another side of the same traumatic German historical experience undermined any real potential for a socialist revolution. This was the fact that Hitler's even more massive and destructive concentration and misuse of state power had instilled in Germans an equally great fear of such power. Post-war Germans of all major political persuasions feared any kind of concentration of power, whether in the hands of large, monopolistic industries or the government. This further complicated the post-war SPD's campaign for socialisation and centralist economic planning.

In essence, while various socio-economic concepts between neo-liberalism and neo-socialism emerged for the political and economic reorganisation of post-war Germany, and were indeed put forward by either German academic schools of thought or political parties, only two played a major role in the political and public discourse. The economic model for the Federal Republic of Germany was strongly debated, but the character of the debate cannot be explained by the confrontation of two fundamentally different economic models described as *laissez-faire* capitalism and a controlled planned economy: neither side stood for an extreme. While the CDU/CSU was not simply propagating a purely free market economy, the SPD did not pursue a permanently government-controlled economy. In fact, both sides shared the goal of pursuing the development of an economic-political system able to overcome both the deficiencies of liberal capitalism and the threats of totalitarianism. However, while both national parties gave priority to the economic issues of the time, the Schumacher SPD wanted to see the primacy of politics despite the wide absence of governmental institutions – in other words, the economic conception of the Social Democrats rested upon unrealistic premises, such as a strong parliamentary government. By contrast, Konrad Adenauer and Ludwig Erhard believed in the primacy of economics: instead of viewing social policy as a prerequisite for economic policy, conversely, the proponents of the Social Market Economy considered economic policy the best social policy to enable the stabilisation and harmonisation of both a liberal economy and democratic society. Thus the citizenry was *the* constitutive element in the socio-economic conception of Alfred Müller-Armack, Ludwig Erhard and Konrad Adenauer, and one, which, in turn, affected the communication of their economic programme. Already at an early stage where contact with both the people and even on an internal party basis was barely existent and inadequately organised, they brought politics closer to the populace – though there was no real use of either modern advertising techniques or public opinion polls, resources that would be fully utilised in future campaigns – and the CDU/CSU consequently aligned its party platform, policies and campaigns – themed 'the economy is our fate' – to include public opinion. In the run-up to the federal elections in August 1949, Adenauer and Erhard complementing each other – while the former unified the party programmatically, it was mainly the latter who introduced the Social Market Economy to both the political and public sphere – campaigned with their pragmatic economic concept and presented the success of their economic policy. While the CDU/CSU was increasingly identified with the economic recovery and the improving economic conditions, the Union also fought more deeply for the public acceptance of its economic model in the battle for a model for post-war Germany, which was arguably not won in offices nor in parliament but rather at the forefront of public opinion.

PART II

POLITICS AND PUBLIC OPINION

Vox populi, vox Dei.[1]

(Hesiod, 700 BC)

Nec audiendi qui solent dicere, Vox populi, vox Dei, quum tumultuositas vulgi semper insaniae proxima sit.[2]

(Flaccus Albinus Alcuinus, 798)

While the previous chapters focused on the academic and bipartisan economic and socio-political concepts and their communication to the public, the following section analyses the sentiment among the populace and the nature of public involvement in the political process.

Following the totalitarianism and despotism of National Socialism both the Allies and the German post-war parties aimed to design and establish a democratic economic and socio-political order derived from the people and consistent with the preferences of the populace.[3] The perpetuation of this regained democracy, in turn, ultimately required the active participation of the people as the actual sovereign.[4] Similarly, public acceptance and civic engagement were equally considered prerequisites for the success of the Social Market Economy.[5] Indeed, both government *by* the people and government *for* the people, that is government in accordance with the people's preferences, ultimately constitute democracy and thus any democratic economic model.[6]

Although it is principally a democratic concept, the tradition of the governors being ultimately constrained by the will of the governed is older than liberal ideology. Its roots lie deep in the past, even though there was no explicit articulation of the idea much before the eighteenth century and no systematic treatment of it until the nineteenth. The concept of popular sovereignty, as the ultimate legitimising authority, can be traced back to Aristotle who remarked 'He who loses the support of the people is a king no longer.'[7] The idea of aligning governmental conduct with public will also became a guiding principle to the fathers of the Constitution of the United States of America. Following the axiom of David Hume that 'it is on opinion only that government is founded',[8] they argued that 'it is the reason, alone, of the public, that ought to control and regulate the government.'[9] The fact that this so-called 'public opinion' is to be taken seriously was indicated by John Locke who used the expression 'Law of Opinion', explaining that the word 'law' was deliberately chosen in order to convey clearly the fact that pressure was being exerted.[10] Jean-Jacques Rousseau, alternating between the expressions general will, public opinion and unwritten laws, went even further by viewing public opinion as the free guardian of morality and traditions and by arguing for the absolute sovereign of the people as community of equal citizens irrespective of their status and property within the nation-state.[11]

The period of confidence in public opinion, based on the belief in the moral judgement of the common man proclaimed in the Age of Enlightenment, was followed by a period of distrust in its capabilities and competence. The first to clearly voice the ambiguous and inherently contradictory role of public opinion was Georg Wilhelm Friedrich Hegel. In contrast to the early liberal belief that the government had to follow the public will, Hegel considered public opinion only the unorganised way in which a people's opinions and wishes are made known, in opposition to the organised state.[12] Similarly, the political-philosophical and social-psychological critiques by Alexis de Tocqueville, John Stuart Mill and James Bryce expressed doubts about the role of public opinion, even referring to the 'tyranny of the majority'.[13] Nevertheless, whether *Vox Populi* was *Vox Dei* or *Vox Diaboli*, public opinion was acknowledged by most to be a force in politics commanding attention.

If it is agreed that public opinion is, or should be, essential for any democratic social system, the first matter at issue is the concept of public opinion itself. What is meant by the 'public' in 'public opinion'? This seemingly simple query belies the complexity at the heart of the matter. What is the essence of defining public opinion – is it the consideration of public, or of opinion, or both? Is the political dimension fundamental to any definition of public opinion, or should we understand it in a much broader, anthropological sense? While the inherent limitations, theoretical assumptions, and social conditions of public opinion have been systematically studied since the rise of empiricism and the sociologisation theories at the beginning of the twentieth century, there remains little agreement on the exact meaning of 'public opinion'.[14] The reason for this lack of consensus may be rooted in the fact that so many researchers and theorists from different disciplines have contributed to the field but have come to the study of public opinion with different assumptions and methodologies. In addition, the meaning of 'public opinion' is also tied to historical circumstances – the sort of political culture that exists, the nature of communication technology, and the importance of public participation in the everyday workings of government. Yet, these are not the only reasons why public opinion is hard to define. Some of the ambiguity in the term simply reflects the problematic nature of the concept, which attempts to unite the seemingly absolutely incompatible, i.e. the public and opinion. Whereas the first aspires to achieve the universal, objective, and rational, the concept of opinion is market by the variable, subjective and uncertain. Thus, for some, public opinion does not exist;[15] others faced difficulties in further defining the concept of public opinion mainly in terms of its scope and representativeness, as expressed in the early circumscription by the historian Hermann Oncken:

> Public opinion is a complex of similar utterances of major or minor social levels on subjects of public life, at times debouching spontaneously, at times artificially created; it expresses itself in various organs, in associations or assemblies, mainly in the press and publishing, or simply in the unuttered sensation of the individual be he an ordinary man on the street or of the small circle of the cultured class; here a respectable sway even statesmen look at, there a factor without political importance; [...] at times consistent rising against the government and experts like a powerful flood wave, at times fragmented [...]; sometimes expressing the plain and natural sensation of the human being, sometimes being a clamorous and absurd burst of wild instincts; always guided but permanently leading; [...], infectious like an epidemic, moody and unfaithful and imperious like people themselves, and after all nothing more than a word by which potentates deceive themselves.[16]

In view of the uncertainty in defining public opinion, it is essential initially to clarify what constitutes a public. The concept of a public emerged from Enlightenment democratic ideals and the many important social transformations that took place in the late nineteenth and early twentieth centuries. A working definition of a public grew from its contrasts to other kinds of social formations, most prominently 'crowds' and 'masses'. While it is considered that the crowd develops in response to shared emotions,[17] the public organises in response to an issue.[18] From the proposition that there is a public opinion only when a large number of people hold an opinion on a specific topic,[19] some would argue that the term 'public' should be confined to those who do, in fact, have an opinion on the issue.[20] From this perspective, the public are the informed, the attentative, or the involved members of the society; the others, i.e. those people who merely inhabit a geographical area, are simply the masses.[21] The problem with this restrictive definition is that it prejudges the question of public interest. In reality, in any society, on any particular issue, there are large numbers who have no knowledge of the issue, no opinions about it, and therefore no will on it. Thus, other attempts to distinguish publics from crowds or masses focused on the idea that divisions of opinion, the existence of debatable demands, were essential characteristics of a public. The clash of contradictory opinions was considered the crucial factor distinguishing a self-aware public reasoning with others from a sentimentally united mass composed of anonymous individuals who engage in very little interaction or communication.[22] Thus, a public may be defined as a group of people who are confronted by an issue, who are divided in the ideas as to how to meet the issue, and who engage in discussion over the issue. Despite the complicated situation regarding access to information, public discourse and democratic attributes in general in post-war West Germany, this chapter adopts the position that the then German population (people, populace, nation) could be considered a public divided over the issue of how to reorganise the post-war economy. Due to this public discourse over the controversy, an opinion, defined as the acceptance of one among two or more inconsistent views, which are capable of being accepted by a rational mind as true, was formed.[23]

In order eventually to attain and assess public opinion, many researchers, policy-makers and journalists have suggested simply aggregating individual opinions.[24] This most common definition of public opinion serves as the justification for using representative surveys and polls, i.e. interviewing randomly selected individuals across social groups, to measure the will of the population; and, further, it resonates with the structure of the popular election. Others argue that public opinion refers to what the majority of individuals opine, say or think.[25] In this context, it is important to distinguish between public opinion proper and opinion that is voiced in public, i.e. popular or published opinion. According to Tom Harrison, 'public opinion is what you will say out loud to anyone. It is an overt, and not necessarily candid, part of your private opinion.'[26] The communication scientist Elisabeth Noelle-Neumann, in introducing the concept of 'the spiral of silence' that determined when opinions could become public, defined public opinion as that 'opinion which can be voiced in public without fear of sanctions and upon which action in public can be based.'[27] Derived from earlier views, as expounded by such philosophers as Locke, Hume, Rousseau and most explicitly de

Tocqueville describing a social pressure to conform, this formulation departs from the more customary definition of a collection of individual opinions and delineates it as a social-system-level concept. Public opinion, from this perspective, imposes sanctions on individuals who are not in step with convention. Fearing sanctions, such as social isolation and unpopularity, individuals are constantly sensitive to the climate of opinion, which differentiates popular from unpopular opinions. The match or mismatch between the personal viewpoint and the perceived majoritarian opinion determines subsequent expression of the individually held opinion. If the personal view is socially dominant or ascendant, it will be expressed willingly in public. However, if the view is in the minority or on the decline, the individual fearing social sanction will be silent. Noelle-Neumann's spiral of silence metaphor attempts to model an opinion winnowing process, wherein perceived majority opinions become self-fulfilling prophecies because uninhibited expressions give the appearance of being more widely held than may actually be the case; and minority opinions, being silenced by their conformist proponents, appear less widely held than they truly are. As minority opinions spiral into silence, people in society are increasingly confronted with one viewpoint that appears dominant. Due to this effect that the opinion of a majority may not always be public and the inherent potential for political communication and media influence over atomised citizens through the use of propaganda and through inclusion or omission of information, it is difficult to limit the assessment of public opinion to the most popular opinion. Finally, other scholars suggest that public opinion is less a reflection of citizens' opinions but rather the projection of what elites, i.e. journalists, politicians, or pollsters, believe. Although this notion that public opinion is a creation of social leaders may seem cynical, it has a large number of adherents. According to Walter Lippmann, the common citizen could not possibly stay informed on all affairs of state and, given this impossibility, could hardly be relied upon to produce intelligent opinion on public affairs. Thus, one could only turn to a government of specialists and see public opinion as the expression of elite opinion; the will of the people can therefore never be any more than the will of some of the people.[28] Similarly, James Best noted that 'one could only conclude that the only public opinion which is relevant in the policy-making process is the opinion of the attentive public or the opinion elite.'[29] While these categories are not mutually exclusive, this assessment considers the aggregated preferences of *all* individuals weighed equally in the conduct of the government that is weighed with no discrimination as to the content or source of the preference, in order to satisfy the claim for a balanced public opinion. Thus, for the purpose of this research and by no means in any final sense, public opinion shall be defined as the aggregation of all citizens' preferences and orientations towards political factual issues expressed in free elections, opinion polls, petitions and newspaper articles.

Considering that ever since the Enlightenment, public opinion bestowed an aura of legitimacy upon laws, policies, decisions and convictions, and, following the Habermasian ideal of a deliberative or discursive democracy in which legitimate lawmaking can only arise from the public deliberation of the citizenry,[30] one may therefore fundamentally expect a high government responsiveness defined by the continuing action of government and policy-makers in accordance with the preferences of its citizens.[31] With regard to both public opinion about the liberalisation of the economy and policy responsiveness of the first parliament, i.e. the Economic Council, in post-war West Germany between 1945 and 1949, however, there exists ambiguity even in scholarly writings and academic research. What little there is appears contradictory and incomplete. Whereas some argue that 'the discontinuation of government control of the economy was embraced by the majority of the public,'[32] others assert that 'the majority [...] could not conceal their appalling surprise'[33] and consider 'the critics of the capitalist economy by no means as hopelessly in a minority.'[34] In order to balance this deficiency, this chapter aims to assess public opinion regarding the implementation of the Social Market Economy in post-war Germany and to examine whether the decisions and policies by the Economic Council were consistent with people's preferences. Although article 20 paragraph 2 of the Basic Law of the Federal Republic of Germany promulgated on 23 May 1949 stated that all state authority is derived from the people,[35] and, similarly, the first Chancellor of the Federal Republic of Germany, Konrad Adenauer, declared in the *Bundestag* on 21 October 1949 that it was not possible for any political organisation in Germany to claim legitimacy for its existence and action unless it rests on the freely expressed will of the people,[36] this chapter argues that the liberalisation process and subsequent implementation of the Social Market Economy were neither in accordance with majority public opinion nor did the Economic Council show a high level of responsiveness to public will.

With regard to the assessment of both public opinion and policy responsiveness, it is essential to focus on salient aspects and elements of the then political discussion and economic policy, such as socialisation, government control of the economy, or the currency reform. In order to gauge representative public opinion and its development over time, this chapter considers representative public opinion surveys conducted by the occupying forces, i.e. the Opinion Survey Section within the Intelligence Branch of OMGUS which, under the direction of Frederick W. Williams, carried out 72 opinion polls between October 1945 and September 1949 testing German opinions on the economy, politics, and society, and German polling institutes, namely the institute for the *Erforschung der öffentlichen Meinung, Marktforschung, Nachrichten, Informationen und Dienstleistungen* (EMNID) founded by the management-consultant Karl-Georg von Stackelberg in Bielefeld in 1945, and the *Institut für Demoskopie* (IfD) established by the pollster Elisabeth Noelle-Neumann in Allensbach in 1947.[37] Although public opinion polling was largely considered the first scientific mastering of public opinion to finally achieve a satisfactory degree of empirical validity,[38] polling was soon criticised for its methodological shortcomings, its negative effects on public opinion and democratic life, and accused of anti-democratic manipulation instead of monitoring public opinion.[39] Nonetheless, due to the ideal situation for drawing random samples in occupied Germany – the then card index of all German inhabitants serving as the distribution basis for food and supply in times of rationing facilitated surveys – this study considers the poll as a significant tool to assess and, thus, reflect public opinion between 1945 and 1949.

In addition, the reports by various local governments on the perceived public sentiment regarding economic issues[40] and the results of democratic elections at local, regional and federal levels will serve as an indicator of public opinion.[41] In connection with this, indeed, it has to be considered that the voting public is not synonymous with the general public – particularly in the local elections 1946 to 1948. Despite a consistent increase in the number of eligible voters in post-war West Germany due to the return of expellees and prisoners of war, the integration of refugees and the readmission of former National Socialists,[42] many people were still denied the right to vote due either to ongoing denazification programmes or to the residency clause. Besides, in some *Länder*, such as Hesse, only political parties receiving a minimum of fifteen percent of the votes obtained a mandate. Further, there were no publicly distinguishable economic conceptions available to the electorate until the run-up to the *Landtag* elections in spring 1947 and concrete competing economic concepts, namely free market or planned economy, did not enter the electoral campaign until the local elections in the second half of the year 1948. Moreover, an individual's electoral behaviour is arguably a function of social structures and influenced by rational choice, i.e. guided by instrumental reason; accordingly, individuals choose what they believe to be the best means to achieve their given ends.[43] Due to these factors the respective election results have limited explanatory power and, thus have to be handled with care.

Furthermore, petitions and resolutions by German individuals and organisations sent to the Economic Council will serve as an indicator of public opinion. The public sentiment also found its expression in various activities, such as strikes and protests. Above all, the public debate accompanying the then economic policy is also reflected in numerous resolutions and articles in the daily press. Ultimately, the latter not only delivered information to the public and, thus was an important element in the process of public opinion formation, but it was also the main means of expression of the public, constituting a virtual public. In addition, the press was a general medium for more restricted means of expression, such as associations, meetings, or demonstrations, whereas the public was always, and nearly exclusively, a newspaper-reading public. While a systematic quantitative content analysis did not prove to be viable due to the small sample size, the author aims to consult a representative selection of articles from numerous newspapers in order to qualitatively gauge the balance of public opinion.[44]

To study the effects of public opinion on government policies, this chapter simply suggests comparing prior majority opinion with subsequent political decisions. Where traceable, the impact of various extra-political actors, as an embodiment of public opinion, on the conduct of the Economic Council shall be considered. While the influence of public opinion on the political decision-making processes is very nebulous and it is cautioned against concluding too quickly that there is a causality between public opinion and policy, this chapter may also help clear the fog in respect to how the Administration for Economics within the Economic Council referred to public opinion when making political and economic decisions. By examining the role of the public during the liberalisation process and consequent implementation of the Social Market Economy as the principal economic system for the Federal Republic of Germany, this chapter seeks to contribute to historical understanding of the political and economic reconstruction of post-war Germany.

3

1945/1946 – STUPOR AND SEARCH FOR DIRECTION

From this war there is no way back to a laissez-faire order of society,
that war as such is the maker of a silent revolution
by preparing the road to a new type of planned order.[1]

(Karl Mannheim, 1945)

The end of the Second World War left Germany in an unprecedented state of defeat, destruction, and disorganisation. Administration virtually disintegrated and German political and economic life had reached 'point zero'.[2] Although there was no *Stunde Null* (zero hour) and anarchy, this notion closely describes the perception of ordinary as well as informed contemporaries. Never did the future of Germany seem less viable, never the chaos more ubiquitous. When US President Harry Truman commissioned a group of experts, led by former President Herbert Hoover, to assess the economic and political situation in post-war Germany on-site, one of the economic experts, Gustav Stolper, reported:

> This, then, is the picture of Germany [...] after the unconditional surrender: A nation irremediably maimed in its biological structure – with a long-term sharp decline of the population inevitable, with a huge preponderance of women and the old, a fateful absence of young, able-bodied men who are indispensable for the regeneration of a race, its intellectual power, its productive efficiency, its moral resistance; a nation intellectually crippled by the horrors of twelve years of Nazi despotism, by isolation from contact and intercourse with the outside world, by a monstrous system of pseudo-philosophical, mystical abstrusities inculcated with the help of police and subservient teachers in schools ruthlessly purged of their

independent minds, with a press and radio system operating under positive direction on the minutest detail of make-up and content; a nation morally ruined by the disruption of its family ties; [...] a nation of an urban and industrial civilisation whose cities are almost all in ruins, its factories smashed; a nation without food and raw materials, without a functioning transport system or a valid currency; a nation whose social fabric has been destroyed by mass flight, mass migration, the compulsory mass settlement of strangers; a nation whose huge national debt has been repudiated, where bank deposits have been either confiscated or rendered worthless by depreciation, and mass expropriation of industrial and commercial property has been ordered or 'voted' as an act of political vengeance; a nation which, having lost provinces that were the source of one-fourth of its food, is in imminent danger of a second partition between its former western and eastern enemies; a nation in which [...] there is no guarantee of personal liberty, no habeas corpus and no democracy, [...] a country where, amidst hunger and fear, hope has died and with it the belief in all the ideals.[3]

This quote is intentionally cited at virtually full length in order to illustrate the political and economic circumstances but also level of morale from which any reconstruction of German political and economic life had to emanate. People were simply disarmed by the facts. Life in post-war Germany in 1945 was dominated by a sense of stupor and by an instinctive search for a direction. The war changed everything and a return to the way things had been before 1933 was out of the question – this included the former capitalist economic system. As capitalism was distinctly associated with the great depression that followed the stock-market crash in 1929, the waste of unemployment, the inequalities, injustices, inefficiencies and the discredited politics of the inter-war years, governmental planning and the enhanced role for the state in social and economic affairs became the political religion in post-war Germany in 1945. The belief in centralist governmental economic planning favoured by 54 per cent of the residents in the American zone in January 1946[4] was matched by the faith in improving economic conditions: in December 1945, 78 per cent of the respondents were optimistic despite their recognition that the road to full recovery was long and only 7 per cent anticipated a worsening economic situation.[5] A very broad constituency took up the idea that a well-planned economy would not only improve economic conditions but also meant a fairer and better-regulated society. Thus most political parties at that time reacted to that socialist *Zeitgeist*, and socialism and socialisation played a distinctive role in their campaign for the forthcoming communal and state legislature elections in 1946.

The first communal elections, held in *Gemeinden* (communities) of less than 20,000 inhabitants, were scheduled in Bavaria, Hesse and Wuerttemberg-Baden for Sunday 20 January and Sunday 27 January 1946. Free elections had returned to Germany and the majority of the Germans, i.e. 82 per cent, proposed to use this first free exercise of the right to ballot since Hitler's rise to power.[6] Finally, and despite the oft-heard charge of political apathy in post-war Germany, old and young, men and women, the well and even the sick had turned out in cold winter weather to record their votes; one contemporary witness even reported that her sickened grandmother was carried to the polling station on a chair in order not to lose a vote.[7] Hence, in Hesse 85.1 per cent and in Wuerttemberg-Baden 86.1 per cent of the eligible voters in the smaller towns and villages went to the polls to select their local councils; in Bavaria, the turnout of voters was even 93.4 per cent. Similarly, the local elections held in *Landkreisen* (rural counties) on 28 April, the municipal assembly elections held in *Stadtkreisen* (municipal counties) and in communities of more than 20,000 inhabitants on 26 May 1946, and also the constituent assembly elections on 30 June 1946, drew between 61.6 and 86.3 per cent of the eligible voters above the age of twenty-one in the American occupation zone to the polls.[8] Final returns in the local elections taking place in Bremen, Hamburg, Lower Saxony, North Rhine-Westphalia, Schleswig-Holstein, Baden, Rhineland-Palatinate, Saarland, Wuerttemberg-Hohenzollern and Berlin on 15 September, 13 and 20 October 1946, also showed an extraordinarily and 'miraculously' high percentage of voter participation.[9] The collapse of the system and the disintegration of the state were indeed accompanied by an intense regionalisation of opinion and a shift of personal identification from the national to private interests.[10] As Theodor Heuss (FDP), later to become the first President of the Federal Republic of Germany, was to put it: 'World catastrophes, which vehemently shake a nation, have at first the strange effect of decentralising the emotions. [...] People attempt to escape to fields where the [...] great political world is not felt so directly.'[11] While such a mood was at best a transient phenomenon and one cannot necessarily refer to political apathy *per se*, in fact there remained a fairly low interest in political activity in the immediate post-war years. Over three-quarters were not and did not intend to become members of a political party[12] – and if they did, often did so because a party membership facilitated obtaining luncheon vouchers and coupons for basic goods.[13] In April 1946, 76 per cent flatly responded that, if they had a son leaving school, they would not like to see him choose politics as a profession. Typical of the comments made by these were 'politics is a dirty business' and 'one is a politician for ten years and then lands in a concentration camp.'[14] Although the percentage seeing politics as a worthy profession was considerably low, levels of political participation in Germany were not inordinately low. Eventually, the then difficult economic circumstances, the unsatisfying political situation and the increased confidence to determine their own future – whereas in 1945, 45, 70 or rather 61 per cent of the respondents thought that the German people as a whole were capable of governing themselves in a democratic way, in 1946, as many as 79 per cent believed in self-government and only 6 per cent did not[15] – drew not only the politically active but also the ordinary German to the polls. Like all the destroyed residential houses in post-war Germany, a new state had to be rebuilt. On this account it is not surprising at all – the then American Military Commander-in-Chief, General Lucius D. Clay, appeared astonished by the high voter participation[16] – that 78 per cent of the eligible voters in the American zone planned to vote[17] in the upcoming state legislature elections taking place in Wuerttemberg-Baden on 24 November and Hesse and Bavaria on 1 December 1946, though often not knowing about the purpose of the elections (74 per cent)[18] or merely out of civic duty (35 per cent).[19] Those least likely to vote in the elections were former Nazi Party members (58 per cent), men (36 per cent), and individuals under the age of 30 (45 per cent);[20] voters belonging to a political party showed by far the highest percentage of those expected to vote (97 per cent).[21] Among the latter, the KPD had the highest percentage of expected voters (89 per cent), followed by the CSU (88 per cent), the CDU (87 per cent), the LDP (86 per cent), and the SPD (85 per cent).[22]

In comparison to voter participation and composition, the electorate's preference for the newly established conservative parties, namely the CDU, the CSU and also the LDP, was rather surprising. According to a special political survey conducted by the OMGUS on 1 April 1946, of the 162 respondents, 67 preferred the CDU or the CSU, 47 the SPD, 9 the KPD, 7 the LDP and 2 the *Deutsche Arbeiterpartei* (German Workers' Party) which existed in the British zone.[23] Eventually, the Union was the most successful party (often by a clear margin) at local and state legislature elections in seven out of thirteen *Länder* in the three western zones of occupation. The victory of the CDU/CSU parties became even more manifest when they gained the majority of popular support in 16 of the 25 local elections although the SPD won four out of six regional elections in the year 1946.[24] These outstanding results of the first free elections in post-war Germany can be attributed to the fact that after 1945, the Union had a near-monopoly of the Catholic vote. At that time, this still mattered a lot: the Catholic vote was still heavily conservative, especially on social questions and in regions of high Catholic practice, such as Bavaria. Traditional Catholic voters in western Germany would rarely vote Socialist and almost never Communist. But, and this was the peculiarity of the post-war era, even conservative Catholics often had no choice but to vote Christian Democrat and Christian Socialist respectively, despite the reformist bent of Christian Democratic politicians and policies, because conventional right-wing parties were either under a shadow or else banned outright. Even non-Catholic conservatives and the middle-class turned increasingly to the Union (or to the Liberal Democrats due to the left tendencies of the CDU, such as most noticeably in Hesse), as a bar to the 'Marxist' left. Thus, the emergence of the parties to the right of Social Democracy as the leading political force was variously regarded as a rejection of extremism, leftism and radicalism in any form.[25] Yet the adoption of the proportional electoral system or rather a combination of the majority vote and proportional representation also helped to stabilise support for the emerging parties in the three western zones.

Thus, in spite of the then predominant socialist *Zeitgeist* and the perceived general preference for centralist governmental macroeconomic planning, for an enhanced role for the state in social and economic affairs, and, ultimately, for universal nationalisation advocated predominantly by the SPD and KPD, both the CDU's economically rather liberal Christian Socialism arguing for *limited* socialisation restricted to core industries, and the CSU's so-called '*soziale Wirtschaftsordnung*' (Social Economic Order) actually *rejecting* collectivisation but recommending private initiatives and free enterprise, became increasingly accepted in the political and public debate in 1945/1946. Indeed, neither the Social Democrats nor the Union put forward a particular economic model in the campaigns to the then upcoming elections and, thus it is arguable whether the electorate voted according to economic considerations and motives. Nonetheless, whereas the political debate between planned and market economy did not expand widely into the public sphere until 1948, there was already an intense public debate on economic regulation and privatisation.[26] In this debate, the majority of informed people eligible to vote in post-war West Germany apparently instead relied on the conservative parties in order to tackle the present and imminent difficulties, such as the food scarcity and housing shortage, and to provide a new direction for a better future.

4

1947 – DISILLUSION AND DISAPPOINTMENT

The all but general opinion seems to be that capitalist methods will be unequal to the task of reconstruction.[1]

(Joseph Alois Schumpeter, 1943)

Optimism about the incipient economic recovery and improving living conditions came to a grinding halt in the severe winter of 1946/1947. Canals froze, roads and railways were impassable for weeks at a time. Coal, still in short supply, could not keep up with domestic demand, and many, not only the 7.5 million homeless – in post-war Germany, at least 3.8 million homes out of a stock of 19 million had been completely destroyed and in the cities hit hardest by the bombing, losses in housing stock ran to 50 per cent[2] – suffered from the extreme cold. By February 1947 it was reported that there had been 305 deaths from hypothermia in the western zones, 1,155 cases had been admitted to hospital and 49,300 people treated for the effects of the frostiness.[3] Infection rates for diphtheria, typhoid and tuberculosis in the British and American zones doubled. Despite economic growth in the western zones, general industrial production slumped to the level of the previous year during which it was merely 32 per cent of the output in 1938.[4] Steel production fell back sharply by 40 per cent compared to the previous year, and agricultural food output fell from 70 per cent in 1946 to 58 per cent of its pre-war level in 1947,[5] a development attributable above all to the lack of transportation caused, in part, by an exceptionally cold winter. The economy hit rock bottom, when lack of energy caused widespread industrial stoppages. But also calorific provision in the western zones of occupation dropped sharply from an average of 1,500 per day per adult in mid 1946 to just 740–800 calories in early 1947.[6] While 30 per cent of the population mentioned food as their chief source of concern in March

1946, this figure now rose to 40 per cent; in Berlin, where the situation was consistently worse, even up to 74 per cent reported insufficient supply of food in February 1947.[7] Those family treasures that had not been destroyed by bombs, stolen or broken were now eaten up; and so-called '*Hamstern*', i.e. the illegal trading with farmers and smallholders, did little to supplement rationing since farmers did not trust the money. In the winter of 1946/47, as many as 60,000 chiefly elderly Germans died of the cold and hunger. In this situation, various hunger demonstrations and even disturbances took place all over the western zones. In Wuppertal the occupying military forces even had to deploy troops and tanks in order to curb the enraged crowd. Confidence in Allied–German cooperation deteriorated radically: in January 1946, 15 per cent were pessimistic regarding the relations; by the spring of 1947 the figure had risen to 70 per cent.[8] Similarly, Germans lost faith in the probability of economic recovery. Whereas in December 1945 nearly eight in ten thought that economic conditions would improve, by April 1947 only 45 per cent believed so.[9] In the course of the first 22 months following the Allied victory the mood among the German populace swung from relief at the mere prospect of peace and a fresh start, to stony resignation and growing disillusion mainly due to the reparations, the privileged situation of the Allies regarding food supply and the magnitude of the tasks still ahead.

Due to the then severe economic situation, complicated even further by the challenge to integrate some 10 million refugees and expellees from the eastern parts of the former Reich and the German-occupied territories, economic and social concerns dominated not only the political but also the public debate in spring 1947. Hence, the political parties' concepts of social and economic policy increasingly came to the fore in the run-up to the *Landtag* elections in North Rhine-Westphalia, Schleswig-Holstein and Lower Saxony on 20 April, and in Baden, Rhineland-Palatinate and Wuerttemberg-Hohenzollern on 18 May 1947. Whereas mainly socio-political issues had dominated election campaigns in the previous year, henceforth socio-economic issues generally displaced these. In contrast to the Social Democrats advocating centralist macroeconomic planning and the nationalisation of core industries in order to overcome the economic and social misery of that time, the Christian Democrats competed with their concept of a *Gemeinwirtschaft.* While both parties endorsed socialisation, the CDU's economic programme set clear limits to collectivisation and governmental control of the economy by maintaining private entrepreneurship. For the time being, however, the Christian Democrats did not venture further economic reforms and, thus, the public believed that it observed political parties competing towards the left.[10] The dire consequences of the war were still too noticeable and most people considered a state-controlled and planned economy necessary to cope with the misery that presented itself in spring 1947.[11] Moreover, many Germans still saw capitalism as largely responsible for the soulless materialism of the modern age and for the alienation of man from his spiritual beliefs and from true religious values. This materialism and this alienation were, according to this view, the main reason for the success of National Socialism. The command economy, unfair, inadequate, and regrettable though it might be, was considered the last bulwark against total chaos.

Due to these realities, and considerations, the SPD was confident about the outcome of both the upcoming state legislature elections and the petition for a referendum on the socialisation debate to be held in the British occupation zone on 20 April 1947. Nevertheless, the public opinion poll was dismissed and it was only in the elections in Lower Saxony and Schleswig-Holstein that the Social Democrats had success. There, however, the SPD's victory was not attributed to its programme for socialisation and a planned economy but mainly to the large number of newly-arrived refugees, who made up nearly 40 per cent of the population and who saw in it their best hope for a redistribution of wealth as a means of compensation for their losses in the East.[12] In all other four states, the Christian Democrats proved to be the most successful party; often by a clear margin, such as in Baden and Wuerttemberg-Hohenzollern.[13] Thus once more after the local and state legislature elections in 1946, the newly established conservative party, whose ideological basis proved broad enough to integrate successfully the variety of political positions to the right of Social Democracy, did surprisingly well in elections which were indeed about economic concerns but not (yet) about economic concepts.

Despite their mediocre performance in the local and *Landtag* elections, the Social Democrats managed to attain the post of Prime Minister in five out of eleven *Länder* parliaments and additionally occupied eight ministries of economics. Thus, the CDU and the CSU, which had both arrived at a common economic programme, i.e. the *Ahlener Programm*, and committed themselves to a joint group in the first post-war parliament, demanded the decisive post of the Director of the Administration for Economics. In the Economic Council constituted on 25 June 1947, the 20 representatives of the Union faced 20 delegates of the SPD and the two different economic agendas of a socialist state-run economy and the more market-oriented *Gemeinwirtschaft* competed in an official and decision-making political body for the first time in post-war West Germany.[14] The Allies considered the ensuing confrontation and conflict of competence between the two major political parties at the start of the Economic Council as a fiasco.[15] In view of the disappointing experiences with the previous bizonal administrations and the still insufficient provision of the population with food and basic goods, a general cooperation was expected between the political parties in order to improve the economic conditions.[16] Similarly, the populace in West Germany, who actually learnt from the press about the appointment of this first German post-war parliament, did not understand the political power struggle about posts under the prevailing circumstances[17] and wished for commonsense cooperation in the intended *democratic* institution for the sake of the public's needs.[18] The people were disappointed by the unrealistic and embarrassing course of action of the Economic Council[19] and wondered whether the delegates themselves had experienced hunger and hardship.[20] A sense of hopelessness and impending disaster had arisen. Thus from the outset the Economic Council was unpopular[21] and the public did not feel themselves to be moving into a better era.[22]

This negative public reception, which possibly affected the next elections,[23] at first reinforced the already prevalent disenchantment with politics: according to an OMGUS survey, 64 per cent of the respondents in the American zone preferred to leave politics to others rather than to concern themselves personally with it, and only 38 per cent perceived any great interest in politics among their contemporaries.[24] In order to counteract both the disenchantment with politics and public criticism, the Economic Council decided to make its plenary meetings open to the public, held regular press conferences for journalists to report about its actions,[25] and edited specific publications providing information to journalists and the general public alike. These decrees, such as the *Gesetz- und Verordnungsblatt des Wirtschaftsrats des Vereinigten Wirtschaftsgebietes*,[26] the *Öffentlicher Anzeiger für das Vereinigte Wirtschaftsgebiet*, edited by the *Rechtsamt* of the VWG, and *Wirtschaftsverwaltung* edited by the Administration for Economics, barely reached the public's attention, however, and the general public hardly became aware of what was happening behind the scenes.[27] In fact, the Economic Council itself was relatively unknown: in October 1947 only about a third (31 per cent) of the AMZON public had heard about the bizonal institution, which by that time had been in operation for some months.[28] This in turn invited speculations about the unclear work of the bizonal administration.[29] Despite various appeals to overcome internal disputes for the sake of concerted action and presentation,[30] the public relations of the Economic Council remained as deficient and dissonant as its image. To many, the public and the media alike, the institution in Frankfurt was still perceived as unregenerate, and even as incapable of making decisions[31] – an impression fuelled by the fact that the parliamentary parties dwelled on political rather than public interests, and hence only six laws were passed in the first six months of the Economic Council's existence.[32] Politics overall was discredited, and people did not have confidence in either the political parties or the institution in Frankfurt to be able to improve the existing economic conditions. While this general sentiment did not markedly affect the communal and state legislature elections taking part in Saarland, Bremen and Wuerttemberg-Baden (both the voter participation and the election results remained in line with previous polls) in the second half of 1947,[33] some newspapers commented on the 'silent legislative machinery without life' and argued that in all likelihood it would be necessary for every German to determine his own future.[34]

In fact, nothing remained to be done except for the Germans to take matters into their own hands. The hot summer after the cold winter had caused an inadequate harvest, and agricultural yields fell by about a third even compared to the previous year's meagre crop. The resultant struggle for bread and coal was dominated by a so-called '*Moral der 1000 Kalorien*' (morale of 1,000 calories) and the traditional values collapsed – necessity knows no law. The black market and the so-called '*Ruinenkriminialität*' (ruin crime rate) prospered: in some regions, criminal offences increased by more than 400 per cent in comparison with pre-war years.[35] While the police and justice instituted legal proceedings, many like the archbishop of Cologne, Cardinal Josef Frings, felt sympathy for the theft of food and the mass stealing of Allied coal in freight depots vernacularly referred to as *Fringsen*.[36] The story of the primate's condoning of theft firstly expressed in his New Year's Eve homily on 31 December 1946 had spread like wildfire. Thereupon trains transporting coal were stormed and more than 17,000 people had been arrested for stealing coal within a few months.[37] There was just too little of everything and to many the year 1947 appeared to be the eighth year of the war. Indeed, the shortfall in coal could be made up in part from imports. Food, too, could be purchased from America and the British Dominions. But all these imports had to be paid for in hard currency, usually dollars. In Germany, however, money had long since ceased to function in any ordinary sense of the word; cigarettes were one accepted medium of exchange. Firms and individuals resorted to illegal barter and to complicated compensation deals, often involving arduously worked out chains of bilateral trade to finally get hold of scarce commodities. Both the need to have a sufficient supply of commodities at hand for bartering and the general *Flucht in Sachwerte* (flight into physical assets) as the only reliable store of value resulted in a large-scale hoarding of raw materials and semi-finished products. The official money had not only lost its value via inflation but also via a spreading reluctance to accept it as a medium of exchange; confidence in the continued value of the *Reichsmark* suffered a further decline after April 1947.[38] In this situation, various individuals and organisations put forth petitions but also proposals for reform of both finances and currency.[39] For many Germans the cry for monetary reform and the demand for a 'new currency' had even become a sort of obsession. In a climate of indubitable and growing malaise, they saw in the new currency the arcanum with which to cure all their ills and evils.

5

1948 – ASPIRATION AND APPREHENSION

Was bewegt uns heut' enorm?
Tag und Nacht?! – Währungsreform!
Kommt sie heute, kommt sie morgen?
Jeder macht sich seine Sorgen.
Manchem Mann ist davor bange,
Manchem währt es viel zu lange.[1]

(*Nürnberger Nachrichten*, 1948)

At the turn of the year 1947/1948, the people's hopes and expectations associated with monetary reform in post-war West Germany increasingly were tempered by scepticism and apprehension: the unilateral declaration of a currency reform for the three western zones would both openly breach the Potsdam Agreement by which the Allies had agreed to treat Germany as a unitary economy and end the negotiations on a pan-German currency reform based on the Colm–Dodge–Goldsmith Plan which in turn would inevitably lead to a forceful response by the Soviet authorities and eventually to the division of Germany. In addition to the political consequences, however, the Germans mainly worried about the economic and financial repercussions.[2] Indeed, there was general agreement that some kind of reform was needed simply to jolt the economy back to life; however, there existed neither the experience nor a manual for such an extensive monetary reform. No other country at that time had suffered such damage and had to integrate so many impecunious refugees and expellees; as many as 16.5 million Germans were driven from their homes.[3] Due to these unparalleled circumstances, more and more people publicly expressed doubts about the success of a reorganisation of the finances and the currency.[4] Such a far-reaching reform required a sensitive approach indeed in order to avoid either inflation or deflation, depending on money supply in relation to the available goods and services, a subsequent increase in unemployment, the complete cancellation of monetary assets (both working capital and private savings) leading to illiquidity of companies and the loss of spending power which in turn were necessary to stimulate the domestic economy, further the increasing public debt and the impoverishment of the population. Most importantly, though, it was fundamental to restore faith in the new currency as well as governance, i.e. the Economic Council; but both increasingly suffered a further decline in spring 1948.

Whereas the Allies were cautious in expressing public criticism, and so merely stated that the Economic Council did not yet live up to its potential,[5] in the view of the German public, by contrast, the economic parliament had gambled away any credibility or authority, and failed as their political representation.[6] Although there were some media, such as the semi-official paper of the American occupying authorities *Die Neue Zeitung*, suggesting a predominantly positive view on the Economic Council,[7] this could not belie the then prevalent public criticism and disappointment about the German authorities' lack of leadership. According to an OMGUS survey on the public reception of the bizonal administration, the confidence that Bizonia would improve living conditions dropped from 73 per cent to 53 per cent between October 1947 and January 1948. In March 1948, 44 per cent said that conditions had been unfavourably affected, while only 36 per cent said that they were better. Thus only 20 per cent of the respondents were satisfied with the work of the Economic Council, whereas 64 per cent expressed dissatisfaction; half of the dissatisfied commented that nothing was getting done.[8] The first post-war parliament was widely discredited and critical petitions sent to what was initially believed to be an effective representation of the people were increasingly replaced by supportive proposals.[9] At this stage, an overwhelming majority was in favour of the popular determination of policy as opposed to its determination by politicians[10] and many an individual saw Germany 'like a rudderless vessel without sails and without captain drifting in [a] tremendous storm and dense fog of political and economic uncertainty more and more towards the rocks which mean economic and political wreck by total impoverishment of state and population.'[11]

As a matter of fact, however, West Germany had a captain and he was everything but irresolute. Quite the contrary, the new Director of the Administration for Economics in the Bizonal Economic Council, Ludwig Erhard, who succeeded Johannes Semler on 2 March 1948, had extensive plans indeed to reorganise the post-war economy. These reforms, centred on economic liberalisation following a currency reform, however, met with incomprehension among politicians and the public alike.[12] Erhard's concept of a so-called 'Social Market Economy', which he introduced to the Economic Council on its fourteenth plenary meeting on 21 April 1948, simply seemed unrealistic and inconceivable in times of prevalent destitution and the absence of market mechanisms. Even the sections of the press, that had supported Erhard's neo-liberal approach, were largely sceptical about his intention to abandon rationing and about market economic measures in general.[13] The economist and journalist of *Die Zeit*, Marion Dönhoff remarked: 'If Germany was not ruined yet, this man with his absurd plan to abandon all rationing will manage to do so. May God prevent him becoming Minister for Economic Affairs. After Hitler, and the fragmentation of Germany, this would be a third catastrophe!'[14] This statement was quite representative of the prevailing German sentiment in spring 1948. The public was not optimistic about a return to a market economy as the economic inequalities made the abolition of state planning and control inconceivable. Thus, due to Erhard's seemingly unreasonable intentions, more and more perceived the Economic Council as unrealistic or even a complete farce.[15]

Despite this prevalent sentiment, nationwide public demonstrations against food shortages, political opposition, albeit mainly on the part of the SPD, and the numerous admonitions for a sensitive procedure with regard to economic, financial and social reform by various charities, the unions and the *Deutscher Städtetag* (Association of German Cities and Towns),[16] to name but a few, there were also supporters of economic liberalisation. For instance, the *Industrie- und Handelskammern*, which had already lobbied for a free market economy via its publication *IHK-Mitteilungen* in the previous year,[17] favoured the abolition of state economic controls.[18] Similarly, German university professors of economics argued for a market-oriented economy and sent a resolution to the Economic Council requesting economic liberalisation and a currency reform they considered essential for the economic reconstruction.[19] Also there were decreasing numbers of adherents of socialisation. According to an OMGUS survey on German opinions on socialisation of industry, only 30 per cent of the respondents said that they would be better off if industry were socialised.[20] The fact that economic liberalism was increasingly standing up to the socialist *Zeitgeist* of the immediate post-war years was also reflected in the election results of the local elections taking part in Bavaria and Hesse on 25 April and 30 May 1948 respectively: while the outcome showed the same winners as in previous elections, namely the CSU in Bavaria (37.8 per cent) and the SPD in Hesse (35.7 per cent), however, the relative percentage of votes revealed that in both states the SPD and the KPD, advocating nationalisation, lost plenty of votes whereas the economically liberal Union parties and the Liberal Democrats in particular attained an extraordinarily good election result; in Hesse, by obtaining 29.1 per cent of the vote, the FDP even came close to becoming the second biggest party.[21] Moreover, according to an EMNID survey of housewives on the topic of 'free market economy or government control of the economy', as many as 74 per cent favoured a free market economy.[22] While the significance of these results is indeed arguable, the debate on the future economic model for Germany had undoubtedly reached the households and marketplaces, the very public sphere.[23]

Henceforth, not only organisations and interest groups, such as the employer and employee associations, but increasingly also ordinary citizens aimed to influence the political and public debate on economic and financial reorganisation. As early as September 1945, professional associations had re-emerged in Germany, in particular in the agricultural sector. This was most pronounced during the years of food shortage when the farmers' unions adopted a mediating role between producers and the administration in Frankfurt. In this function, the associations criticised the intended economic policy of the Economic Council, and exerted influence through the CSU. Next to the farmers' unions the industrial associations are to be mentioned at this stage. Although the Allies initially did not grant the employers an effective organisation, seeing it as tainted by National Socialism, this did not mean that the industry was unable to articulate its interests. On the contrary, various trade associations, such as the *Wirtschaftsvereinigung Eisen- und Stahlindustrie*, the *Wirtschaftsverband Eisen-, Blech- und Metallwarenindustrie*, the *Arbeitsgemeinschaft Eisen und Metall*, or the *Arbeitsgemeinschaft der Bauindustrie in den Vereinigten Westzonen*, and chambers of industry and commerce formed and were finally recognised; by autumn 1948, around 1,500 such industrial associations were accredited in the Bizone. The economically liberal employers and industrial associations aimed to influence the Economic Council mainly through the liberal and conservative parties in order to push economic developments in their favour. In opposition to the employers' associations, the zonal precursor of the *Deutscher Gewerkschaftsbund* (DGB) (Federation of German Trade Unions) which was formally founded as an umbrella organisation of sixteen national trade unions organised on industrial lines later on 13 October 1949, sent proposals to the *Länder* governments, the Economic and the Parliamentary Council regarding uniform labour law, the freedom to form trade unions, the right to strike, and also socialisation, which it wished to see inserted into the Basic Law.[24] The two major political parties obliged on many of these requests, sometimes over the protests of the FDP/DVP. Similarly, the DGB urged that the future federal government be empowered with authority to establish bodies of social or economic self-government without a formal constitutional amendment. The trade unions feared, in particular, that the safeguards of federalism against the administrative expansion of the centre might interfere with their plans for 'economic democracy'; a system of economic chambers in which labour and business organisations would share the control of the economy. For this reason, they also complained about the rigidity of the strict division between the powers of the federation and the *Länder*.[25] A delegation of the Council of Trade Unions of the western zones also requested several amendments to the Basic Law, including the right to strike, a guarantee of the status of works councils, a commitment to the socialisation of basic industries, economic democracy, the federal financial administration, the exclusive legislature jurisdiction of the federation on income, corporation and property taxes, and its concurrent jurisdiction over all other taxes.[26] Besides numerous other interest groups, such as the *Zentralverband der Fliegergeschädigten* representing the interests of air raid victims and arguing for a moderate and acceptable economic and financial reorganisation,[27] however, there were also many petitions and proposals on the part of the populace. Born out of either the ambition to contribute to the success of an economic and monetary reform or out of mere frustration or even both, many an individual appealed to the economic parliament in Frankfurt.[28]

That such public attempts were heard – though how well considered is difficult to establish – is exemplified in a response to a petition and an accompanying memorandum by the merchant Hellmut Sommer in which he requested to avoid imposition of policies without public referendum, but argued for the involvement of the populace in the upcoming currency reorganisation in order to gain credibility and confidence in the new currency.[29] Here, the 'man in the street' demanded democratic rights and the voice of the people to be heard. These lines embody the will and hopes of an individual to contribute to political decision-making. The impact of this attempt to influence political decision takers is documented in an internal statement by the AG CDU/CSU: 'The [...] memorandum by Mr Hellmut Sommer on the upcoming currency reform is the intelligent and elaborate work of a German [...] merchant. [...] It was undoubtedly interesting to get more precise proposals [...] by Mr Sommer'.[30] The CDU/CSU even considered applying the proposal to the preparation of the financial reform,[31] about which the general public had already begun to speculate.

With rumours that the old money was shortly to go, there was frenzied buying to get rid of potentially worthless currency. The pubs were filled with people drinking away their reserves. By May prices had fallen but were rising again shortly afterwards as the new money did not come. At the beginning of June, for instance, a pound of coffee cost 2,400 RM. These developments increasingly reminded many of the traumatic hyperinflation of 1923 in which countless Germans lost both their savings and their faith in government. Awaited and feared in equal measure, the upcoming currency reform at first led to a state of disconcertment. In some regions the churches offered special services and prayers to help people cope with the volatile climate which permeated Germany; there were even fears of suicide attempts.[32] The days preceding the currency reform, people gathered in the streets and in front of shops, which were often closed for the most spurious of reasons; business claimed to be out of stock or on company holidays or to be inventory-checking. The discussions centred primarily around one question: what to do with the old currency? Some suggested depositing the old *Reichsmark* in the bank, others made investments. Panic and confusion were considerable. Many carried out last-minute transactions and bought panic-proof tangible goods. This often took bizarre forms: '70-year-olds buying baby soothers [...] and the granny next door purchased seven lipsticks.'[33]

Finally, on Friday 18 June, the first two laws for the implementation of the long expected currency reform on Sunday 20 June were promulgated by the three western Military Governments, the Chairman of the Executive Committee, Hermann Pünder, and the president of the Economic Council, Erich Köhler. The 'First Law for Monetary Reform (Currency Law)' established the *Deutsche Mark* (DM) as the only legal currency valid from Monday 21 June and allocated every inhabitant in exchange for old currency of the same nominal amount a maximum of 60 DM of which not more than 40 DM were paid in cash immediately and the remainder within two months.[34] The old *Reichsmark* was to be surrendered at specific institutions, primarily banks and *Sparkassen*. The 'Second Law for Monetary Reform (Issue Law)' outlined the terms of reference of the *Bank Deutscher Länder*, the newly formed central bank for the three western zones of occupation, and established reserve requirements for the *Landeszentralbanken* (Federal State Central Banks).

Thus, after these laws came into effect and people received their *Kopfgeld* (bounty) of 40 DM, which corresponded to almost a week's pay of a skilled worker, to many in West Germany, the situation on Monday 21 June when public trading resumed and the black market disappeared seemed surreal and fairytale-like. The shops presented full displays of goods held back for days and weeks in anticipation (similarly, manufacturers had built up stocks of semi-finished goods and raw materials) and the Germans were often literally 'drunk' with the opportunities the new *Deutsche Mark* gave them.[35] One contemporary described: 'The shop windows were bursting with long-missed products;

relatively low prices and a flexible handling of rationing instructions [...] lured the consumer and opened the moneybags.'[36] While one day apathy was mirrored on German faces, on the next a whole nation looked hopefully into the future.[37]

The initial euphoria in West Germany was subdued when the Soviet Union countered with the introduction of its own currency in the eastern zone on 23 June and blockaded entry into West Berlin the following day leading to the feared definite division of Germany. It eventually came to a sudden end with the proclamation of the 'Third Law for Monetary Reform (Conversion Law)' that was announced later the week on 26 June. It stated that

> the old currency credit balances [...] shall be converted so that the owner is credited with one *Deutsche Mark* for every ten *Reichsmark*. Of this, one half shall be credited to a free *Deutsche Mark* account (*Freikonto*) and the other half to a blocked *Deutsche Mark* account (*Festkonto*), with regard to which regulations will be issued within 90 days.[38]

These regulations, which eventually formed the so-called '*Festkontengesetz*' (Fixed Account Law) issued later on 7 October, determined that saving deposits were reduced to just 10 per cent of the original nominal value and half the deposit was frozen for a fixed period, after which 70 per cent of that nominal sum was again taken away on the release date. Thus all savings were actually not converted at a ratio of 10:1, a rate originally envisaged in the Colm–Dodge–Goldsmith Plan of April 1946,[39] but proportionately 10:0.65. Consequently, for 100 RM one merely received 6.50 DM.[40] This currency devaluation annihilated massive private wealth, yet left wealth in estate and production unaffected. Whereas debtors benefited, the accounts of savers were diminished and many lost their savings – though it is estimated that 28 per cent of the adult population at that time had no bank accounts and that another quarter of the population had less than 2,000 RM in bank and savings accounts.[41]

In addition to the currency reform which involved both the substitution of the *Reichsmark* by the *Deutsche Mark* and the sterilisation of the excessive money supply, people had to cope with rising prices as a consequence of the enormous demand and relatively low production. After the Economic Council had adopted Ludwig Erhard's draft for the Guiding Principle Law cancelling existing economic controls at the same time to currency reform on 18 June, price ceilings were maintained only for a limited number of essential foods, rents and some basic materials, such as coal and steel; clothing and footwear were freed of controls but subject to rationing.

On the basis of – justifiable – uncertainty in regard to public reception of the consequences of the currency reform which made clear the dichotomy between market economy and planned economy, Erhard commissioned the IfD to assess public opinion in two surveys in June and July 1948. These showed that 71 per cent and 74 per cent respectively welcomed the currency reform. Furthermore, 44 per cent of the interviewees considered the future of Germany after the reform more optimistic, while 22 per cent were undecided and 24 per cent remained sceptical and pessimistic.[42] However, these opinion polls also revealed that the majority (79 per cent) considered the currency reform unfair and inconsiderate because it was seen to privilege certain sectors of society; for example, 62 per cent felt that mainly businesses benefited.[43] These results were widely confirmed by an OMGUS survey in July 1948 in which the currency reform received hearty approval in the American zone of occupation. Nine in ten termed the reform drastic but necessary to jolt the economy back to life, and over half (53 per cent) thought it should have taken place earlier. It tended to create an optimistic mood: 54 per cent expected the new currency to retain its value, 58 per cent believed that they would get along better during the coming year because of the reform. Even so, dissatisfaction increasingly pervaded society, particularly small savers who felt disadvantaged compared to proprietors.[44] Although worries over the availability of basic necessities tended to decrease after the currency reform to nearly manageable proportions, anxiety over the means of obtaining them skyrocketed. By midsummer, for instance, half of the population in the American zone (48 per cent) said that they had no means of livelihood, and by August this figure had risen to 59 per cent.[45] Furthermore, while in June 78 per cent of the people in West Germany did not fear unemployment against 14 per cent who did,[46] by August of that year, 77 per cent expected – correctly, as it turned out – that the currency reform would lead to greater unemployment.[47] In fact, the unemployment rate increased from 3.2 per cent in June to 12.2 per cent in December 1948.[48] Whereas many enjoyed the benefits of the currency reform, more and more Germans did not and became mere onlookers of economic life. Many felt betrayed by the Economic Council and their representatives. This bitterness was, for instance, documented in a monthly report of the district president of Upper and Middle Franconia sent to the Bavarian government on 9 July 1948.[49] After living expenses further increased by up to 200 per cent and simultaneously a general pay freeze had been imposed, confrontations between employees and employers grew and lawsuits in labour courts proliferated. For instance in Bavaria, the number of pending lawsuits increased from 4,000 to 7,500 between December 1948 and December 1949.[50] Public discord also became occasionally visible in the harassment of shopkeepers and merchants; protests on occasion turned into riots in various cities.

The people blamed mainly Ludwig Erhard for this misery and economic inequality. Eventually, to him, as former Chairman of the Special Bureau for Money and Credit and Director of the Administration for Economics in the Bizonal Economic Council, were assigned both the task to prepare the currency reform (though the scheme was actually devised by the Western Allies, and German involvement was restricted to the subordinate task of drafting the laws and regulations) and that of cancelling existing economic controls. The *Wirtschaftsdiktator* (economic dictator) as Erhard was then often named became one of the most unpopular politicians,[51] and his economic programme of a Social Market Economy seemed to have failed. Multiple protest rallies of thousands of unionised workers and civil servants took place and various unions led by the Chairman of the Federation of German Trade Unions, Hans Böckler, criticised in particular the pricing policy and the pay freeze.[52] The majority of the public (between 81 and 94 per cent depending on the merchandise in question) considered prices far too high, and consequently 70 per cent favoured a return to price control.[53] Thus, Erhard was vehemently criticised for his timing of economic liberalisation within the CDU/CSU[54] and even within his circle of (political) friends as he remarked at a later stage: 'It was worse that even good friends should have gone so wrong as to think that my economic policy would land Germany in disaster.'[55]

After increasing explicit criticism on the part of the political left and right,[56] various organisations, such as the *Deutscher Rentnerbund* (Union of Retired Persons), the *Wirtschaftsgemeinschaft selbständiger Ingenieure* (Economic Community of Self-Employed Engineers), the *Verband der Versicherungsunternehmen* (Association of Insurance Companies) or the *Reichsbund der Körperbeschädigten, Sozialrentner und Hinterbliebenen* (Federation of the Maimed, Retired and Bereaved), numerous municipal councils and mayors,[57] but also individuals who considered the introduction of a market economy at that stage most antisocial,[58] the CDU/CSU ran indeed the risk of losing votes at large in the upcoming local elections taking place in seven out of thirteen *Länder* in late autumn 1948.[59] Increasingly, the SPD, which had already unsuccessfully submitted a motion of no confidence against the Director of the Administration for Economics on 17 August 1948, seemed to be right after all and Schumacher was perceived as the most competent politician at that time.[60] Despite the public's criticism of Erhard's economic policy and the prevalent unpopularity of the Economic Council,[61] considered to be unable to correct the disparity between wages and price level,[62] against expectations, the majority of the Germans (65 per cent) did not intend to alter their voting behaviour after the currency reform; only 4 per cent stated that they would vote differently in the next elections.[63] And indeed, the respective election results – and also the voter participation – differed only marginally from the previous ones or even remained exactly the same as in North Rhine-Westphalia. Solely in Rhineland-Palatinate was there a shift in the relative strength in favour of the SPD whereas the CDU won even more votes in other states, such as Lower Saxony, Schleswig-Holstein or Wuerttemberg-Hohenzollern.[64] Whereas votes in local elections generally offer limited evidence of the popularity of regional or federal policies, it is safe to infer that the Union benefited from the SPD's inability to take advantage of the situation and to provide both a viable alternative to the CDU's socially acceptable market economy and a leading personality able to confront the charismatic Ludwig Erhard.

Nonetheless, in late autumn 1948, Erhard's popularity was under considerable strain at both elite and mass level among the public.[65] Thereupon, the Administration for Economics responded to former pleas on the part of officials and the public for frequent information about the administration's activities[66] though mainly by urging the media to be more supportive and the people to show more respect for the Frankfurt achievements.[67] Nevertheless, periodical price comparison lists were issued in order to inform consumers. In addition, the *Gesetz gegen Preistreiberei* which enabled the prosecution of the forcing up of prices was passed by the Economic Council on 7 October and the so-called '*Jedermann-Programm*' which provided reasonably priced and specifically marked goods to the people was started in November 1948. While the majority of the Germans welcomed these actions (the *Jedermann-Programm* in particular was embraced by 71 per cent of the respondents),[68] all these measures had mixed success because they were limited in range and merely aimed at appeasing the public.

In fact, an increasing number of people threatened by destitution and unemployment showed their resentment. Spontaneous strikes and frantic demonstrations took place. Alarmed and worried by this anarchy, the Federation of German Trade Unions led by the labour union official Hans Böckler requested a 'sensible government control of the economy'[69] and eventually called for a general strike to be held on Friday 12 November 1948.[70] While 9.2 million out of 11.7 million workers and employees in the Bizone followed the appeal in protest against the rising prices, and for economic democracy and socialisation,[71] many of the strikers perceived the work stoppage, deliberately called by Böckler for a Friday in order to avoid further non-productive time, as a half-hearted holiday or warning strike that would be ineffective at daunting Ludwig Erhard. Nonetheless, the general strike and the SPD's second – albeit unsuccessful – motion of no confidence against the Director of the Administration for Economics in November 1948 marked the climax of public and political criticism.

In the following months the economy began to cool off. After the inflationary burst in summer and early autumn, the price level was approaching the limit set by the monetary frame and the fiscal surplus; in addition the anticipation of the first Marshall-Plan imports may have eased inflationary pressures somewhat. Between October and December the annualised increase of consumer prices dropped to 8.8 per cent and that of producer prices to 2.9 per cent. The final victory of the *Deutsche Mark* became evident in the exchange rate against commodity substitutes, i.e. in the prices of tobacco and coffee. In December 1948, these goods were traded for half of their pre-reform prices.[72] Due to this generally noticeable turnaround in the German post-war economy, which, contrary to popular belief, was not caused by the currency reform in June 1948, but rather by the overall steady economic growth experienced since 1947,[73] the criticism of Erhard's economic policy abated though did not fall silent in view of the still high unemployment.[74] Essentially, however, after one of the most dramatic and indeed decisive years in German political and economic history, economic liberalism was firmly anchored in both the political and the public debate about Germany's post-war economic model,[75] and the sense of doom and gloom prevalent in previous years was replaced by a growing sense of optimism and economic recovery.

6

1949 – CONTENTMENT AND CONFIDENCE

In the federal elections, the people unambiguously decided for the Social Market Economy.[1]

(Konrad Adenauer, 1949)

When in spring 1949 prices noticeably and sustainably stabilised, faith both in the *Deutsche Mark* and in improving economic conditions grew among the German people. According to an EMNID survey, by February 1949, 66 per cent of respondents believed in the stability of the new currency whereas in July 1948 only 53.1 per cent and in August 1948 merely 42.5 per cent of interviewees had done so; even more significant were the respective percentages of respondents not having faith in the DM: 46.9 per cent, 53.0 per cent, and, finally, 13.2 per cent.[2] Similarly, an OMGUS opinion poll on economic affairs documented the upward trend in confidence in the new currency, gaining twenty points from July 1948 to February 1949. Approval of currency reform measures remained at a high level, averaging about nine out of ten. Although money and high prices in general were great cause of concern (in fact, 57 per cent mentioned financial problems, far exceeding the figure of 10 per cent that then mentioned food as a major concern), at the turn of the year, majorities felt that prices would go down. Thus, in January 1949, 52 per cent of the respondents claimed to be better off than they had been a year earlier, at which time 57 per cent had said they were worse off than the year before.[3] According to a contemporary EMNID survey, people similarly calculated their personal economic situation: in consecutive opinion polls, in the months of August, September, November 1948 and February 1949, there was a fluctuation – 43.6 per cent, 65 per cent, 47.8 per cent, and 70 per cent – in those interviewed who thought themselves better off than before the currency reform. The analogous figures reflecting those considering their personal situation worse than before June 1948 were: 30.3 per cent, 17.5 per cent, 24.9 per cent and 4.8 per cent.[4] By July 1949, 48 per cent in the American occupation zone (57 per cent in West Berlin, and 61 per cent in Bremen) felt that their economic situation was better than it had been just a year earlier. Those who felt they were worse off (17 per cent in the American zone and West Berlin, 14 per cent in Bremen) did not form any cohesive or well-defined group.[5] These survey results reflected the improving economic conditions in spring 1949 and revealed a public sentiment which could be characterised by relative material contentment and confidence.

Despite its evidently successful economic and financial policy, the Economic Council remained relatively unpopular mainly due to tenacious unemployment and widely felt social disparities.[6] To many employees and employers, the Social Market Economy was of doubtful success and anything but social, since Erhard's promises seemed to becoming true only for a minority,[7] an impression which was also not altered by an image campaign initiated mainly by the Economic Council and the CDU.[8] The unpopularity of the Economic Council and the lack of confidence in government and political parties,[9] however, were also due to a perceived lack of transparency in political decision-taking and a low policy responsiveness to public concerns.[10] Then again indeed, the public's receptiveness to political arguments was low in the immediate post-war years and politics seemed far detached from everyday life;[11] daily concerns, such as housing (22.9 per cent), missing family members (21.34 per cent) and unemployment (13.2 per cent), took clear priority over tax reform (7.3 per cent) and land reform (2.5 per cent). Even the issue of socialisation, hotly debated in the Economic Council, was of minor importance to the general public; foreign and cultural affairs were not mentioned at all.[12] Nonetheless, the populace felt widely mis- or even wholly uninformed by their government. For instance, only 40 per cent of the respondents in the American occupation zone knew that German authorities had adopted the so-called '*Lastenausgleichsgesetz*' for the equalisation of war losses and burdens among the people. Large numbers of Germans were not even aware that a Basic Law had been framed for a West German Federal Republic. In western Germany, only 18 per cent of those who did know that it had been enacted knew something about it.[13]

Hence the majority of Germans showed a low level of interest in politics and at least initially wished to keep themselves to themselves.[14] For instance, while the DGB continued to protest for higher wages, the rights of labour, a federal financial administration, and the exclusively federal jurisdiction on economic and social policy,[15] fewer and fewer Germans cherished hopes for improvements by public protests. In fact, the majority of the Germans in the American zone (68 per cent), Bremen (72 per cent), and Berlin (72 per cent), explicitly disapproved of strikes. The main criticism was that such strikes were useless and would accomplish nothing.[16] Only 20 per cent of the residents in the American zone felt that, if called upon to decide, political parties would opt for the good of the country, as opposed to 62 per cent who thought that the parties would pursue their own interests. Somewhat over a third (38 per cent) felt that people could influence the activities of political parties. The majority of those who perceived little chance of influence (34 per cent) argued that the parties would do as they pleased without regard for the wishes of the people. Two-thirds of those who thought that the people could exert influence believed that this would be desirable, as did three-quarters of the more pessimistic. Regarding the *Länder* parliaments, only 41 per cent thought their members were in touch with public opinion, 30 per cent felt that their members welcomed expressions of opinion from the public, and merely 29 per cent felt their own interests as citizens were sufficiently represented in these parliaments. Nor were the prospects for political participation any greater: 71 per cent of Germans voiced their unwillingness to take a responsible position in the political life of their community if they were requested to. Only 40 per cent were aware of so-called 'citizens' meetings' in their communities; as few as 13 per cent claimed to have attended such a forum. Indeed, fewer than one in five (19 per cent) had attended any political meeting since the end of war. Roughly half this number (11 per cent) had attended an election meeting during the campaign going on at the time of the survey. Nonetheless, the majority of the Germans (80 per cent) indicated their intention to vote in the upcoming federal elections; but two weeks before polling day, 69 per cent had not decided for whom they would vote.[17]

Eventually, on Sunday 14 August 1949, around 31 million Germans were called to cast a vote for the first German *Bundestag* and to decide between a controlled economy and a Social Market Economy. Of those eligible to vote 25 million actually went to the ballot boxes often set up in restaurants and public houses; only the citizens of West Berlin were not allowed to vote, though they were indirectly represented in the federal parliament by 20 non-voting delegates. Thus, contrary to the Allies' apprehensions for a democratic Germany, 78.5 per cent of the eligible voters exercised their right to vote, which was interpreted as clear commitment to democracy. Asked why they voted, the largest number (27 per cent) responded that it was their duty, 18 per cent hoped to defeat communism, an equally large percentage expressed partisan reasons (voting for or against a particular party), and 14 per cent hoped to achieve better conditions.[18]

Out of the 19 political parties available for elections, 11 were finally elected to parliament (the hurdle that a party had to poll at least 5 per cent of the votes to be seated in parliament applied then only to *Länder* parliaments). Although the SPD, gaining 29.12 per cent of the votes, turned out to be the most successful single party, the CDU/CSU combined attracted 424,109 more votes, totalling 31 per cent, and 139 mandates compared to 131 for the Social Democrats. Konrad Adenauer interpreted this victory by a slim majority as clear support for the CDU/CSU and their concept of the Social Market Economy:

> The question of Planned Economy or Social Market Economy played a decisive role in the election. The German people have spoken with a great majority against the Planned Economy. A [grand] coalition between the parties that oppose the Planned Economy and those that support the Planned Economy has been rejected by the will of the majority of the voters.[19]

This study has revealed, however, that in fact both *Volksparteien*, the SPD and the CDU/CSU, had suffered large percentage losses over their previous *Land* election totals by failing to capture a comparable share of the enlarged electorate – since the elections in 1946/1947, the electorate had been expanded from some 39 million to around 48 million by returning prisoners of war, by the influx of expellees and refugees, and by the reenfranchisement of large numbers of individuals previously barred from voting because of former connections with National Socialism.[20] The most remarkable advance by winning over a million extra votes – in comparison, the SPD increased its by 850,000, and the CDU/CSU by merely 800,000 – and achieving 11.9 per cent of the total votes was that made by the FDP.[21] Contrary to the expectations of many observers,[22] the politically progressive and economically conservative Free Democrats were in fact the only political party consistently gaining percentage of votes between 1946 and 1949.[23] Most notably in Hesse, the nationalisation plans of the governing SPD and left-leaning tendencies of the CDU swayed many of the middle classes to vote for the FDP. But also on a national level, supporters of socialisation were in continuous decline. According to a nationwide opinion poll at that time, a majority of the Germans in summer 1949 (68 per cent) actually considered private initiatives and market competition more likely than socialisation (22 per cent) to enable economic recovery and to increase social income[24] – quite contrary to Kurt Schumacher's belief that the majority of the German people wanted socialisation.[25] In doing so, the rejection of socialisation by civic groups seemed more broad-based than the denial of private initiatives by socialist devotees and the working class. Given that generally only 10 per cent of the public understood the meaning of socialisation,[26] however, it is arguable whether these findings were more than superficial. Nonetheless, 45 per cent of the interviewees mentioned that they deemed governmental interference as consequence of socialisation to be harmful to the economy and a mere 4 per cent wanted government agencies (unions 9 per cent and workers' councils 14 per cent) to get involved in socialised companies rather preferring the former proprietor (29 per cent) or private experts (30 per cent).[27] These results clearly affirmed the then general pro-market trend in public opinion. Whereas in 1947 a majority among the German people had wanted macroeconomic planning and nationalisation, by mid-1949 this opinion was largely changed; nonetheless, the socialisation of private property for the well-being of the general public was anchored as part of an elaborate compromise in the Basic Law promulgated on 23 May 1949.[28] In this development, the poor social and economic performance of the communist Soviet regime – a lesson which millions of Germans learned from first-hand experience during their uninvited visits to Soviet territory – and the negative headlines about the failed nationalisation attempts of the then British Labour Government as well as the hostility of the American authorities to socialist experiments and the founding of the Federal Republic under the leadership of a bourgeois coalition government all militated against socialisation and a socialist economic democracy. The widespread anti-capitalist and pro-socialist rhetoric of the immediate post-war period indeed created a mood for the radical socialisation of both the economy and society, but, at the same time, the National Socialists' even more massive and destructive concentration and misuse of state power had instilled in Germans a comparably great fear of such power; post-war Germans of all major political persuasions feared any kind of concentration of power, whether in the hands of large, monopolistic industries or the government. Even the fact that, in contrast to the Union parties, the SPD lacked an economic concept and instead merely advocated socialisation and centralist economic planning both complicated the parliamentary work of the party in the Economic Council and gave their political opponents the opportunity to present them as pursuing a command economy similar to the one of the former hated totalitarian regime, did not decidedly swing the decision in favour of the CDU/CSU. Eventually, the electorate made its decision contingent on the satisfaction of its practical needs rather than on any particular theoretical economic system; in fact, most were relatively ignorant with only 12 per cent of respondents able to correctly identify the Social Market

Economy.[29] The advantage of the CDU and the CSU lay precisely in the fact that they were quasi-governing across the Bizone.

Whereas the SPD had acquired the post of Prime Minister in five out of eleven *Länder* parliaments and had additionally occupied eight ministries of economics, it left the key position within the Bizonal Economic Council with regard to economic policy, i.e. the post of the Director of the Administration for Economics, to the Union parties. This fateful decision was unambiguously attributed to the leader of the SPD, Kurt Schumacher, who considered both the Economic Council and its Administration for Economics in Frankfurt as mere provisional institutions and not as decisive political instruments. But the latter is exactly what they were: both the quasi-parliament and the ministry-like *Verwaltung für Wirtschaft* in particular were in fact not only administering but also determining and ultimately implementing economic policy. This in turn enabled the CDU/CSU adequately to communicate their socio-political and economic ideas to both the party base and the general public. In aligning their campaigns themed 'the economy is our fate' and in relentlessly promoting their economic concept, Alfred Müller-Armack, Konrad Adenauer, and Ludwig Erhard, in particular, created increasing confidence in economic liberalisation as the means to a Social Market Economy. After the economic and monetary reforms eventually turned out to be widely successful, the population was not only more open to liberal economic arguments[30] but the CDU/CSU even acquired a governmental or incumbency bonus and its socio-economic programme was increasingly seen as progressive and appealing economic and social policy. Erhard's manner spread optimism, and more and more people relied upon the Christian Union to improve both their material and psychological situation in the post-war years. Eventually, a prevailing mood of confidence in economic recovery characterised the months before the federal elections of August 1949.[31]

Nonetheless, to some socialism and economic planning still presented a magnetic attraction. In a public opinion survey conducted by the *Forschungsstelle für Volkspsychologie*, a research centre to assess the condition of the German people, many respondents still considered the SPD to have the better political and economic programme for a prosperous post-war Germany.[32] Assured in his pursuit of a socialist controlled economy, Kurt Schumacher continued to proclaim socialisation and macroeconomic planning despite widespread misgivings among the public and the apparently improved economic conditions. The confrontation of two opposed economic concepts and ideologies led to a hard-fought election campaign. In both the political as well as in the public arena, the two people's parties competed for support for their programmes. Fuelled by a

CDU publication which claimed that the Pope would not only excommunicate communists but furthermore that he condemned any form of socialism limiting personal freedom,[33] this contest assumed the form of a cultural conflict for all intents and purposes.[34] Once the Union parties occupied the field of socially oriented economic competence, it became difficult for the SPD to respond adequately. Instead of providing a viable economic alternative, Schumacher lapsed into anchorless destructive criticism of Erhard's economic policy. Whereas the latter could legitimately claim credit for a constructive approach leading to economic recovery, the aggressive class struggle polemic of the leader of the German Social Democratic Party was increasingly perceived as obstructive to the growing prosperity.[35] Thus Kurt Schumacher forfeited public favour – whereas in October 1948 he had been regarded as the most competent politician, by March of the following year, the public preferred Konrad Adenauer[36] – and the SPD lost votes among its former natural supporters.[37] At the same time, the CDU/CSU increased their share of votes among their target groups, namely refugees who had mainly voted for the SPD in previous elections, and women who would have realised the economic improvement soonest. As a matter of fact, 33 per cent of the former opted for the Union parties and 29 per cent for the SPD whereas among locals the percentages were exactly the other way round. Similar was the relative voting behaviour of women: whereas 41 per cent of all eligible female voters cast a ballot for the CDU/CSU and only 24 per cent for the SPD, conversely 21 per cent of all men gave their vote to the Union parties and 34 per cent to the Social Democrats.[38] Indeed, the CDU/CSU was increasingly identified with the economic and social recovery which assured many Germans to vote for the union parties, but the Union also fought more deeply for the public acceptance of its economic model in the battle to choose such a model for post-war West Germany. In abstaining from issuing merely dogmatic, ideological programme statements that appealed to the party's most faithful members and a narrow segment of society, the CDU/CSU rather formed and projected a party image that effectively attracted votes from varied sociological groups.

After a relatively successful campaign in the run-up to the federal elections dominated by economic policy, the political parties which had campaigned for a common socio-political and economic programme, namely the CDU, the CSU, and the FDP, formed a bourgeois coalition to serve as West Germany's first democratically elected federal government. Given a favourable party ratio with the help of the DP, which had received 4 per cent of the votes corresponding to 17 mandates, and also due to fundamental ideological differences, an alliance with the SPD was not seriously considered.[39] By a majority of a single vote (202 out of 402 seats), namely his own, Konrad Adenauer (CDU) was eventually invested as Chancellor on 15 September, Franz Blücher (FDP) becoming Vice-Chancellor. Kurt Schumacher, who furthermore had just lost against Theodor Heuss (FDP) in the poll to be the first President of the Federal Republic, then chaired the SPD parliamentary group in the *Bundestag*, which convened for the first time on 7 September 1949. The Social Market Economy's strongest proponent, Ludwig Erhard, was appointed Minister for Economic Affairs.

The Bizonal Economic Council, which was according to the Basic Law officially replaced by the democratically elected *Bundestag* as parliament of a new trizonal state,[40] formally dissolved by act and ordinance of the American and the British Military Government on 1 September 1949.[41] Until its end, this first post-war quasi-parliament had been relatively unpopular despite its achievements in both the economic and the political spheres. In its two years of existence, the Economic Council submitted 171 bills of which 131 became law in the Bizone and Trizone respectively. Political power struggles and conflicts of competence between the political parties, however, meant that in 1947 just 6 and in 1948 merely 49 bills were legislated.[42] This in turn had led to prevalent disappointment and disenchantment with politics; due to the economic and psychological malaise at the time, people expected from the Economic Council commonsense cooperation for the sake of their needs. While the economic situation gradually began to improve as early as 1947, the institution in Frankfurt remained unloved mainly due to tenacious unemployment and widely perceived inequity intensified by the monetary reform. Moreover, the unpopularity of the Economic Council and the lack of confidence in governance were also due to a perceived lack of transparency in political decision-making and a low policy responsiveness to public concerns. Although the Economic Council neither formed part of a direct democracy nor were its members publicly elected representatives, one may assume that the quasi-government in this economic parliament was indirectly guided and influenced by the public and its preferences. Indeed, it is arguable how much political consideration could be given to public preferences especially in these times of economic and political reconstruction. But precisely due to these extraordinary economic and political circumstances and following the dictatorship of National Socialism, it was more essential to restore faith in government and its economic and socio-political agenda. The establishment and perpetuation of both the Social Market Economy and democracy in general in post-war Germany ultimately required an individual's active political engagement on the one hand but also the inclusion of the populace in political decision-making on the other hand. Despite their initial low level of political interest, Germans gave expression to a norm of participation: almost three in four (73 per cent) considered it a good idea that people were able directly to make a proposal for a law; 65 per cent thought it a good idea for the people directly to be able to vote on the acceptance of a law, instead of its going through the parliament. As opposed to 23 per cent who favoured a government by experts, fully two-thirds (68 per cent) of the Germans thought it best that all the people determine the political and economic direction that the government should follow.[43] Expecting to codetermine the political debate, the German electorate produced remarkable turnouts in every local, regional or federal election between 1946 and 1949. This voter participation often described as *Wahlwunder* (election miracle) and civic political engagement in general, however, were not matched by the government. Although there was indeed an awareness that it was not possible for any political organisation to claim democratic legitimacy unless it rested on the freely expressed will of the people as the actual sovereign and principal in an institutional economic order, and even though article 20 paragraph 2 of the Basic Law of the Federal Republic of Germany promulgated on 23 May 1949 stated that 'all state authority is derived from the people',[44] politics hardly rose to the popular challenge. Even though Ludwig Erhard, who was constantly concerned about public opinion, aimed at popularising his liberal economic concept and policy which in turn stimulated the public debate on the future economic model for Germany, the Administration for Economics was little responsive to the public and most of its laws never reached the public sphere enabling only a relatively limited public debate about the economic reconstruction in comparison to the public debate about the political reorganisation of post-war Germany.[45]

Thus merely 13 per cent (as against 51 per cent) of the people in post-war West Germany believed that politics had done everything to improve the prevailing economic situation.[46] Although the populace was relatively mis- or even uninformed about actual governmental policies and the electorate was widely subject to partisan and often misleading messages disseminated by the political parties, 51 per cent (as against 19 per cent) of the eligible voters were in general satisfied with the outcome of the first federal elections[47] and the majority (47 per cent) had faith in the victors mainly due to the noticeably improving economic situation.[48] Furthermore, the object-lesson on a planned economy versus a Social Market Economy as offered by the press influenced the electorate in that direction.[49] In essence, however, just as little public relations was done by the Economic Council and the Administration for Economics, the newspaper editorial offices also hardly met their obligation factually to inform the general public on effective economic policies but tolerated selectivity and distortions.[50] Indeed, media policy just as much as democratic action at large had to be learnt and practised anew, in view of the emphasis on and claim for democracy at that time, namely that the public had to be central in both politics and the media. Despite this lack of information, the public in contrast took an interest by every available means in the ongoing debate on economic policy and, furthermore, on the development of an economic and socio-political model for a democratic post-war Germany.[51]

While policy responsiveness seems very plausible for the most salient issues about which policy-makers were likely to receive clear indications of public attitudes, there remains some uncertainty in the findings and evidence reported, as well as how to use them, concerning how much actual public control of policy-making there was. Whether it can be judged either that the public only loosely constrained policy-making or that it only on very few occasions forced the government's hand, there is no evidence that government policies were responsive to public opinion in the timeframe examined nor that the implementation of the Social Market Economy met with public approval.

CONCLUSION

Can capitalism survive? No. I do not think it can.
Can socialism work? Of course it can.[1]

(Joseph Alois Schumpeter, 1943)

As this study about the economic and political reorganisation of post-war West Germany has sought to demonstrate, neither the political decisions regarding the economic reconstruction of post-war West Germany nor the academic discussion on reinvigorating the philosophical and economic standing of liberalism in post-war Europe were confined to the political strategy units and schools of economic thought in Paris, London and Washington. Quite the contrary: several German think tanks, political parties and individuals gave impulse to and then shaped academic, political and economic developments in occupied Germany, whether they were based there or abroad. While the Allies, indeed, set the political, economic and institutional framework in times of occupation, Germans were throughout formative actors rather than passive recipients in both reorganising the post-war economy and in redefining political and economic liberalism – and indeed socialism. United on one front, conservatives and socialists alike aimed to develop a viable socio-political and economic order between the extremes of unbridled capitalism and collectivist central planning. The lessons gained from the historical experiences of both failed economic liberalism in the early 1930s and the inhumane totalitarianism of National Socialism, and, in addition, Germany's preoccupation with the social question since the late nineteenth century led to the eventual development of a so-called 'Third' or 'Middle Way' not as a compromise but as a combination of greater state provision for social security with the preservation of individual freedom. Despite common starting points, the various interpretations differed significantly, mainly regarding the importance attached to the state and to the individual. This research has recalled and contrasted the principal academic and political approaches of that time, namely the economic and socio-political ideas of the *Arbeitsgemeinschaft Erwin von Beckerath* within the Freiburg Circles, the Freiburg and the Cologne School of Economics, the West German Social Democratic Party, the Christian Democratic Union and Christian Social Union, as well as the programmes of the less influential but by no means negligible Liberal Democrats and the Communist Party. In so doing, the focus has been neither on the genesis nor the definition of individual concepts of economic policy, formed by academics or politicians, but on their respective communication to the public.

In their endeavours to anchor their particular economic ideas – often diametrically opposed to one another, of course – the individual parties stimulated not only the academic and political but also the public debate on the political and economic reconstruction of occupied post-war West Germany. Viewing in particular the extreme unparalleled depth of Germany's experience of totalitarianism, there was a broad consensus that not only any political but also any economic system had to be democratic in nature. The establishment and perpetuation of both political and economic democracy thus required the inclusion of the populace in decision-making which, in turn, had an effect on the communication of socio-economic ideas. While the various neo-liberal approaches all attached to the people the status of actual sovereign in an institutional economic order, and recognised the interdependence of politics, economics and the public, one particular school of economic thought outpaced the others in communicating a model of coordinated economic and social policy, namely the Social Market Economy. While that model has been much praised and studied, its communication to and eventual acceptance by the public have received considerably less attention. By examining both the constitutive involvement of German parties in post-war reconstruction and the role of the public during the process of economic liberalisation, this research provided alternative explanations for why the Social Market Economy prevailed as the socio-political and economic model for the Federal Republic of Germany.

While the Communist Party would have faced restrictions on the implementation of its programme due to guidelines issued by the Allied authorities, and the Social Democrats did not put forth their own economic concept, the Social Market Economy was by no means the most elaborate or well defined socio-political or economic idea brought before the public at that time; in fact, it was more a mélange of socio-political ideas than a precise theoretical order. But what set the Social Market Economy apart from other institutional approaches to economic management was its communication to both the political classes and the public. Its adherents fought more consistently – and eventually with greater success – for acceptance of their economic model as the model for post-war Germany, which was arguably not won in offices nor in parliament but rather at the centre of public debate. In particular Ludwig Erhard, as the Social Market Economy's most passionate proponent, realised the potential of subtle and systematic marketing to transform the concept from an economic theory, or even abstract economic policy, into the basis of a political party's propaganda and public image that held broad appeal. Due to the inherent potential which media influence had, when combined with political communication skills, for impact upon an atomised citizenry, Erhard cultivated the company of selected journalists and influential personages. Contacts with these 'opinion leaders' proved to be most beneficial in promoting his socio-economic programme and in presenting the success of his economic policy effectively. Although the implementation of the Social Market Economy benefited also from other crucial factors – including the east-west conflict and a favourable political and social climate within Germany and abroad, sustained domestic economic growth, the primacy of economics over politics, the stabilising alliance between the conservative and liberal parties, the pro-market composition of the Economic Council and the Federal Republic's own *Grundgesetz* which stressed individual freedom, human dignity, and the subsidiarity of societal organisation – it was mainly the following efforts at political communication of the cooperative and corporate model that led to the implementation and eventual electoral validation of the Social Market Economy in post-war West Germany.

Moreover, the process of political communication accommodated the demand for democratic political action, and stimulated the deliberation and discussion crucial to the formation of voting preferences regarding issues of political substance. Yet, despite the Social Market Economy's adherents' ambition to stimulate both political and public debate, they widely failed with regard to the latter. Indeed, both sides had to relearn and rehearse democratic mentalities and behaviour patterns; politics and the media had to regain credibility lost in twelve years of Nazi despotism; and, furthermore, the satisfaction of elementary needs as *the* priority in post-war Germany implied a reluctance to engage politically; and the generally noticeable lack of either transparency or responsiveness on the part of the bizonal and later trizonal political institutions permitted only very limited public debate. On this basis, findings showing public disapproval of economic liberalisation and the subsequent implementation of the Social Market Economy in post-war West Germany are certainly questionable in that public opinion varied according to both time and region. Decisive for the legitimacy of the emerging political institutions and the introduction of the Social Market Economy as a democratic economic system for the Federal Republic of Germany, however, were not the degree of public acceptance and whether most laws were approved *by* the people but rather that the first post-war government and parliament evidently acted *for* the people; and, furthermore, they committed themselves to political communication and policy responsiveness *per se*. In their effort to encourage the general public to partake in the policy discourse as politically mature actors rather than objects, and by their ambitious media policy geared to create a public sphere, the campaigners for the Social Market Economy were the main ancestors of the evolving democracy in post-war Germany. For it is that democracy is government for the people, but equally it is the role of the governed to enter directly and/or indirectly into a political and constitutional dialogue in order to determine the possible consistency between a preferred policy option and a preferred constitutional structure. In addition, the academic, political and public debate about the socio-political and economic model for a democratic, liberal and social post-war Germany, and the mutually accepted reciprocity between political conduct and public opinion not only led to the formation, implementation, and validation of the Social Market Economy in Germany, but also to international respect and emancipation for the legal successor of the Third Reich, which thereupon began its return to the table of power politics. Thus the period of Allied occupation, from 1945 right up to the birth of the Federal Republic of Germany in 1949, cannot be characterised as a mere interlude between collapse and restart; but, rather, it must instead be seen as a definitive phase of German economic, constitutional and democratic reconstruction.

What is past is prologue;
the fate of our civilisation will ultimately depend on
how we solve the economic problems we shall then face.

APPENDICES

APPENDIX 1: List of Licensed Political Parties at Zonal Level (1945–1949)

Soviet occupation zone
(Brandenburg, Mecklenburg, Saxony, Saxony-Anhalt, Thuringia)
CDU, KPD, LDPD, SPD

American occupation zone
(Bavaria, Bremen, Hesse, Wuerttemberg-Baden)
AP, BP, BDV, BHE, CSU, DB, DDB, DPD, DVP, EVD, FDP, GB, KPD, LDP, NDP, SPD, WAV, Z

British occupation zone
(Hamburg, Lower Saxony, North Rhine-Westphalia, Schleswig-Holstein)
BHE, CDU, CDP (later CDU), DKP/DRP (former DAP and DKP), DP, DZP, FDP, GB, KPD, NLP (later DP), PFD (later FDP), RPD, RSF, SHB, SPD, SPF, SSV (later SSW), VBH, Z

French occupation zone
(Baden, Rhineland-Palatinate, Saarland, Wuerttemberg-Hohenzollern)
BCSV, CDU, CVP, Demokratische Partei Rheinland-Pfalz, DPS, FDP, KP, KPD, Liberale Partei, Sozialer Volksbund, SPS

Greater Berlin was divided into four sectors by the Allies under the London Protocol of 1944: one each for the United States, consisting of the boroughs of Neukölln, Kreuzberg, Tempelhof, Schöneberg, Steglitz and Zehlendorf; the United Kingdom, consisting of the boroughs of Tiergarten, Charlottenburg, Wilmersdorf and Spandau; France, consisting of the boroughs of Wedding and Reinickendorf; the Soviet Union, consisting of the boroughs of Mitte, Prenzlauer Berg, Pankow, Weissensee, Friedrichshain, Lichtenberg, Treptow and Köpenick.

Source: Own compilations based on available sources published by the various *Länder* governments or political foundations. This list is not exhaustive due to limited sources.

APPENDIX 2: Administration of American Zone of Occupation (1946)

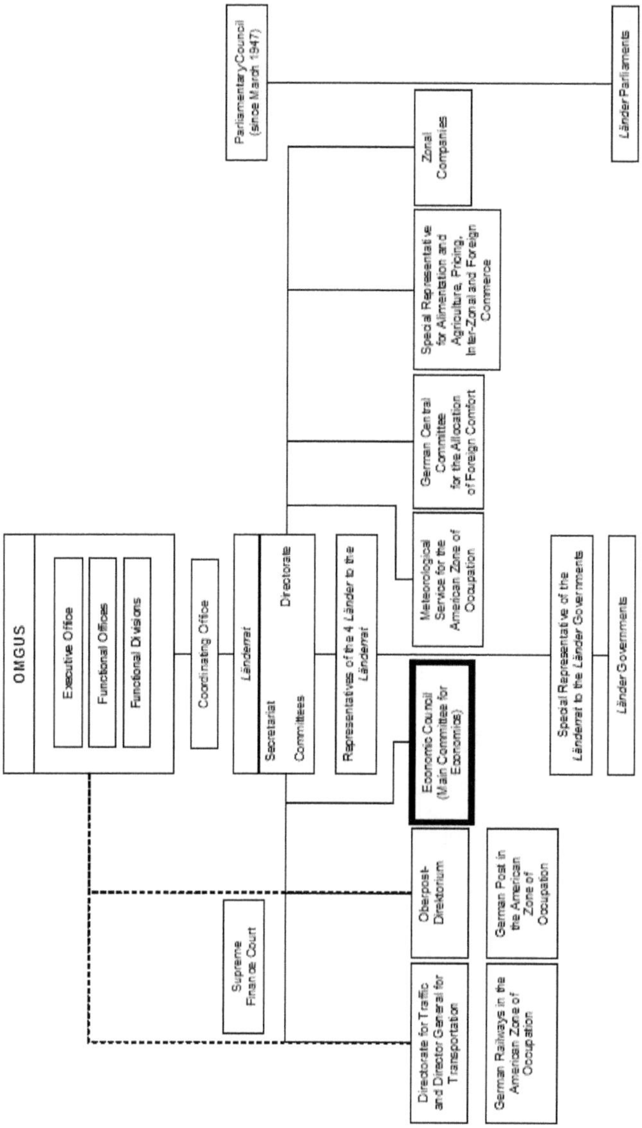

Source: Ambrosius, G., l.c., p. 51.

APPENDIX 3: Administration of British Zone of Occupation (1946)

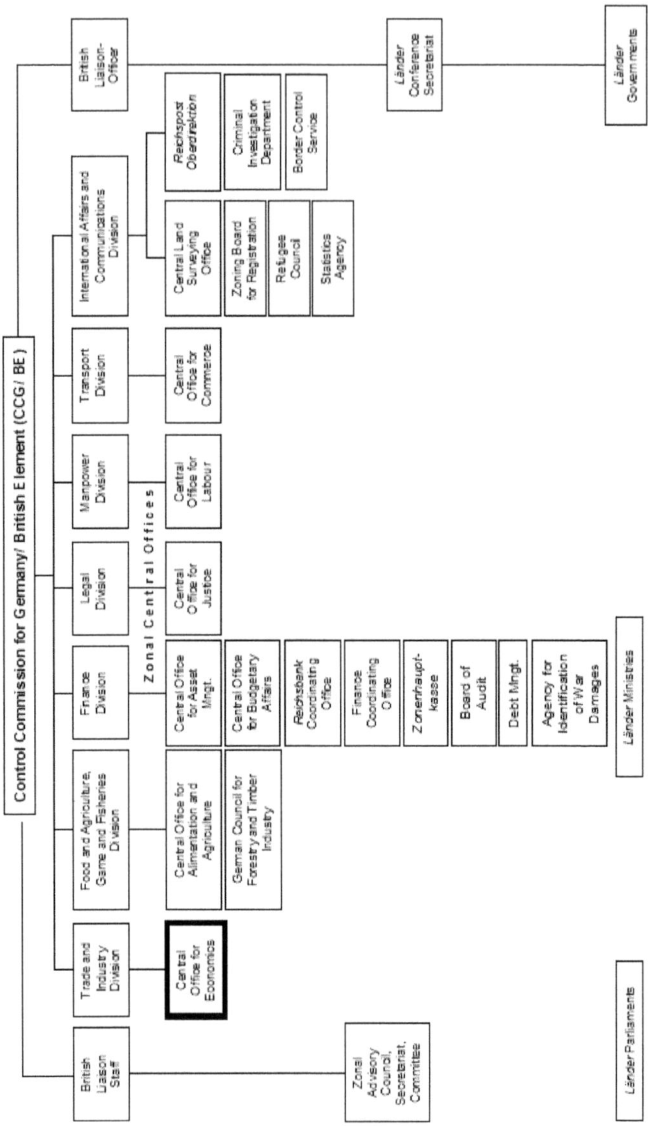

Source: Ambrosius, G., l.c., p. 49.

APPENDIX 4: Geographical Illustration of Anglo-American Bizone (1949)

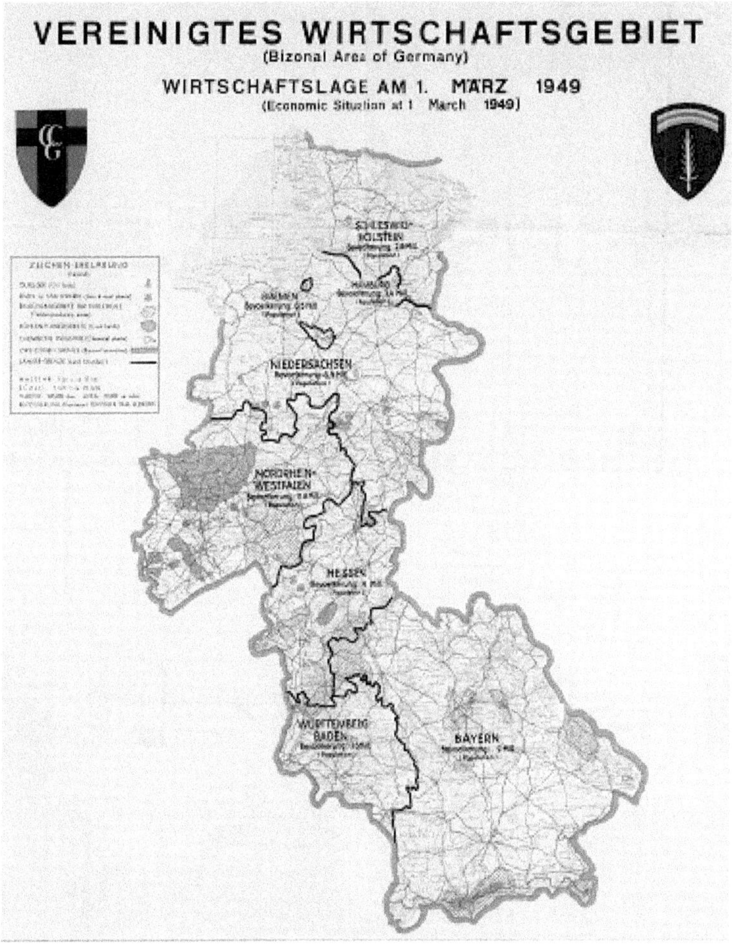

Source: Map of the Anglo-American Bizone documenting the economic situation on 1 March 1949. Original print 30 x 21 cm, EB-Nr.: 1997/06/0260, in: *Haus der Geschichte*, Bonn/Germany.

APPENDIX 5: Administration of Bizonal Economic Area (1949)

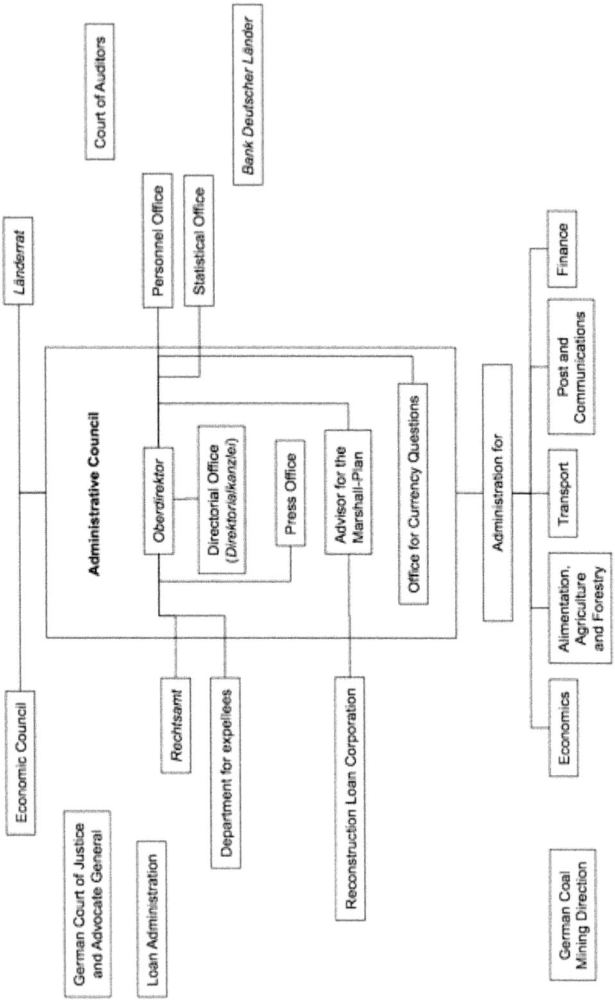

Source: Own compilation based on Vogel, W., l.c., vol. I, Koblenz, 1956.

APPENDIX 6: Composition of First Economic Council (1947–8)

	CDU CSU	SPD	FDP LDP DVP	Z	WAV	DP	KPD	
North Rhine-Westphalia	16	6	5	1	2	-	-	2
Bavaria	12	6	3	1	-	1	-	1
Lower Saxony	8	2	4	-	-	-	2	-
Hesse	5	2	2	1	-	-	-	-
Wuerttemberg-Baden	5	2	2	1	-	-	-	-
Schleswig-Holstein	3	1	2	-	-	-	-	-
Hamburg	2	1	1	-	-	-	-	-
Bremen	1	-	1	-	-	-	-	-
Total	52	20	20	4	2	1	2	3

Source: Stamm, C., l.c., p. XX.

APPENDIX 7: Composition of Second Economic Council (1948–9)

	CDU CSU	SPD	FDP LDP DVP	Z	WAV	DP	KPD	
North Rhine-Westphalia	32	12	10	2	4	-	-	4
Bavaria	24	12	6	2	-	2	-	2
Lower Saxony	16	4	8	-	-	-	4	-
Hesse	10	4	4	2	-	-	-	-
Wuerttemberg-Baden	10	4	4	2	-	-	-	-
Schleswig-Holstein	6	2	4	-	-	-	-	-
Hamburg	4	2	2	-	-	-	-	-
Bremen	2	-	2	-	-	-	-	-
Total	104	40	40	8	4	2	4	6

Source: Stamm, C., l.c., p. XXIII.

APPENDIX 8: List of Members of Economic Council (1947–9)

CDU/CSU parliamentary group

Prof. Dr. Baur, Georg
Blank, Theodor
Boysen, Georg Wilhelm
Braun, Josef
Brese, Wilhelm
Dr. Bucerius, Gerd
Dr. Burghartz, Arnold (–3 Feb 1949 *Zentrum*)
Dr. Butz, Wolfgang
Dr. Dengler, Fritz
Elsen, Franz-Michael
Eplée, Hermann A.
Flörl, Fritz
Fromm, Kurt-Wilhelm
Gehring, Albrecht
Günther, Bernhard
Dr. Haffner, Alex
Dr. Henle, Günter
Dr. Hermes, Andreas
Hohl, Heinrich
Dr. Holzapfel, Friedrich
Hoogen, Matthias (–6 Apr 1949 *Zentrum*)
Horn, Peter
Jakob, Josef (–3 Mar 1949 *Zentrum*)
Karpf, Hugo
Kaufmann, Theophil H.
Ketels, Max-Detlef
Dr. Köhler, Erich
Lang-Brumann, Thusnelda
Loibl, Alfons
Naegel, Wilhelm
Niggemeyer, Maria
Dr. Otto, Paul
Dr. Pferdmenges, Robert
Rattenhuber, Ernst
Schlack, Peter
Dr. Schmidt, Hanno
Schütz, Hans
Dr. Seeling, Otto
Siara, Walter
Storch, Anton
Strauss, Franz-Josef
Strunk, Heinrich
Struve, Detlev
Dr. Vogel, Rudolf
Weinkamm, Otto
Winkelheide, Bernhard
Wolf, Chr. Heinrich
Dr. Zwicknagl, Max

SPD parliamentary group

Dr. Agartz, Viktor (–8 May 1948)
Altwein, Erich
Dr. Arndt, Adolf
Ballof, Walter (8 June 1948–)
Baur, Valentin
Baurichter, Kurt
Dr. Berger, Georg
Dr. Bleiß, Paul
Dr. Cahn-Carnier, Fritz († 8 June 1949)
Cramer, Johann
Dahrendorf, Gustav
Daum, Robert
Krahnstöver, Anni
Dr. Kreyssig, Gerhard
Kriedemann, Herbert
Leddin, Bruno
Lücker, Willi
Mellies, Wilhelm (30 Apr 1948–)
Meyer, Heinz
Dr. Mommer, Karl
Dr. Potthoff, Erich
Remmele, Adam
Reuter, Georg
Richter, Willi

SPD parliamentary group

Eichler, Willi
Enderle, Irmgard
Dr. Dr. h.c. Heimerich, Hermann
Heinen, Franz
Hemsath, Heinrich
Herberts, Hermann
Heukelum, Gerhard van (–3 June 1948)
Hewusch, Franz
Hölkeskamp, Walter
Kiesel, Wilhelm
Köhler, Anton
Korspeter, Lisa
Rupprecht, Fritz
Schoettle, Erwin
Dr. Schöne, Joachim
Schulze, Karl
Schulze, Oskar
Seuffert, Walter
Strahringer, Wilhelm
Dr. Veit, Hermann
Voss, Otto
Wohlers, Robert
Zinn, Georg August

FDP/ DVP/ LDP parliamentary group

Blücher, Franz
Dr. Bungartz, Everhard
Euler, August M.
Fassbender, Heinrich
Krämer, Alfred
Dr. Oellers, Fritz
Quilling, Karl (–10 July 1949)
Dr. Schwamberger, Emil
Dr. Wellhausen, Hans

Z parliamentary group

Dr. Bunghartz, Arnold (10 Sep 1947–3 Feb 1949)
Hoogen, Matthias (6 Apr 1948–3 Mar 1949)
Jakob, Josef (24 Feb 1948–3 Mar 1949)
Dr. Spiecker, Carl (25 June 1947–10 Sep 1947/ 24 Feb 1948–6 Apr 1948)
Dr. Stricker, Fritz

WAV parliamentary group

Kuehne, Erich
Quilling, Karl (25 June 1947–1 Oct 1948)

DP parliamentary group

Dr. Bode, Wolfgang (25 June 1947–16 Feb 1949)
Dr. Campe, Karl von
Kuhlemann, Christian
Dr. Mühlenfeld, Hans
Dr. Zimmermann, Heinrich

KPD parliamentary group

Becker, Ludwig (25 June–10 Dec 1947)
Ficker, Ludwig (25 June–10 Dec 1947†)
Dr. Kroth, Alfred
Müller, Kurt
Niebes, Heinrich
Reimann, Max
Rische, Friedrich
Sperling, Fritz

Without party affiliation

Quilling, Karl (1 Oct 1948–22 Apr 1949)

Source: *Der Wirtschaftsrat des Vereinigten Wirtschaftsgebietes 1947-1949*, edited by the Office of the Economic Council, n.l., n.d., pp. 61 ff.

APPENDIX 9: Social Structure of Members of Economic Council

Profession	CDU CSU	SPD	FDP LDP DVP	Z	WAV	DP	KPD
Self-employed, fabricants	7	5	4	2	1	-	1
Directors, executives	6	9	2	-	-	3	-
Publishers, editors	2	8	-	-	-	-	1
Unionists	3	5	-	1	1	-	2
Civil servants	6	8	-	-	-	-	-
Former civil servants	3	1	2	1	-	1	-
Workers	-	-	-	-	-	-	2
Craftsmen	2	1	-	-	-	-	-
Employees	4	3	-	-	-	-	-
Agriculturists	6	-	-	-	-	-	-
Without profession	1	-	-	-	-	-	-

Source: *Frankfurter Neue Presse, Von Altwein bis Zwicknagl – Die soziale Struktur des Wirtschaftsrates*, 2 November 1948; WB, l.c., vol. 1, pp. 27–34.

APPENDIX 10: List of Plenary Meetings of Economic Council

1st Economic Council (25 June 1947–23 Feb 1948)

1.	Plenary Meeting	25 June 1947	in: WB VV, l.c., pp.	1 ff.
2.	"	22-24 July 1947	"	1 ff.
3.	"	9 Aug 1947	"	57 ff.
4.	"	4/5 Sep 1947	"	61 ff.
5.	"	29/30 Sep/3 Oct 1947	"	111 ff.
6.	"	11 Oct 1947	"	139 ff.
7.	"	29/30 Oct 1947	"	149 ff.
8.	"	21 Nov 1947	"	197 ff.
9.	"	18 Dec 1947	"	235 ff.
10.	"	21/23 Jan 1948	"	265 ff.

2nd Economic Council (24 Feb 1948–1 Sep 1949)

11.	Plenary Meeting	24 Feb 1948	in: WB VV, l.c., pp.	307 ff.
12.	"	2 Mar 1948	"	319 ff.
13.	"	16/17 Mar 1948	"	355 ff.
14.	"	21/22 Apr 1948	"	419 ff.
15.	"	28 Apr 1948	"	513 ff.
16.	"	25/26 May 1948	"	549 ff.
17.	"	14 June 1948	"	599 ff.
18.	"	17/18 June 1948	"	613 ff.
19.	"	8/9 July 1948	"	683 ff.
20.	"	17/19/20 Aug 1948	"	757 ff.
21.	"	31 Aug 1948	"	847 ff.
22.	"	27/28/30 Sep/1 Oct 1948	"	871 ff.
23.	"	19 Oct 1948	"	1045 ff.
24.	"	9/10 Nov 1948	"	1073 ff.
25.	"	19/20 Nov 1948	"	1131 ff.
26.	"	30 Nov/1 Dec 1948	"	1155 ff.
27.	"	2/3 Dec1948	"	1199 ff.
28.	"	14 Dec 1948	"	1249 ff.
29.	"	17 Dec 1948	"	1277 ff.
30.	"	7 Jan 1949	"	1327 ff.
31.	"	19 Jan 1949	"	1343 ff.
32.	"	15 Feb 1949	"	1384 ff.
33.	"	18 Feb 1949	"	1411 ff.
34.	"	4 Mar 1949	"	1479 ff.
35.	"	24/25 Mar 1949	"	1511 ff.
36.	"	3/4 May 1949	"	1587 ff.
37.	"	23/24/25 May 1949	"	1643 ff.
38.	"	23/24 June 1949	"	1775 ff.
39.	"	19/20 July 1949	"	1873 ff.
40.	"	8 Aug 1949	"	1973 ff.

Source: WB VV, l.c.

APPENDIX 11: Overview of Licensed Newspapers (1945–9)

	No. of licensed newspapers	No. of licensees	Party membership of licensee					
			CDU CSU	SPD	FDP LDP DVP	KPD	misc.	n.p.a.
American Zone of Occupation								
Bavaria	26	48	8	18	1	-	-	21
Berlin	2	5	1	1	-	-	-	3
Bremen	2	4	-	1	-	-	-	3
Hesse	15	23	2	9	1	-	-	11
Wuerttemberg-Baden	15	32	5	8	6	-	-	13
	60	**112**	**16**	**37**	**8**	**-**	**-**	**51**
British Zone of Occupation								
Berlin	6		1	2	2	-	-	1
North Rhine-Westphalia	26		8	7	2	4	2	3
Lower Saxony	10		2	2	-	1	2	3
Schleswig-Holstein	10		1	2	1	1	2	3
Hamburg	6		1	1	1	1	1	1
	58		**13**	**14**	**6**	**7**	**7**	**11**
French Zone of Occupation								
Baden	9		1	1	1	1	-	5
Berlin	1		-	-	-	-	-	1
Rhineland-Palatinate	9		1	1	1	1	-	5
Saarland	4		1	1	1	1	-	-
Wuerttemberg-Hohenzollern	7		1	1	1	1	-	3
	30		**4**	**4**	**4**	**4**	**-**	**14**
Total	**148**		**33**	**55**	**18**	**11**	**7**	**76**

Source: Own compilation based on Fischer, H.-D., l.c., 1971, pp. 52–71. This list representing the status in 1949 is not exhaustive due to limited sources.

APPENDIX 12: List of Individual Licensed Newspapers (1945–9)

Title of Newspaper/ Place of Publication	Zone of Occupation	Editor/ Licence Holder	Political Affiliation	Circulation
Aachener Nachrichten Aachen	BOZ	H. Hollands E. Stadthagen H. Schäfer	SPD	40,000; 3/wk
Aachener Volkszeitung Aachen	BOZ	J. Hofmann A. Maas J. Schmitz	CDU	87,000; 3/wk
Allgemeine Kölnische Rundschau Cologne	BOZ	F. Wester F. Fuchs J. Baumhoff H. Mönning R. Heinen	CDU	158,000; 3/wk
Allgemeine Zeitung Mainz	FOZ	*Mainzer Verlags-GmbH*	Ind.	250,000; 7/wk
Augsburger Tagespost Augsburg	AOZ	J. W. Naumann	CSU	51,200; 3/wk
Badener Tagblatt Baden-Baden	FOZ		Ind.	38,000; 7/wk
Badische Zeitung Freiburg im Breisgau	FOZ	J. Knecht H. Rombach O. Stark	Ind.	220,000; 2/wk
Berliner Montagsecho Berlin	BOZ	C.-H. Schwennicke R. Markewitz H. Reif E. E. Torenburg	LDP	125,000; 5/wk
Braunschweiger Zeitung Braunschweig	BOZ	H. Eckensberger A. Neumann	SPD	100,000; 3/wk
Darmstädter Echo Darmstadt	AOZ	P. Rodemann J. S. Dang H. J. Reinowski	Ind.	75,200, 6/wk

Title of Newspaper/ Place of Publication	Zone of Occupation	Editor/ Licence Holder	Political Affiliation	Circulation
Deutsche Volkszeitung Celle	BOZ	H.-C. Seebohm	DP	85,000; 3/wk
Flensburger Tageblatt Flensburg	BOZ	L. Iversen T. Andresen G. Macknow W. Petersen	Ind.	82,000; 3/wk
Frankfurter Hefte Frankfurt am Main	AOZ	E. Kogon W. Dirks	CDU	75,000; 1/m
Frankfurter Neue Presse Frankfurt am Main	AOZ	H. Stenzel	CDU	164,000; 6/wk
Frankfurter Rundschau Frankfurt am Main	AOZ	A. Rudert K. Gerold H. Etkorn P. Rodemann W. Knote W. K. Gerst E. Carlebach	Ind.	186,650; 7/wk
Freiheit Düsseldorf	BOZ		KPD	
Freie Presse Bielefeld	BOZ	E. Groß P. Eilers J. Triem	SPD	124,000; 3/wk
Hamburger Abendblatt Hamburg	BOZ	A. Springer	Ind.	100,000; 6/wk
Hamburger Allgemeine Zeitung Hamburg	BOZ	F. Beyrich A. Haßler	CDU	138,000; 3/wk
Hamburger Echo Hamburg	BOZ	W. Grabbert J. Richter K. Meitmann	SPD	230,000; 3/wk
Hamburger Freie Presse Hamburg	BOZ	P. Heile H. Sommerhäuser	FDP	100,000; 3/wk

Title of Newspaper/ Place of Publication	Zone of Occupation	Editor/ Licence Holder	Political Affiliation	Circulation
Hamburger Volkszeitung Hamburg	BOZ		KPD	
Hannoversche Neueste Nachrichten Hanover	BOZ	R. Boese A. Fratzscher A. Storch	CDU	128,000; 3/wk
Hannoversche Presse Hanover	BOZ	F. Heine E. Franke R. Hoffmeister	SPD	340,000; 3/wk
Hannoversche Volksstimme Hanover	BOZ		KPD	
Hessische Nachrichten Kassel	AOZ	W. Bartels W. Pöschl G. Römer	Ind.	126,750; 6/wk
Kasseler Zeitung Kassel	AOZ	A. W. Diehl	Ind.	49,950; 6/wk
Kieler Nachrichten Kiel	BOZ	W. Koch	CDU	130,000; 3/wk
Der Kurier Berlin	FOZ	P. Bourdin	Ind.	200,000; 6/wk
Lübecker Freie Presse Lübeck	BOZ		SPD	83,000
Lüneburger Landeszeitung Lüneburg	BOZ	E. Riggert H. Bumann W. Bergmann E. Wiesemann	Ind.	110,000; 3/wk
Mannheimer Morgen Mannheim	AOZ	K. Ackermann L. F. Schilling v. Canstatt	Ind.	86,214; 4/wk
Münchner Merkur Munich	AOZ	H. Heinrich F. Buttersack	CSU	171,800; 3/wk

Title of Newspaper/ Place of Publication	Zone of Occupation	Editor/ Licence Holder	Political Affiliation	Circulation
Neue Ruhr Zeitung Essen	BOZ	D. Oppenberg W. Nieswand A. Frisch F. Feldens	SPD	113,000; 3/wk
Neue Volkszeitung Dortmund	BOZ	H. Renner W. Blumenthal P. Dastig A. Sand	KPD	150,000; 3/wk
Neue Zeit Saarbrücken	FOZ	F. Nikolay F. Bäsel	KPD	30,000; 3/wk
Neue Zeitung Munich	AOZ	US Military Government		630,000; 2/wk
Neuer Vorwärts Hanover	BOZ		SPD	
Neuer Westfälischer Kurier Werl	BOZ	H. Wessel F. Erhart J. Weiser	Z	115,000; 3/wk
Niedersächsische Volksstimme Hanover	BOZ	R. Lehmann E. Jungmann H. Heyne	KPD	66,000; 3/wk
Norddeutsches Echo Kiel	BOZ	A. Oertel A. Heitmann L. Böckmann	KPD	30,000; 3wk
Nordsee Zeitung Bremen, Bremerhaven	AOZ	B. Stöwsand W. Gong	Ind.	85,000; 4/wk
Nordwestdeutsche Rundschau Wilhelmshaven	BOZ	O. Hünlich H. Wunderlich J. Kramer	SPD	100,000; 3/wk
Nouvelles de France/ West Echo Konstanz	FOZ	F Military Government		

Title of Newspaper/ Place of Publication	Zone of Occupation	Editor/ Licence Holder	Political Affiliation	Circulation
Rhein Echo Düsseldorf	BOZ	G. Stoever L. Ingenhut E. Kobusch	SPD	152,000; 3/wk
Rhein Zeitung Koblenz	FOZ	W. Twer O. Richardt M. Weber	Ind.	250,000; 3/wk
Rhein-Neckar-Zeitung Heidelberg	AOZ	R. Agricola H. Knorr T. Heuss	Ind.	
Rheinisch-Pfälzische Rundschau Bad Kreuznach	FOZ	F. R. G. Ringel	FDP	25,000; 3/wk
Rheinische Post Düsseldorf	BOZ	A. Betz K. Arnold	CDU	282,200; 27wk
Rheinische Zeitung Cologne	BOZ	J. Pedrotti R. Görlinger H. Böckler H. Braubach H. Reifferscheidt	SPD	98,000; 3/wk
Rheinischer Merkur Koblenz	FOZ	F. A. Kramer	CDU	162,040; 1/wk
Die Rheinpfalz Neustadt	FOZ	*Rheinpfalz Verlag*	Ind.	220,000; 2/wk
Rhein-Ruhr Zeitung Essen	BOZ	W. Hamacher	Z	130,000; 3/wk
Saarländische Volkszeitung Saarbrücken	FOZ	J. Hoffmann	CVP	100,000; 7/wk
Schleswig-Holsteinische Volkszeitung Kiel	BOZ	K. Ratz	SPD	96,000; 3/wk

Title of Newspaper/ Place of Publication	Zone of Occupation	Editor/ Licence Holder	Political Affiliation	Circulation
Schwabenecho Oberndorf	FOZ	*Schwabenwarte GmbH*	DVP	45,000; 2/wk
Schwäbisches Tagblatt Tübingen	FOZ		Ind.	40,000; 7/wk
Schwäbische Post Aalen	AOZ	J. Binkowski K. Theiss	Ind.	
Schwäbische Zeitung Leutkirch	AOZ	*Schwäbischer Verlag*	CDU	180,000; 7/wk
Schwarzwälder Post Oberndorf	FOZ	H. Biesenberger	CDU	160,000; 3/wk
Stuttgarter Zeitung Stuttgart	AOZ	F. K. Maier E. Schairer J. Eberle H. Bernhard K. Ackermann	Ind.	155,851; 3/wk
Süddeutsche Zeitung Munich	AOZ	A. Schwingenstein E. Goldschagg F. J. Schoeningh W. Friedmann	Ind.	185,200; 3/wk
Südkurier Konstanz	FOZ	*Südkurier Verlag*	Ind.	165,000; 3/wk
Südwestdeutsche Volkszeitung Freiburg im Breisgau	FOZ	*Christl.-Soz. Verlag*	CDU	54,500; 3/wk
Der Tag Berlin	BOZ	J. Kaiser	CDU	100,000; 6/wk
Tagesspiegel Berlin	AOZ	W. Karsch E. Redslob E. Reger	Ind.	240,000; 7/wk
Telegraf Berlin	BOZ	P. Löbe A. Leber A. Scholz	Ind.	400,000; 7/wk

Title of Newspaper/ Place of Publication	Zone of Occupation	Editor/ Licence Holder	Political Affiliation	Circulation
Trierische Volkszeitung Trier	FOZ	N. Koch	Ind.	85,000; 3/wk
Das Volk Freiburg im Breisgau	FOZ	P. Martzloff F. Leibbrandt F. Geiler	SPD	60,000; 2/wk
Volksstimme Cologne	BOZ	I. Heilborn K. Bachmann	KPD	60,500; 3/wk
Die Welt Hamburg	BOZ	R. Küstermeier	SPD (liberal)	896,000; 7/wk
Weser Kurier Bremen	AOZ	H. Hankmach F. v. Eckardt	Ind.	125,000; 4/wk
Westdeutsche Allgemeine Bochum	BOZ	E. Brost	Ind.	250,000; 3/wk
Westdeutsche Rundschau Wuppertal	BOZ	F. Middelhauve C. Wirths E. Richter C. Gehring	FDP	90,500; 3/wk
Westdeutsche Zeitung Düsseldorf	BOZ	W. Elfes	Ind.	250,000; 3/wk
Westdeutsches Tageblatt Dortmund	BOZ	H. Kauffmann	FDP	70,000; 3/wk
Westdeutsches Volksecho Dortmund	BOZ		KPD	
Westfalenpost Soest	BOZ	A. Sträter	CDU	270,000; 3/wk
Westfalen Zeitung Bielefeld	BOZ	A. Hausknecht D. Lausenstein	CDU	129,500; 3/wk
Westfälische Nachrichten Münster	BOZ	G. Hasenkamp F. Bornefeld-Ettmann F. L. Hüffer	CDU	6/wk

Title of Newspaper/ Place of Publication	Zone of Occupation	Editor/ Licence Holder	Political Affiliation	Circulation
Westfälische Rundschau Dortmund	BOZ	F. Henßler P. Sattler H. Sträter	SPD	338,500, 3/wk
Der Württemberger Reutlingen	FOZ	K. Gall	SPD	75,000; 2/wk
Die Zeit Hamburg	BOZ	G. Bucerius L. H. Lorenz R. Tüngel E. Schmidt di Simoni	Ind.	110,000; 1/wk

Source: Koszyk, K., l.c., 1986, pp. 471–91; Gardner J., l.c., pp. 300–10. This list is not exhaustive due to limited sources.

APPENDIX 13: Overview of Party Conventions (1945–50)

SPD

1. Party Convention	9–11 May 1946	Hanover
2. Party Convention	29 June–2 July 1947	Nuremberg
3. Party Convention	12 Sep–14 Sep 1948	Düsseldorf
4. Party Convention	21–5 May 1950	Hamburg

CDU

Party Convention*	14–16 Dec 1945	Bad Godesberg
Party Convention	1 Mar 1946	Neheim-Hüsten
Party Convention	3 Feb 1947	Ahlen
Party Convention	15 July 1949	Düsseldorf
Constitutive Party Convention	20–2 Oct 1950	Goslar

* In view of the fact that the CDU was a 'Union' of various Christian-oriented parties and not a uniform party on a national level until 1950, one can hardly speak of representative party conventions. However, several congresses of national importance took place before the constitutive CDU Party Convention in Goslar in 1950.

CSU

1. Party Convention	17 May 1946	Munich
2. Party Convention	14/15 Dec 1946	Eichstätt
3. Party Convention	30/31 Aug 1947	Eichstätt
4. Party Convention	24/25 Jan 1948	Marktredwitz
5. Party Convention	27–9 May 1949	Straubing

FDP

1. Party Convention	11/12 Dec 1948	Heppenheim
2. Party Convention	12 June 1949	Bremen

Source: Own compilation based on available data published by the various political parties.

APPENDIX 14: Overview of Elections (1946–9)

	1946 Communal/ Local	*Landtag*	1947 *Landtag/* Local	1948 Communal/ Local	*Landtag*	1949* Local
Baden	15 Sep 13 Oct		18 May	14 Nov		
Bavaria	20/27 Jan 28 Apr 26 May 30 June	1 Dec		25 Apr 30 May		
Berlin**		20 Oct			5 Dec (West Berlin)	
Bremen**		13 Oct	12 Oct			
Hamburg**		13 Oct				
Hesse	20/27 Jan 28 Apr 26 May 30 June	1 Dec		25 Apr		
Lower Saxony	15 Sep 13 Oct		20 Apr	28 Nov		
North Rhine-Westphalia	15 Sep 13 Oct		20 Apr	17 Oct		
Rhineland-Palatinate	15 Sep 13 Oct		18 May	14 Nov		
Saarland	15 Sep		5 Oct			27 Mar
Schleswig-Holstein	15 Sep 13 Oct		20 Apr	24 Oct		
Wuerttemberg-Baden	20/27 Jan 28 Apr 26 May 30 June	24 Nov	7 Dec			
Wuerttemberg-Hohenzollern	15 Sep 13 Oct		18 May	14 Nov 5 Dec		

* The federal elections to the first *Bundestag* were scheduled for 14 August 1949.

** In the city states Berlin (Stadtverordnetenversammlung Gross-Berlin), Bremen and Hamburg (Bürgerschaftswahlen), municipal elections correspond to *Landtag* elections in the other states.

1 The first municipal elections in 2,618 communes.

Source: Own compilation based on relevant statistics published by the various *Länder* governments or political foundations.

APPENDIX 15: Election Results (1946–9) [in %]

	Date	Turnout	CDU CSU	SPD	FDP	KPD	misc.
AMERICAN ZONE OF OCCUPATION							
Bavaria (pop. 9,119,154)							
Communal Elections[1]	20./27.1.1946	93.4	42.7	16.5	0.9	2.3	37.6
Rural County Elections[2]	28.4.1946	73.1	68.6	23.6	-	3.9	3.9
Municipal Assembly Elections[3]	26.5.1946	86.3	48.2	38.1	4.5	5.4	3.8
Constituent Assembly Elections	30.6.1946	71.7	58.3	28.9	2.5	5.3	5.0
State Legislature Elections	1.12.1946	75.7	52.3	28.6	5.7	6.1	7.3
Local Elections[4,5]	25.4./30.5.1948	84.8	37.8	23.7	5.1	4.6	28.8
Federal Elections	14.8.1949	81.1	29.2	22.7	8.5	4.1	35.5
Bremen (pop. 581,035)							
City Council Elections[6]	13.10.1946	85.2	18.9	47.6	-	11.5	22.0
City Council Elections	12.10.1947	67.8	22.0	41.7	5.4	8.8	22.1
Federal Elections	14.8.1949	81.9	16.9	34.4	12.9	6.7	29.1
Hesse (pop. 4,392,534)							
Communal Elections[1]	20./27.1.1946	85.1	31.0	44.7	2.2	5.7	16.4
Rural County Elections[2]	28.4.1946	76.1	38.1	43.9	6.2	8.4	3.4
Municipal Assembly Elections[3]	26.5.1946	76.1	34.5	41.1	9.8	11.6	3.0
Constituent Assembly Elections	30.6.1946	71.7	37.2	44.3	8.1	9.8	0.6
State Legislature Elections	1.12.1946	73.2	30.9	42.7	15.7	10.7	-
Local Elections[4]	25.4.1948	81.3	29.1	35.7	21.9	7.9	5.4
Federal Elections	14.8.1949	77.3	21.3	32.1	28.1	6.7	11.8
Wuerttemberg-Baden (pop. 3,982,212)							
Communal Elections[1,7]	20./27.1.1946	86.1	25.6	20.0	9.4	4.2	40.8
Rural County Elections[2]	28.4.1946	61.6	54.3	22.6	8.7	3.0	11.4
Municipal Assembly Elections[3]	26.5.1946	79.9	26.2	34.1	21.3	12.3	6.1
Constituent Assembly Elections	30.6.1946	68.2	40.9	32.3	16.8	10.0	-
State Legislature Elections	24.11.1946	71.7	38.4	31.9	19.5	10.2	-
Communal Elections[4,7]	7.12.1947	72,7	24.4	31.3	17.0	9.1	18.2
Federal Elections	14.8.1949	72.5	31.0	25.2	18.3	7.4	18.1

	Date	Turnout	CDU CSU	SPD	FDP	KPD	misc.
BRITISH ZONE OF OCCUPATION							
Hamburg (pop. 1,658,038)							
City Council Elections	13.10.1946	79.0	26.7	43.1	18.2	10.4	1.6
Federal Elections	14.8.1949	81.2	19.7	39.6	15.8	8.5	16.4
Lower Saxony (pop. 6,710,974)							
Communal Elections[8]	15.9.1946	77.0	15.0	37.1	4.4	4.0	39.5
Rural & Municipal County Elections[8]	13.10.1946	68.5	22.5	41.9	8.2	5.1	22.3
State Legislature Elections	20.4.1947	65.1	19.9	43.3	8.8	5.7	22.3
Rural County Elections	28.11.1948	71.9	24.3	39.6	9.4	3.0	23.7
Municipal County & Communal Elections[9]	28.11.1948	75.6	22.7	36.3	8.4	1.7	30.9
Federal Elections	14.8.1949	77.7	17.6	33.4	7.5	3.1	38.4
North Rhine-Westphalia (pop. 13,598,633)							
Communal Elections[8]	15.9.1946	73.3	49.9	29.9	2.1	6.6	11.5
Rural & Municipal County Elections[8]	13.10.1946	74.4	46.0	33.4	4.3	9.4	6.9
State Legislature Elections	20.4.1947	67.3	37.6	32.0	5.9	14.0	10.5
Municipal County & Communal Elections	17.10.1948	69.3	37.6	35.9	6.9	7.8	11.8
Federal Elections	14.8.1949	79.6	36.9	31.4	8.6	7.6	15.5
Schleswig-Holstein (pop. 2,486,779)							
Communal Elections[8]	15.9.1946	77.2	31.8	35.2	7.1	4.4	21.5
Rural & Municipal County Elections[8]	13.10.1946	70.6	37.3	41.0	6.1	5.1	10.5
State Legislature Elections	20.4.1947	69.8	34.5	44.5	5.1	4.8	11.1
Municipal County & Communal Elections	24.10.1948	78.1	37.8	39.7	5.8	3.3	13.4
Federal Elections	14.8.1949	82.7	30.7	29.6	7.4	3.1	29.2

	Date	Turnout	CDU CSU	SPD	FDP	KPD	misc.
FRENCH ZONE OF OCCUPATION							
Baden (pop. 1,391,394)							
Municipal County & Communal Elections[10]	15.9.1946	88.8	53.2	14.0	8.3	6.0	18.5
Rural County Elections	13.10.1946	67.5	60.4	17.3	14.4	7.6	0.3
State Legislature Elections	18.5.1947	67.7	55.9	22.3	14.2	7.6	-
Municipal County & Communal Elections	14.11.1948	66.4	43.1	21.0	13.6	4.8	17.5
Rural County Elections	14.11.1948	65.0	49.3	25.6	19.1	6.0	-
Federal Elections	14.8.1949	69.9	51.1	23.7	17.4	4.2	3.6
Rhineland-Palatinate (pop. 3,111,012)							
Municipal County & Communal Elections[10]	15.9.1946	88.3	45.1	24.7	-	6.7	23.5
Rural County Elections	13.10.1946	78.9	54.7	30.2	5.9	7.6	1.6
State Legislature Elections	18.5.1947	77.9	47.2	34.3	5.7	8.7	4.1
Municipal County & Communal Elections	14.11.1948	73.7	44.6	34.1	10.5	7.2	3.6
Rural County Elections	14.11.1948	77.9	37.7	40.2	9.9	9.9	2.3
Federal Elections	14.8.1949	79.6	49.0	28.6	15.8	6.6	-
Wuerttemberg-Hohenzollern (pop. 1,273,738)							
Municipal County & Communal Elections[10]	15.9.1946	86.6	38.2	13.6	5.6	5.0	37.6
Rural County Elections	13.10.1946	69.7	62.8	19.9	10.4	6.9	-
State Legislature Elections	18.5.1947	66.4	54.3	20.8	17.7	7.2	-
Municipal County & Communal Elections	14.11.1948	67.0	20.0	10.5	6.1	3.4	60.0
Rural County Elections	5.12.1948	73.9	41.0	15.2	8.6	4.0	31.2
Federal Elections	14.8.1949	64.5	59.1	18.9	15.3	5.2	1.5
Saarland (pop. 944,700)							
Municipal Elections	15.9.1946	93.8	52.4[8]	25.5[9]	-	9.1	13.0
State Legislature Elections	5.10.1947	95.7	51.2	32.8	7.6	8.4	-
Municipal Elections	27.3.1949	88.6	49.7	31.2	6.6[10]	8.6	3.9
Federal Elections[11]	14.8.1949						

	Date	Turnout	CDU CSU	SPD	FDP	KPD	misc.
BERLIN (pop. 2,172,000)							
City Assembly Elections	20.10.1946	88.5	24.3	51.7	10.3	13.7	-
City Assembly Elections	5.12.1948	86.6	19.4	64.5	16.1	-	-
Federal Elections[12]	14.8.1949						
FEDERAL REPUBLIC OF GERMANY (pop. 48,305,783)							
Local Elections (acc.)		76.6 [ø]	40.4	30.1	8.1	6.3	15.1
State Legislature Elections (acc.)		72.5 [ø]	35.5	36.8	9.5	9.6	8.6
Federal Elections (acc.)	14.8.1949	78.5	31.0	29.2	11.9	5.7	22.2

1 Held in communities (*Gemeinden*) of less than 20,000 inhabitants.
2 Held in rural counties (*Landkreise*).
3 Held in municipal counties (*Stadtkreise*) and in communities (*Gemeinden*) of more than 20,000 inhabitants.
4 Held throughout the state in communities, rural and municipal counties.
5 Each voter could cast a number of ballots equal to the number of members in the county or community council – in communities with up to 3,000 inhabitants that have fewer council members, they had twice as many votes. Each voter could accept a list of candidates without change or they could split their ballots among the different lists of candidates or they could give up to three ballots to any one candidate.
6 In 1946 Bremen was still in the British area of control. Each voter had 3, and in exceptional cases up to 5 ballots.
7 In the Baden area of Wuerttemberg-Baden, each voter had one ballot only. In the Wuerttemberg area each voter could cast a number of ballots equal to the number of members in the village or town council (4–24); they could split their ballots among the various party tickets, and they could give more than one (up to a maximum of three) ballots to a particular candidate.
8 In 1946 each voter had 3, in exceptional cases up to 6 ballots.
9 Generally each voter had 3 ballots in 1948.
10 Held in municipal counties (*Stadtkreise*) and in the smaller communities (*Gemeinden*) without municipal status.
11 The Saarland did not participate in the federal elections.
12 Although West Berliners became citizens of the Federal Republic of Germany, they were not eligible to vote in the federal elections. Instead, they were indirectly represented in the *Bundestag* by 20 non-voting delegates chosen by the West Berlin House of Representatives. Similarly, the West Berlin Senate sent non-voting delegates to the *Bundesrat*.

Source: Own calculations based on statistics provided by the respective *Statistische Landesämter*. This list is not exhaustive due to limited sources.

APPENDIX 16: Evolution of Major Party Vote (1946–9)

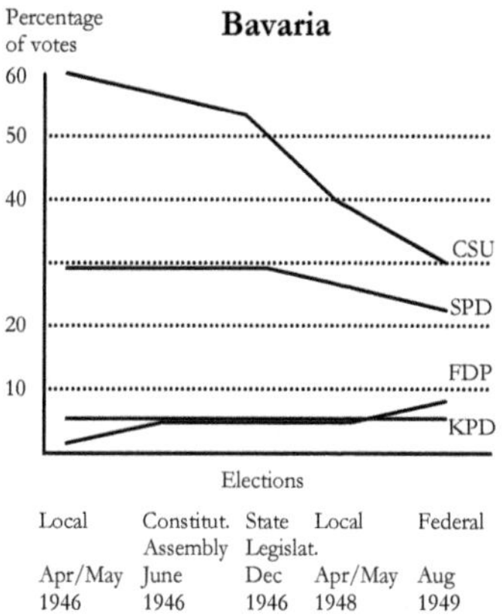

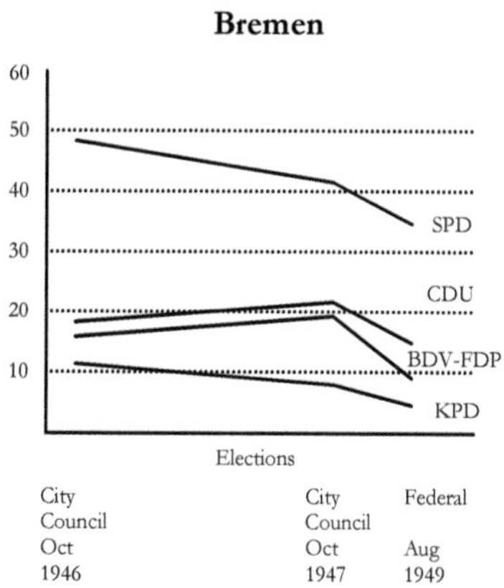

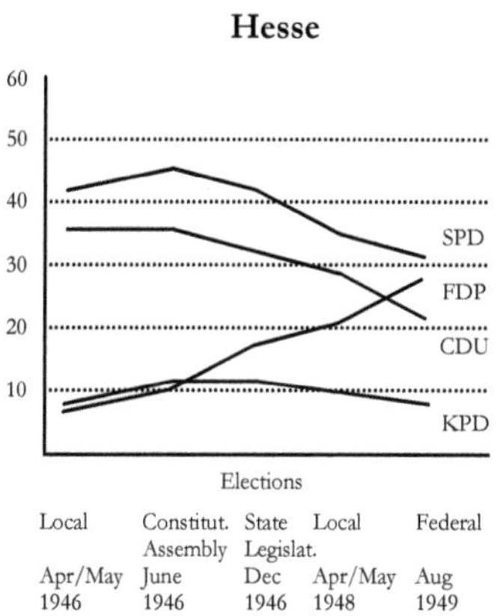

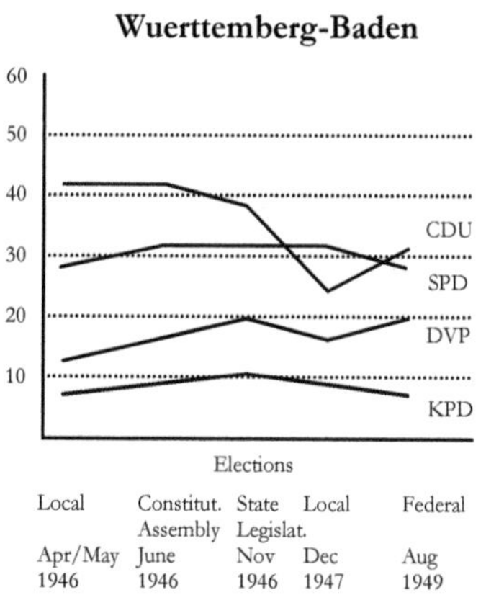

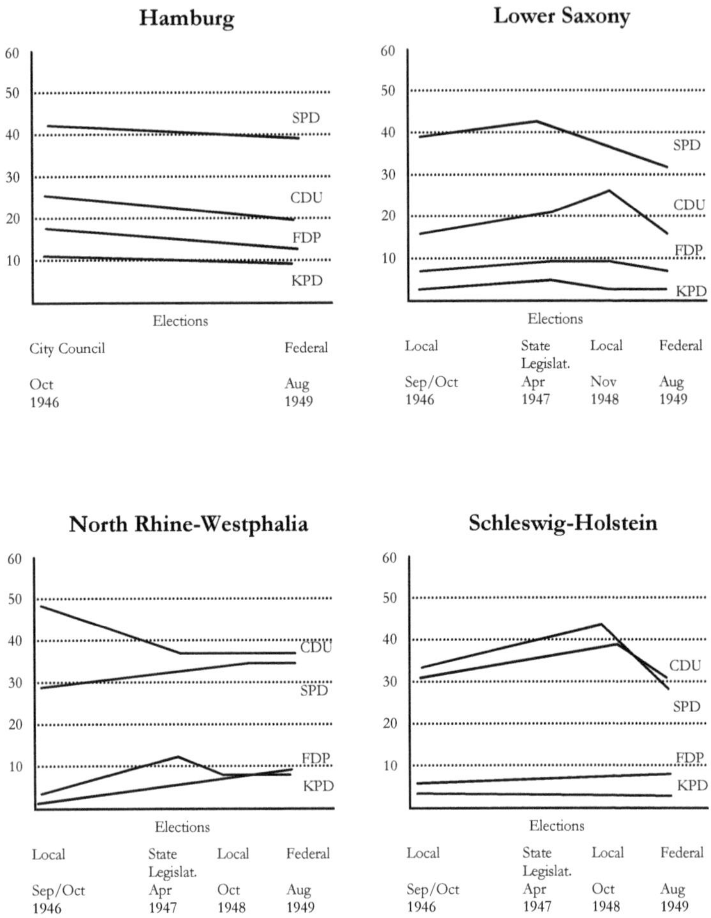
Hamburg
60
50
40
30
20
10
SPD
CDU
FDP
KPD
Elections
City Council
Federal
Oct 1946
Aug 1949
Lower Saxony
60
50
40
30
20
10
SPD
CDU
FDP
KPD
Elections
Local
State Legislat.
Local
Federal
Sep/Oct 1946
Apr 1947
Nov 1948
Aug 1949
North Rhine-Westphalia
60
50
40
30
20
10
CDU
SPD
FDP
KPD
Elections
Local
State Legislat.
Local
Federal
Sep/Oct 1946
Apr 1947
Oct 1948
Aug 1949
Schleswig-Holstein
60
50
40
30
20
10
CDU
SPD
FDP
KPD
Elections
Local
State Legislat.
Local
Federal
Sep/Oct 1946
Apr 1947
Oct 1948
Aug 1949

Baden

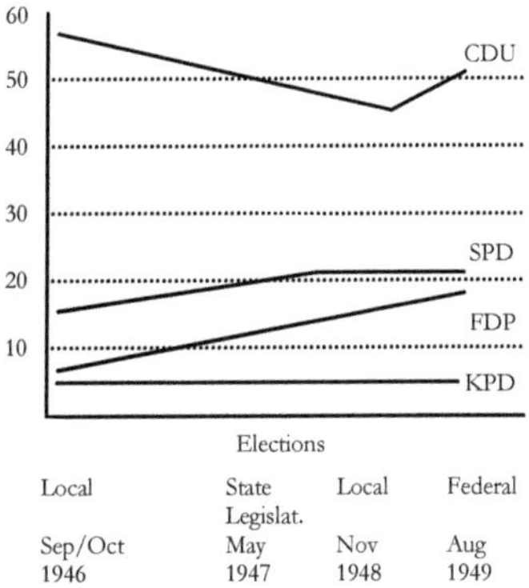

Rhineland-Palatinate

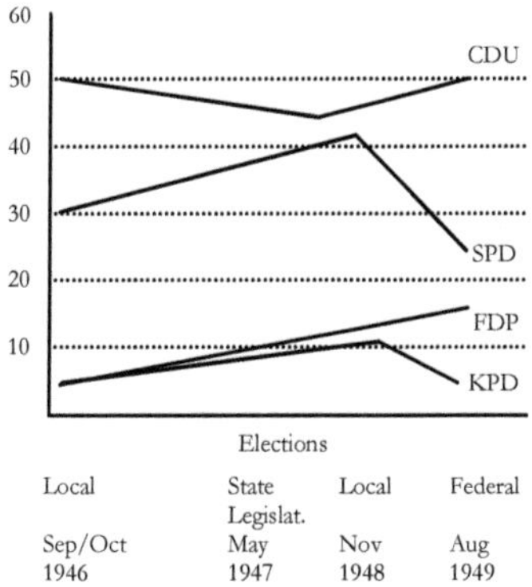

Wuerttemberg-Hohenzollern

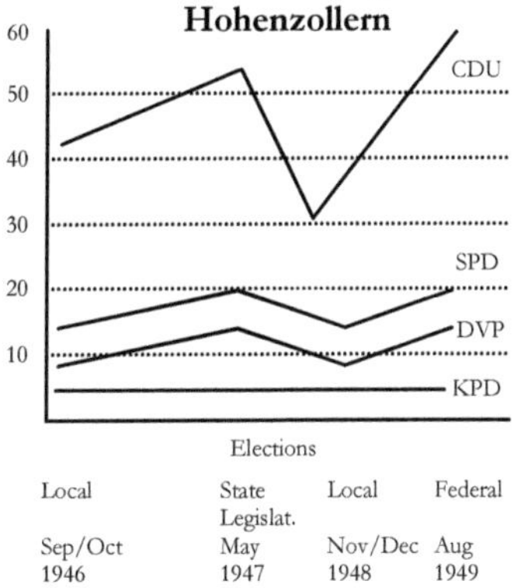

Saarland

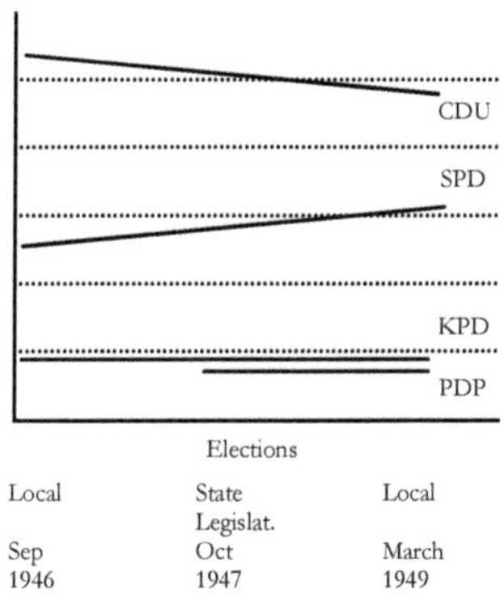

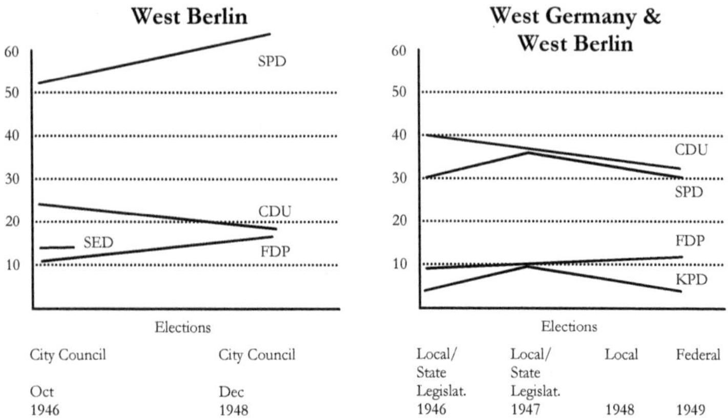

Source: Own calculations based on statistics provided by the respective *Statistische Landesämter*.

NOTES

Introduction

1 Abelshauser, W., *Wirtschaftsgeschichte der Bundesrepublik Deutschland (1945-1980)*, Frankfurt am Main, 1983, p. 8. Annotation: All translations from German are, if not otherwise specified, my own.

2 Article 3 para. 3 Draft Treaty establishing a Constitution for Europe, Brussels, 2003.

3 Krieger, W., *Germany*, in: Reynolds, D. (ed.), *The Origins of the Cold War in Europe. International Perspectives*, New Haven/London, 1994, p. 166.

4 Schwarz, H.-P., *Vom Reich zur Bundesrepublik. Deutschland im Widerstreit der aussenpolitischen Konzeptionen in den Jahren der Besatzungsherrschaft 1945-1949*, Stuttgart, 1966; Eschenburg, T., *Jahre der Besatzung 1945-1949*, Stuttgart/Wiesbaden, 1983; Graml, H., *Die Alliierten und die Teilung Deutschlands. Konflikte und Entscheidungen 1941-1948*, Frankfurt am Main, 1985; Benz, W., *Deutschland unter alliierter Besatzung 1945-1949/1955*, Berlin, 1999.

5 Krautkrämer, E., *Deutsche Geschichte nach dem Zweiten Weltkrieg. Eine Darstellung der Entwicklung von 1945 bis 1949 mit Dokumenten*, Hildesheim, 1962; Deuerlein, E., *Deutschland nach dem Zweiten Weltkrieg 1945-1955*, Konstanz, 1964; Gimbel, J., *Amerikanische Besatzungspolitik in Deutschland 1945-1949*, Frankfurt am Main, 1968; Morsey, R., *Die Bundesrepublik Deutschland: Entstehung und Entwicklung bis 1969*, Munich, 1995.

6 *Akten zur Vorgeschichte der Bundesrepublik Deutschland* edited by Walter Vogel, Christoph Weisz, Wolfram Werner, Bernd Steger, Hans-Dieter Kreikamp, and Günter Plum, Munich etc., 1976/1979/1981/1982/1983 (in the following AV_{BRD}); Becker, J.; Stammen, T.; Waldmann, P. (eds.), *Vorgeschichte der Bundesrepublik Deutschland – Zwischen Kapitulation und Grundgesetz*, Munich, 1979; Bracher, K. D.; Eschenburg, T.; Fest, J.; Jäckel, E., *Geschichte der Bundesrepublik Deutschland*, 5 vols., Stuttgart, Wiesbaden, Mannheim, 1981–7; Dönhoff, M., *Von gestern nach übermorgen – Zur Geschichte der Bundesrepublik Deutschland*, Hamburg, 1981.

7 Schwarz, H.-P., l.c., preface.

8 Eschenburg, T., *Regierung, Bürokratie und Parteien 1945-1949 – Ihre Bedeutung für die politische Entwicklung der Bundesrepublik*, in: *Vierteljahreshefte für Zeitgeschichte* (VfZ) 24/1, Munich, 1976, pp. 58–74; Winkler, H. A. (ed.), *Politische Weichenstellungen im Nachkriegsdeutschland 1945-1953*, Göttingen, 1979; Görtemaker, M., *Geschichte der Bundesrepublik Deutschland: Von der Gründung bis zur Gegenwart*, Munich, 1999; Benz, W., *Die Gründung der Bundesrepublik Deutschland – Von der Bizone zum souveränen Staat*, Munich, 1999a; Edinger, L. J., *West German Politics*, New York, 2006.

9 Judt, T., *Postwar: A History of Europe since 1945*, London, 2007, p. 355. In this connection, see also Tooze, A., *The Wages of Destruction – The Making and Breaking of the Nazi Economy*, London, 2006.

10 Abelshauser, W., *Wirtschaft in Westdeutschland, 1945-1948: Rekonstruktion und Wachstumsbedingungen in der amerikanischen und britischen Zone*, Stuttgart, 1975; Idem, l.c.; Buchheim, C., *Die Wiedereingliederung Westdeutschlands in die Weltwirtschaft, 1945-1958*, Munich, 1990.

11 Nicholls, A. J., *Freedom with Responsibility – The Social Market Economy in Germany, 1918-1963*, Oxford, 1994; Van Hook, J. C., *Rebuilding Germany: The Creation of the Social Market Economy, 1945-1957*, Cambridge, 2004.

12 Blum, R., *Soziale Marktwirtschaft. Wirtschaftspolitik zwischen Neoliberalismus und Ordoliberalismus*, Tübingen, 1969; Ambrosius, G., *Die Durchsetzung der sozialen Marktwirtschaft in Westdeutschland 1945-1949*, Stuttgart, 1977; Heusgen, C., *Ludwig Erhards Lehre von der Sozialen Marktwirtschaft: Ursprünge, Kerngehalt, Wandlungen*, Bern, 1981; Müller, G., *Die Grundlegung der westdeutschen Wirtschaftsordnung im Frankfurter Wirtschaftsrat*, Frankfurt am Main, 1982; Berghahn, V. R., *Ideas into Politics: The Case of Ludwig Erhard*, in: Bullen, R. J.; Pogge von Strandmann, H. J. O.; Polonsky, A. B. (eds.), *Ideas into Politics*, London, 1984; Wünsche, H. F., *Ludwig Erhards Gesellschafts- und Wirtschaftskonzeption, Soziale Marktwirtschaft als politische Ökonomie*, Bonn/Stuttgart, 1986; Biedenkopf, K. H., *Ludwig Erhards Ringen um eine politische Gesamtordnung*, in: Hohmann, K.; Schönwitz, D.; Weber, H. J.; Wünsche, H. F. (eds.), *Grundtexte zur Sozialen Marktwirtschaft*, vol. 2, *Das Soziale in der Sozialen Marktwirtschaft*, Stuttgart/New York, 1988, pp. 453–70; Schlecht, O., *Die Soziale Marktwirtschaft ist der Dritte Weg, Ein Model macht Karriere*, in: Fack, F. U.; Fromme, F. K.; Nonnenmacher, G. (ed.), *Das deutsche Modell, Freiheitlicher Rechtsstaat und Soziale Marktwirtschaft*, Munich, 1991.

13 Blumenberg-Lampe, C., *Das Wirtschaftspolitische Programm der "Freiburger Kreise"*, Berlin, 1973; Idem, *Der Weg in die Soziale Marktwirtschaft: Referate, Protokolle, Gutachten der Arbeitsgemeinschaft Erwin von Beckerath 1943-1947*, Stuttgart, 1986; Idem, *Oppositionelle Nachkriegsplanung: Wirtschaftswissenschaftler gegen den Nationalsozialismus*, in: Eckhard, J.; Martin, B.; Mück, M.; Ott, H. (eds.), *Die Freiburger Universität in der Zeit des Nationalsozialismus*, Freiburg/Würzburg, 1991, pp. 207–19; Kluge, U., *Der "Freiburger Kreis" 1938-1945 – Personen, Strukturen und Ziele kirchlich-akademischen Widerstandsverhaltens gegen den Nationalsozialismus*, in: *Freiburger Universitätsblätter* 27/102, Freiburg im Breisgau, 1988, pp. 19–40; Rüther, D., *Der Widerstand des 20. Juli auf dem Weg*

in die Soziale Marktwirtschaft. Die wirtschaftspolitischen Vorstellungen der bürgerlichen Opposition gegen Hitler, Paderborn, 2002; Grossekettler, H., *Adolf Lampe, die Transformationsprobleme zwischen Friedens- und Kriegswirtschaften und die Arbeitsgemeinschaft Erwin von Beckerath*, in: Goldschmidt, N. (ed.), *Wirtschaft, Politik und Freiheit*, Freiburg im Breisgau, 2005, pp. 91–119; Klump, R., *Der Beitrag der Freiburger Kreise zum Konzept der sozialen Marktwirtschaft*, in: Goldschmidt, N. (ed.), l.c., 2005, pp. 383–401; Peukert, H., *Die wirtschafts- und sozialpolitischen Zielsetzungen des Freiburger Kreises*, in: Goldschmidt, N. (ed.), l.c., 2005, pp. 267–88.

14 Götz, H. H., *Die geistigen Väter der sozialen Marktwirtschaft*, in: Eick, J. (ed.), *So nutzt man den Wirtschaftsteil einer Tageszeitung*, Frankfurt, 1971, pp. 57–61; Grossekettler, H., *On Designing an Economic Order. The Contributions of the Freiburg School*, in: Walker, D. A. (ed.), *Perspectives on the History of Economic Thought*, vol. II, Aldershot, 1989, pp. 38–84; Oberender, P., *Der Einfluß ordnungstheoretischer Prinzipien Walter Euckens auf die deutsche Wirtschaftspolitik nach dem Zweiten Weltkrieg: Eine ordnungspolitische Analyse*, in: *ORDO, Jahrbuch für die Ordnung von Wirtschaft und Gesellschaft* (in the following *ORDO*) 40, Stuttgart, 1989; Hollerbach, A., *Juristische Lehre und Forschung in Freiburg in der Zeit des Nationalsozialismus*, in: Eckhard, J. *et al.* (eds.), *Die Freiburger Universität in der Zeit des Nationalsozialismus*, Freiburg im Breisgau, 1991, pp. 91–113; Streit, M. E., *Economic Order, Private Law and Public Policy. The Freiburg School of Law and Economics in Perspective*, in: *Journal of Institutional and Theoretical Economics* 148, Bad Feilnbach, 1992, pp. 675–704; Idem, *Freiburger Beiträge zur Ordnungsökonomik*, Tübingen, 1995; Rieter, H.; Schmolz, M., *The Ideas of German Ordoliberalism 1938-1945: Pointing the Way to a New Economic Order*, in: *The European Journal of the History of Economic Thought* 1, London, 1993, pp. 87–114; Albrecht, C.; Behrmann, G. C.; Bock, M.; Homann, H.; Tenbruck, F. H., *Die intellektuelle Gründung der Bundesrepublik. Eine Wirkungsgeschichte der Frankfurter Schule*, Frankfurt am Main/New York, 1999.

15 Watrin, C., *Principles of the Social Market Economy – its Origins and Early History*, in: *Zeitschrift für die gesamte Staatswissenschaft* 135, Tübingen, 1979; Zweig, K., *The Origins of the Social Market Economy – The leading ideas and their intellectual roots*, London, 1980; Starbatty, J., *Alfred Müller-Armacks Beitrag zur Theorie und Politik der Sozialen Marktwirtschaft*, in: *Soziale Marktwirtschaft im vierten Jahrzehnt ihrer Bewährung*, edited by the *Ludwig-Erhard-Stiftung* (LES), Stuttgart/New York, 1982; Schlecht, O., *Die Genesis des Konzepts der Sozialen Marktwirtschaft*, in: Hohmann, K.; Schönwitz, D.; Weber, H. J.; Wünsche, H. F. (eds.), l.c., 1988, pp. 131–45; Deter, G., *Ursprung und Entwicklung der Sozialen Marktwirtschaft*, in: Rüther, G. (ed.), *Soziale Marktwirtschaft. Entstehung, Grundlagen, Instrumente*, Bonn, 1994; Wünsche, H. F., *Erhards Soziale Marktwirtschaft. Von Eucken programmiert, von Müller-Armack inspiriert?*, in: *Soziale Marktwirtschaft als historische Weichenstellung – Bewertungen und Ausblicke. Eine Festschrift zum 100. Geburtstag von Ludwig Erhard*, edited by the LES, Bonn, 1998, pp. 131–69.

16 Schmidt, M. E., *Die Ordnungsfrage in der Wirtschaftspolitik der deutschen Sozialdemokratie nach den Programmen der SPD*, doctoral thesis, Freiburg, 1956;

Kaden, A., *Einheit oder Freiheit. Die Wiedergründung der SPD 1945/46*, Hanover, 1964; Pirker, T., *Die SPD nach Hitler. Die Geschichte der Sozialdemokratischen Partei Deutschlands 1945-1964*, Munich, 1964; Ehni, H. P., *Sozialistische Neubauforderung und Proklamation des "Dritten Weges". Richtungen sozialdemokratischer Wirtschaftspolitik 1945-1947*, in: *Archiv für Sozialgeschichte* 13, Bonn, 1973; Abelshauser, W., *Freiheitlicher Sozialismus oder Soziale Marktwirtschaft? Die Gutachtertagung über Grundfragen der Wirtschaftsplanung und Wirtschaftslenkung am 21. und 22. Juni 1946*, in: VfZ 24 (4), Munich, 1976; Huster, E.-U., *Die Politik der SPD 1945-1950*, Frankfurt am Main/New York, 1978; Miller, S.; Potthoff, H., *Kleine Geschichte der SPD. Darstellung und Dokumente 1848-1990*, Bonn, 1991; Dowe, D. (ed.), *Kurt Schumacher und der „Neubau" der deutschen Sozialdemokratie nach 1945, Referate und Podiumsdiskussion eines Kolloquiums des Gesprächskreises Geschichte der Friedrich-Ebert-Stiftung in Bonn am 12./13. Oktober 1995, Heft 13*, Bonn, 1996.

17 Flechtheim, O. K. (ed.), *Dokumente zur parteipolitischen Entwicklung in Deutschland seit 1945*, vols. I–IX, Berlin, 1962–71; Schwering, L., *Frühgeschichte der Christlich-Demokratischen Union*, Recklinghausen, 1963; Langner, A., *Wirtschaftliche Ordnungsvorstellungen im deutschen Katholizismus 1945-1963*, in: Idem (ed.), *Katholizismus, Wirtschaftsordnung und Sozialpolitik 1945-1963*, Paderborn/ Munich/Vienna/Zurich, 1980, pp. 27 ff.; Uertz, R., *Christentum und Sozialismus in der frühen CDU. Grundlagen und Wirkungen der christlich-sozialen Ideen in der Union 1945-49*, Stuttgart, 1981; Wenzel, R., *Konrad Adenauer und die Gestaltung der Wirtschafts- und Sozialordnung in Westdeutschland 1945-1951/52*, doctoral thesis, Augsburg, 1981; Heitzer, H., *Die CDU in der britischen Zone: Gründung, Organisation, Programm und Politik 1945-1949*, Düsseldorf, 1988; Henning, F.-W., *Konrad Adenauer und die Soziale Marktwirtschaft bis 1956*, in: Pohl, H. (ed.), *Adenauers Verhältnis zu Wirtschaft und Gesellschaft*, in: *Rhöndorfer Gespräche*, vol. 12, Bonn, 1992; Kleinmann, H.-O., *Geschichte der CDU*, Stuttgart, 1993; Becker, F., *Kleine Geschichte der CDU*, edited by the *Konrad-Adenauer-Stiftung*, Stuttgart, 1995.

18 Berberich, W., *Die historische Entwicklung der Christlich-Sozialen Union in Bayern bis zum Eintritt in die Bundesrepublik*, doctoral thesis, Würzburg, 1965; Deuerlein, E.; Gruner, W. D., *Die politische Entwicklung Bayerns 1945 bis 1972*, in: Spindler, M. (ed.), *Handbuch der bayerischen Geschichte*, vol. 4/1, Munich, 1974; Mintzel, A., *Die CSU. Anatomie einer konservativen Partei 1945-1972*, in: *Schriften des Zentralinstituts für sozialwissenschaftliche Forschungen der Freien Universität Berlin*, vol. 26, Opladen, 1975; Idem, *Political and Socio-economic Developments in the Postwar Era: The Case of Bavaria, 1945-1989*, in: Rohe, K. (ed.), *Elections, Parties and Political Traditions: Social Foundations of German Parties and Party Systems 1867-1987*, (*German Historical Perspectives* 4), New York/ Oxford, 1990, pp. 145–78; Gelberg, K-U., *Hans Ehard – Die Föderalistische Politik des Bayerischen Ministerpräsidenten 1946-1954*, Düsseldorf, 1992; Kleinhenz, G. D., *Wirtschafts- und Sozialpolitik: Die Verwirklichung einer Sozialen Marktwirtschaft durch die Landespolitik der CSU*, in: Baumgärtel, M. (ed.), *Geschichte einer Volkspartei: 50 Jahre CSU 1945-1995*, edited by the *Hanns-Seidel-Stiftung* (HSS), Munich, 1995.

[19] Deuerlein, E., *CDU/CSU 1945-1957. Beiträge zur Zeitgeschichte*, Cologne, 1957b; Becker, W., *CDU und CSU 1945-1950. Vorläufer, Gründung und regionale Entwicklung bis zum Entstehen der CDU-Bundespartei*, Mainz, 1987; Otto, K. (eds.), *Die Gründung der Union. Tradition, Entstehung und Repräsentanten*, Munich, 1990.

[20] Gutscher, J. M., *Die Entwicklung der FDP von ihren Anfängen bis 1961*, Meisenheim, 1967; Juling, P., *Programmatische Entwicklung der FDP 1946 bis 1969. Einführung und Dokumente*, in: Kaak, H. (ed.), *Studien zum politischen System der Bundesrepublik Deutschland*, Meisenheim am Glan, 1977; Cerratti, R., *The Development of the Free Democratic Party in West Germany, 1945-1956*, doctoral thesis, Oxford, 1982; Leuschner, U., *Die Geschichte der FDP – Metamorphosen einer Partei zwischen rechts, sozialliberal und neokonservativ*, Münster, 2005.

[21] Stamm, C., *Die SPD-Fraktion im Frankfurter Wirtschaftsrat 1947-1949: Protokolle, Aufzeichnungen, Rundschreiben*, Bonn, 1993.

[22] Salzmann, R. (ed.), *Die CDU/CSU im Frankfurter Wirtschaftsrat. Protokolle der Unionsfraktion 1947-1949*, Düsseldorf, 1988.

[23] Wettstein, K. P., *Die Politik der sozialdemokratischen Fraktion im Zweizonen-Wirtschaftsrat (1947-1949) unter besonderer Berücksichtigung ihrer wirtschaftspolitischen Konzeption*, Heidelberg, 1966; Schara, S., *Die SPD im Frankfurter Wirtschaftsrat 1947 bis 1949*, Cologne, 1988.

[24] Vanberg, V., *'Ordnungstheorie' as Constitutional Economics – The German Conception of a 'Social Market Economy'*, in: *ORDO* 39, Stuttgart, 1988, pp. 17–31; Idem, *Die Verfassung der Freiheit: Zum Verhältnis von Liberalismus und Demokratie*, in: Berthold, N.; Gundel, E. (eds.), *Theorie der sozialen Ordnungspolitik*, Stuttgart, 2003, pp. 35–51; Commun, P., *Erhards Bekehrung zum Ordoliberalismus: Die grundlegende Bedeutung des wirtschaftspolitischen Diskurses in Umbruchszeiten*, in: *Freiburg Discussion Papers on Constitutional Economics* 04/4, Freiburg im Breisgau, 2004; Ptak, R., *Vom Ordoliberalismus zur Sozialen Marktwirtschaft – Stationen des Neoliberalismus in Deutschland*, doctoral thesis, Hamburg, 2003; Goldschmidt, N. (ed.), l.c., 2005; Ptak, R., *Neoliberalism in Germany: Revisiting the Ordoliberal Foundations of the Social Market Economy*, in: Mirowski, P.; Plehwe, D. (eds.), *The Road from Mont Pèlerin – The Making of the Neoliberal Thought Collective*, Cambridge, Mass., 2009, pp. 98–138.

[25] Riedl, A., *Liberale Publizistik für Soziale Marktwirtschaft – Die Unterstützung der Wirtschaftspolitik Ludwig Erhards in der Frankfurter Allgemeinen Zeitung und in der Neuen Zürcher Zeitung 1948/49 bis 1957*, Regensburg, 1992.

[26] Spicka, M. E., *Selling the Economic Miracle – Economic Reconstruction and Politics in West Germany, 1949-1957*, New York/ Oxford, 2007.

[27] Erhard, L., *Wohlstand für alle*, Gütersloh, 1963[2], p. 11.

[28] Koslowski, P., *Das Ausgleichsprinzip der Sozialen Marktwirtschaft zwischen Solidarität und Korporatismus*, in: Goldschmidt, N.; Wohlgemuth, M. (eds.), *Die Zukunft der Sozialen Marktwirtschaft – Sozialethische und Ordnungsökonomische Grundlagen*, Freiburg im Breisgau, 2004, pp. 57–61.

29 Koslowski, P., *Solidarism, Capitalism, and Economic Ethics in Heinrich Pesch*, in: Idem (ed.), *The Theory of Capitalism in the German Economic Tradition: Historism, Ordo-Liberalism, Critical Theory, Solidarism*, Berlin/New York, 2000, pp. 371–94.

30 Luhmann, N., *Politische Theorie im Wohlfahrtsstaat*, Munich, 1981, pp. 44 f.; see also Sarcinelli, U., *Politikvermittlung und demokratische Kommunikationskultur*, in: Idem (ed.), *Politikvermittlung. Beiträge zur politischen Kommunikationskultur*, Bonn, 1987, p. 19.

31 Habermas, J., *Strukturwandel der Öffentlichkeit: Untersuchungen zu einer Kategorie der bürgerlichen Gesellschaft*, Frankfurt, 1999[6], preface to reprint 1990, pp. 11–53.

32 Hume, D., *Of the First Principles of Government*, in: Hendel, Ch. W. (ed.), *David Hume's Political Essays*, New York, 1953, p. 24. In connection with this, see also Lijphart, A., *Democracies. Patterns of Majoritarian and Consensus Government in Twenty-One Countries*, New Haven/London, 1984, p. 2; Dahl, R. A., *Polyarchy. Participation and Opposition*, New Haven/London, 1971, p. 1.

33 Art. 20 para. 2 *Grundgesetz für die Bundesrepublik Deutschland vom 23. Mai 1949* (GG), in: *Bundesgesetzblatt* (BGBl.) I.

34 E.g. Berg-Schlosser, D., *Die Konstituierung des Wirtschaftssystems*, in: Becker, J.; Stammen, T.; Waldmann, P. (eds.), l.c.; Benz, W., l.c., 1999a.

Part I

1 Kardorff, U. v., *Aufzeichnungen 1942-1945*, Munich, 1994, pp. 319–20.

2 Vogel, W., *Westdeutschland 1945-1950. Der Aufbau von Verfassungs- und Verwaltungseinrichtungen über den Ländern der drei westlichen Besatzungszonen*, vol. I, *Geschichtlicher Überblick; oberste beratende Stellen und Einrichtungen für Gesetzgebung, Verwaltung und Rechtsprechung; einzelne Verwaltungszweige: Ernährung, Landwirtschaft und Forsten*, Koblenz, 1956; vol. II, *Einzelne Verwaltungszweige: Wirtschaft, Marshallplan, Statistik*, Boppard, 1964; vol. III, *Einzelne Verwaltungszweige: Finanzen; Post und Verkehr; Arbeit und Soziales; Flüchtlinge, Suchdienst und Kriegsgefangene; Justiz, Inneres*, Boppard, 1963.

3 Berghahn, V., *Modern Germany*, Cambridge, 1987, pp. 182–6; Kettenacker, L., *Germany since 1945*, Oxford, 1997, pp. 5–36, 80–105.

4 Siegler, H. V., *Dokumente zur Deutschlandfrage. Von der Atlantik-Charta 1941 bis zur Berlin-Sperre 1961*, 3 vols., Bonn/Vienna/Zurich, 1961, vol. 1, pp. 5–35; Deuerlein, E. (ed.), *Potsdam 1945. Quellen zur Konferenz der „Grossen Drei"*, Munich, 1963.

5 Due to the federal approach in contrast to the centralisation of political and administrative institutions and powers, the *Länder* became the principal political units and basis for post-war Germany's federal structure. However, with a few exceptions, such as Bavaria and Saxony, the *Länder* were established in a haphazard way.

6 Potsdam Agreement, Political Principles, para. 9 (i), (ii) and (iii), in: Stolper, G., *German Realities*, New York, 1948, p. 266. See also *A Decade of American Foreign Policy: Basic Documents, 1941-49 Prepared at the request of the Senate Committee on Foreign Relations by the Staff of the Committee and the Department of*

State, Washington, D.C., Government Printing Office, 1950; Bittel, K. (ed.), *Das Potsdamer Abkommen und andere Dokumente*, Berlin, 1959, pp. 80 f.

7 Ibid., para. 9 (iv), in: Stolper, G., l.c., p. 266.

8 Ibid., para. 14, in: Stolper, G., l.c., p. 267.

9 Eschenburg, T., l.c., 1976, pp. 58–74.

10 Sternberger, D., *Block und Koalition. Eine Studie zur Entstehung der deutschen Parteiensysteme nach 1945*, in: Idem (ed.), *Lebende Verfassung. Studien über Koalition und Opposition*, Meisenheim a. Glan, 1956, pp. 51 ff.; Pulzer, P. G. J., *German Politics, 1945-1995*, Oxford, 1995, pp. 32–7.

11 Sternberger, D., *Lebende Verfassung*, Meisenheim, 1956, p. 89.

12 However, there is dispute about the exact date of zonal authorisation. Whereas Ludwig Bergsträsser states that political parties were also admitted to act on a zonal level in the British zone already on 14 Sep 1945, Heinz-Dietrich Fischer argues that parties were only admitted at county level expanding their activities at a later stage. Compare Bergsträsser, L., *Geschichte der politischen Parteien in Deutschland*, Munich/Vienna, 1965, p. 264 with Fischer, H.-D., *Parteien und Presse in Deutschland seit 1945*, Bremen, 1971, p. 53. Notwithstanding, there is general agreement in academic literature that American authorities admitted German political parties at zonal level on 1 Sep, the British Military Government on 15 Sep 1945.

13 For a list of licensed political parties at local, regional, and zonal levels, see appendix 1, p. 152.

14 In disagreement with Vogel, B.; Nohlen, D.; Schultze, R.-O., *Wahlen in Deutschland: Theorie – Geschichte – Dokumente 1848-1970*, Berlin/New York, 1971, p. 176.

15 Pulzer, P. G. J., l.c., p. 38.

16 Byrnes, J. F., *Restatement of US Policy in Germany*, Stuttgart, 6 Sep 1946 (US Government Print Office, Dept. of State publication, 2616, 1946), pp. 9–11.

17 Ruhm von Oppen, B. (ed.), *Documents on Germany under Occupation 1945-1954*, London/New York/Toronto, 1955, p. 19.

18 Directive JCS 1779 printed in: *Germany, 1947–1949; the story in documents*, edited by US Dept. of State, Washington, 1950, pp. 33–41.

19 Para. 6 (c), in: *New directive, approved by the State, War and Navy Departments, to Gen. Lucius D. Clay, United States Commander in Germany, on the Military Government of that country*, Washington, D.C., 15 July 1947, in: Stolper, G., l.c., p. 314.

20 Ibid., para. 8 (a).

21 Coles, H. L.; Weinberg, A. K., *Civil Affairs: Soldiers become Governors*, Washington, D.C., 1964; Donnison, F. S. V., *Civil Affairs and Military Government, North West Europe 1944-1946*, London, 1961; Niethammer, L., *Die Amerikanische Besatzungsmacht zwischen Verwaltungstradition und politischen Parteien in Bayern 1945*, in: VfZ 15 (2), Munich, 1967, pp. 153–210; Peterson, E. N., *The American Occupation of Germany – Retreat to Victory*, Detroit, 1977.

22 Concerning the administration of the American zone of occupation, see appendix 2, p. 153.

23 In the course of the three generations, Germany has tried various electoral systems. To replace the absolute majority system, which since 1871 had served in the appointment of delegates to the German national parliament, proportional representation was introduced for elections to the *Reichstag* after the First World War. In the discussion after the Second World War on the establishment of parliamentary representation, the opponents of the system of proportional representation charged that from 1918 to 1933 it had furthered the rise of numerous splinter parties and pressure groups, many of which in the course of time achieved parliamentary representation. The National Socialists' rise to power was also, in part, blamed upon certain aspects of proportional representation, which had progressively narrowed the foundations for the establishment of workable government coalitions. The adherents of proportional representation, on the other hand, stressed the inequities in majority vote. Regarding the electoral system for post-war Germany, see Golay, J. F., *The Founding of the Federal Republic of Germany*, Chicago, 1958; Beyme, K. v., *The Political System of the Federal Republic of Germany*, Aldershot, 1983.

24 Clay, L. D., *Decision in Germany*, Garden City/New York, 1950, p. 88.

25 Regarding particular election dates, see appendix 14, p. 172.

26 Regarding the administration of the British zone of occupation, see appendix 3, p. 154.

27 Vogelsang, T., *Die Bemühungen um eine deutsche Zentralverwaltung 1945/46*, in: VfZ 18 (4), Munich, 1970, p. 514.

28 Deuerlein, E., *Die Einheit Deutschlands. Ihre Erörterung und Behandlung auf den Kriegs- und Nachkriegskonferenzen 1941-1949. Darstellung und Dokumentation*, Frankfurt am Main/Berlin, 1957a, p. 114.

29 For a geographical illustration of the *Bizone*, see appendix 4, p. 155.

30 Kettenacker, L., l.c., p. 27.

31 For exact wording of the Bevin–Byrnes agreement, see Pünder, T., *Das Bizonale Interregnum. Die Geschichte des Vereinigten Wirtschaftsgebiets 1946-1949*, Waiblingen, 1966, pp. 383–7; AV_{BRD}, vol. 2, *Documents on Germany*, Munich, 1979, pp. 195–9; *Institut für Zeitgeschichte* (IFZ), NL Wilhelm Hoegner, ED 120/133. Regarding the then American *Deutschlandpolitik* see also Gimbel, J., *Byrnes' Stuttgarter Rede und die amerikanische Nachkriegspolitik in Deutschland*, in: VfZ 20, 1972, pp. 39–62; Idem, *Byrnes und die Bizone – Eine amerikanische Entscheidung zur Teilung Deutschlands?*, in: Benz, W.; Graml, H. (eds.), *Aspekte deutscher Aussenpolitik im 20. Jahrhundert*, Stuttgart, 1976, pp. 193–210; Kreikamp, H.-D., *Die amerikanische Deutschlandpolitik im Herbst 1946 und die Byrnes-Rede in Stuttgart*, in: VfZ 29, 1981, pp. 269–85.

32 Potsdam Agreement, Economic Principles, para. 11–19, in: Stolper, G., l.c., p. 267. Certainly, international power struggles and political interests were additional arguments that led to the setting up of the bizonal economic authorities. However, it is not part of this book to analyse those. For comprehensive depictions, see Benz, W., *Von der Besatzungsherrschaft zur Bundesrepublik. Stationen einer Staatsgründung 1946-1949*, Frankfurt am Main,

1985; Overesch, M., *Deutschland 1945-1949. Vorgeschichte und Gründung der Bundesrepublik*, Königstein im Taunus etc., 1979; AV_{BRD}, vol. 1, Munich etc., 1976.

33 *Vorläufige Abkommen über die Bildung einer deutschen Ernährungs- und Landwirtschaftsverwaltung, Verkehrsverwaltung, Wirtschaftsverwaltung, eines Finanzrates, einer Verwaltung des Post- und Fernmeldewesens*, signed on 10/11/13 Sep and 1 Oct 1946, in: *Deutscher Bundestag, Parlamentsarchiv* (DBt PA), 2/3.

34 Strauß, W., *Entwicklung und Aufbau des Vereinigten Wirtschaftsgebiets*, Heidelberg, 1948.

35 For causes of the failure of the first manifestation of the *Bizone*, see Werner, W., *Einleitung*, in: AV_{BRD}, vol. 2, Munich, 1979, pp. 11 f.; Pünder, T., l.c., pp. 83 ff.

36 Dorondo, D. R., *Bavaria and German Federalism: Reich to Republic, 1918-33, 1945-49*, New York, 1992.

37 Agreement published as 'Appendix A to Proclamation no. 5' (American occupation zone) and 'Ordinance no. 88' (British occupation zone) respectively entitled 'Economic Council' (EC); *Gesetz- und Verordnungsblatt des Wirtschaftsrats des Vereinigten Wirtschaftsgebietes* (WiGBl.), addendum no. 1, p. 1; also Pünder, T., l.c., pp. 370 ff.; Ruhm von Oppen, B. (ed.), l.c., pp. 227–31.

38 For organisation of the bizonal administration, see appendix 5, p. 156.

39 *Der Wirtschaftsrat des Vereinigten Wirtschaftsgebietes 1947-1949*, edited by the Office of the EC, n.l., n.d., p. 10; Pünder, T., l.c., pp. 370 ff.

40 For composition of the first EC, see appendix 6, p. 200.

41 *Gesetz über den vorläufigen Aufbau der Wirtschaftsverwaltung des Vereinigten Wirtschaftsgebietes (Überleitungsgesetz)*, 9 Aug 1947, in: DBt PA, 2/5.

42 Regarding the constructional deficiencies and unsettled questions on the part of German officials see Steger, B., *Konstruktionsfehler der bizonalen "Verfassung". Vorschläge Edmund Kaufmanns zur Überwindung struktureller Mängel des Vereinigten Wirtschaftsgebiets 1947/1948*, in: VfZ 29, 1982, pp. 286 ff. and the German analysis of the Proclamation no. 5, in: DBt PA, 2/3.

43 The statute was published as 'Proclamation no. 7' (American occupation zone) and 'Ordinance no. 126' (British occupation zone) respectively; cf. Pünder, T., l.c., p. 377.

44 Regarding a detailed composition of the second economic parliament see appendix 7, 8, and 9, pp. 157–60. An overview of its plenary meetings is provided in appendix 10, p. 161. Concerning the formation, reformation and development of the EC, see Närger, H. A., *Der Wirtschaftsrat des Vereinigten Wirtschaftsgebietes. Entwicklung, Verfassung und staatsrechtliche Würdigung* (status of 1 Jan 1949), Munich, 1949; Vogel, W., l.c., vol. II, Boppard, 1964; Pünder, T., l.c., pp. 97 ff.; Weisz, Ch.; Woller, H. (eds.), *Wörtliche Berichte und Drucksachen des Wirtschaftsrates des Vereinigten Wirtschaftsgebietes 1947-1949* (in the following WB), by the IFZ and the *Deutschen Bundestag, Wissenschaftliche Dienste*, Munich etc., 1977, vol. 2, *Wörtliche Berichte 1-22* (25.06.1947-01.10.1948), pp. 35 ff.; Plum, G., *Einleitung*, in: AV_{BRD}, vol. 3, Munich, 1982, pp. 49 ff.; Weisz, Ch., *Einleitung*, in: AV_{BRD}, vol. 4, Munich, 1983, pp. 36 ff.

45 Lippmann, W., *Public Opinion*, New York, 1922, p. 20.

46 Lazarsfeld, P. F.; Berlson, B.; Gaudet, H., *The People's Choice*, New York, 1948, p. 151.

47 Lenart, S., *Shaping Political Attitudes – The Impact of Interpersonal Communication and Mass Media*, London, 1994, p. 6.

48 Knower, F. H., *Experimental Studies of Change in Attitudes: I. A Study of the Effect of Oral Argument on Changes of Attitudes*, in: *Journal of Abnormal and Social Psychology* 6(1), Washington, D.C., 1935, pp. 315–47.

49 Belloc, H.; Chesterton, C., *The Party System*, London, 1921, p. 226.

50 There are various examinations dealing with the reconstruction of the press, and media in general, in the period of transition between 1945 and 1949. Unfortunately, these studies are widely fragmentary due to limited sources: Bitter, G., *Zur Typologie des deutschen Zeitungswesens in der Bundesrepublik Deutschland*, Munich, 1951; Mannhart, F., *Entwicklung und Strukturwandel der Tagespresse in der Bundesrepublik Deutschland seit 1945 und ihre Position im öffentlichen Raum*, Munich, 1957; Hofmann, J., *The CDU Press of the German Federal Republic*, in: *Gazette* 5/1, Leiden, 1959, pp. 31 ff.; Koszyk, K., *German Newspapers with Socialist Tendency since 1945*, in: Ibid., pp. 41 ff.; Idem, *Die Inhaltsanalyse der deutschen Presse*, in: *Publizistik* 7, 1962, pp. 142–6; Idem, *Deutsche Presse im 19. Jahrhundert. Geschichte der deutschen Presse*, vol. II, Berlin, 1966; Idem, *Kontinuität oder Neubeginn. Massenkommunikation in Deutschland 1945-1949*, Siegen, 1981; Idem, *Pressepolitik für Deutsche 1945-1949. Geschichte der deutschen Presse Teil IV* (*Abhandlungen und Materialien zur Publizistik*, vol. 10), Berlin, 1986; Hurwitz, H., Die *Pressepolitik der Alliierten*, in: Pross, H. (ed.), *Deutsche Presse seit 1945*, Bern/Munich/Vienna, 1965; Idem, *Die Stunde Null der deutschen Presse. Die amerikanische Pressepolitik in Deutschland 1945-1949*, Cologne, 1972; Pross, H. (ed.), *Deutsche Presse seit 1945*, Bern/Munich/Vienna, 1965; Wuerstlein, G., *Zur Problematik der deutschen Presse nach 1945*, doctoral thesis, Erlangen, 1971; Fischer, H.-D., l.c., 1971; Welsch, E.-J., *Die hessischen Lizenzträger und ihre Zeitungen*, doctoral thesis, Dortmund, 2002; Deissler, D., *Die entnazifizierte Sprache – Sprachpolitik und Sprachregelung in der Besatzungszeit*, Frankfurt am Main/Berlin/Bern/Bruxelles/New York/Oxford/Vienna, 2006.

51 Schmidt, F., *Presse in Fesseln – Eine Schilderung des NS-Pressetrusts*, Berlin, 1948; Oron, J. H., *The Captive Press in the Third Reich*, Princeton/New Jersey, 1964.

52 Zink, H., *The United States in Germany, 1944-1955*, Princeton/Toronto/London/New York, 1957, p. 235; Pross, H., l.c., pp. 131–2; Matz, E., *Die Zeitungen der US-Armee für die deutsche Bevölkerung (1944-1946)*, Münster, 1969, p. 37.

53 *The Psychological Warfare Division, Supreme Headquarters Allied Expeditionary Force. An Account of its Operations in the Western European Campaign 1944-1945*, Bad Homburg, 1945, p. 101.

54 Manual edited by the US Forces European Theater (USFET), i.e. the American military headquarter under General Dwight D. Eisenhower, Frankfurt am Main, 20 Sep 1945.

55 Potsdam Agreement, para. 10, printed in: Stolper, G., l.c., p. 266.

56 SHAEF Law No. 191, in: *Gazette US Military Government Germany*, 24 Nov 1944; *Amtsblatt der Militärregierung Deutschland. Britisches Kontrollgebiet*, no. 3, n.d., p. 36.

57 *Nachrichtenkontrollvorschrift Nr. 1* or Information Control Instruction No. 1, 12 May 1945, printed in: Greuner, R., *Lizenzpresse. Auftrag und Ende. Der Einfluss der anglo-amerikanischen Besatzungspolitik auf die Wiedererrichtung eines imperialistischen Pressewesens in Westdeutschland*, Berlin, 1962, pp. 266–8.

58 *Nachrichtenkontrollanweisung Nr. 2* or Information Control Instruction No. 2, 2 June 1945, printed in: Fait, B.; Mintzel, A.; Schlemmer, Th. (eds.), *Die CSU 1945-1948. Protokolle und Materialien zur Frühgeschichte der Christlich-Sozialen Union*, 3 vols., Munich, 1993, vol. 1, pp. 1759 f.

59 Runge, K., *Urheber- und Verlagsrecht*, Bonn/Hanover, 1948, p. 630.

60 Stöss, R.; Schmollinger, H. W., *Die Parteien und die Presse der Parteien und Gewerkschaften in der Bundesrepublik Deutschland, 1945-1974*, Munich, 1975.

61 Clay, L. D., l.c., p. 286.

62 A critique of the system that recruited these licensing officers is provided by the former chief of the PWD, James P. Warburg, in: Warburg, J. P., *Deutschland – Brücke oder Schlachtfeld*, Stuttgart, 1949, p. 81.

63 *The Psychological Warfare Division*, l.c., p. 102.

64 *Kontrollratsdirektive no. 40 über Richtlinien für die deutschen Politiker und die deutsche Presse*, 12 Oct 1946, in: *Amtsblatt des Kontrollrats in Deutschland* edited by the Allied Secretariat, no. 11, Berlin, 31 Oct 1946, p. 212.

65 Para. 8 (b), in: *New directive,* l.c., p. 314.

66 Clay, L. D., l.c., p. 158.

67 Leuschner, U., *Die neue Gleichschaltung*, Mannheim, 2005.

68 Bitter, G., *Zur Typologie des deutschen Zeitungswesens in der BRD*, Munich, 1951, p. 52. See also Welsch, E.-J., l.c., p. 46.

69 Clay, L. D., l.c., p. 319.

70 Hurwitz, H., l.c., p. 152.

71 Newspaper article titled *77 Prozent bevorzugen die überparteiliche Zeitung*, in: *Deutsche Zeitung* (DZ), vol. 1 (3), 25 Nov 1946, p. 11.

72 Hurwitz, H., l.c., 1972, p. 46.

73 Kogon, E., *Vom Elend unserer Presse*, in: *Frankfurter Hefte* (FH) 3/7, Frankfurt am Main, July 1948, p. 616.

74 Complaint by the chairman of the FDP in Bavaria, Thomas Dehler, in: *Die Neue Zeitung*, vol. 4 (17), Munich, 11 July 1948, p. 2.

75 Regarding the political orientation of licensed newspapers in the American zone in 1949, see appendix 11/12, pp. 162–70.

76 Hurwitz, H., l.c., 1972, p. 36.

77 See appendix 11/12, pp. 162–70.

78 Fischer, H.-D., l.c., 1971, pp. 53–65; Hurwitz, H., l.c., 1972, pp. 27–55; Pross, H., l.c., pp. 127–71.

79 Clay, L. D., l.c., p. 396.

80 *Zeitungen aus der britisch besetzten Zone*, in: *Mitteilungen des Nordwestdeutschen Zeitungsverleger-Vereins e. V. für die britische Zone* (MITT.), vol. 1 (2), Aug 1946, p. 6, printed in: Fischer, H.-D., l.c., 1971, p. 56.

81 Directive no. 81, in: *Amtsblatt der Militärregierung Deutschland*, l.c., p. 497.

82 Directive no. 108, Art. II, 5, in: *Die Deutsche Zeitung* (DDZ), vol. 1 (6), Nov 1947, p. 11.

83 *Amtsblatt der Militärregierung Deutschland*, l.c., 604.

84 Bitter, G., l.c., p. 112. See also appendix 11/12, pp. 162–70.

85 *Bilan d'Activité de la Sous-Direction Presse – depuis le début de l'occupation*, edited by the *Commandement en chef Français en Allemagne, Division de l'information* (*Sous-Direction Presse*), Baden-Baden, 1949, p. 3.

86 Hädler, Ch., *Die Versorgung der deutschen Tagespresse mit Zeitungsdruckpapier*, doctoral thesis, Nuremberg, 1961, p. 122.

87 Gardner, J., *The public debate about the formulation of the Basic Law of the Federal Republic of Germany, 1948-1949*, D.Phil. thesis, Oxford, 2004, pp. 33–5.

88 Schildt, A., *Hegemon der häuslichen Freiheit: Rundfunk in den 50er Jahren*, in: Schildt, A; Sywottek, A., *Modernisierung im Wiederaufbau: Die westdeutsche Gesellschaft der 50er Jahre*, Bonn, 1998, p. 459.

89 Mehnert, K.; Schulte, H., *Deutschland-Jahrbuch 1949*, Essen, 1949, p. 462.

90 Regarding listening patterns at that time, see Gardner, J., l.c., pp. 36–8.

91 For detailed accounts, see Pilgert, H. P.; Dobbert, H., *Press, Radio and Film in West Germany*, Office of US High Commissioner for Germany, 1953; Bausch, H., *Rundfunkpolitik nach 1945*, vol. 1 1945–1962, Munich, 1980; Frei, N., *Hörfunk und Fernsehen*, in: Benz, W. (ed.), *Die Bundesrepublik Deutschland. Geschichte in drei Bänden*, vol. 3, Frankfurt am Main, 1983, pp. 319–57.

92 Fischer, H.-D., l.c., 1971, pp. 52–71. See also appendix 11/12, pp. 205–11.

93 Interview with Swiss media expert Ernst Bollinger, Geneva, 13 Aug 2005.

94 Wiskemann, E., *A Great Swiss Newspaper. The Story of the Neue Zürcher Zeitung*, London/New York/Toronto, 1959, p. 80.

95 Fischer, H. D., *Die grossen Zeitungen. Portraits der Weltpresse*, Munich, 1966, p. 58.

96 Letter Konrad Adenauer to Paul Silverberg, 30 May 1947, in: *Stiftung Bundeskanzler-Adenauer-Haus* (StBKAH), NL Konrad Adenauer, 07.03; see also Jahn, H. E., *An Adenauers Seite. Sein Berater erinnert sich*, Munich/Vienna, 1987, p. 119.

97 For further investigation, see Arnold, F., *Anschläge. 220 politische Plakate als Dokumente der deutschen Geschichte 1900-1980*, Ebenhausen, 1985.

98 *Gesetz no. 5 über die Presse, den Rundfunk, die Berichterstattung und die Unterhaltungsstätten*, in: Glain, G. P. (ed.), *Amtsblatt der Hohen Alliierten Kommission in Deutschland*, no. 1, Bonn-Petersberg, 23 Sep 1949, pp. 7 ff.

99 Mettler, B., *Demokratisierung und Kalter Krieg. Zur amerikanischen Informations- und Rundfunkpolitik in Westdeutschland 1945-1949*, Berlin, 1975.

Chapter 1

1 Hayek, F. A. v., *The Road to Serfdom*, Chicago, 1944, p. 23.

2 The *Verein für Socialpolitik* was founded in 1872 and reestablished in 1948. The association composed of personalitites from academia, politics, business, and media argued for an academic discussion of economic and socio-political issues in order to achieve social balance by reforms. What became known as *Kathedersozialismus* (lectern socialism) with its representatives Adolf Wagner (1835-1917), Lujo Brentano (1844-1931), Gustav von Schmoller (1838-1917), and Werner Sombart (1863-1941), was later institutionalised as *Verein für Socialpolitik – Gesellschaft für Wirtschafts- und Sozialwissenschaften* (Association for Social Policy – Society for Economic and Social Science) in Frankfurt am Main in 1956.

3 Becker, H. P., *Die soziale Frage im Neoliberalismus*, Heidelberg/Leuven, 1965.

4 Wenz, R., *Wirtschafts- und Sozialordnung*, in: Becker, J.; Stammen, T., Waldmann, P. (eds.), l.c., pp. 293–330.

5 Schlecht, O., l.c., 1988, pp. 131–45.

6 Zweig, K., l.c.; Wünsche, H. F., l.c., 1998, pp. 131–69; Goldschmidt, N. (ed.), l.c., 2005.

Chapter 1.1

1 Adolf Lampe (1897–1948) in his report entitled *Massnahmen der Übergangswirtschaft nach dem Kriege zur Wiederingangsetzung marktlicher Wirtschaftslenkung*, in: Blumenberg-Lampe, C., l.c., 1986, p. 114.

2 The notion 'neo-liberalism' was termed by Friedrich August von Hayek (1899–1992), Wilhelm Röpke (1899–1966) and Walter Eucken (1891–1950) at a conference on the apparent crisis of liberalism in Europe at the *Institut International de Coopération Intellectuelle* in Paris in August 1938. However, there is no single school of thought known under this name but the notion covers a wide spectrum of various schools and interpretations, such as monetarism, libertarianism, or ordo-liberalism.

3 Referring to the famous words '*laissez faire, laissez passer, le monde va de lui-même*' presumably first enunciated by the French liberal economist and supporter of physiocracy, Jean Claude Marie Vincent Marquis de Gournay (1712–59).

4 E.g. Götz, H. H., l.c., pp. 57–61 or Rieter, H.; Schmolz, M., l.c., pp. 87-114.

5 Blumenberg-Lampe, C., l.c., 1973; Idem, l.c., 1986; Idem, l.c., 1991, pp. 207–19.

6 Rüther, D., l.c.; Klump, R., l.c., 2005, pp. 383–401; Oswalt, W., *Liberale Opposition gegen den NS-Staat: Zur Entwicklung von Walter Euckens Sozialtheorie*, in: Goldschmidt, N. (ed.), l.c., 2005, pp. 315–53.

7 Christine Blumenberg-Lampe, l.c., 1973; Daniela Rüther, l.c.; Grossekettler, H., l.c., 2005, pp. 91–119.

8 With the exception of the meetings in Rhöndorf, Jena and Bad Godesberg, the AG_{EvB} convened eight times in Freiburg between March 1943 and July 1944. The sessions, usually taking place in private homes, were in each case dedicated to particular subjects and intensively prepared. For an overview of

the (changing) participants, proceedings and results of the private meetings of the AG$_{\text{EvB}}$, see Blumenberg-Lampe, C. (ed.), l.c., 1986, pp. 619–22.

9 Blumenberg-Lampe, C., l.c., 1973, pp. 7, 52.

10 Idem, l.c., 1986.

11 *Wirtschaftsfibel*, in: *Bundesarchiv* in Koblenz (BA), *Nachlass* (NL) Johannes Popitz, 262/87. See also Rüther, D., *Der Einfluss Freiburger Nationalökonomen auf die wirtschaftspolitischen Vorstellungen und Planungen der Widerstandsbewegung des 20. Juli 1944 – dargestellt am Beispiel der „Volkswirtschaftsfibel" von 1941/42*, in: Goldschmidt, N. (ed.), l.c., 2005, pp. 355–81.

12 Blumenberg-Lampe, C., l.c., 1973, pp. 49 ff.

13 Grossekettler, H., l.c., 2005, p. 104 and Blumenberg-Lampe, C., l.c., 1973, p. 64 (footnote).

14 Draft report by Lampe entitled *Probleme der Übergangswirtschaft nach dem Krieg und Voraussetzung für das Wiederingangbringen marktlich geordneter Wirtschaft*, Freiburg, Jan 1943 (in the following cited as report no. 3), in: Blumenberg-Lampe, C. (ed.), l.c., 1986, p. 71 (footnote).

15 Statement by Edith Eucken, in: *Archiv der Christlich-Demokratischen Politik* (ACDP), NL Adolf Lampe, I-256-041.

16 Report no. 3, in: Blumenberg-Lampe, C. (ed.), l.c., 1986, p. 70.

17 Exposé by Lampe entitled *Wiederaufbau der Friedenswirtschaft = Wiederaufbau der Marktwirtschaft*, Freiburg, Nov 1942 (in the following cited as report no. 1), in: Ibid., pp. 40–52.

18 Discussion paper *Entwurf. Umrisse eines Systems wirtschaftspolitischer Wiederaufbau-Massnahmen nach dem Kriege. Zweiter Abschnitt: Die Notwendigkeit der Rückkehr zu primär marktlich geordneter Wirtschaft*, Freiburg, Sep 1943 (in the following cited as report no. 14), in: Ibid., pp. 189–91.

19 Letter by von Beckerath (1889–1964) to the AG$_{\text{EvB}}$, 19 Nov 1943, in: common report *Wichtigste Probleme des Wiederaufbaus der Friedenswirtschaft und ihre Lösung durch primär marktwirtschaftliche Wirtschaftsordnung*, Freiburg, 24/25 Sep 1943 (in the following cited as report no. 18), in: Ibid., p. 243.

20 Blumenberg-Lampe, C., l.c., 1973, pp. 62 ff.

21 Contribution by Lampe entitled *Material zur Diskussion über "Vorschläge zur Wiederingangsetzung der Marktwirtschaft nach Kriegsende"*, Freiburg, 17 Feb 1943 (in the following report no. 4), in: Blumenberg-Lampe, C. (ed.), l.c., 1986, p. 76.

22 Lampe in the contributions *Massnahmen der Übergangswirtschaft nach dem Kriege zur Wiederingangsetzung marktlicher Wirtschaftslenkung – Nachträgliche Niederschrift des Einleitungsvortrages zum erstatteten Vorgutachten*, Freiburg, March 1943 (in the following cited as report no. 6), in: Ibid., p. 114.

23 Report no. 14, in: Blumenberg-Lampe, C. (ed.), l.c., 1986, p. 192.

24 Ibid., pp. 500–6.

25 Letter Lampe to Holstein, 21 July 1947, in: Blumenberg-Lampe, C., l.c., 1973, p. 133.

26 Lampe to Böhm, 5 Aug 1946, in: ACDP, NL Adolf Lampe, I-256-037/2. See also Blumenberg-Lampe, C., l.c., 1973, pp. 134 ff.

27 These reports are available at *Archives de l'Occupation Française en Allemagne et en Autriche* (AOC) in Colmar. Two of the documents are published as report no. 47 (*Währungsordnung = Wirtschaftsordnung*) and no. 48 (*Währungsordnung und Wirtschaftsordnung*), in: Blumenberg-Lampe, C. (ed.), l.c., 1986, pp. 507–27 and pp. 528–34.

28 Criticism in *Vorgutachten über die Gesamtrichtung der Wirtschaftspolitik*, Jan 1946, in: ACDP, NL Adolf Lampe, I-256-037/2.

29 Letter von Beckerath to Lampe, 17 Dec 1945, in: ACDP, NL Adolf Lampe, I-256-037/2.

30 Letter Lampe to von Beckerath, 1 March 1946, in: Ibid.

31 E.g. Lampe in *Ein Weg zur Wirtschaftsordnung* published posthumously, in: *Die Gegenwart*, 1 March 1948, pp. 31–3.

32 *Volkswirtschaftliche Probleme des deutschen Aussenhandels*, pp. 105–33; also in: Blumenberg-Lampe, C. (ed.), l.c., 1986, pp. 593–604.

33 Koch, W., *Der Wissenschaftliche Beirat beim Bundesminister für Wirtschaft*, in: *Probleme der normativen Ökonomik und der wirtschaftspolitischen Beratung. Schriften des Vereins für Socialpolitik – Gesellschaft für Wirtschafts- und Sozialwissenschaften*, vol. 29, Frankfurt, 1963, pp. 405–20.

34 Johannes Semler cited in minutes of the first meeting of the WB_{VfW} in Königstein im Taunus on 23/24 Jan 1948, in: IFZ, NL Hans Möller, ED 150/30.

35 *Der Wissenschaftliche Beirat beim Bundeswirtschaftsministerium, Band 2, Gutachten vom Juni 1950 bis November 1952*, edited by the *Bundeswirtschaftsministerium*, Göttingen, 1953.

36 Blumenberg-Lampe, C., l.c., 1973, p. 62.

37 Hentschel, V., *Ludwig Erhard – Ein Politikerleben*, Berlin, 1998, p. 49.

38 Letter from Lampe to Preiser, 26 Oct 1945, in: ACDP, NL Adolf Lampe, I-256-037/2.

39 Letter by Blumenberg-Lampe to the author of this book, 12 Feb 2004.

40 Interview with Blumenberg-Lampe, Bonn, 16 Dec 2003.

Chapter 1.2

1 Eucken, W., *Wissenschaft im Stile Schmollers*, in: *Weltwirtschaftliches Archiv* 52, Berlin/Heidelberg, 1940a, pp. 490 f.

2 This conclusion was reached in the following studies: Hagemann, W., *Grundzüge der Publizistik. Als Einführung in die Lehre von der sozialen Kommunikation*, Münster, 1966, p. 81; Vetter, E. G., *Wirtschaftspublizistik*, in: *Handwörterbuch der Betriebswirtschaft* I/3.4., Stuttgart, 1976, pp. 4644–51; Fischer, H. D., *Reeducations- und Pressepolitik unter britischem Besatzungsstatus. Die Zonenzeitung „Die Welt" 1946-1950. Konzeption, Artikulation und Rezeption*, Düsseldorf, 1978, p. 160 and p. 450.

3 Regarding the historical roots of the Freiburg School and its members, see Grossekettler, H., l.c., 1989, pp. 38–84; Hollerbach, A., l.c., pp. 91–113; Streit, M. E., l.c., 1992, pp. 675–704.

4 As the term 'order' is central to the concept of the Freiburg School, it is important to note that it consistently relates to the order needed to underpin political economy and does not contain any wider conservative connotation, still less an authoritarian one.

5 Böhm, F.; Eucken, W.; Großmann-Doerth, H., *Unsere Aufgabe. (Einleitung der Herausgeber)*, in: Böhm, F.; Eucken, W.; Großmann-Doerth, H. (eds.) *Ordnung der Wirtschaft*, 1, Stuttgart/Berlin, 1937, pp. 7–21.

6 Böhm, F., *Die Ordnung der Wirtschaft als geschichtliche Aufgabe und rechtsschöpferische Leistung*, in: Idem, l.c., Stuttgart/Berlin, 1937, pp. 101 f.

7 The German Historical School of Economics (1850–1950) and its members, such as Gustav von Schmoller (1838–1917), Karl Bücher (1847–1930) and Lujo Brentano (1844–1931), did not in principle oppose economic theory or even economic laws, but instead were against premature deductive theorising and deductive theories divorced from empirical facts and tests. For the historical economists history was never an end in itself but merely a tool of social and economic research. Sometimes 'historical' implied nothing more than a vague commitment to history, ethical issues, or policy in economics. Cf. Böhm-Bawerk, E., *Historische und theoretische Nationalökonomie*, in: Weiss, F. X. (ed.), *Gesammelte Schriften von Eugen Böhm-Bawerk*, Wien/Leipzig, 1924, pp. 157–88; Grimmer-Solem, E., *The Rise of Historical Economics and Social Reform in Germany 1864-1894*, New York, 2003.

8 Herrmann-Pillath, C., *Methodological Aspects of Eucken's Work*, in: *Journal of Economic Studies* 21, 1994, pp. 46–60.

9 Eucken, W., *Kapitaltheoretische Untersuchungen. Mit einer Einleitung in die Sammlung: Was leistet die nationalökonomische Theorie?*, Jena, 1934, p. 39; Idem, l.c., 1940.

10 Eucken, W., *Wissenschaft im Stile Schmollers*, in: *Weltwirtschaftliches Archiv* 52, Berlin/Heidelberg, 1940a, pp. 468–506; Idem, *Grundsätze der Wirtschaftspolitik*, Tübingen, 1952; Vanberg, V., *The Freiburg School: Walter Eucken and Ordoliberalism*, in: *Freiburg Discussion Papers on Constitutional Economics* 04/11, Freiburg im Breisgau, 2004.

11 Streit, M. E., l.c., 1995; Vanberg, V., *Die normativen Grundlagen von Ordnungspolitik*, in: *ORDO* 48, Stuttgart, 1997, pp. 707–26; Buchanan, J., *The Economics and the Ethics of Constitutional Order*, Ann Arbor, 1991.

12 Sombart, W., *Der moderne Kapitalismus. Historisch-systematische Darstellung des gesamteuropäischen Wirtschaftslebens von seinen Anfängen bis zur Gegenwart*, Munich/Leipzig, 1922.

13 Weber, M., *Die Protestantische Ethik und der Geist des Kapitalismus*, orig. in: *Archiv für Sozialwissenschaft u. Sozialpolitik* 20 (1904), pp. 1–54 and 21 (1905), pp. 1–110. Reprint: Munich, 2004. Idem, *Wirtschaft und Gesellschaft*, Tübingen, 1922.

14 Eucken, W., *Die Überwindung des Historismus*, in: *Schmollers Jahrbuch* 62, Berlin, 1938, pp. 63–86; Idem, l.c., 1952, pp. 374 f.; Böhm, F., l.c., 1937, pp. 120 f.

15 Eucken, W., *Staatliche Strukturwandlungen und die Krisis des Kapitalismus*, in: *Weltwirtschaftliches Archiv* 36, Berlin/Heidelberg, 1932, pp. 297–321.

16 Note by Böhm, in: ACDP, NL Franz Böhm, I-200-044/1; Böhm, F., *Wettbewerb und Monopolkampf. Eine Untersuchung zur Frage des wirtschaftlichen*

Kampfrechts und zur Frage der rechtlichen Struktur der geltenden Wirtschaftsordnung. Berlin, 1933.

17 Eucken, W., l.c., 1940a, pp. 490 f.

18 Böhm, F., *Freiheit und Ordnung in der Marktwirtschaft*, Baden-Baden, 1980, p. 158.

19 Eucken, W., l.c., 1952, pp. 325–38.

20 Private note *Liberalismus-Sozialismus*, n.d., pp. 4 f., in: ACDP, NL Franz Böhm, I-200-044/3.

21 Rüstow, A., *Zwischen Kapitalismus und Kommunismus*, in: *ORDO* 2, Stuttgart, 1949.

22 Röpke, W., *Grundfragen rationeller Wirtschaftspolitik*, in: *Zeitschrift für Schweizer Statistik & Volkswirtschaft*, no. 1, 1941, p. 112; *Der Dritte Weg*, in: *Ostschweiz (St. Gallen)*, 4 April 1942; *Der Dritte Weg*, in: *Seeländer Volksstimme (Biel)*, 11 June 1942; Röpke, W., *Weltwirtschaft und internationale Geldordnung nach dem Kriege – Der „Dritte Weg" in der Weltwirtschaft*, in: *Schweizer Monatshefte* 10/10, Jan 1943.

23 Görtemaker, M., l.c., p. 151; Albrecht, C.; Behrmann, G. C.; Bock, M.; Homann, H.; Tenbruck, F. H., l.c.; Klump, R., l.c., 2005, pp. 384–401.

24 Letter by Eucken to von Beckerath, 3 Feb 1950, in: Oswalt, W., l.c., 2005, p. 320.

25 Röpke, W., l.c., 1944, pp. 75–7; Rüstow, A., *Soziale Marktwirtschaft als Gegenprogramm gegen Kommunismus und Bolschewismus*, in: Hunold, A. (ed.), *Wirtschaft ohne Wunder*, Erlenbach-Zurich, 1953.

26 Röpke, W., *Blätter der Erinnerung an Walter Eucken*, in: *ORDO*, Düsseldorf/Munich, 1961, pp. 101 f.

27 Note by Eucken, in: *Walter Eucken Archiv* (WEA), Frankfurt am Main; comment in Eucken's diary, Sep 1942, in: personal property Christoph Eucken, cited in: Oswalt, W., l.c., 2005, p. 318.

28 *Währungssanierung durch Kaufkraftabschöpfung mit anschliessender Geldumlaufs-auffüllung*, Freiburg, 3 and 11 Aug 1945 respectively, in: Blumenberg-Lampe, C. (ed.), l.c., 1986, pp. 500–6.

29 Blumenberg-Lampe, C., l.c., 1973, p. 133.

30 Letter by Eucken to Gerhard Albrecht dated 24 July 1947, in: *Nordrhein-Westfälisches Hauptstaatsarchiv in Düsseldorf* (HStAD), RW 189–93, sheet 118.

31 *Centre d'Organisation et d'Etudes Economiques de Fribourg en Breisgau* (COEE) to the *Section Economie Générale*, 13 Feb 1946, in: AOC, Série: Bade, 5812 A.

32 Klump, R., *Wege zur Sozialen Marktwirtschaft – Die Entwicklung ordnungspolitischer Konzeptionen in Deutschland vor der Währungsreform*, in: Streissler, E., (ed.), *Studien zur Entwicklung der ökonomischen Theorien XVI. Die Umsetzung wirtschaftspolitischer Grundkonzeptionen in die kontinentaleuropäische Praxis des 19. und 20. Jahrhunderts*, part I, Berlin, 1997, pp. 129–60.

33 Report *Maßnahmen der Verbrauchsregelung, der Bewirtschaftung und der Preispolitik nach der Währungsreform*, 1 April 1948, in: *Der Wissenschaftliche Beirat bei der VfW des VWGs; Gutachten 1948 - Mai 1950*, edited by the *Bundeswirtschaftsministerium*, Göttingen, n.d., pp. 25–30.

34 WiGBl. 1948, pp. 59 f., preamble, attachment 1 and 2.

35 Reports *Investitionspolitik nach der Währungsreform*, 11 July 1948; *Währungs-, Preis-, Produktions- und Investitionspolitik*, 3 Sep 1948; *Expansive und kontraktive Kreditpolitik*, 8 May 1949; *Geldordnung und Wirtschaftsordnung*, 18 Sep 1949, in: Ibid..

36 Erhard on Miksch, in: *Landesarchiv Baden-Württemberg, Staatsarchiv Freiburg*, C 25/2, no. 137.

37 Nicholls, A. J., l.c., 1994, p. 252.

38 Miksch, L., *Das Problem der künftigen Wirtschaftsformen: Gedanken zur Wirtschaftsordnung*, in: *Der Wirtschaftsspiegel. Wirtschaftspolitische Halbmonatsschrift*, 1947a, pp. 401–55; Idem, *Wirtschaftsmoral und Wirtschaftsordnung*, in: *Wirtschaftsverwaltung* 1/14, 1948a, pp. 2–5; Idem, *Zur Theorie des Gleichgewichts*, in: *ORDO* 1, Stuttgart, 1948b, pp. 175–96; Idem, *Die Wirtschaftspolitik des Als-Ob*, in: *Zeitschrift für die gesamte Staatswissenschaft* 105, Tübingen, 1949, pp. 310–38.

39 Gillessen, G., *Die Frankfurter Zeitung im Dritten Reich*, Berlin, 1986, p. 430.

40 Miksch, L., *Wirtschaftspolitik in der Demokratie*, in: *Die Zeit*, 3 July 1947b, p. 5; Idem, *Die Zinspolitik am Scheideweg*, in: *Neue Zürcher Zeitung* (NZZ), 6 Sep 1948c.

41 Eucken, W., *Wettbewerb, Monopol und Unternehmer*, in: *Wirtschaft und Gesellschaft*, Bad Nauheim, 1953.

42 Eucken, W., *Das ordnungspolitische Problem*, in: *ORDO* 1, Stuttgart, 1948, pp. 56–90; Idem, *Die Wettbewerbsordnung und ihre Verwirklichung*, in: *ORDO* 2, Stuttgart, 1949, pp. 1–99.

43 Welter served as editor-in-chief of the *Vossisches Zeitung* in Berlin from 1932 to 1934 and was on the *Frankfurter Zeitung* editorial staff from 1935 to 1943. In 1946 he launched the *Wirtschafts-Zeitung* in Stuttgart and also wrote for the *Allgemeine Zeitung* in Mainz from 1948 onwards.

44 Letter Eucken to Welter, 3 June 1946, in: BA, NL Erich Welter, no. 57, 530.

45 Eucken, W., *Wirtschaftspolitik am toten Punkt*, in: NZZ, 20 July 1948a; Idem, *Der Kurs der Wirtschaftspolitik*, in: *Wirtschafts-Zeitung*, 4 Dec 1948b; Idem, *Von der alten zur neuen Wirtschaftspolitik*, in: FAZ, 31 Dec, 1949, p. 11.

46 Rüstow, A., *Interessenpolitik oder Staatspolitik*, in: *Schriften des Vereins für Socialpolitik* 187, Munich, 1933; Idem, *Das Versagen des Wirtschaftsliberalismus*, Heidelberg, 1950a; Idem, *Ortsbestimmung der Gegenwart*, Erlenbach-Zurich, 1950b.

47 Röpke, W., *Die Grundlagen der Nationalökonomie I*, in: NZZ, 22 Feb 1942; Idem, *Grundlagen der Nationalökonomie II*, in: NZZ, 24 Feb 1942; Idem, *Das Echo eines Buches I-IV*, in: NZZ, 23–6 July 1942; Idem, *Internationale Wirtschaftsprobleme nach dem Kriege*, in: NZZ, n.d.; Idem, *Gerechte Rohstoffverteilung zwischen den Völkern*, in: NZZ, 14 June 1944; *Vereinigte Staaten von Deutschland*, in: NZZ, 21 Sep 1946.

48 Apart from Switzerland, Röpke also lectured at Hungarian universities; György, P., *Gondolatok egy könyvsiker felett*, in: *Magyar Nemzet*, 26 Feb 1944.

49 Correspondence between Röpke and the Director of the IUHEI in Geneva, William E. Rappard, 3 March 1946, in: *Archiv Wilhelm Röpke*, IUHEI, Bibliothèque, Genève.

50 *Ausblick in die Nachkriegswirtschaft*, in: *Tagesanzeiger (Zurich)*, 22 Jan 1942; *Wirtschaft im und nach dem Krieg*, in: *Hochwacht (Winterthur)*, 30 Jan 1942; *Prospettive economiche del dopo-guerra*, in: *Il Contadino Svizzero*, Feb 1942; *Die Gesellschaftskrisis der Gegenwart*, in: *Vaterland (Luzern)*, 16 Mar 1942; *Die Gesellschaftskrisis der Gegenwart*, in: *Thurgauer Zeitung (Frauenfeld)*, 31 Mar 1942; *Die Gesellschaftskrisis der Gegenwart*, in: *Tagesanzeiger (Zurich)*, 6 June 1942; *La Crise de Notre Temps*, in: *Gazette de Lausanne*, 18 May 1942; *L'Example de la Suisse*, in: *Journal de Genève*, 4 June 1943; *La société saine et malade*, in: *Journal de Genève*, 30 Nov 1943; *Une conférence de M. Röpke sur „La société saine et malade"*, in: *La Tribune de Genève*, 1 Dec 1943; György, P., l.c.; Braichet, R., *Le Problème Allemand*, in: *Feuille d'Avis de Neuchâtel*, 24 May 1945; Ladame, P.-A., *La crise de notre temps et le néo-libéralisme du professeur Röpke*, in: *La Tribune de Genève*, 29 June 1945.

51 Röpke, W., *Um die deutsche Wirtschaftsheilung I*, in: NZZ, 19 Feb 1948a; Idem, *Um die deutsche Wirtschaftsheilung II*, in: NZZ, 20 Feb 1948b; Idem, *Kollektivistischer Starrkrampf in Deutschland*, in: NZZ, 1 June 1948c; Idem, *Die Rettung Westdeutschlands*, in: NZZ, 30 June 1948d.

52 Röpke, W., *Die Gesellschaftskrisis der Gegenwart*, Erlenbach-Zurich, 1942, p. 9; Idem, *Civitas Humana – Grundfragen der Gesellschafts- und Wirtschaftsordnung*, Erlenbach-Zurich, 1944, p. 46; Idem, *Internationale Ordnung*, Zurich, 1945.

53 Appreciation of Röpke and his work was expressed in numerous Swiss newspaper articles e.g. when the economist was appointed to a professorship in New York in Feb 1943; e.g. *Prof. W. Röpke nach Amerika berufen*, in: NZZ, 9 Feb 1943; *Berufung von Prof. W. Röpke*, in: *Neues Winterthurer Tagblatt*, 9 Feb 1943; *Le professeur Röpke appelé à New York*, in: *Gazette de Lausanne*, 9 Feb 1943; *De Genève à New York*, in: *Journal de Genève*, 9 Feb 1943; *Wilhelm Röpke verlässt Genf*, in: *Express (Biel)*, 9 Feb 1943; *Wissenschaftliche Nachrichten*, in: *National Zeitung (Basel)*, 10 Feb 1943; *Wilhelm Röpke geht nach New York*, in: *Neue Zürcher Nachrichten*, 10 Feb 1943; *Geht Professor Röpke nach Amerika?*, in: *Die Tat*, 10 Feb 1943; *Röpke nach New York berufen*, in: *Bund*, 10 Feb 1943; *Le professeur Wilhelm Röpke*, in: *La Suisse*, 10 Feb 1943; *Wilhelm Röpke nach Amerika berufen*, in: *Echo vom Zürichberg (Oerlikon)*, 11 Feb 1943; *So etwas wie ein geistiger Führer…*, in: *Das Volk (Olten)*, 24 June 1944; *Le Professeur Röpke*, in: *Journal de Montreux*, 5 Dec 1944. However, there were also negative views about the German economist, mainly in left-wing newspapers; e.g. *Antiroepke*, in: *Arbeiter Zeitung (Schaffhausen)*, 21 April 1944.

54 Mötteli, C., *Das Problem der internationalen Ordnung – Zur Neuauflage eines Buches von Wilhelm Röpke*, in: NZZ, 5 Aug 1954, p. 1.

55 E.g. Röpke, W., *Ein neuer Typ der Wirtschaftspolitik*, in: *Stuttgarter Zeitung*, 27 Feb 1946.

56 Böhm, F., *Schutz vor den „Großen"?* in: FAZ, 17 April 1953; Rüstow, A., *Die Bewältigung des Wohlstandes*, in: FAZ, 7 Dec 1960, p. 11.

57 Letter Welter to Röpke, 28 Sep 1953, in: BA, NL Erich Welter, no. 219.

58 Letter Röpke to Welter, 5 Feb 1952, in: BA, NL Erich Welter, no. 154.

59 Röpke, W., *Sozialismus in Deutschland?*, in: NZZ, 12 April 1947; homonymous document dated 22 July 1947, in: *Deutsche Bundesbank, Historisches Archiv* (BuBa), B 331-HMS, no. 566, 569.
60 Heitzer, H., l.c., p. 507.
61 Letter Konrad Adenauer to Maurice W. Altaffer, 10 Aug 1947, in: Adenauer, K., *Briefe 1947-1949*, edited by Hans Peter Mensing, Berlin, 1983, p. 44; letter to Röpke, 12 July 1949, in: Adenauer, K., *Briefe 1949-1951*, edited by Hans Peter Mensing, Berlin, 1984, p. 56.
62 Adenauer, K., *Erinnerungen 1945-1953*, Stuttgart, 1965, p. 337; letter to Semler, 15 Dec 1947, in: Adenauer, K., l.c., 1983, p. 123.
63 Eschenburg, T., *„Aus persönlichem Erleben: Zur Kurzfassung der Denkschrift 1943/44" zur Kriegsschrift Ludwig Erhards „Kriegsfinanzierung und Schuldenkonsolidierung"*, Frankfurt am Main, 1977, pp. 15-21; Nicholls, A. J., l.c., 1994; Hieronymi, O., *Wilhelm Röpke, The Social Market Economy and Today's Domestic and International Order*, in: *Cahiers HEI 2002, no. 6, Colloque Wilhelm Röpke (1899-1966), The Relevance of his Teaching Today: Globalization and the Social Market Economy*, Geneva, 2002.
64 Hentschel, V., l.c., pp. 77 f.
65 Initially, 37 scholars were invited. In the early 1950s, the society had around 200 members increasing to about 500 nowadays.
66 Erhard felt honoured by the invitation: letter to Eucken, 13 Feb 1950, in: *Ludwig-Erhard-Archiv* (LEA), NL Ludwig Erhard, I. 4) 41.
67 Cockett, R., *Thinking the Unthinkable – Think-Tanks and the Economic Counter-Revolution 1931-1983*, London, 1994, pp. 100–21.
68 Röpke, W., l.c., 1944, pp. 45, 76.

Chapter 1.3

1 Müller-Armack, A., *Soziale Marktwirtschaft – Handwörterbuch der Sozialwissenschaften*, vol. 9, Göttingen, 1956, p. 249.
2 Müller-Armack, A., *Wirtschaftslenkung und Marktwirtschaft*, Hamburg, 1946, p. 88. Regarding the authorship of the Social Market Economy see also Franz Böhm's handwritten amendment to his drafted speech, n.d., p. 13, in: ACDP, NL Franz Böhm, I-200-044/1. However, the question of the origins of the term *Soziale Marktwirtschaft* is still controversial. In his autobiography *Wahrheit und Wirklichkeit. Der Weg aus den Weltkriegen in die Soziale Marktwirtschaft und eine künftige Weltordnung*, Homburg-Saarplatz, 1996, pp. 571 ff., Karl Günther Weiss, academic assistant to the former permanent representative of the State Secretary in the Reich Ministry of Economics, Otto Ohlendorf, argues, the term 'Social Market Economy' was the outcome of a discussion with Ludwig Erhard on 12 Jan 1945. There is also some evidence that Harold Rasch, who in 1946/47 was deputy head of the inter-zonal economic administration in Minden, used the term in late 1947 and early 1948 independently of Müller-Armack (1901–78); cf. Rasch, H., *Grundlagen der Wirtschaftsverfassung*, Bad Godesberg, 1948.

3 The literature on the Social Market Economy is vast, however, for a detailed account of the genesis and concept, see Blum, R., l.c.; Watrin, C., l.c., 1979; Müller-Armack, A., *Genealogie der Sozialen Marktwirtschaft. Frühschriften und weiterführende Konzepte*, Bern/Stuttgart, 1981; Tribe, K., *Strategies of Economic Order: German Economic Discourse, 1750-1950*, Cambridge, 1995.

4 Müller-Armack, A., l.c., 1956, p. 390; Idem, *Wirtschaftsordnung und Wirtschaftspolitik, Studien und Konzepte zur Sozialen Marktwirtschaft und zur Europäischen Integration*, Freiburg im Breisgau, 1966, p. 245.

5 Hayek, F. A. v., *Was ist und was heisst "sozial"?*, in: Hunold, A. (ed.), *Masse und Demokratie*, Erlenbach-Zurich/Stuttgart, 1957, pp. 71 ff. See also the contributions of Horst Friedrich Wünsche *Welcher Marktwirtschaft gebührt das Beiwort „sozial"?* and Christian Watrin *Zur sozialen Dimension marktwirtschaftlicher Ordnungen*, in: Hohmann, K.; Schönwitz, D.; Weber, H. J.; Wünsche, H. F. (eds.), l.c., 1988, pp. 21–31, and pp. 411–15.

6 Nicholls, A. J., *The Bonn Republic – West German Democracy 1945-1990*, London/New York, 1997, pp. 59 ff.

7 Röpke, W., l.c., 1944.

8 Müller-Armack, A., *Soziale Irenik*, in: *Weltwirtschaftliches Archiv* 64, Berlin/Heidelberg, 1950, pp. 181–203.

9 Müller-Armack, A., *Auf dem Weg nach Europa. Erinnerungen und Ausblicke*, Tübingen/Stuttgart, 1971, pp. 50 ff.

10 In regard to the different conceptions of the state see the study Lange-von Kulessa, J.; Renner, A., *Die Soziale Marktwirtschaft Alfred Müller-Armacks und der Ordoliberalismus der Freiburger Schule – Zur Unvereinbarkeit zweier Staatsauffassungen*, in: *ORDO* 49, Stuttgart, 1998, pp. 79–104.

11 Schlecht, O., l.c., 1991, p. 215. The expression 'Third Way' in regard to Germany evolved from historical experiences. Whereas the western European nations practised 'freedom without regulation' or 'freedom through equality' (in reference to the formula of the French Revolution *liberté, égalité, fraternité* in 1789), German freedom had been defined by Johann Gottlieb Fichte as 'freedom through the state'.

12 Nipperdey, Th., *Deutsche Geschichte 1866-1918. Erster Band: Arbeitswelt und Bürgergeist*, Munich 1993, p. 336.

13 Oppenheimer, F., *System der Soziologie* (III/1). *Band 3: Theorie der reinen und politischen Ökonomie, Teil 1: Grundlagen*, Jena, 1910, p. 9. The economist Franz Oppenheimer (1864–1943) also published his economic conception in *Sprung über ein Jahrhundert*, Bern/Leipzig, 1935 under the pseudonym F. D. Pelton.

14 Oppenheimer, F., *Weder so – noch so. Der dritte Weg*, Potsdam, 1933.

15 Oppenheimer supervised Erhard's doctoral thesis titled '*Wesen und Inhalt der Werteinheit*', namely a study on various historical schools' perception of character and content of value, in the years 1922 to 1925.

16 Erhard, L., *Franz Oppenheimer, dem Lehrer und Freund* (1964), in: Hohmann, K. (ed.), *Ludwig Erhard. Gedanken aus fünf Jahrzehnten, Reden und Schriften*, Düsseldorf/Vienna/New York, 1988b, p. 861.

17 Regarding the influence of Oppenheimer on Erhard, see Wünsche, H. F., *Der Einfluss Oppenheimers auf Erhard und dessen Konzeption von der Sozialen Marktwirtschaft*, in: Caspari, V.; Schefold, B. (eds.), *Franz Oppenheimer und Adolph Lowe, Zwei Wirtschaftswissenschaftler der Frankfurter Universität*, Marburg, 1996, pp. 141–61; Hentschel, V., l.c., pp. 15–18; Haselbach, D., *Franz Oppenheimer's Theory of Capitalism and of a Third Path*, in: Koslowski, P. (ed.), *The Theory of Capitalism in the German Economic Tradition. Historism, Ordo-Liberalism, Critical Theory, Solidarism*, Berlin *et al.*, 2000, pp. 54–86.

18 Erhard, L., *Wirtschaft und Bildung* (17 Aug 1957), reprinted in: Hohmann, K. (ed.), l.c., 1988b, p. 515.

19 Comparative study Goldschmidt, N., *Alfred Müller-Armack and Ludwig Erhard: Social Market Liberalism*, in: *CREPHE-CREA Histoire du Liberalisme en Europe*, Brochure no. 21, Paris, 2004.

20 Erhard, L., *Wirken und Reden,* Ludwigsburg, 1966, p. 320.

21 Commun, P., l.c..

22 Erhard, L., l.c., 1992, p. 592.

23 Wünsche, H. F., l.c., 1986; Nicholls, A. J., l.c., 1994; Hieronymi, O., l.c., 2002.

24 Letter Erhard to Röpke, 7 Oct 1959, in: LEA, NL Ludwig Erhard, I. 4) 59.

25 Letter Erhard to Röpke, 22 May 1950, in: Ibid., I. 4) 59; Hentschel, V., l.c., 1998, pp. 75–8.

26 Ibid., p. 25.

27 WB, l.c., p. 799.

28 Erhard, L., *Marktwirtschaft im Streit der Meinungen*, printed in: Erhard, L., *Deutsche Wirtschaftspolitik – Der Weg der Sozialen Marktwirtschaft*, Düsseldorf/Vienna/New York/Moscow, 1992, p. 70. Finally, Erhard used and described the term in an article in the *Berliner Tagesspiegel* on 23 April 1949.

29 Müller-Armack, A., *The Social Market Economy as an Economic and Social Order*, in: *Review of Social Economy* 36, Washington, D.C., 1978a, pp. 326 f.

30 Müller-Armack, A., *Religion und Wirtschaft*, Bern/Stuttgart, 1950a, pp. 559 ff.

31 Erhard, L., l.c., 1963, p. 11.

32 *Symposion I – Soziale Marktwirtschaft als nationale und internationale Ordnung*, edited by LES, issue 59, Stuttgart, 1978, pp. 116 f.

33 In this connection, see also Erhard's definition of advertising, in: Erhard, L., *Werbewirtschaft und Werbegestaltung*, in: *Die Deutsche Fertigware*, Teil A, Heft 3, 1937, p. 53.

34 Erhard, L., *Ich bin mein eigener Werbeleiter. Möglichkeiten und Grenzen der Werbung in der Marktwirtschaft.* (*Vortrag Erhards vor dem Zentralausschuss der Werbewirtschaft am 7. Oktober 1955 in Essen*), in: LEA, NL Ludwig Erhard, 1520.

35 Erhard, L., *Ein Notweg*, in: *Das Tage-Buch*, 1 Aug 1931.

36 Erhard, L., *Marktwirtschaft und Werbung gehören untrennbar zusammen*, in: *Wirtschaft und Werbung*, 12 Dec 1952, pp. 327 f.

37 Müller-Armack, A., l.c., 1966, p. 109.

38 Erhard, L., *Sprachverwirrung um die Wirtschaftsordnung*, in: *Die Neue Zeitung*, 23 June 1947, printed in: Idem, l.c., 1992, p. 23.

39 Erhard, L., *Ausblicke*, in: *Deutsche Zeitung und Wirtschaftszeitung*, 15 May 1945; Idem, *Zur Jahreswende 1945/46*, in: *Die Neue Zeitung*, 31 Dec 1945; Idem, *Politischer Föderalismus und wirtschaftlicher Zentralismus*, in: *Die Neue Zeitung*, 9 Oct 1946; Idem, *Ist eine dezentralisierte Planwirtschaft möglich?*, in: *Die Neue Zeitung*, 26 May 1947. Müller-Armack, A., *Soziale Marktwirtschaft*, in: *Der Wirtschaftsspiegel*, vol. 21 (2), Dec 1947; Idem, *Soziale Marktwirtschaft*, in: *Telegraf*, 31 July 1947; Idem, *Sicherung der Marktwirtschaft*, in: *Der Tagesspiegel*, 28 Sep 1948.

40 Müller-Armack, A., *Die Konzeption der Sozialen Marktwirtschaft*, in: Altvater, E.; Arndt, H.; Besters, H. (eds.), *Unsere Wirtschaft: Basis, Dschungel, Dogma? – Marktwirtschaft in der gegenwärtigen Auseinandersetzung*, Cologne, 1974, p. 90.

41 Goldschmidt, N., l.c., 2004; Wulff, M., *Die neoliberale Wirtschaftsordnung, Versuch einer dynamischen Analyse der Konzeption und Realität*, Tübingen, 1976.

42 Noelle-Neumann, E., *Soziale Marktwirtschaft im Bewusstsein der Bevölkerung*, in: *Soziale Marktwirtschaft als historische Weichenstellung*, l.c., pp. 607–27.

43 Erhard, L., *Kriegsfinanzierung und Schuldenkonsolidierung. Faksimiledruck der Denkschrift von 1943/44*, Frankfurt/Berlin/Vienna, 1977, preface, p. VII.

44 Hentschel, V., l.c., pp. 44–50.

45 Erhard, L., *Zur Jahreswende 1945/46*, in: *Die Neue Zeitung*, 31 Dec 1945; Idem, *Freie Wirtschaft und Planwirtschaft*, in: *Die Neue Zeitung*, 14 Oct 1946.

46 Nicholls, A. J., l.c. 1994, p. 158.

47 Kordes, W.; Pollmann, H., *Das Presse- und Informationsamt der Bundesregierung (Ämter und Organisation der Bundesrepublik Deutschland, Band 18)*, Düsseldorf, 1985.

48 Cf. appendix 5, p. 156.

49 *Direktorialsitzung*, 23 March 1948, in: AV_{BRD}, vol. 4, Munich, 1983, p. 411.

50 *Geschäftsordnung des Verwaltungsrates des Vereinigten Wirtschaftsgebietes*, in: BA, B 102, no. 9114.

51 Plenary meeting of the EC, 27/28 Sep 1948, in: WB, l.c., pp. 890 ff.

52 Binder, P., *Sozialisierung und Planwirtschaft*, in: *Schwäbische Zeitung*, no. 7, vol. 4, 23 Jan 1948; Idem, *Deutschlands Rückkehr in die Wirtschaft*, in: *Schwäbische Zeitung*, no. 27, vol. 4, 2 April 1948; Neumann, C., *Marktwirtschaft unverletzlich!*, in: *Industriekurier*, 12 Dec 1948;

53 *Rundverfügung* or ordinance by Ludwig Erhard no. 76/48 and 94/48, 17 July 1948 and 7 Sep 1948, in: BA, 102, no. 9114.

54 Erhard in *Zeitungs-Verlag und Zeitschriften-Verlag*, 19 Oct 1957, in: LEA, NL Ludwig Erhard, 1534.

55 Erhard's request sent to OMGUS on 20 Nov and letter to then State Secretary in the Bavarian Ministry of Justice, Hans Ehard, on 28 Nov 1946, in: *Bayerisches Hauptstaatsarchiv* (BayHStA), NL Hans Ehard, no. 681.

56 Minutes of the press conference in Frankfurt, 2 April 1948, p. 1, in: LEA, NL Ludwig Erhard, 1593.

57 Minutes of the press conference of the VfW, 14 April 1948, pp. 1–6, in: Ibid., 1516.

58 Erhard, L., *Mengenkonjunktur als wirtschaftspolitisches Ziel*, in: *Industrie-Anzeiger*, 30 June 1953, p. 670, in: LEA, NL Ludwig Erhard, H0.

59 In an ironic allusion, the name was derived from the former homonymous *Freikorps Brigade Erhard* which took part in the Kapp-Lüttwitz-Putsch in March 1920. The less familiar denomination *Neuhauser Kreis* referred to Neuhaus in Bavaria where the mentor Hans-Henning Zencke held a summer residence.

60 However, the index of names varies over time; cf. Koerfer, D., *Kampf ums Kanzleramt, Erhard und Adenauer*, Stuttgart, 1987, p. 783; Fack, F. U., *'Ich brauche mich Ihnen nicht vorzustellen"*, in: FAZ, 1 Feb 1997, p. 15.

61 Although the Allies initially did not grant the employers an effective organisation as considered accessory to National Socialism, various trade associations (re)formed and were finally recognised by the military authorities. By fall 1948, around 1,500 industrial associations were accredited in the *Bizone*.

62 Plumpe, W., *Die Entstehungsphase des industriellen Spitzenverbandes im britischen und amerikanischen Besatzungsgebiet nach dem Zweiten Weltkrieg im Spiegel der öffentlichen Meinung*, manuscript, Bochum, 1979, pp. 80–9; Prowe, D., *Unternehmer, Gewerkschaften und Staat in der Kammerneuordnung in der britischen Besatzungszone bis 1950*, in: Petzina, D.; Euchner, W. (eds.), *Wirtschaftspolitik im britischen Besatzungsgebiet 1945-1949*, Düsseldorf, 1984, pp. 235–54; Idem, *Economic Democracy in Post-World War II Germany: Corporatist Crisis Response, 1945-1948*, in: *Journal of Modern History* 57, Chicago, 1985, pp. 451–82.

63 Ibid., p. 454.

64 Statement, in: *IHK-Mitteilungen*, Frankfurt am Main, 25 April 1948.

65 Langer, W., *Wer ist denn eigentlich dieser Ludwig Erhard?*, in: FAZ, 1 Feb 1997, p. 16.

66 Ockhardt, K., *Der Vater des Wohlstandes*, in: Schröder, G.; Müller-Armack, A.; Hohmann, K.; Gross, J.; Altmann, R. (eds.), *Ludwig Erhard – Beiträge zu seiner politischen Biographie, Festschrift zum 75. Geburtstag*, Frankfurt, 1972, p. 583.

67 Schulz, K., D., *Unternehmerinteresse und Wirtschaftssystem. Beiträge der Unternehmer zur politischen Entwicklung der Bundesrepublik Deutschland*, Frankfurt, 1986.

68 Preamble of the principles of the *Wirtschaftspolitische Gesellschaft von 1947 e.V.*, in: BA, Z1, no. 703 (see also Zsg 1-98).

69 Ibid., p. 8 (attachment specifying all charter members).

70 Gather, G., *Wirtschaft – Politik – Gesellschaft. Die Wirtschaftspolitische Gesellschaft 1947/71 und das Bildungswerk Offene Welt. Ulrich von Pufendorf zum 70. Geburtstag, 12. Oktober, 1971*, Frankfurt, 1971, p. 13; Muthesius, V., *Augenzeuge von drei Inflationen. Erinnerungen und Gedanken eines Wirtschaftspublizisten*, Frankfurt, 1973, p. 101.

71 Letter of member of EC Paul Binder to Müller-Armack, 1 Oct 1947, in: ACDP, NL Paul Binder, I-105-020. Regarding Erhard's affiliation, see also the association's website (http://www.wipog.de).

72 Letter by Mueller including the exposé '*Die Wirtschaftsordnungen, sozial gesehen*' to the delegate Paul Binder, Munich, 19 Aug 1947 in: ACDP, NL Paul Binder, I-105-020; letter and exposé '*Vorschläge zur Verwirklichung der Sozialen Marktwirtschaft*' to the delegate Fritz Dengler, Hamburg, 15 June 1948 in: ACDP, NL Fritz Dengler, I-002-001/3; see also in: *Archiv für Christlich-Soziale Politik* (ACSP), NL Franz Elsen, 9.1.9.

73 Gather, G., l.c., p. 12; Muthesius, V., *Erinnerungen an den "Befreiungskrieg"*, in: Schröder, G.; Müller-Armack, A.; Hohmann, K.; Gross, J.; Altmann, R. (eds.), l.c., 1972, p. 159.
74 *Marktwirtschaft als politisches Element*, in: *Der Wirtschaftsspiegel*, 15 Dec 1947.
75 Jahn, H. E., *Lebendige Demokratie: Die Praxis der politischen Meinungspflege in Deutschland*, Frankfurt am Main, 1956, pp. 229–31.
76 Letter by Mueller to Erhard, 9 Dec 1949, in: LEA, NL Ludwig Erhard, I. 4) 54. See also Riedl, A., l.c., p. 62.
77 According to the recollections of the former Managing Director of the *Frankfurter Allgemeine Zeitung GmbH*, Werner G. Hoffmann; cf. minutes of a meeting between Hoffmann, Erich Welter and Max H. Schmid, 7 June 1961, p. 1, in: BA, NL Erich Welter, 73. However, there is dissension whether Erhard only *initiated* the foundation or was also actively engaged in the establishment of the FAZ; Riedl, A., l.c., p. 64.
78 The meeting was initiated by the Director of the *Salamander AG* in Kornwestheim, Alex Haffner; Korda, R. M., *Für Bürgertum und Business. "Die Frankfurter Allgemeine Zeitung"*, in: Thomas, M. W. (ed.), *Porträts der deutschen Presse. Politik und Profit*, Berlin, 1980, pp. 81–96.
79 Schulz, K. D., l.c., pp. 151 f. and Riedl, A., l.c., pp. 65–7.
80 Gillessen, G., l.c.; Paupié, K., *Frankfurter Zeitung (1856-1943)*, in: Fischer, H.-D. (ed.), *Deutsche Zeitungen des 17. bis 20. Jahrhunderts (Publizistik-Historische Beiträge, Band 2)*, Munich, 1972, pp. 241-256; Sänger, F., *Zur Geschichte der „Frankfurter Zeitung"*, in: *Publizistik* 22, 1977, pp. 275–94.
81 *Zeitung für Deutschland*, in: FAZ, 1 Nov 1949, p. 1.
82 Greiser, F., *Die westdeutschen Tageszeitungen – Tatsachen und Tendenzen*, in: *Wirtschaftsdienst* 34, Heidelberg, 1954, pp. 553–9.
83 Schulz, K. D., l.c., pp. 151 and 164.
84 Riedl, A., l.c., pp. 87–92; Welter, E., *Die Wirtschaftspolitische Bildungsaufgabe*, in: Hunold, A. (ed.), *Wirtschaft ohne Wunder*, Zurich, 1953, pp. 342 f..
85 Miksch, L., *Wettbewerb als Aufgabe. Grundsätze einer Wettbewerbsordnung*, Godesberg, 1947, p. 13.; Rüstow, A., *Die Bewältigung des Wohlstandes*, in: FAZ, 7 Dec 1960. Alexander Rüstow also became a shareholder and chairman of the FAZIT foundation, namely the holding of the FAZ.
86 Schwarz, H.-P., *Die Ära Adenauer. Gründerjahre der Republik 1949-1957. Geschichte der Bundesrepublik Deutschland*, vol. 2, Wiesbaden, 1981, p. 79 f.
87 E.g. Erhard, L., *Die Wirtschaftsordnung für freie Menschen*, in: FAZ, 1 June 1957.
88 Letter Welter to Miksch, 2 Aug 1948, in: BA, NL Erich Welter, 434.
89 Ilau, H., *Künstliche Verwirrung*, in: FAZ, 13 June 1953, p. 7; Greiss, F., *Erhards Soziale Marktwirtschaft und die Waage*, in: Schröder, G.; Müller-Armack, A.; Hohmann, K.; Gross, J.; Altmann, R. (eds.), l.c., 1972, pp. 89–110; Schmidt, K.-D., *Soziale Gerechtigkeit durch unternehmerische Initiative: Der Bund Katholischer Unternehmer, 1949-1990*, Munich, 1994, pp. 32–5; Schindelbeck, D.; Ilgen, V., *„Haste was, biste was!" Werbung für die Soziale Marktwirtschaft*, Darmstadt, 1999; Löffler, B., *Soziale Marktwirtschaft und administrative Praxis. Das Bundeswirtschaftsministerium unter Ludwig Erhard*, Wiesbaden, 2002, pp. 280 ff.

90 Noelle, E.; Neumann, E. P. (eds.), *Jahrbuch der Öffentlichen Meinung 1947-1955*, Allensbach, 1956, p. 192.

91 Huebner, R., *Werbung für alle*, in: FAZ, 20 Jan 1953, p. 7; Spicka, M. E., l.c., pp. 86–139.

92 Fack, F. U., l.c., p. 15.

93 Comment by Klaus Hildebrand, printed in: Schwarz, H.-P., *Ludwig Erhard – ein grosser Unzeitgemässer*, in: FAZ, 1 Feb 1997, p. 13.

94 Altmann, R.; Gross, J., *Gespräch über Erhard*, in: Schröder, G.; Müller-Armack, A.; Hohmann, K.; Gross, J.; Altmann, R. (eds.), l.c., 1972, pp. 30 ff.

95 Hentschel, V., l.c., p. 107.

96 Ibid., p. 66.

97 WB VV, l.c., pp. 436 ff.; see also Erhard, L., l.c., 1992, p. 60.

98 Görtemaker, M., l.c., p. 148.

99 Although Volker Hentschel refers to a bad performance and inane speech, there is wide agreement about the enthusiasm after Erhard's appearance; cf. Hentschel, V., l.c., p. 99 and Stoltenberg, G., *Konrad Adenauer und die Soziale Marktwirtschaft*, in: *Die Politische Meinung*, edited by the *Konrad-Adenauer-Stiftung* (KAS) 45/373, Sankt Augin, 2000, pp. 21 f.

100 Erhard, L., l.c., 1992, pp. 69–85.

101 Müller-Armack, A., l.c., 1971, p. 247.

102 Schwarz, H.-P., *Adenauer. Der Aufstieg. 1876-1952*, Stuttgart, 1986, p. 602.

103 Erhard, L., *Was uns trennte, was uns einte*, in: *Deutsche Zeitung*, 26 Dec 1975, p. 3.

104 Lukomski, J. M., *Ludwig Erhard. Der Mensch und der Politiker*, Düsseldorf, 1965, pp. 59 f.

105 Clay, L. D., l.c., pp. 225 ff.

106 Görtemaker, M., l.c., p. 151.

107 Hombuger Plan, in: Möller, H. (ed.), *Zur Vorgeschichte der Deutschen Mark. Die Währungsreformpläne 1945-1948*, Basel/Tübingen, 1961, pp. 477 ff.

108 Wandel, E., *Die Entstehung der Bank deutscher Länder und die deutsche Währungsreform 1948. Die Rekonstruktion des westdeutschen Geld- und Währungssystems 1945-1949 unter Berücksichtigung der amerikanischen Besatzungspolitik*, Frankfurt am Main, 1980, pp. 188–91.

109 Broadcast address by Köhler, 19 June 1948, in: DBt PA, 2/508.

110 Statement by Erhard during press conference given by Pünder, 28 May 1948, in: DBt PA, 2/508.

111 *Der Neue Kurs*, 21 June 1948, in: Erhard, L., l.c., 1992, pp. 62–8.

112 Speech titled *Auf die Reform der Wirtschaft kommt es an* held at EC, 28 Sep 1949, in: Erhard, L., l.c., 1992, pp. 86–95.

113 *Streitgespräch Erhard-Nölting*, in: *Rheinische Post*, 15 Nov 1948.

114 *Zonenausschussprotokoll* (ZA) 24/25 Feb 1949 in Königswinter, in: Pütz, H. (ed.), *Konrad Adenauer und die CDU der britischen Besatzungszone 1946-1949. Dokumente zur Gründungsgeschichte der CDU Deutschlands*, Bonn, 1975, p. 853.

115 To this day, Ludwig Erhard's party membership is controversial. The *Ludwig-Erhard-Archiv* in Bonn holds Erhard's membership card which records a CDU membership as early as 1 March 1949. However, this card is without any, then

common, adhesive stamps certifying payed membership fees. Erhard probably joined the party not until 1962/63. The exact date is not documented and there is no evidence neither in the *Bundes*-CDU, nor the *Landesverband* Wuerttemberg-Baden, nor the *Kreisverband* Ulm nor in the ACDP. However, in an interview in Jan 1962, Ludwig Erhard stated that he was not a member (cf. *Das Parlament*, no. 21–2, 27 May 1988, p. 21). Other sources suggest that he became a member of the CDU in conjunction with the taking over of the party chairmanship in March 1966. On 5 March 1966, the public questioned Erhard's status and the *Saarbrücker Zeitung* published an article titled *Muss Erhard Parteibeiträge nachzahlen?* In view of Ludwig Erhard's engagement in campaigns for the CDU, Adenauer in written form asked him to join the party on 14 Feb 1966. However, Erhard did not attribute much importance to the party membership. In connection with this, see also *Ludwig Erhard soll nie CDU-Mitglied gewesen sein*, in: *Der Spiegel online*, 25 April 2007.

116 Wengst, U., *Die CDU/CSU im Bundestagswahlkampf 1949*, in: VfZ 34, no. 1, Munich, 1986, p. 25.

117 Narr, W.-D., *CDU-SPD. Programm und Praxis seit 1945*, Stuttgart, 1966, p. 95; Koerfer, D., l.c., p. 56; see also Laitenberger, V., *Ludwig Erhard. Der Nationalökonom als Politiker*, Göttingen, 1986.

118 Fack, F. U., l.c., p. 15.

119 Erhard in a public audio transmission, 6 June 1949, published in: Erhard, L., l.c., 1992, p. 105.

120 E.g. speech given by Erhard during his stump tour throughout West Germany, in: BA, 102, no. 9085.

121 Dreher, K., *Der Weg zum Kanzler. Adenauers Griff nach der Macht*, Düsseldorf/Vienna, 1972, p. 225.

122 Hentschel, V., l.c., p. 107.

123 Böhm, F., *Der Sprung in die Marktwirtschaft*, in: Schröder, G.; Müller-Armack, A.; Hohmann, K.; Gross, J.; Altmann, R. (eds.), l.c., 1972, p. 417.

124 Müller-Armack on Erhard, cited, in: Müller-Armack, A., l.c., 1971, p. 246.

125 Jeske, J., *Die Marktwirtschaft – das war er*, in: FAZ, 1 Feb 1997, p. 13.

126 Goldschmidt, N., l.c., 2004, p. 3.

127 Hentschel, V., l.c., p. 89. See also part II chapter 3 of this book, pp. 165 ff.

128 Götz, H. H., *Er suchte kompetente Gesprächspartner*, in: FAZ, 1 Feb 1997, p. 14.

Chapter 2

1 Friedrich Hölderlin cited in: Hayek, F. A. v., l.c., 1944, p. 18.

2 *Documents on the Creation of the German Federal Constitution*, edited by the OMGUS, Civil Administration Division, Berlin, 1949, p. 86.

Chapter 2.1

1 Grebing, H., *Neubau statt Wiederaufbau der SPD – Die Lehren aus der Weimarer Republik*, in: Dowe, D. (ed.), l.c., p. 76.

2 Müller, G., l.c., p. 13; Schwarz, H.-P., l.c., 1966, pp. 484–504.

3 Schütz, K., *Die Sozialdemokratie im Nachkriegsdeutschland*, in: *Parteien in der Bundesrepublik. Studien zur Entwicklung der deutschen Parteien bis zur Bundestagswahl 1953*, *Schriften des Instituts für politische Wissenschaft*, vol. 6, Stuttgart/Düsseldorf, 1955.

4 Immediately after the arrival of the Allies in Hanover in April 1945, Schumacher started the reconstruction of the SPD and the *Büro Dr. Schumacher* became the inofficial party headquarters. In August, he successfully applied for a licence for the SPD in the British occupation zone.

5 Concerning the politician Kurt Schumacher (1895–1952) and his politics, see Albrecht, W., *Kurt Schumacher. Ein Leben für den demokratischen Sozialismus*, Bonn, 1985; Idem, *Kurt Schumacher als deutscher und europäischer Sozialist*, Bonn, 1988; Merseburger, P., *Der schwierige Deutsche. Kurt Schumacher*, Stuttgart, 1995; Dowe, D. (ed.), l.c.. Regarding the claim for leadership, see Pirker, T., l.c., pp. 16 f.; Albrecht, W. (ed.), *Kurt Schumacher. Reden – Schriften – Korrespondenzen 1945-1952*, Berlin/Bonn, 1985a, pp. 375–84, 463–74.

6 Vieritz, J., *Die SPD im Meinungsbild der ersten Kriegsjahre in Briefen an Kurt Schumacher 1945-1949*, state examination thesis, University of Göttingen, 1988.

7 Brockway, F., *The New Leader*, in: Scholz, A.; Oschilewski, W. G. (eds.), *Turmwächter der Demokratie – Ein Lebensbild von Kurt Schumacher*, vol. II, Berlin, 1953, pp. 62 f.

8 Speech entitled *Wir verzweifeln nicht* held by Schumacher in Hanover on 6 May 1945.

9 Brandt, P., *Demokratischer Sozialismus – Deutsche Einheit – Europäische Friedensordnung. Kurt Schumacher in der Nachkriegspolitik 1945-1952*, in: Dowe, D. (ed.), l.c., p. 44.

10 For an overview of party conventions at that time, see appendix 13, p. 171.

11 *Protokoll der Verhandlungen des Parteitages der Sozialdemokratischen Partei Deutschlands vom 9. bis 11. Mai 1946 in Hannover* (in the following *Protokoll SPD-Parteitag 1946*), Hamburg, 1947, p. 38; see also Pirker, T., l.c., p. 52.

12 *Politische Leitsätze* adopted at the party convention in Hanover on 11 May 1946, in: Flechtheim, O. K. (ed.), l.c., vol. III, Berlin, 1963, p. 20.

13 *Protokoll SPD-Parteitag 1946*, l.c., p. 47. In his statements, however, Schumacher neither concretised whom the middle class included nor did he formulate differentiated policies. Rather his appeals to the bourgeoisie were politically motivated. Concerning this issue, see Ritter, W., *Kurt Schumacher. Eine Untersuchung seiner politischen Konzeption und seiner Gesellschafts- und Staatsauffassung*, Hanover, 1964, p. 172; Klotzbach, K., *Der Weg zur Staatspartei. Programmatik, praktische Politik und Organisation der deutschen Sozialdemokratie 1945-1965*, Berlin/Bonn, 1982, pp. 58 f.; Lösche, P.; Walter, F., *Die SPD. Klassenpartei, Volkspartei, Quotenpartei*, Darmstadt, 1992, pp. 2 ff.

14 Wesemann, F., *Kurt Schumacher*, Frankfurt am Main, 1952, p. 109; Klotzbach, K., l.c., p. 58; Lösche, P., *Abschied von der Klassenpartei – Das Ringen der SPD um die Mittelschichten*, in: Dowe, D. (ed.), l.c., pp. 93–112.

15 Grebing, H., *Zur Problematik der personellen und programmatischen Kontinuität in den Organisationen der Arbeiterbewegung in Westdeutschland 1945/46*, in: *Herkunft und Mandat. Beiträge zur Führungsproblematik in der Arbeiterbewegung*, Frankfurt am Main/Cologne, 1976, pp. 171–94; Idem, *Von der Traditionskompanie zur Staatspartei. Die Modernisierung der Sozialdemokratie in den 1950er und 1960er Jahren im regionalen Vergleich*, in: Kocka, J.; Puhle, H.-J.; Tenfelde, K., *Von der Arbeiterbewegung zum modernen Sozialstaat. Festschrift für Gerhard A. Ritter zum 65. Geburtstag*, Munich, 1994, pp. 205–21; Idem, *„Neubau" statt „Wiederaufbau" der SPD – die Lehren aus der Weimarer Republik*, in: Dowe, D. (ed.), l.c., pp. 73–89; Wolfrum, E., *Französische Besatzungspolitik und deutsche Sozialdemokratie. Politische Neuansätze in der „vergessenen" Zone bis zur Bildung des Südweststaates 1945-1952*, Düsseldorf, 1991; Tomin, W., *Die Geschichte der SPD in Hamburg 1945 bis 1950*, Hamburg, 1995.

16 This pursuit can be found in various speeches held by Schumacher, e.g. in a talk given to social democratic officials in Hanover on 6 May 1945, in his political directives for the SPD on 25 Aug 1945, in the programmatic declarations at the conferences of Wennigsen and Hanover on 5/6 Oct 1945, as well as in the speeches held at the party conference in Hanover on 9–11 May 1946, further in a statement during the congress of the *Sozialistischer Deutscher Studentenbund* (SDS) in Hamburg on 4 Sep 1946, printed in: Albrecht, W. (ed.), l.c., pp. 203–36, pp. 256–6, pp. 301–19, pp. 385–422, pp. 463–74. Additionally, see the talk given in Kiel on 27 June 1945 and the article in the *Tagesspiegel*, 17 April 1946, in: Scholz, A.; Oschilewski, W. G. (eds.), l.c., vol. II, Berlin, 1953, pp. 25–50 and pp. 71–4.

17 Schumacher, K., *Die Wandlungen um den Klassenkampf*, in: Idem, *Reden und Schriften*, Berlin, 1962, pp. 297 ff.

18 Braunthal, J., *Kurt Schumacher und die Sozialistische Internationale*, in: Scholz, A.; Oschilewski, W. G. (eds.), l.c., vol. I, Berlin, 1954, pp. 510 ff.

19 *Politische Leitsätze*, l.c., p. 20.

20 Ehni, H. P., l.c., pp. 131–89, here pp. 144–7.

21 Talk given by Schumacher in Frankfurt am Main on 1 June 1947; cited in: Scholz, A.; Oschilewski, W. G. (eds.), l.c., vol. II, Berlin, 1953, pp. 424 ff.

22 Schumacher, K., *Aufgaben und Ziele der deutschen Sozialdemokratie*, presentation given on the party conference of the SPD in 1946, edited by the SPD Greater-Hesse, Frankfurt am Main, 1946, p. 12.

23 Sering, P. (alias Richard Löwenthal), *Jenseits des Kapitalismus*, Lauf, 1946, p. 168; Huster, E.-U., l.c., p. 31.

24 Scholz, A.; Oschilewski, W. G. (eds.), l.c., vol. II, Berlin, 1953, p. 37.

25 As prophet of democratic socialism, already Ferdinand Lasalle (1825–1864) campaigned for the abolition of private property and a solidarian society. While he fundamentally agreed with Marxian ideas, the committed democrat advocated a socialist reform by universal suffrage instead of a proletarian revolution. His political conviction was expressed in the foundation of the first German labour party, namely the *Allgemeiner Deutscher Arbeiterverein* (ADAV) or General German Workers' Association, in Leipzig on 23 May

1863. When the ADAV merged with the *Sozialdemokratische Arbeiterpartei* (SDAP) or Social Democratic Workers' Party, in Gotha on 27 May 1875, the *Sozialistische Arbeiterpartei Deutschlands* (SAP) or Socialist Workers' Party of Germany which was renamed the *Sozialdemokratische Partei Deutschlands* (SPD) or Social Democratic Party of Germany in 1890, emerged.

26 Schumacher at the SPD party congress in Hanover on 9–11 May 1946, cited in: Ehni, H. P., l.c., p. 144. See also Ritter, W., l.c., p. 91.

27 Schumacher, K., *Aufgaben und Ziele der deutschen Sozialdemokratie*, presentation given on the party conference of the SPD in 1946, edited by the SPD Greater-Hesse, Frankfurt am Main, 1946, p. 3.

28 Klingelhöfer, G., *Analyse der Weltlage 1945 und ihrer wahrscheinlichen Entwicklung*, presentation held at the second meeting of the SPD's central economic policy committee on 31 Aug 1945, in: *Landesarchiv Berlin* (LAB), Rep 200/Acc 2435 (Klingelhöfer) 22.

29 *Grundgedanken eines sozialistischen Wirtschaftsprogramms. Wege und Ziele sozialdemokratischer Wirtschaftspolitik* edited by the *Vorstand der Sozialdemokratischen Partei Deutschlands*, Hamburg, n.d..

30 Apart from diverse economic conceptions, Schumacher's centralised action was often incompatible with the interests of individual *Länder* and encountered resistance from some sovereigns, such as the Prime Minister of Lower Saxony, Hinrich Kopf, and the Bavarian Prime Minister, Wilhelm Hoegner; Eschenburg, T., l.c., 1976, p. 66.

31 Schütz, K., l.c., pp. 157 ff; Blum, R., l.c., pp. 13 ff; Ehni, H. P., l.c., pp. 131ff.

32 Agartz, V., *Sozialistische Wirtschaftspolitik*, presentation given at the party conference in 1946, edited by the SPD Greater-Hesse, Frankfurt, 1946.

33 *Protokoll PT 1946*, l.c.

34 Naphtali, F., *Wirtschaftsdemokratie – Ihr Wesen, Weg und Ziel*, Frankfurt am Main, 1928. In this context, it is interesting to note, that Fritz Naphtali lectured at the *Erste Deutsche Hochschule für das Volk der Arbeit* (founded in 1921; today *Akademie der Arbeit in der Universität Frankfurt am Main*) at the same time as Franz Oppenheimer who supervised Erhard's doctoral thesis between 1922 and 1925. See also Schmidt, M. E., l.c.; Köser, H., *Die Grundsatzdebatte in der SPD von 1945/46 bis 1958/59*, doctoral thesis, Freiburg, 1971.

35 *Politische Leitsätze*, l.c..

36 SPD Hamburg (ed.), *Leitsätze der Sozialdemokratischen Partei Deutschlands zur Gestaltung einer sozialistischen deutschen Wirtschaftsverfassung*, Hamburg, 1946, p. 3.

37 Abelshauser, W., l.c., 1976, p. 415.

38 *Protokoll der Gutachtertagung über Grundfragen der Wirtschaftsplanung und Wirtschaftslenkung*, in: DBt PA, 1/55, pp. 9 f.

39 Galbraith, J. K., *The German Economy*, in: Harris, S. E., *Foreign Economic Policy for the United States*, Cambridge, Mass., 1948, pp. 94 f.

40 Nölting, E., *Freiheit und Bindung in der sozialistischen Wirtschaft. Referat auf der wirtschaftspolitischen Tagung am 19./20.6.1947 in Bad Wildungen*, in: Weber, A., *Erik Nölting, Sozialistische Wirtschaftsordnung. Beiträge zur Diskussion*, Hamburg, 1948, pp. 17–20.

41 *Protokoll der Verhandlungen des Parteitages der Sozialdemokratischen Partei Deutschlands vom 29. Juni bis 2. Juli 1947 in Nürnberg* (*Protokoll SPD-Parteitag 1947*), Hamburg, n.d., pp. 158–61.

42 Nölting, E., l.c., pp. 15–22.

43 Eynern, G. von, *Freiheit in der Planwirtschaft*, in: *Das Sozialistische Jahrhundert* I, 7/8, Berlin, 1947, pp. 99 ff.

44 *Protokoll SPD-Parteitag 1947*, l.c., pp. 227 f.

45 *Protokoll der Verhandlungen des Parteitages der Sozialdemokratischen Partei Deutschlands vom 11. bis 14. Septmeber 1948 in Düsseldorf* (*Protokoll SPD-Parteitag 1948*), Hamburg, n.d., reprint, Berlin/Bonn, 1976, pp. 133–59, here p. 147.

46 Ibid., pp. 144–9.

47 Ibid., pp. 210 f.

48 Ibid., p. 162.

49 Ibid..

50 SPD (ed.), *Was wir wollen*, n.l., 1949, pp. 32 f.

51 Later description of Schumacher by Clay in the *New York Times*, 31 July 1949, cited in: Edinger, L. J., *Kurt Schumacher. Persönlichkeit und politisches Verhalten*, Cologne/Opladen, 1967, pp. 262 f.

52 *Sozialdemokratischer Pressedienst* (spd), no. 7, 12 June, no. 13, 20 July, no. 16, 7 Aug 1946.

53 Letter of spd to the editor in chief of various independent newspapers dated 26 Nov 1946, in: *Archiv der sozialen Demokratie* (AdsD), SPD – *Sozialdemokratischer Pressedienst*, signatory MF 1324, microfilm no. 001.

54 Schäfer, O., *Für die Wirtschaftsdemokratie*, in: *Hessische Nachrichten*, no. 12, 3 Nov 1945; Agartz, V., *Unternehmertum – Trotz Planung*, in: *Wirtschafts-Zeitung*, 24 May 1946; Idem, *Um den Neubau der Wirtschaft*, in: *Rheinische Zeitung*, 27 July 1946; Kronberger, P., *Warum Wirtschaftsdemokratie*, in: *Frankfurter Rundschau*, 9 April 1946; Idem, *6760 Milliarden Kriegskosten – Beweis für die Notwendigkeit sozialistischer Planwirtschaft*, in: *Hannoversche Presse*, 11 Oct 1946; Stampfer, F., *Klare Wirtschaftspolitik*, in: *Der Sozialdemokrat*, 25 Jan 1947; Skopp, P., *Wirtschaft und Verfassung – Auf dem Wege zur Wirtschaftsdemokratie*, in: *Neuer Vorwärts*, 2 Oct 1948; Zorn, R., *Von der regulierten Marktwirtschaft*, in: *Sozialistische Monatshefte* 4/1 and 4/2, Stuttgart, 1949; Idem, *Die regulierte Marktwirtschaft*, in: *Die Gegenwart*, 1 Feb 1949, p. 10; Weisser, G., *Wohin wird die westdeutsche Wirtschaft gesteuert?*, in: *Hamburger Echo*, 14 Oct 1949.

55 For a detailed overview of the elections taking place in Germany between 1946 and 1949, see appendix 14, p. 172.

56 SPD poster *Alle wahren Christen wählen Sozialisten*, sign. 6/PLKA003308, 1947, in: AdsD, *Plakatsammlung* (PS).

57 Pamphlets *Was wäre wenn…*, sign. 6/FLBL001634, 1947; *Der Grundinstinkt des deutschen Volkes ist antikapitalistisch*, sign. 6/FLBL001640, 1947; *Bereitet den Boden für neue Saaten*, sign. 6/FLBL001407, 1947, in: AdsD, *Flugblattsammlung* (FS).

58 *Die Sozialdemokratische Partei ist die Partei der Hilfe für alle Armen und Hilflosen*, sign. 6/FLBL001571, 1947, in: AdsD, PS.

59 *SPD – Sozialisierung!*, sign. 6/PLKA001642, 1947; *Gerechter Lohn durch Sozialisierung! Darum Sozialdemokraten*, sign. 6/PLKA002530, 1947; *Sozialisierung – Darum SPD*, sign. 6/FLBL001621, 1947; *Sozialismus ist kein Experiment…Sozialismus ist Gegenwartsaufgabe*, sign. 6/PLKA003800, 1947, in: AdsD, PS.

60 *Kein Glücksspiel mehr – deshalb selbständig politisch denken – SPD Sozialismus, Planwirtschaft, Demokratie*, sign. 6/PLKA001478, 1947, in: AdsD, PS.

61 Poster *CDU – gegen Vermassung für Verantwortung und soziale Wirtschaft*, sign. X-008-7, 1947, in: ACDP, PS, printed in: Langguth, G. (ed.), *Politik und Plakat – 50 Jahre Plakatgeschichte am Beispiel der CDU*, Bonn, 1995, p. 41.

62 Pamphlet *Lockerung der Bewirtschaftung?*, sign. 6/FLBL002129, July 1947 – Jan 1948, in: AdsD, FS.

63 Ibid., p. 6.

64 Poster *Für demokratische Mitbestimmung in der Wirtschaft oder kapitalistische Wirtschaftsdiktatur?*, sign. 6/FLBL002194, 1947, in: AdsD, FS.

65 Poster *Für Gemeinwirtschaft kämpft die CDU*, sign. X-009-86, 1947, in: ACDP, PS, printed in: Langguth, G. (ed.), l.c., p. 46.

66 *Gegen das Volk*, in: *Rheinische Zeitung*, 8 March 1947.

67 *Das ganze Volk wird entscheiden*, in: *Hannoversche Volksstimme*, 14 Feb 1947.

68 For election results, see appendix 15, pp. 173–6.

69 Schachtner, R., *Die deutschen Nachkriegswahlen*, Munich, 1956, pp. 48 ff.

70 Minutes of the meeting no. 2-6 of 22/23/25 July 1947, in: Salzmann, R. (ed.), l.c., pp. 45–53.

71 WB, l.c., pp. 25–36. Regarding the contention for the post of Director for Economics in the Bizonal Administration, see Ambrosius, G., l.c., pp. 86–95.

72 Miller, S.; Potthoff, H., l.c., p. 189.

73 Pamphlet *Klare Fronten*, sign. 6/FLBL001973, 1947, in: AdsD, FS. See also Schumacher's statement *Über Deutschland und Europa*, in: spd, *Parteitag-Sonderdienst*, no. 3, 1 July 1947, p. 4; further the article *Nach Frankfurt* by Herbert Kriedemann, in: spd, no. II/60, 29 July 1947, p. 2.

74 Record of the third plenary assembly of EC on 9 Aug 1947 by the delegate Gerhard Kreyssig (SPD), in: AdsD, NL Waldemar von Knoeringen, 371.

75 Weisz, Ch., *Einleitung*, in: AV$_{\text{BRD}}$, vol. 4, Munich, 1983, pp. 41 f.

76 *Frankfurt – eine Chance*, in: *Die Welt*, 7 June 1947, in: AdsD, NL Gerhard Kreyssig, no. 89/90; *Protokoll SPD-Parteitag 1948*, l.c., p. 150.

77 Stamm, C., l.c..

78 Pamphlet *Klare Fronten*, l.c..

79 Wettstein, K. P., l.c.; Schara, S., l.c.; Stamm, C., l.c..

80 Memorandum by Emil Kaufmann, 10 Dec 1947, in: BA, Z4, no. 130, pp. 1 ff.

81 Demand note, 5 Aug 1947, in: BA, Z4, no. 31.

82 Wilhelm Naegel (CDU) in: *7. Vollversammlung des Wirtschaftsrates* (VV WR) or seventh plenary meeting of EC on 30 Oct 1947, in: *Wörtliche Berichte über die 1.-40. Vollversammlung des Wirtschaftsrates des Vereinigten Wirtschaftsgebietes (Zweizonen-Wirtschaftsrat) in Frankfurt am Main* (WB VV), vol. 2, Wiesbaden/Frankfurt, 1947–9, p. 158; Viktor Agartz (SPD), in: Ibid., pp. 162 f.

83 Ibid., pp. 173 ff.; printed in: *Gesetz- und Verordnungsblatt des Wirtschaftsrats des Vereinigten Wirtschaftsgebietes* (WiGBl.) 1948, pp. 3–7.

84 WB VV, l.c., pp. 169 f.

85 Ibid., pp. 244 ff.

86 Contributions by Groß and Caspary, *Protokoll SPD-Parteitag 1946*, l.c., pp. 115/148.

87 See appendix 15, pp. 173–6.

88 *Protokoll SPD-Parteitag 1947*, l.c., p. 55.

89 Record of fourth plenary assembly of EC on 4 and 5 Sep 1947 by the delegate Kreyssig, printed in: Stamm, C., l.c., no. 17, p. 34; minutes of the 21st caucus on 15 Dec 1947, in: Stamm, C., l.c., no. 28, p. 68; on this issue, see also later record of the meeting of the party executive, the committee and the parliamentary group in the EC on 18 Feb 1948 by the delegate Gerhard Kreyssig (SPD), printed in: Stamm, C., l.c., no. 40, p. 96.

90 For particular polling days, see appendix 14, p. 172.

91 *Der Spiegel*, 6 March 1948, p. 4.

92 WB VV, l.c., p. 332.

93 WiGBl. 1948, pp. 27 f.

94 WB VV, l.c., p. 380.

95 Ibid., p. 386.

96 WB VV, l.c., pp. 436–42.

97 Note by Schlange-Schöningen, 23 April 1948, BA, Z6 I/17, p. 192.

98 WB VV, l.c., p. 455.

99 *Protokoll SPD-Parteitag 1948*, l.c., p. 163.

100 WB VV, l.c., p. 1264.

101 Ibid., p. 629.

102 WiGBl. 1948, pp. 59 f., preamble, attachment 1 and 2.

103 Eschenburg, T., l.c., 1983, p. 431.

104 Minutes of the eleventh meeting of the Administrative Council on 28 May and minutes of the fourth meeting of the Economic Committee of the *Länderrat* on 4 June 1948, in: BA, Z13, no. 87, folio 2 and Z4, no.162, folio 166, p. 4 respectively; minutes of 22nd meeting of the Economic Committee of EC on 10/11 June 1948, in: DBt PA.

105 WB VV, l.c., pp. 623 ff.

106 Ibid., p. 629.

107 Ibid..

108 Galbraith, J. K., l.c., 1948, pp. 94 ff.; Eschenburg, T., l.c., 1983, p. 430.

109 WB VV, l.c., p. 654.

110 Ibid., p. 630.

111 Ibid., p. 657. See also minutes of the meeting of the SPD parliamentary group on 16 April 1948, in: AdsD, holding Kurt Schumacher, no. J 88.

112 Ibid., pp. 623–38, 652–64.

113 Minutes of the public meeting of the *Länderrat*, 21 June 1948, in: BA, Z4, no. 531; *Protokoll SPD-Parteitag 1948*, l.c., p. 124.

114 Pünder, H., *Die Entstehung der Sozialen Marktwirtschaft*, in: Schröder, G.; Müller-Armack, A.; Hohmann, K.; Gross, J.; Altmann, R. (eds.), *Ludwig Erhard – Beiträge zu seiner politischen Biographie, Festschrift zum 75. Geburtstag*, Frankfurt a. Main, 1972, p. 190.

115 *Entwurf eines Gesetzes zur Neuordnung des Geldwesens* (*Homburger-Plan*). *Vorgelegt von der Verwaltung für Finanzen des VWGs*, Heidelberg, 1948.

116 Müller, G., l.c., p. 131.

117 Broadcast *Der Neue Kurs*, 21 June 1948, in: Erhard, L., l.c., 1992, pp. 62–8.

118 Regarding the intention to dismiss Erhard, see minutes of the 43rd caucus on 16 Aug 1948, in: Stamm, C., l.c., no. 68, pp. 168 ff.; circular no. 16/48 of the SPD parliamentary group in the EC on 24 Nov 1948, in: Ibid., no. 87, p. 215; WB, l.c., vol. 4, pp. 478 and 757.

119 WB VV, l.c., vol. 2, pp. 800 f.

120 Report *Frankfurter Wochenbericht* prepared by the envoy of the Bavarian CSU in the EC, 24–30 Jan 1948, in: ACSP, NL Anton Besold, no. 57.

121 Letter of chairman of the SPD district Hesse-South, Willi Knothe, to the *Parteivorstand* (PV) or party executive, 18 Aug 1948, in: AdsD, holding Kurt Schumacher, no. J 46; letter of SPD district East-Westphalia-Lippe to Kriedemann, 23 Aug 1948, in: AdsD, holding Kurt Schumacher, no. J 87; letter of the SPD parliamentary group in the *Landtag* of Lower Saxony to the parliamentary group in the EC, 2 Sep 1948, in: AdsD, *Landtagsfraktion Niedersachsen*, no. 53; circular of the press and propaganda department of the SPD party executive, 27 Aug 1948, in: AdsD, NL Erwin Schoettle, no. 185.

122 Letter of SPD party executive to Kreyssig, 14 Aug 1948, in: AdsD, NL Gerhard Kreyssig, no. 62.

123 *Die SPD in der Krise*, in: *Rheinischer Kurier*, 19 Sep 1948.

124 Letter of Käthe Richters (SPD Hesse-Kassel) to Kriedemann, 19 Oct 1948, in: AdsD, holding Kurt Schumacher, no. J 87.

125 Correspondence Kriedemann with the *Gewerkschaftsbund Württemberg-Baden*, 6 Nov 1947, in: AdsD, holding Kurt Schumacher, no. J 86.

126 Minutes of the 55th caucus on 9 Nov 1948, in: Stamm, C., l.c., no. 83, pp. 207 f.; WB, l.c., vol 3, p. 1127.

127 E.g. articles *Aus dem Wirtschaftsrat*, in: *Nordwestdeutsche Rundschau*, 3 Oct 1947; *Allerlei aus Frankfurt*, in: *Die Welt*, 28 Oct 1947; *Zwei Angestellte – ein Referent*, in: *Darmstädter Echo*, 29 April 1948.

128 For exact dates of the various elections in 1948, see appendix 14, p. 172.

129 Pamphlets *Was hineinkommt – bestimmt die Politik*, sign. 6/FLBL001859, 1948; *Volle Schaufenster, leere Geldtaschen!*, sign. 6/FLBL002668, n.d., in: AdsD, FS.

130 Pamphlets *Wenn das Preisthermometer steigt, dann denk daran…*, sign. 6/FLBL003812, 1948; *Warum haben wir Wucherpreise?*, sign. 6/FLBL003825, 1948; *Bilanz der „freien Wirtschaft"*, sign. 6/FLBL002636, 1948, in: AdsD, FS.

131 Pamphlets *Täglich 8000000 Arbeitsstunden*, sign. 6/FLBL002634, 1948, in: Ibid..

132 Montag, A., *Die Aera Erhard*, in: *Volks-Wirtschaft – Sozialdemokratischer Pressedienst*, vol. vw/III/30, 29 July 1948; Kriedemann, H., *Positive Wirtschaftspolitik*, in: spd, III/34, 26 Aug 1948; Idem, *Freie Wirtschaft und die*

Folgen, in: spd, III/106, 3 Sep 1948; Idem, *Deutsche Wirtschaft 1948*, in: spd *Sonderdienst*, 21 Dec 1948; Stampfer, F., *Zwang und Arbeit*, in: spd, III/139, 15 Nov 1948.

133 *Protokoll SPD-Parteitag 1948*, l.c., pp. 39 f.

134 Eschenburg, T., l.c., 1976, p. 430.

135 *Entscheidung der Massenprotestkundgebung der Bayerischen Gewerkschaften*, 25 Aug 1948, in: AdsD, NL Erwin Schoettle, no. 35.

136 Beier, G., *Der Demonstrations- und Generalstreik vom 12. November 1948*, Frankfurt am Main/Cologne, 1975, p. 41. In connection with this, see also the claim for socialisation of individual companies, e.g. by the *Elektrizitäts-Aktiengesellschaft Mitteldeutschland*, 14 Sep 1948, in: DBt PA, 2/717.

137 *Neuer Vorwärts*, I/11, 20 Nov 1948.

138 Declaration of party board, in: *Neuer Vorwärts*, I/10, 13 Nov 1948, p. 1.

139 *Streitgespräch Erhard-Nölting*, in: *Rheinische Post*, 15 Nov 1948.

140 Recker, M.-L., *Wahlen und Wahlkämpfe in der Bundesrepublik Deutschland, 1949-1969*, in: Ritter, G. A. (ed.), *Wahlen und Wahlkämpfe in Deutschland: Von den Anfängen im 19. Jahrhundert bis zur Bundesrepublik*, Düsseldorf, 1997, p. 296.

141 Broadcasting address by Schumacher, 21 April 1949, in: *Stiftung Deutsches Rundfunk Archiv* (DRA), *Stimmen des 20. Jahrhundert: Nach bestem Wissen und Gewissen – Die Beratungen zum Grundgesetz im Parlamentarischen Rat 1948/49*, Frankfurt, 1998, no. 17.

142 Election posters *Mit Professor Erhard (CDU) in den Abgrund!*, sign. 6/PLKA025087, 1949; *Prof. Erhard – CDU ruiniert die Wirtschaft…Wer SPD wählt – wählt den Aufbau*, sign. 6/PLKA009971, 1949; *Wir verlangen Antwort!... Das deutsche Volk will endlich die Wahrheit wissen. Es hat genug vom kapitalistischen Wirtschaftssystem und will endlich einen Sozialismus der Tat! SPD*, sign. 6/PLKA008771, 1949, in: AdsD, PS.

143 Pamphlet *„Wirtschaft Horatio" Ein Drama in 5 Akten*, sign. 6/FLBL002609, 1949, in: AdsD, FS.

144 Speech held by Schumacher in Koblenz, 28 July 1949, in: AdsD, holding Kurt Schumacher, no. J 48.

145 Kriedemann, H., *Bilanz der „freien Wirtschaft"*, in: spd, IV/54, 9 May 1949; Grote-Mißmahl, U., *Gewerkschaftliche Forderungen*, in: *Die Freiheit*, 16 June 1949; Gleitze, B., *Gefahren der freien Marktwirtschaft*, in: *Lübecker Freie Presse*, 1 Nov 1949.

146 Poster *Katholische Wählerinnen und Wähler…Viele Tausende gläubiger Katholiken sind Mitglied der Sozialdemokratischen Partei…Es widerspricht dem Christentum und der Lehre der katholischen Kirche, den Kapitalismus zu verteidigen*, sign. 6/PLKA007358, 1949, in: AdsD, PS. See also Benz, W., l.c., 1985, p. 266.

147 Schumacher's speeches in Hamburg on 30 July and on the Römerberg in Frankfurt on 3 Aug 1949, in: AdsD, holding Kurt Schumacher, no. Q 10.

148 *„Für ein freies Deutschland in einem neuen Europa", Wahlaufruf der Sozialdemokratischen Partei Deutschlands, Sonderversand*, in: *SPD-Pressedienst*, 1949.

149 SPD (ed.), l.c., pp. 32 f.

150 Speech given by Schumacher in Bremen, 14 Jan 1948, in: DRA, 76 U 3459/4.

Chapter 2.2

1 Adenauer in his first government policy statement on 20 Sep 1949, in: DRA, *Stimmen des 20. Jahrhunderts: Wir sind wieder wer*, Frankfurt am Main, 2000, no. 2. See also Henning, F.-W., l.c., p. 26.

2 Wieck, H. G., *Die Entstehung der CDU und die Wiedergründung des Zentrums im Jahre 1945*, in: *Beiträge zur Geschichte des Parlamentarismus und der politischen Parteien*, vol. 2, Düsseldorf, 1953; Schulz, G., *Die CDU – Merkmale ihres Aufbaus*, in: Lange, M. G.; Schulz, G.; Schütz, K. *et al., Parteien in der Bundesrepublik. Studien zur Entwicklung der deutschen Parteien bis zur Bundestagswahl 1953*, in: *Schriften des Instituts für politische Wissenschaften*, vol. 6, Stuttgart/Düsseldorf, 1953; Deuerlein, E., l.c., 1957b; Mintzel, A., l.c., 1975; Becker, W.; Morsey, R. (eds.), *Christliche Demokratie in Europa. Grundlagen und Entwicklungen seit dem 19. Jahrhundert*, Cologne/Vienna, 1988; Buchstab, G.; Otto, K. (eds.), l.c., 1990; Kleinmann, H.-O., l.c., 1993; Baumgärtel, M. (ed.), l.c., pp. 69–89.

3 Regarding the interpretation of Thomas Aquinas' (1225–74) social doctrine and the definition of Christian Socialism see Uhl, B., *Die Idee des Christlichen Sozialismus in Deutschland 1945-1947*, Mainz, 1975; Uertz, R., l.c., pp. 7–22; Langner, A., l.c., pp. 27 ff.

4 Ortlieb, H. D., *Der sozialistische Gedanke unter liberalistischer Kritik*, in: Idem, *Wandlungen des Sozialismus. Fünf Aufsätze zur Gegenwartslage des Sozialismus*, Hamburg 1947, p. 9.

5 While Uertz refers to the *Köln-Walberberger Kreis*, it is important to distinguish between the *Kölner* and the *Walberberger Kreis* with regard to the socio-political conception; cf. Uertz, R., l.c., pp. 7–22; Bücker, V., *Der Kölner Kreis und seine Konzeption für ein Deutschland nach Hitler*, in: *Historisch-politische Mitteilungen* 2, Cologne, 1995, pp. 49–82. Concerning the socio-economic agenda, however, this distinction is negligible.

6 Welty, E., *Die Entscheidung in die Zukunft. Grundsätze und Hinweise zur Neuordnung im deutschen Lebensraum*, Heidelberg, 1946; Idem, *Christlicher Sozialismus*, in: *Die neue Ordnung* 1, 1946/47, pp. 39 ff. and 132 ff.

7 *Kölner Leitsätze – Vorläufiger Entwurf zu einem Programm der Christlich Demokratischen Union Deutschlands* put forward by the Christian Democrats in Cologne on 24 June 1945; principles printed in: Hintze, P. (ed.), *Die CDU Parteiprogramme: Eine Dokumentation der Ziele und Aufgaben*, Bonn, 1995, pp. 9–12.

8 Written statement *Sozialismus* by (presumably) Michael Rott, in: ACDP, NL Michael Rott, I-101; the speech *Der soziale und sittliche Geist in der Demokratie* by Karl Arnold in Düsseldorf on 24 Nov 1945, in: StBKAH, NL Konrad Adenauer, 08.56; Johannes Albers' address *Die Aufgabe der Christlich Demokratischen Union im Leben des deutschen Volkes*, printed in: *Schriftenreihe der Christlich-Demokratischen Union des Rheinlandes* 2, Cologne, 1945, pp. 5 ff.

9 Kaiser, J., *Um Deutschlands Schicksal*, in: *Deutschland und die Union, Die Berliner Tagung 1946. Reden und Aussprache*, in: *Schriftenreihe der CDU Berlin: Wege in die neue Zeit*, no. 4, Berlin, 1946, pp. 9 ff.; Kaiser's speech *Der soziale und*

staatspolitische Wille der Christlich-Demokratischen Union Deutschlands in Berlin on 13 Feb 1946, in: StBKAH, NL Konrad Adenauer, 08.56; the presentation given by Kaiser at the party conference of the CDU in Berlin on 13 Feb 1946, printed in: Albers, J., *Grundgedanken zum Thema Christlicher Sozialismus*, p. 8, in: *Stadtarchiv Köln* (SAK), NL Leo Schwering. See also Conze, W., *Jakob Kaiser. Politiker zwischen Ost und West 1945-1949*, Stuttgart/Berlin/Cologne/Mainz, 1969.

10 *Gründungsaufgruf der CDU „Deutsches Volk!"*, Berlin, 26 June 1945.

11 Later appeal by the CDU in South Wuerttemberg-Hohenzollern on 23 June 1946, in: Flechtheim, O. K. (ed.), l.c., vol. II, Berlin, 1962, pp. 47 ff.; *Suedwestdeutsche Union*, vol. 2, no. 1, Jan 1947, p. 1; Ambrosius, G., l.c., pp. 15 f.

12 Dirks, W., *Das Wort Sozialismus*, in: FH 1/7, 1946, p. 639.

13 Idem, *Das Abendland und der Sozialismus*, in: FH 1/3, 1946, pp. 67–76; Idem, *Die Zweite Republik*, in: FH 1/1, 1946, pp. 23 ff.; Kogon, E., *Der Weg zu einem Sozialismus der Freiheit in Deutschland*, in: FH 2/9, 1947, pp. 877–96.

14 Kogon, E., l.c., 1947, p. 889.

15 *Frankfurter Leitsätze*, printed in: Flechtheim, O. K. (ed.), l.c., vol. II., Berlin, 1962, pp. 36 ff.

16 Regarding Konrad Adenauer's (1876–1967) socio-political and economic views in the style of the ordo-liberal Freiburg School and Wilhelm Röpke in particular, see Rodens, F., *Konrad Adenauer – Der Mensch und Politiker*, Munich/Zurich, 1963; Schwarz, H.-P., l.c., 1986. Further, see the contributions *Visionär, Taktiker, Patriot* by Angela Merkel, *Konrad Adenauer und die Soziale Marktwirtschaft* by Gerhard Stoltenberg, *Adenauer und das Christentum* by Otto B. Roegele, and, *Die politische Sprache Konrad Adenauers* by Wolfgang Bergsdorf, in: *Die Politische Meinung, Zum 125. Geburtstag von Konrad Adenauer*, no. 373, edited for the KAS, Sankt Augin, 2000, pp. 7–10, 21–4, 79–88, 97–104.

17 For an analysis of Adenauer's attitude towards Christian Socialism, see Schwarz, H.-P., l.c., 1966, pp. 436 ff.; Uertz, R., l.c., p. 75; Wenzel, R., l.c.; Ambrosius, G., l.c., 24–32. See also Adenauer's later speeches on 19 Nov 1946 and 28 March 1947, in: HStAD, RW 26-1026 and StBKAH, NL Konrad Adenauer, 06.04.

18 Notes by secretary general of the CDP, Karl Zimmermann, in: HStAD, RWV 26-2363.

19 Uertz, R., l.c., p. 47; Morsey, R., *Konrad Adenauer und der Weg zur Bundesrepublik Deutschland 1946-1949*, in: Idem (ed.), *Konrad Adenauer und die Bundesrepublik Deutschland*, in: *Rhöndorfer Gespräche*, vol. 3, Stuttgart/Zurich, 1979, p. 13; Pohl, H. (ed.), l.c., p. 16.

20 Minutes of the meeting on 5 Oct, in: HStAD, RWV 26-2364.

21 Party platform of the CDP, in: StBKAH, NL Konrad Adenauer, 08.06.

22 Zimmermann, K., *Erste Reichstagung der Christlich-Demokratischen Union in Godesberg am 14., 15. und 16. Dezember 1945*, in: *Schriftenreihe der Christlich-Demokratischen Union des Rheinlandes* 3, Cologne, 1946, pp. 7 ff. Regarding the subsequent debate among Christian Democrats in Berlin about the application

of the term Christian Socialism, see the minutes of the meeting on 18 Dec 1945, in: BA, NL Jakob Kaiser, no. 88.

23 Regarding the naming, see Baumgärtel, M. (ed.), l.c., pp. 76–90.

24 Memo regarding party formation, Munich, 17 July 1954, pp. 8 ff., in: ACSP, NL Josef Müller.

25 *Gründungsprogramm der Partei der Christlich-sozialen Einigung in Bayern* (later renamed as CSU), 15 Nov 1945, in: ACSP, NL Josef Müller, no. 161.

26 *Die zehn Punkte der Christlich-Sozialen Union 1945*, in: ACSP, NL Wilhelm Arnold, no. 4. Further printed in: *Gründungsurkunde Programme seit 1945* (in the following *Gründungsurkunde*) edited by the CSU, n.l., n.d..

27 Archival sources regarding study groups, in: ACSP, NL Josef Müller, no. 38.

28 Leaflet *Programm der Christlich Sozialen Union* edited by the journalist Georg Pix and printed by the *Süddeutsche Zeitung* in Munich, n.d., in: ACSP, NL Hannes Schinagl, no. 2; handbill *Aufruf*, in: ACSP, *Handakte* (HA) Werner Dollinger; handout *Aufruf der Christlich-Sozialen Union an alle Deutschen*, 1946, in: ACSP, *Flugblattsammlung* (Fslg.), *Flugblatt* (FL) 1945–8, no. 3.

29 Resolution *Die fünf Punkte der Union* passed at the first party convention in Munich on 17 May 1946, in: ACSP, *Landesgeschäftsführer-Parteivorstand* (LGF-PV), no. 2.

30 Section 1 article 151 para. 1 and 2, articles 152 and 154, section 2 article 160 para. 1 and 2 in: *Verfassung des Freistaates Bayern*, published in: *Bayerisches Gesetz- und Verordnungsblatt*, 8 Dec 1946.

31 Article 15, in: *Die dreissig Punkte der Union. Richtlinien der Christlich-Sozialen Union in Bayern zur Überwindung der inneren und äusseren Not unseres Volkes* decided upon at the second party convention in Eichstätt on 14/15 Dec 1946 and edited by the party chairman Josef Müller under Political Party Publications Licence No. US-E-1, printed in: *Gründungsurkunde*, l.c., p. 35; ACSP, DS 1/3.

32 Section IV *Wirtschaftsordnung* or economic order, para. 1-5, in: *Grundsatz-Programm der Christlich-Sozialen Union in Bayern*, 14/15 Dec 1946, printed in: *Gründungsurkunde*, l.c., p. 23.

33 Calling of public meetings no. 2966, 2962, 3192, 3191, in: ACSP, *Plakatsammlung* (Pslg.).

34 Hurwitz, H., l.c., 1972, p. 171.

35 Party organ *Der Gerade Weg – Organ der Christlich-Sozialen Union*, Munich, 1948, in: ACSP, Z-LL.

36 Ambrosius, G., l.c., pp. 16 ff.; Wenzel, R., l.c., p. 39; Müller, G., pp. 26–53.

37 Pütz, H. (ed.), l.c., p. 87.

38 In contradiction to Müller, G., l.c., p. 26.

39 Schwarz, H.-P., l.c., 1986, p. 492.

40 Concept presented to the committee for the formulation of a CDU party platform in Herford on 22/23 Jan 1946, in: StBKAH, NL Konrad Adenauer, 08.07; final party platform printed in: Flechtheim, O. K. (ed.), l.c., vol. II., Berlin, 1962, pp. 48–53.

41 Statement by Adenauer in Cologne on 24 March 1946, printed in: Adenauer, K.; Poppinga, A. (ed.), *"Seid wach für die kommenden Jahre". Grundsätze, Erfahrungen, Einsichten*, Bergisch Gladbach, 1997, p. 235.

42 Adenauer on the programme of the CDU on 6 March 1946, in: DRA, *Stimmen des 20. Jahrhunderts: Überleben im Nachkriegsdeutschland*, Frankfurt, 2000, no. 7.

43 Schulz, G., *Konrad Adenauers gesellschaftspolitische Vorstellungen*, in: Pohl, H. (ed.), l.c., p. 168.

44 Relevant document, in: BA, NL Jakob Kaiser, no. 57.

45 StBKAH, NL Konrad Adenauer, 08.54.

46 Speeches held in Cologne on 24 March, in Bonn on 7 April and in Wuppertal on 5 May 1946, in: Adenauer, K., *Reden 1917-1967. Eine Auswahl*, edited by Hans-Peter Schwarz, Stuttgart, 1975, or rather HStAD, RWV 26-1051.

47 *Sieben-Punkte-Entschliessung*, in: BA, NL Friedrich Holzapfel, no. 249.

48 Pamphlet of the CDU in Essen, in: Ibid.. See also the precedent *Entschliessung zur Frage der Wirtschaftsverfassung* adopted in Neuenkirchen on 2 Aug and the resolution *Zehn-Punkte Wirtschaftsprogramm der CDU* drafted in Herford on 19 Aug 1946, in: ACDP, NL Georg Stickrodt, I-085-047 or rather BA, NL Friedrich Holzapfel, no. 249.

49 Circular to the CDU party members in the British sovereign territory, 26 Aug 1946, in: Ibid..

50 For particular polling days in 1946, see appendix 14, p. 172.

51 *Grundstein für eine neue Wirtschaftsdemokratie*, in: zonal CDU organ *Informations-dienst* 1/46, n.d..

52 Deuerlein, E., l.c., 1957b, p. 79. See also Pohl, H. (ed.), l.c., p. 18 and Ambrosius, G., l.c., p. 22.

53 Poster *Mit uns bau wieder auf – Eiserner Wille und das nötige Gottvertrauen haben es immer noch am sichersten und besten geschafft*, sign. X-024-155, 1946; placards for local elections in North Rhine-Westphalia on 15 Sep and 13 Oct 1946 *Die Union – Die Sammlung aller Christen auf der politischen Ebene*, sign. X-017-1, 1946 and *Gott…im Dienst der öffentlichen Sache – Das ist das Grundgesetz der CDU*, sign. X-017-30, 1946; posters *Die Frau als Hüterin der christlichen Familie*, sign. X-017-3, 1946; *Die Not überwinden – Hilf mit in der CDU*, sign. X-017-4, 1946, in: ACDP, PS, printed in: Langguth, G. (ed.), l.c., pp. 30, 32/33, 53.

54 Posters *Nie wieder Tod und Zerstörung*, sign. X-002-850, n.d.; *Für Wahrheit und Recht*, sign. 024-184, 1946; *Menschenwürde, Recht und Freiheit*, sign. X-024-178, 1946; placards for local elections in North Rhine-Westphalia on 15 Sep and 13 Oct 1946 *Ein neues, freies Deutschland*, sign. X-017-71, 1946; *Alle Kraft dem Wiederaufbau*, sign. X-017-50, 1946; *Gerechte Verteilung der Lasten beim Wiederaufbau*, sign. X-020-21, 1946; poster for communal elections in Bremen on 13 Oct 1946 *CDU – Die Partei für den Aufbau*, sign. X-005-1, 1946; placard for local elections in Lower Saxony on 15 Sep 1946 *Mit der CDU gegen Zersplitterung für den Neuaufbau Deutschlands*, sign. X-016-4; posters for local elections in Schleswig-Holstein on 15 Sep and 13 Oct 1946 *Wieder Fesseln? Wieder Diktatur? Für Deine Freiheit bürgt die CDU*, sign. X-020-4, 1946 and *CDU – Das Tor zur wahren Demokratie*, sign. X-020-1, 1946, in: Ibid., pp. 22–66.

55 Placards *CDU – Christentum, Demokratie, Sozialismus dies sind unsere Ziele*, sign. X-024-171, 1946 and *Die CDU: Die politische Einheit des christlichen Volkes – Neu und gross sind auch ihre Ziele: … Sozialismus der Tat aus Christlicher Verantwortung*, sign. X-017-29, 1946, in: Ibid., pp. 47 and 50. Furthermore, see the public statement *Deutschland wird demokratisch sein oder es wird nicht sein – Deutschland wird christlich sein oder es wird Erschütterungen seines Daseins nicht mehr durchhalten – Deutschland wird sozialistisch sein oder es ist den Nöten unserer Zeit nicht mehr gewachsen* on CDUD poster *Es geht um Deutschland*, sign. X-024-193, 1946, in: Ibid., p. 23.

56 Appeals *Adenauer und die Politik der CDU* in Dortmund on 28 July 1946, sign. X-017-83, 1946 and *Jakob Kaiser spricht über Christlichen Sozialismus* in Dortmund on 6 Oct 1946, sign. X-017-81, 1946, in: Ibid., p. 48.

57 Poster *Aus den Leitsätzen der Union … Eine planvoll gelenkte Wirtschaft muss Allen ausreichende Nahrung, Kleidung und Wohnung sichern*, sign. X-017-28, 1946, in: Ibid., p. 45.

58 Adenauer, K., l.c., 1983, p. 387. Regarding exact dates of the seven regional elections in 1947, see appendix 14, p. 172.

59 Pütz, H. (ed.), l.c., pp. 260–78.

60 Placard *Die Christlich-Soziale Union warnt* and broadsheet *Die Union kämpft für/gegen*, in: ACSP, Fslg., FL 1945-1948, no. 8 and 24.

61 Draft law for the *Gesetz zur Überführung von Konzernen und sonstigen gemeinwirtschaftlichen Unternehmungen in Gemeineigentum* submitted to the city council of Berlin on 12 Dec 1946.

62 Economic proposal *Die CDU zur Neuordnung der Wirtschaft*, n.d., in: HStAD, NL Guido Ziersch, RWN 116 no. 3 folio 293–7. Regarding the interal decision-making process to substitute the term socialisation by *Gemeinwirtschaft*, see Schwering, L., *Auf der Suche nach dem neuen Kurs – Zur Erinnerung an die Gründung der CDU im Rheinland vor 25 Jahren*, Cologne, 1970, pp. 116 f.

63 Report entitled *Stellungnahme der CDU zur Gemeinwirtschaft*, in: BA, NL Friedrich Holzapfel, no. 249.

64 *Informationsdienst* 3/47, n.d..

65 *Ahlener Programm*, in: Heck, B. (ed.), *Die CDU und ihr Programm – Programme, Erklärungen, Entschliessungen*, Melle/Sankt Augin, 1979, pp. 3–5.

66 *Programm von Ahlen*, para. II *Neue Struktur der deutschen industriellen Wirtschaft*, in: Ibid., pp. 5–7.

67 However, dissent regarding Adenauer's actual contribution to the formulation of the *Ahlener Programm* prevails. While Hans-Peter Schwarz refers to the 'Adenauer Programm', Bruno Heck states: 'One can say that the *Ahlener Programm* was not Adenauer's programme.' Cf. Schwarz, H.-P., l.c., 1986; Heck, B., *Adenauer und die Christlich-Demokratische Union Deutschlands*, in: *Konrad Adenauer und seine Zeit. Politik und Persönlichkeit des ersten Bundeskanzlers. Beiträge von Weg- und Zeitgenossen*, vol. I, Stuttgart, 1976, p. 196. Regardless of this academic dispute, it is commonly accepted that Konrad Adenauer significantly influenced the programmatic debate and preliminary work resulting in the party platform adopted in Ahlen.

68 Uertz, R., l.c., p. 185.

69 Heidenheimer, A. J., *Adenauer and the CDU. The Rise of the Leader and the Integration of the Party*, The Hague, 1960, p. 128.

70 Pütz, H. (ed.), l.c., p. 149; Woerdehoff, B., *Die Adenauersche Mumie*, in: *Die Zeit*, Feb 1987.

71 *Christliche Demokratie in Deutschland. Analysen und Dokumente zur Geschichte und Programmatik der Christlich-Demokratischen Union Deutschlands und der Jungen Union Deutschlands*, edited by the KAS (*Handbücher der Politischen Akademie Eichholz*, vol. 7), Melle, 1978, pp. 21 ff.

72 E.g. socialisation debate in the parliament of North Rhine-Westphalia on 4 March, in: *Landtagsdrucksache* (LD) I 109-114 printed in: John, A., *Ahlen und das Ahlener Programm. Dokumente, Ereignisse, Erinnerungen*, Ahlen, 1977, pp. 127 ff. and speech by Adenauer in Wuppertal on 10 March 1947, in: *Rheinische Post*, 15 March 1947. See also *Grundzüge einer bayer. Wirtschaftspolitik*, in: *Mitteilungen der Christlich-Sozialen Union*, 22 Feb 1947, in: ACSP, NL Wilhelm Arnold, 5.1.

73 Placards *CDU gegen Vermassung für Verantwortung und soziale Wirtschaft*, sign. X-008-7, 1947; *Vertriebene – Eure Not ist unsere Not*, sign. X-008-1, 1947; *Vertriebene, nicht verzweifeln!*, sign. X-009-27, 1947, in: ACDP, PS, printed in: Langguth, G. (ed.), l.c., pp. 40, 55–6.

74 Posters for *Landtag* elections in Lower Saxony and North Rhine-Westphalia *Die CDU – Die Brücke in eine neue Zeit!*, sign. X-008-6, 1947; *Neuen Ufern zu mit der CDU*, sign. X-012-7, 1947; *Eine grosse Partei … nach christlichen Grundsätzen in demokratischem Geiste*, sign. X-009-6, 1947; *Auch in der Politik gelten die Zehn Gebote*, sign. X-009-3, 1947; election posters in Rhineland-Palatinate *Ich rufe die Jugend von Rheinland-Pfalz – Hilf mit am Aufbau der Heimat*, sign. X-010-5, 1947, in: ACDP, PS, printed in: Langguth, G. (ed.), l.c., pp. 21, 26, 31, 33, 53.

75 *Für Gemeinwirtschaft kämpft die CDU*, sign. X-009-86, 1947, in: Ibid., p. 46.

76 Kaff, B. (ed.), *Die Unionsparteien 1946-1950. Protokolle der Arbeitsgemeinschaft der CDU/CSU Deutschlands und der Konferenzen der Landesvorsitzenden*, Düsseldorf, 1991.

77 Ambrosius, G., l.c., p. 87; Baumgärtel, M. (ed.), l.c., pp. 137, 571, 574; Müchler, G., *Zum frühen Verhältnis von CDU und CSU*, in: *Politische Studien* 23/202, Munich, 1972, p. 609. See also Idem, *CDU/CSU. Das schwierige Bündnis*, Munich, 1976.

78 Holzapfel in the first plenary meeting of the EC on 25 June 1947, in: WB VV, l.c., p. 8.

79 Regarding composition of the first EC, see appendix 6, p. 157.

80 WB VV, l.c., pp. 25–36.

81 Minutes of the caucuses no. 2–6 of 22/23/25 July 1947, in: Salzmann, R. (ed.), l.c., pp. 45–53.

82 Minutes of the caucus no. 1 of 21 July 1947, in: Ibid., p. 44.

83 Letter by Adenauer to then Bavarian Prime Minister, Hans Ehard, 23 July 1947, in: BayHStA, NL Hans Ehard, no. 1610.

84 Höpfinger, R., *Bayerische Lebensbilder 2 – Biografien, Erinnerungen, Zeugnisse: Franz Josef Strauß, Ludwig Bölkow, Sepp Hort*, edited by the HSS, Munich, 2004, p. 131.

85 WB VV, l.c., pp. 38 f.

86 Semler, J., *Wirtschaftslage und Wirtschaftsgestaltung*, in: *Fragen der Zeit, Schriftenreihe der Christlich-Sozialen Union Bayerns* 1, Munich, 1946. See also minutes of the caucus no. 18 of 12 Oct 1947, in: Salzmann, R. (ed.), l.c., p. 86.

87 Minutes of the caucus no. 6 of 25 July 1947, in: Salzmann, R. (ed.), l.c., p 53.

88 Letter by Adenauer to the *Kreistag* delegate August Osberghaus, 2 Sep 1947, in: StBKAH, NL Konrad Adenauer, 07.16.

89 Letter by Adenauer to then Director of the Administration for Nutrition, Agriculture and Forestry, Schlange-Schöningen, 21 Aug 1947, in: Ibid., 08.61.

90 Pütz, H. (ed.), l.c., pp. 330–7.

91 Letter by Adenauer to Holzapfel dated 16 Aug and the writing to Schlange-Schöningen dated 21 Aug 1947, in: Adenauer, K., l.c., 1983, pp. 45–54.

92 Morsey, R. (ed.), l.c., p. 77.

93 Minutes of the caucuses, in: Salzmann, R. (ed.), l.c., pp. 43–442. See also the statement by Adenauer in a speech delivered in Heidelberg on 21 July 1949, in: Adenauer, K., l.c., 1975, p. 141.

94 Petitions by various party members and the initiative by the Hessian CDU on 24 Oct 1947, in: BA, NL Friedrich Holzapfel, no. 269. See also the resolution by *Junge Union*, 10 Aug 1947, in: AdsD, NL Gerhard Kreyssig, no. 62 and the letter by Bavarian Prime Minister Hans Ehard to Adenauer in Aug 1947, in: BayHStA, NL Hans Ehard, no. 1610. Even the editor in chief of the business section of the *Neue Zeit* (Union publishing), Hans E. Roos, suggested an economic association in order to coordinate the economic policy between the party and parliamentary group; cf. letter to Paul Binder (CDU), 14 Oct 1947, in: ACDP, NL Paul Binder, I-105-022.

95 Müller, G., l.c., pp. 278–82.

96 The former district administrator in Lower Franconia, Hanns Seidel (1901–61), succeeded the resigning Social Democrat Rudolf Zorn (1893–1966) on 20 Sep 1947.

97 Seidel, H., *Zeitprobleme. Gesammelte Aufsätze und Vorträge*, Aschaffenburg, 1960a, pp. 38–41, 44 ff.; Klump, R., *Historische Wurzeln*, in: Vaubel, R.; Barbier, H. D. (eds.), *Handbuch Marktwirtschaft*, Pfullingen, 1986, p. 139; Groß, H. F., *Hanns Seidel 1901-1961: Eine politische Biographie*, edited by the HSS, Munich, 1992, pp. 68–72.

98 *Wirtschafts- und Sozialprogramm der CSU*, 31 Aug 1947, printed in: Fait, B.; Mintzel, A.; Schlemmer, Th. (eds.), l.c., Munich, 1993, vol. 3, pp. 1723–8.

99 Minutes of the meeting of the Council of Ministers on 24 Sep 1947, in: BayHStA, *Akten der Bayerischen Staatskanzlei* (BayStKA), no. 111525/1.

100 Seidel, H., l.c., 1960a, pp. 28 f. Regarding his concern with public opinion, see Seidel, H., *Vom Mythos der öffentlichen Meinung*, Aschaffenburg, 1961.

101 Speech by Seidel in the Bavarian Parliament on 5 Dec 1947, in: *Verhandlungen des Bayerischen Landtags, Stenographische Berichte* (in the following LT SB), Munich, 1947, pp. 333–6. See also Seidel's broadcast address on 28 Sep 1948, in: ACSP, NL Hanns Seidel, no. 1. Further, Seidel, H., l.c., 1960a, pp. 107 f.

102 Minutes of the meeting of the Council of Ministers on 19 Jan 1948, in: Ibid., no. 111526.

103 *Der Rücktritt des sozialdemokratischen Wirtschaftsministers schlägt – nach der Frankfurter Entscheidung – die zweite Bresche in das Primat der SPD für die Wirtschaft*, in: *Süddeutsche Zeitung*, 23 Sep 1947.

104 Speech by Seidel in the Bavarian Parliament on 28 Nov 1947, in: LT SB, l.c., p. 256; also in: ACSP, NL Hanns Seidel, no. 1a. Regarding Seidel's ethical attitude in politics and economics, see Seidel, H., *Wirtschaftspolitik und Soziale Ethik*, Munich 1952; Ibid., *Weltanschauung und Politik. Ein Beitrag zum Verständnis der Christlich-Sozialen Union in Bayern*, Munich, 1960b.

105 Term used in a talk given by Seidel at the chamber of industry and commerce in Bayreuth on 13 Oct 1948, in: Ibid., no. 1; see also the article in the party journal *Der Gerade Weg – Organ der Christlich-Sozialen Union* on 30 Nov 1948, in: ACSP, Z-LL. Further, Seidel, H., l.c., 1960a, pp. 29/109.

106 Statement on 12 Nov 1947, in: ACSP, NL Hanns Seidel, no. 1.

107 Seidel on 28 Nov and 5 Dec 1947, in: LT SB, l.c., pp. 256/334.

108 Erhard, L., *Politischer Föderalismus und wirtschaftlicher Zentralismus. Aufgaben und Grenzen zentraler Wirtschaftsverwaltungsstellen*, in: *Der Wirtschaftsspiegel* 1/2, Jan/Feb 1947; Miksch, L., *Gedanken zur Wirtschaftsordnung*, in: *Der Wirtschaftsspiegel*, vol. 18 (2), Nov 1947; Müller-Armack, A., *Zur Diagnose unserer wirtschaftlichen Lage*, Bielefeld, 1947; Nölting, E.; Kromphardt, W., *Marktspaltung und Kernplanung in der Volkswirtschaft*, in: *Dortmunder Schriften zur Sozialforschung* 3, Dortmund, 1947; Ortlieb, H. D., *Wandlungen des Sozialismus. Fünf Aufsätze zur Gegenwartslage des Sozialismus*, Hamburg, 1947; Rasch, H., *Grundlagen der Wirtschaftsverfassung*, Godesberg, 1948; Weber, A.; Nölting, E. (eds.), *Sozialistische Wirtschaftsordnung. Beiträge zur Diskussion*, Hamburg, 1948.

109 *Landesversammlung der CSU am 24. und 25.1.1948 in Marktredwitz*, printed in: Fait, B.; Mintzel, A.; Schlemmer, Th. (eds.), l.c., Munich, 1993, vol. 2, pp. 1500–14; minutes of the caucus no. 35 of 23 Feb 1948, in: Salzmann, R. (ed.), l.c., p. 141.

110 Minutes of the caucus no. 37 of 24 Feb 1948, in: Ibid., p. 148.

111 Minutes of the CDU/CSU caucus no. 43 and 44 of 1 and 2 March 1948, in: Ibid., pp. 156 f.; also Müller, G., l.c., p. 285; Pünder, T., l.c., pp. 147 f.

112 WB VV, l.c., pp. 8 and 169. See also Ambrosius, G., l.c., p. 156.

113 Minutes of the caucus no. 35 of 23 Feb 1948, in: Salzmann, R. (ed.), l.c., p. 143.

114 Minutes of the fourteenth meeting of the committee on industry and trade, 3 March 1948, in: BA, Z4, no. 11.

115 Risse, R., *Alltag mit Erhard*, in: Schröder, G.; Müller-Armack, A.; Hohmann, K.; Gross, J.; Altmann, R. (eds.), l.c., p. 591. See also the statement by Alex Haffner at the fourteenth plenary meeting of the EC on 21 April 1948, in: WB VV, l.c., pp. 445–6.

116 Statement by Erhard, in: Ibid., pp. 426 ff. It is interesting to note that this speech was already published in the official journal of the Bizonal VfW; cf. Erhard, L., *Wirtschaftspolitik im Zeichen der Währungsreform und der Aktivierung des Marshallplans*, in: *Wirtschaftsverwaltung* 1, May 1948, pp. 4–15.

117 Party platform *Stellungnahme der CDU zur Wirtschaftsordnung*, 3 May 1948, in: StBKAH, NL Konrad Adenauer, 07.18.

118 Speech by Theodor Blank (CDU) at the eighteenth plenary meeting of the EC on 18 June 1948, in: WB VV, l.c., pp. 655 f.

119 Minutes of the party congress in Recklinghausen on 28/29 Aug, in: Pütz, H. (ed.), l.c., pp. 657–712.

120 Broadcast address by Seidel, 28 Sep 1948, in: ACSP, NL Hanns Seidel, no. 1. Further, Seidel's advocacy for a Christian economic order; cf. *Um die künftige Wirtschaftsform*, in: *Deutschland-Union-Dienst* (DUD) – *Pressedienst der CDU/CSU*, 28 Dec 1948, in: ACDP, *Sammlung Bundesgeschäftsstelle* (Slg. BGS), VII-005-59/2. Regarding demands on the part of public and trade unions, see Laitenberger, V., l.c., pp. 73 f. The CSU even distanced itself from Erhard and then Bavarian Deputy Prime Minister, Josef Müller, requested his resignation; cf. ZA 28/29 Oct 1948, in: Pütz, H. (ed.), l.c., pp. 738 ff.

121 Letter by Seidel to the Bavarian trade associations, 21 July 1948, in: BayHStA, *Akten des Bayerischen Staatsministeriums für Wirtschaft und Verkehr* (MWi), no. 9725.

122 Müller-Armack, A., l.c., 1971, p. 247; Erhard, L., *Was uns trennte, was uns einte*, in: *Deutsche Zeitung*, 26 Dec 1975, p. 3; Schwarz, H.-P., l.c., 1986, p. 602.

123 E.g. article *Preissteigerungen ohne Ende* by the deputy chairman of the CDU in North-Wuerttemberg, Paul Bausch, in: *Hannoversche Presse*, volume 3, no. 98, 31 Aug 1948. See also the critique of the CDU's social committees, in: *Informationsdienst* 19, 11 Dec 1948 and the letter of the CDU in Cologne to the parliamentary group, 13 Dec 1948, in: BA, Z13, no. 332.

124 Statement by Adenauer at a presentation of the CDU on 21 July 1948, in: StBKAH, NL Konrad Adenauer, 02.04, printed in: Adenauer, K.; Poppinga, A. (ed.), l.c., pp. 236 f.

125 Letters by Adenauer to Erhard, 9 Aug 1948, and then Minister for Economic Affairs in North Rhine-Westphalia, Erik Nölting (SPD), 5 Oct 1948, in: StBKAH, NL Konrad Adenauer, 07.18 and 08.63. Further, see telegrams to Erhard and then Director of the Administration for Labour, Anton Storch (CDU), 4 Oct 1948, in: Adenauer, K., l.c., 1983, pp. 316 f.

126 *Gesetz gegen Preistreiberei*, 7 Oct 1948, in: WiGBl.,1948, p. 99.

127 Broadcast address by Erhard, 11 Nov 1948, in: DRA, WDR doc. 564/2.

128 Pirker, T., *Die blinde Macht. Die Gewerkschaftsbewegung in Westdeutschland*, vol. 1, Munich, 1960, p. 109.

129 For specific polling days, see appendix 14, p. 172.

130 Remarks by Adenauer in minutes of the caucus no. 96 A of 18 Oct 1948, in: Salzmann, R. (ed.), l.c., p. 284.

131 Posters *Es geht uns besser*, sign. X-017-201, 1948; *Endlich wieder kaufen können*, sign. X-017-202, 1948; *An den Früchten werdet ihr sie erkennen...und der Erfolg unserer Frankfurter Politik*, sign. X-017-230, 1948, in: ACDP, PS, printed in: Langguth, G. (ed.), l.c., pp. 42–4.

132 Posters *Frei von Zwangswirtschaft*, sign. X-017-248, 1948; *Was Zwang und Plan hat nicht geschafft, bewirkt die freie Marktwirtschaft*, sign. X-017-231, 1948; *Der neue Weg*

– *Freie Wirtschaft*, sign. X-017-285, 1948, in: ACDP, PS, printed in: Langguth, G. (ed.), l.c., p. 42.

133 Letter by Adenauer to the chairman of the CDU/CSU parliamentary group in the EC, Holzapfel, 30 Oct 1948, in: BA, NL Friedrich Holzapfel, no. 256; printed in: Adenauer, K., l.c., 1983, p. 331. See also letter to Pünder, 31 Aug 1948, in: BA, NL Hermann Pünder, no. 483, sheet 169.

134 Statement by Erhard in minutes of the caucus no. 64, 24 May 1948, in: Salzmann, R. (ed.), l.c., p. 200.

135 Minutes of the meeting no. 35 and 64, 23 Feb and 24 May 1948, in: Ibid., pp. 143, 200; article *Der Prüfstein*, in: *Die Neue Zeitung*, 3 Oct 1947; Erhard, L., l.c., 1963, pp. 15 f.

136 E.g. letter of complaint by the local politician and publisher of the *Kölnische Rundschau*, Reinhold Heinen (CDU), to Adenauer, 29 Oct 1948; petitions by the *Zentralverband der Haus- und Grundbesitzer* and the *Zentralverband der Fliegergeschädigten*, in: BA, NL Friedrich Holzapfel, no. 22. Furthermore, see the complaint by the consultancy *Hang & Rehm* sent to the CSU on 16 March 1948, in: ACSP, NL Franz Elsen, 6.7.2 and the resolutions by the Bavarian trade unions, 25 Aug, 15 Oct, 6 Nov 1948, in: BayHStA, NL Hans Ehard, no. 1326.

137 Letter by Adenauer to then Minister of the Interior in Lower Saxony, Günther Gereke (CDU), on 9 June 1948, in: Adenauer, K., l.c., 1983, p. 257.

138 Letters by Adenauer to Holzapfel and Pünder, 30 Oct 1948, in: StBKAH, NL Konrad Adenauer, 08.61. See also the note to Holzapfel and the Directors in the EC, in: BA, NL Friedrich Holzapfel, no. 256.

139 Häußermann, E., *Konrad Adenauer und die Presse vor 1933*, in: Stehkämper, H. (ed.), *Konrad Adenauer. Oberbürgermeister von Köln*, Cologne, 1976, pp. 243 ff; statement by Adenauer at a meeting of the party executive on 24 July 1946, in: HStAD, RWV 26-14; letters to Heinen on 9 Dec 1946 and 7 March 1947, and to the industrialist Hermann Knuth on 2 March 1947, in: StBKAH, NL Konrad Adenauer, 07.12, 07.14, 08.28. Regarding Adenauer's stance over the press see also Fischer, H.-D., l.c., 1978, p. 368.

140 Schwarz, H.-P., *Konrad Adenauer: A German Politician and Statesman in a Period of War, Revolution, and Reconstruction*, vol. 2, Providence, 1997, p. 71.

141 Spicka, M. E., l.c., pp. 151, 154.

142 Schachtner, R., l.c., pp. 48 ff.

143 ZA 28/29 Oct 1948, in: Pütz, H. (ed.), l.c., pp. 739 f.

144 ZA 24/25 Feb 1949, in: Ibid., p. 853.

145 Uertz, R., l.c., p. 196.

146 ZA 24/25 Feb 1949, in: Pütz, H. (ed.), l.c., pp. 885 f.

147 Etzel, F.; Scharnberg, H.; Böhm, F.; Erhard, L., *Entwurf eines Wirtschafts-programms (Frankfurter Fassung)*, 19 March 1949, in: BA, NL Friedrich Holzapfel, no. 264.

148 Letter by Johannes Albers to Konrad Adenauer, 15 May 1948, in: StBKAH, NL Konrad Adenauer, 08.11; ZA 24/25 Feb 1949, in: Pütz, H. (ed.), l.c., p.

858; Siebrecht, V., *Die Arbeitspolitik nach der Währungsreform*, in: FH 3/6, 1948, pp. 491 ff.

149 Economic principles *Wirtschaftspolitische Richtlinien der CSU in Bayern*, n.l., n.d. (supposedly end of 1948), in: ACSP, NL Franz Elsen, 3.1.1.; speech by Seidel given at the party convention in Straubing, 27–9 May 1949, in: BayHStA, NL Hans Ehard, no. 685.

150 *Wirtschaftspolitische Leitsätze der Arbeitsgemeinschaft der CDU/CSU*, n.d. (presumably April 1949), in: BA, NL Friedrich Holzapfel, no. 264.

151 Stoltenberg, G., l.c., p. 22.

152 *Düsseldorfer Leitsätze über Wirtschaftspolitik, Landwirtschaftspolitik, Sozialpolitik, Wohnungsbau vom 15. Juli 1949*, in: Heck, B. (ed.), l.c., 1979, p. 26.

153 Ibid., p. 31.

154 Ibid., p. 38.

155 Internal party circular by Bruno Dörpinghaus to the chairmen of the regional organisations of the CDU and CSU in the British and American zones of occupation, 12 Jan 1949, in: ACDP, NL Bruno Dörpinghaus, I-009-012/7; see also ZA 2/3 June 1949, in: Pütz, H. (ed.), l.c., p. 100.

156 Kaff, B. (ed.), l.c., pp. 402–4.

157 Spicka, M. E., l.c., p. 59.

158 Adenauer at the meeting of the executive committee of the CDU in the British zone of occupation; cf. ZA 24/25 Feb 1949, in: Pütz, H. (ed.), l.c., p. 858. Furthermore, see the party chairman's speech in Heidelberg on 21 July 1949, in: Adenauer, K., l.c., 1975, p. 141.

159 Kaff, B. (ed.), l.c., pp. 456–7.

160 Election posters *Soziale Marktwirtschaft oder Zwangswirtschaft?*, sign. X-001-57, 1949 and *Am Scheideweg der Wirtschaft*, sign. X-001-6, 1949, in: ACDP, PS, printed in: Langguth, G. (ed.), l.c., pp. 74 f.

161 Portrait 'Erhard', in: *Union im Wahlkampf: Informations- und Rednerdienst der Arbeitsgemeinschaft der CDU/CSU Deutschlands*, 13 July 1949, p. 1.

162 E.g. posters *Für den Frieden, Freiheit und die Einheit Deutschlands*, sign. X-001-104, 1949; *Einigkeit, Recht, Freiheit*, sign. X-001-122, 1949; *Das ganze Deutschland soll es sein*, sign. X-001-14, 1949; *Die Rettung – CDU*, sign. X-001-11, 1949, in: ACDP, PS, printed in: Langguth, G. (ed.), l.c., pp. 77–80

163 Kaff, B. (ed.), l.c., pp. 455, 625; Spicka, M. E., l.c., p. 65.

164 CDU placard *1948 – 1949, Das brachte Dir unsere Wirtschaftspolitik*, sign. X-001-5, 1949; poster series *1947 Hunger-Not-Elend, 1949 Vorwärts! Aufwärts!*, sign. X-001-22-29, 1949; *Wir wollen keine Marken und Bezugsscheine, wir brauchen freie Marktwirtschaft*, sign. X-001-43, 1949; *Wir können nicht zaubern aber arbeiten. Hilf mit! Wähl CDU*, sign. X-001-4, 1949; *Gemeinsam schaffen wir's*, sign. X-001-16, 1949; *Es geht um Deutschland*, sign. X-001-2, 1949, in: Ibid., pp. 73, 75 f., 82-85. Regarding the CSU's position, see the posters *Wir können nicht zaubern aber wir bauen auf. Gegen Sozialisierung wählt CSU*, sign. X-001-243, 1949, in: Ibid., p. 81; *Nie wieder Zwangswirtschaft* (showing Erhard); *Kampf dem Sozialismus*, in: ACSP, Pslg. PL 319, 1323. See also the broadsheet *Die SPD hat abgewirtschaftet… Die von der CDU/CSU vertretene Wirtschaftspolitik der Marktwirtschaft brachte uns*

hingegen…, in: ACSP, Fslg. FL 1949, no. 4; also the handouts *Die Deutschen Wahlen vom 14. August 1949*, in: ACSP, DS 3187 and *Bundeswahlen und Wirtschaftspolitik*, 17 July 1949, in: BayHStA, NL Hans Ehard, no. 685.

165 Own calculations based on demography B15 (1950) and the study *Die deutschen Vertriebenen in Zahlen Teil II – 40 Jahre Eingliederung in der Bundesrepublik Deutschland* provided by the *Statistisches Bundesamt* (StBA), Wiesbaden.

166 According to Rudolf Morsey, still in fall 1949 Konrad Adenauer was less well-known to the general public than his counterpart Kurt Schumacher; cf. comment by Rudolf Morsey, in: Pohl, H. (ed.), l.c., p. 68. Further, a survey by Elisabeth Noelle-Neumann a year earlier revealed that the German people considered the SPD chairman to be the more competent politician; cf. Noelle, E.; Neumann, E. P. (eds.), l.c., p. 193.

167 Erhard in a public radio transmission, 6 June 1949, published in: Erhard, L., l.c., 1992, p. 105.

168 E.g. Art. 14 GG, in: BGBl. I.

169 Art. 15, in: Ibid..

170 Röpke, W., l.c., 1942, p. 131; Idem, l.c., 1949, p. 67; Böhm, F., l.c., 1933; Idem, l.c., 1937, pp. 101 ff. Similarly, later academic literature argued that the Social Market Economy was the only adequate economic system for a liberal democracy; cf. Gutmann, G.; Hochstrate, H.-J.; Schlüter, R., *Die Wirtschafts-verfassung der Bundesrepublik Deutschland. Entwicklung und ordnungspolitische Grundlagen*, Stuttgart, 1964; Papier, H.-J., *Grundgesetz und Wirtschaftsordnung*, in: Benda, E.; Maihofer, W.; Vogel, H.-J. (eds.), *Handbuch des Verfassungsrechts der Bundesrepublik Deutschland*, Berlin, 1983, pp. 609 ff.; Schockenhoff, V., *Wirtschaftsverfassung und Grundgesetz. Die Auseinandersetzungen in den Verfassungsberatungen 1945-1949*, doctoral thesis, Frankfurt am Main, 1986. While few authors addressed the correlation between the economic and political order in examining the reconstruction of the German post-war economy, an in-depth analysis considering the mutual interdependence and interplay between Economic and Parliamentary Council is still missing.

171 In this context, see also Gardner, J., l.c..

172 Barbier, H. D., *Die Freiheit als Sozialprogramm*, in: FAZ, 1 Feb 1997, p. 13.

173 N.B. the Social Market Economy was first constitutionally anchored in article 1-3 para. 3 of the Treaty establishing a Constitution for the European Union signed in 2004.

174 Weekly reports by the authorised agent of the CSU at the EC, 17 Jan to 3 April and the notice no. 6, 7 May 1948, in: ACSP, NL Anton Besold, no. 57. See also minutes of the meeting about the coordination of the cooperation between Bavarian ministries and the bizonal administration in the Bavarian *Staatskanzlei* on 26 April 1948, in: BayHStA, NL Hans Ehard, no. 1614.

175 WB VV, l.c., p. 454.

176 Ibid., 448.

177 Notice *Wohin gehört Prof. Erhard?* by the chairman of the FDP in the British zone, Franz Blücher, n.d., in: *Archiv desLiberalismus* (ADL), NL Franz Blücher, D 2-1, no. II. See also the reminiscence of Everhard Bungartz *Erinnerungen an*

die Grundlegung der sozialen Marktwirtschaft, 27 Feb 1978, pp. 3–5, in: ADL, NL Everhard Bungartz, N 33-9. To the disappointment of the FDP, however, Erhard publicly clarified that he campaigned for the Christian Democrats; cf. newspaper article *Erhard an die CDU*, in: *Stuttgarter Zeitung*, issue 138, 12 Aug 1949. Nonetheless, Ludwig Erhard arguably acted for the FDP once in a while; cf. comment by Max Schulze-Vorberg, in: Pohl, H. (ed.), l.c., p. 70.

178 Proclamations and party platforms *Programm der Demokratischen Partei in Süd- und Mittelbaden*, 20 Jan 1946; *Programmatische Richtlinien der Freien Demokratischen Partei der Britischen Zone*, 4 Feb 1946; *Programm der Freien Demokratischen Partei Bayern*, 28 March 1946; *Wahlaufruf und Programm der Demokratischen Volkspartei Wuerttemberg-Baden*, 14 June 1946; *Programmatische Leitsätze der Freien Demokratischen Partei Hamburg*, Aug 1946; *Programm der Demokratischen Partei Rheinland-Pfalz*, 1947; *Wirtschaftsprogramm der FDP der Britischen Zone. Protokoll der Inseltagung des Zonenvorstands der FDP in Wangerooge*, 3–10 Jan 1948; *Heppenheimer Proklamation der Bundes-FDP*, 12 Dec 1948; *Bremer Plattform 1949. Beschlüsse des 1. Bundesparteitages*, 11/12 June 1949, printed in: Juling, P., l.c., pp. 9-87. Further, see the declarations *Freie Demokratische Partei, Landesverband Nord-Rheinprovinz*, 21 Aug 1946, in: BA, NL Franz Blücher, no. 154, and *Das wirtschaftliche Programm der Mitte*, 14 Feb 1947, in: ADL, NL Franz Blücher, N 37-32. Regarding the programmatic development of the FDP see Gutscher, J. M., l.c., 1967; Cerratti, R., l.c., 1982.

179 Nicholls, A. J., l.c. 1994, pp. 146–9; see also Gutscher, J. M., l.c., pp. 95–6.

180 Letter by the *Fraktionelle Arbeitsgemeinschaft* (parliamentary working group) to Hermann Pünder, 17 Dec 1948, in: BA, NL Hermann Pünder, no. 481, sheet 87; notice *Bericht aus dem Wirtschaftsrat*, 21 Dec 1948, in: ADL, NL Franz Blücher, D 2-1, no. XXXX.

181 Programmatic declarations *Zwölf-Punkte Programm der FDP-Fraktion des Wirtschaftsrates*, 10 Nov 1948, in: ADL, NL Franz Blücher, D 2-1, no. XXX, and *Ein Jahr liberale Wirtschaft in Westdeutschland*, in: *Algemeen Handelsblad*, Amsterdam, 5 July 1949.

182 Election posters *Wer hilft im Kampfe ... gegen den Behördensozialismus?*, sign. P 3-10, 1946; *Sozialismus bedeutet Zwangswirtschaft*, sign. P 5-38, 1947; *Sozialisierung ist Bürokratie*, sign. P 5-40, 1947; *Warum lehnt die FDP den Sozialismus ab?*, sign. P 2-49, 1948; *Unsere Plattform*, sign. P 2-83, 1948; *CDU+FDP*, sign. P 1-22, 1949; *FDP/CDU*, sign. P 3-92, 1949, in: ADL, Pslg.. See also the public advocacy for economic liberalisation by the spokesperson of the Liberal Democrats in the Hessian *Landtag*, Hans Ilau, *Planwirtschaft als politische Utopie*, in: *Die Gegenwart*, 15 Dec 1948, pp. 9 ff.

183 Cerratti, R. l.c., p. 190.

184 Minutes of the press and propaganda committee, 8 May 1949, in: ACDP, NL Bruno Dörpinghaus, I-009-006/2.

185 Spicka, M. E., l.c., p. 87.

186 Kaff, B. (ed.), l.c., p. 624.

187 Election posters/slogans *Sozialisierung – Hände Weg vom Eigentum*; *Schluss mit Planwirtschaft*; *Entscheide dich für die Freiheit*, *Wer nicht wählt, wählt den*

Kommunismus, 1948, n.s., in: ADL, Pslg.. See also Schmollinger, H. W., *Die Deutsche Partei*, in: Stöss, R. (ed.), *Parteien-Handbuch. Die Parteien der Bundesrepublik Deutschland 1945-1980*, (*Schriften des Zentralinstituts für Sozialwissenschaftliche Forschung der Freien Universität Berlin vol. 38*), Opladen, 1986, pp. 1025–111.

188 Election posters *Schluss mit der Diktatur des Grosskapitals – Art. 41 Ja! Wählt Kommunisten*, in: *Institut für Stadtgeschichte Frankfurt*, KPD Hessen (Leo Bauer), 1946, published in: *Digitales Archiv Marburg* (DigAM), doc. 212; *Fortschrittliche Verfassung Ja! Großbanken, Großindustrie in die Hände des Volkes Ja!...wählt Kommunisten*, in: *Hessisches Hauptstaatsarchiv, Wiesbaden* (HHStA), KPD Hessen (Leo Bauer) 1946, also in: DigAM, doc. 201; *Grossindustrie in des Volkes Hand – gibt den Menschen Brot und Brand*, 1947/1948, in: AdsD, PS.

189 *Bericht vom 15. Parteitag der Kommunistischen Partei Deutschlands*, Berlin, 1946.

190 Potthoff, H., *Kurt Schumacher – Sozialdemokraten und Kommunisten*, in: Dowe, D. (ed.), l.c., pp. 133–48.

191 For election results, see appendix 15, pp. 173–6.

192 See appendix 9, p. 160.

193 Gotto, K., *Die deutschen Katholiken und die Wahlen in der Adenauer-Ära*, in: Langner, A. (ed.), *Katholizismus im politischen System der Bundesrepublik, 1949-1963*, Paderborn, 1978, pp. 22–5.

194 Weber, A., *Sozialistische Marktwirtschaft*, in: DSJ IV/1, Berlin, 1950, pp. 3 ff.

Part II

1 '*The voice of the people* [is] *the voice of God*', in: Hesiod, *Theogony, Works and Days, Testimonia*, edited and translated by Glenn W. Most, Cambridge, Mass./London, 2006, p. 149, line 763.

2 '*And those people should not be listened to who keep saying the voice of the people is the voice of God, since the riotousness of the crowd is always very close to madness*', in: Flaccus Albinus Alcuinus cited in: *The Concise Oxford Dictionary of Quotations*, Oxford, 1993^{3}, p. 3.

3 Para. 6 (c), 8 (a) and (b), in: *New directive*, l.c., Washington, D.C., 15 July 1947, in: Stolper, G., l.c., p. 314.

4 In this connection, see Adenauer's broadcast address on *Nordwestdeutscher Rundfunk* on 6 March 1946, printed in: Flechtheim, O. K. (ed.), l.c., vol. VI, Berlin, 1968, p. 1.

5 Müller-Armack, A., l.c., 1978a, pp. 326 f.; Idem, l.c., Bern/Stuttgart, 1950, pp. 559 ff.; Erhard, L., l.c., 1963, p. 11.

6 Lijphart, A., l.c., p. 2.

7 Aristotle; Gigon, O. (ed.), *Politik*, Munich, 1986, p. 1313.

8 Hume, D., l.c., p. 24.

9 Hamilton, A.; Jay, J.; Madison, J., *The Federalist. A Commentary on the Constitution of the United States. Being a Collection of Essays written in Support of the Constitution agreed upon September 17, 1787, by the Federal Convention*, New York, 1937, p. 331.

10 Locke, J., *An Essay Concerning Human Understanding*, New York, 1959, p. 477.

11 Rousseau, J. J., *The Social Contract*, New York, 1762 (reprint 1947).

12 Hegel, G. W. F., *Philosophy of Right* (translated with notes by T. M. Knox), London, 1821 (1971), p. 197.

13 Tocqueville, A. de, *Democracy in America*, New York, 1840; Mill, J. S., *On Liberty*, London, 1859, Bryce, J., *The American Commonwealth*, Indianapolis, 1888.

14 Tarde, G., *L'opinion et la foule*, Paris, 1901; Park, R., *The Crowd and the Public*, Chicago, 1904; Lippmann, W., l.c., 1922; Speier, H., *Historical Development of Public Opinion*, in: *American Journal of Sociology* 55, 1950, pp. 376–88; Childs, H. L., *Public Opinion: Nature, Formation, and Role*, Princeton, *et al.*, 1965; Davison, W. Ph., *Public Opinion. Introduction*, in: Sills, D. L. (ed.), *International Encyclopedia of the Social Sciences*, vol. 13, New York, 1968, pp. 188–97; Hennessy, B. C., *Public Opinion*, Belmont, 1970. Regarding the historical development of the concept of public opinion, see also Glynn, C. J., *Public Opinion*, Oxford, 1999, pp. 31–64.

15 Bourdieu, P., *Public Opinion Does Not Exist*, in: Mattelart, A.; Siegelaub, S. (eds.), *Communication and Class Struggle*, vol. I, New York, 1979, pp. 124–30; Herbst, S., *Surveys in the public sphere: Applying Bourdieu's critique of opinion polls*, in: *International Journal of Public Opinion Research* 4/3, Oxford, 1992, pp. 220–9.

16 Oncken, H., *Politik, Geschichtsschreibung und öffentliche Meinung*, in: Idem, *Historisch-Politische Aufsätze und Reden*, vol. 1, Munich/Berlin, 1914, p. 236.

17 Price, V., *Public Opinion*, Newbury Park, 1992, p. 26. In this context, see also the classic treatment of the notion 'crowds', in: Le Bon, G., *The Crowd: A Study of the Popular Mind*, New York, 1896.

18 Glynn, C. J., l.c., p. 16.

19 Albig, W., *Public Opinion*, New York/London, 1939, p. 3.

20 E.g. Rosenau, J. N., *Public Opinion and Foreign Policy*, New York, 1961, p. 19.

21 Albig, W., *Modern Public Opinion*, New York, 1956, p. 5.

22 Lasswell, H. D., *Democracy Through Public Opinion*, Menasha, 1941, p. 20; Baur, E. J., *Public Opinion and the Primary Group*, in: *American Sociological Review* 25, Columbus, 1960, pp. 209 f.; Blumer, H., *Collective Behaviour*, New York, 1946.

23 Lowell, A. L., *Public Opinion in War and Peace*, Cambridge, Mass., 1923, p. 23.

24 E.g. Dahl, R. A., l.c., p. 2; Monroe, A. D., *Public Opinion in America*, New York, 1975; Sartori, G., *The Theory of Democracy Revisited*, Chatham, 1987.

25 Bauer, W., *Die öffentliche Meinung in der Weltgeschichte*, Wildpart-Potsdam, 1930, p. 19; Schmidtchen, G., *Die befragte Nation. Über den Einfluss der Meinungsforschung auf die Politik*, Freiburg, 1959, p. 237.

26 Harrison, T., *What is Public Opinion?*, in: *Political Quarterly* 11, Oxford, 1940, p. 374.

27 Noelle-Neumann, E., *The Spiral of Silence: A Theory of Public Opinion*, in: *Journal of Communication* 24, Oxford, 1974, p. 44.

28 Lippmann, W., *The Phantom Public*, New York, 1925, pp. 155 f.

29 Best, J., *Public Opinion: Micro and Macro*, Homewood, 1973, p. 216. See also Hennis, W., *Meinungsforschung und repräsentative Demokratie. Zur Kritik politischer Umfragen*, Tübingen, 1957, p. 25; Mahrenholz, E. G., *Medien und Macht – Wie*

sichern wir Pluralismus und Transparenz?, in: *Bertelsmann Briefe*, Heft 129, Gütersloh, 1993, p. 5.

30 Habermas, J., l.c., pp. 11–53, 340–52.

31 Pennock, J. R., *Responsiveness, Responsibility, and Majority Rule*, in: *American Political Science Review 46*, Los Angeles, 1952, pp. 790–807; Pitkin, H. F., *The Concept of Representation*, Berkeley/Los Angeles, 1967; Etzioni, A., *The Active Society. A Theory of Societal and Political Processes*, London/New York, 1968.

32 Berg-Schlosser, D., l.c., p. 114. Similarly, Konrad Adenauer in his first government policy statement on 20 Sep 1949, in: DRA, l.c., no. 2.

33 Görtemaker, M., l.c., p. 148.

34 Benz, W., l.c., 1999a, p. 85.

35 Art. 20 para. 2 GG, in: BGBl. I.

36 Ruhm von Oppen, B. (ed.), l.c., p. 432.

37 Merritt, A. J.; Merritt, R. L. (eds.), *Public Opinion in Occupied Germany. The OMGUS Surveys, 1945-1949*, Urbana/Chicago/London, 1970 (sample size 331-3,000 persons; mainly in American zone of occupation); Cantril, H.; Strunk, M., *Public Opinion 1935-1946*, Princeton, 1951 (~ 3,000; drawing on OMGUS surveys); EMNID surveys published in selected newspapers (sample size unknown); IfD, *Bericht über die erste Umfrage der wirtschaftspolitischen Gesellschaft von 1947 über die deutsche Situation*, Allensbach, 1949 (unpublished) (2,100); Noelle, E.; Neumann, E. P. (eds.), l.c. (2,000).

38 Gallup, G.; Rae, S. F., *The Pulse of Democracy: The Public Opinion Poll and How It Works*, New York, 1940; Woodward, J. L., *Public Opinion Polls as an Aid to Democracy*, in: *Political Science Quarterly* 61, New York, 1946, p. 238; Hennessy, B. C., l.c., p. 130.

39 Blumer, H., *Public Opinion and Public Opinion Polling*, in: *American Sociological Review* 13, Columbus, OH, 1948, pp. 542–9; Marsh, C., *The Survey Method: The Contribution of Surveys to Sociological Explanation*, London, 1982; Miller, W., *The Survey Method in the Social and Political Sciences: Achievements, Failures, Prospects*, London, 1983.

40 *Bayerisches Staatsministerium für Arbeit und soziale Fürsorge, Monatsbericht über Arbeit und Wirtschaft in Bayern* and *Berichterstattung Regierungspräsident an Bayerische Staatsregierung*, in: BayHStA, *Berichte des Landesarbeitsamtes* or *Regierung von Ober- und Mittelfranken, Berichterstattung 1947/1948*. Further, the reports of individual mayors to the respective provincial government or district president will be considered.

41 Results of local, regional and federal elections provided by the StBA and by the respective *Statistische Landesämter* (StLA). See also *Elections and Political Parties in Germany, 1945-1952*, edited by Policy Reports Secretary Office of Executive Secretary (Office of the U.S. High Commissioner for Germany), 1 June 1952; Vogel, B.; Nohlen, D.; Schultze, R.-O., *Wahlen in Deutschland: Theorie – Geschichte – Dokumente 1848-1970*, Berlin/New York, 1971.

42 The highest increase was recorded in Bavaria where the number of eligible voters increased from 3.6 million in June 1946 to 6 million in Aug 1949. Faul, E. (ed.), *Wahlen und Wähler in Westdeutschland*, Villingen, 1960, p. 35.

43 Marsh, D.; Stoker, G. (eds.), *Theory and Methods in Political Science*, New York, 1995, p. 74.

44 Regarding the party affiliation and orientation of applied newspapers, see appendix 11/12, pp. 162–70.

Chapter 3

1 Karl Mannheim cited in: Judt, T., l.c., p. 63.

2 Sueskind, W. E., *Der politische Rohstoff*, in: Moras, J.; Paeschke, H. (eds.), *Deutscher Geist zwischen Gestern und Morgen*, Stuttgart, 1954, p. 54.

3 Stolper, G., *German Realities*, New York, 1948, pp. 135 f. Although this assessment was recorded in 1947, it best describes the situation in Germany in the immediate post-war years.

4 Report no. 17 (14 Jan 1946), in: Cantril, H.; Strunk, M., l.c., p. 269. See also report no. 19 of that day according to which 59 per cent thought that a central government should be set up for all four zones of Germany and survey results no. 24 and 25 (25 July 1946) which revealed that most respondents in the American zone (31 per cent) favoured a strong central government directing the zone from Berlin; cf. Ibid., pp. 269 f. Indeed, these responses must be seen in connection with the general wish for German political unification; however, the priority was given to economic unity (63 per cent); cf. report no. 32 (25 Nov 1946), in: Ibid., p. 271.

5 Report no. 35 (6 Dec 1945), in: Ibid., p. 177.

6 Report no. 1 (11 Dec 1945), in: Ibid., p. 194.

7 Interview with contemporary witness Helga Seifert, 13 Dec 2006.

8 See appendix 15, pp. 173–6.

9 Ibid..

10 Merkl, P. H., *The Origin of the West German Republic*, New York/Oxford, 1963, p. 28.

11 *Documents on the Creation of the German Federal Constitution*, edited by the OMGUS, Civil Administration Division, Berlin, 1949, p. 86.

12 Merritt, A. J.; Merritt, R. L. (eds.), l.c., p. 44.

13 Interview with contemporary witnesses Max and Maria Beyer, 30 May 2006.

14 Merritt, A. J.; Merritt, R. L. (eds.), l.c., p. 44.

15 Report no. 11, 12, 15 and 31 (5 and 26 Nov, 27 Dec 1945, 9 Aug 1946), in: Cantril, H.; Strunk, M., l.c., pp. 269, 271.

16 Clay, L. D., l.c., p. 88.

17 Report no. 4 (3 Sep 1946), in: Cantril, H.; Strunk, M., l.c., p. 195. See also report no. 26 (13 Nov 1946), in: Merritt, A. J.; Merritt, R. L. (eds.), l.c., p. 110.

18 Report no. 2 (3 Sep 1946), in: Cantril, H.; Strunk, M., l.c., p. 194.

19 Report no. 3 (15 March 1946), in: Merritt, A. J.; Merritt, R. L. (eds.), l.c., p. 72.

20 Ibid..

21 Report no. 26 (13 Nov 1946), in: Ibid., p. 110.

22 Ibid..

23 Report no. 5 (1 April 1946), in: Merritt, A. J.; Merritt, R. L. (eds.), l.c., p. 75.

24 See appendix 15, pp. 173–6.
25 In connection with this, see also Cerratti, R., l.c., p. 111 and Judt, T., l.c., p. 80.
26 Newspaper articles *Plan- oder Privatwirtschaft*, in: NZZ, 23 Oct 1945; Schiller, K., *Wirtschaft am Scheideweg*, in: *Schleswig-Holsteinische Volkszeitung*, 13 April 1946; *Über die wirtschaftliche Freiheit*, in: *Die Gegenwart*, 24 July 1946, p. 37; Schumpeter, J., *Der Übergang zum Sozialismus*, in: *Wirtschafts-Zeitung* 12, 26 July 1946; *Bayern proklamiert Planwirtschaft*, in: *Aachener Nachrichten*, 27 Aug 1946; *Der Ruf nach der Wirtschaftsfreiheit*, in: *Freie Presse*, 24 Dec 1946.

Chapter 4

1 Joseph Schumpeter cited in: Judt, T., l.c., p. 63.
2 Tooze, A., l.c., p. 672.
3 MacDonogh, G., *After the Reich. From the Fall of Vienna to the Berlin Airlift*, London, 2007, p. 368.
4 Abelshauser, W., l.c., 1975, pp. 15–18.
5 StBA, *Statistisches Jahrbuch* 1953, p. 15.
6 Ibid., p. 1; Judt, T., l.c., pp. 21, 86; Balabkins, N., *Germany under Direct Controls*, New Brunswick, 1964, p. 115.
7 Report no. 15 (27 July 1946) and report no. 85 (17 Dec 1947), in: Merritt, A. J.; Merritt, R. L. (eds.), l.c., pp. 92/93, 191.
8 Ibid., p. 192.
9 Report no. 60 (April 1947), in: Ibid., pp. 160 f.
10 *Im Westen „sozialisiert" die CDU*, in: *Telegraf*, 30 March 1947.
11 In this connection, see the depiction by Ludwig Erhard, l.c., 1963, p. 12.
12 Jürgensen, K., *Die Gründung des Landes Schleswig-Holstein nach dem Zweiten Weltkrieg. Der Aufbau der Demokratischen Ordnung in Schleswig-Holstein unter dem ersten Ministerpräsidenten Theodor Steltzer 1945-1947*, Neumünster, 1969, pp. 43 ff.
13 For a detailed overview of election results, see appendix 15, pp. 173–6.
14 Regarding a detailed composition of the first EC, see appendix 6, p. 157.
15 *Die Neue Zeitung*, 28 July 1947.
16 *Die Schlacht von Minden*, in: *Gewerkschaftliche Informationen*, no. 9, 1 June 1947; *Besser als nichts*, in: *Wirtschafts-Zeitung*, 6 June 1947; *Die neue Obrigkeit*, in: *Neues Deutschland*, 12 June 1947; *Wirtschaftseinheit und Länderrecht*, in: *Handelsblatt*, 19 June 1947; *Die Organisation der Bi-Zone*, in: *Neue Zeit*, 27 June 1947; *Die Zukunft der Zweizonenwirtschaft*, in: *Handelsblatt*, 10 July 1947.
17 *Verkannte Aufgaben*, in: *Rhein-Neckar-Zeitung*, 26 July 1947.
18 *Das Streiflicht*, in: *Süddeutsche Zeitung*, 29 July 1947; *Verpasste Gelegenheit*, in: *Weser-Kurier*, 29 July 1947; *Sachliche Opposition*, in: *Die Gegenwart*, 31 Aug 1947, p. 2.
19 *Bürokratie – wirklichkeitsfremd*, in: *Die Zeit*, 12 June 1947.
20 *Nichts dazugelernt*, in: *Frankfurter Neue Presse*, 28 July 1947.
21 *Keine Begeisterung*, in: *Neues Deutschland*, 27 June 1947.
22 *Die Wirtschaftseinheit für zwei Zonen*, in: *Die Gegenwart*, 30 June 1947, p. 34.
23 *Über die Grenzen schauen*, in: *Kasseler Zeitung*, 8 Aug 1947.
24 Merritt, A. J.; Merritt, R. L. (eds.), l.c., pp. 45 ff.

25 E.g. *Aus dem Wirtschaftsrat*, in: *Nordwestdeutsche Rundschau*, 3 Oct 1947; *Allerlei aus Frankfurt*, in: *Die Welt*, 28 Oct 1947.

26 From no. 19/48 onwards *Gesetzblatt der Verwaltung des Vereinigten Wirtschafts-gebietes.*

27 Erhard, L., l.c., 1963, pp. 15 f.

28 Merritt, A. J.; Merritt, R. L. (eds.), l.c., pp. 220–1.

29 *Der Prüfstein*, in: *Die Neue Zeitung*, 3 Oct 1947.

30 E.g. resolution by *Junge Union*, 10 Aug 1947, in: AdsD, NL Gerhard Kreyssig, no. 62 and the letter by Bavarian Prime Minister Ehard to Adenauer in Aug 1947, in: BayHStA, NL Hans Ehard, no. 1610.

31 *Das Streiflicht*, in: *Süddeutsche Zeitung*, 23 Sep 1947; *Der Prüfstein*, in: *Die Neue Zeitung*, 3 Oct 1947; *Aus Prinzip*, in: *Wiesbadener Kurier*, 18 Oct 1947.

32 *Hinweg mit dem Länder-Egoismus*, in: *Telegraf*, 7 Oct 1947; Ficker, L., *Aus dem Zweizonen-Wirtschaftsrat*, in: *Informationsblatt der Kommunistischen Partei* 20, 15 Oct 1947. In connection with this, see also the explanation by the Bavarian Prime Minister; cf. Ehard, H., *Vor einer neuen Fehlentwicklung? – Kritik am Frankfurter Wirtschaftsrat*, in: *Süddeutsche Zeitung*, 4 Oct 1947.

33 Appendix 15/16, pp. 173–80.

34 Frentzel-Wagner, H., *Bremsklötze weg!*, in: *Die Zeit*, 28 Aug 1947; *Neuaufbau oder Wiederaufbau?*, in: *Süddeutsche Zeitung*, 4 Nov 1947.

35 *Muckefuck und Eichelsuppe*, in: *Die 50er Jahre – Vom Trümmerland zum Wirtschaftswunder, Spiegel Spezial* 1, 2006, p. 37.

36 Trippen, N., *Josef Kardinal Frings (1887-1978): Sein Wirken für das Erzbistum Köln und für die Kirche in Deutschland*, vol. I, Paderborn, 2003, p. 251.

37 Meehan, P., *A Strange Enemy People: Germans under the British, 1945–1950*, London, 2001, p. 240.

38 Report no. 41 (15 Jan 1947) and report no. 60 (April 1947), in: Merritt, A. J.; Merritt, R. L. (eds.), l.c., pp. 133, 160 f.

39 E.g. proposals *Neuordnung des Geldwesens* by Siegfried Rentrop, 17 Oct 1946; *Vorschlag zur Ordnung der Geld- und Kapitalverhältnisse* by Friedrich Schamann, 28 Jan 1947; *Währungsreform* by Herbert Gudehus, 25 July 1947 sent to then Chairman of the Financial Committee of the EC and Minister of Finance in North Rhine-Westphalia, Franz Blücher, in: ADL, NL Franz Blücher, A 3-75, no. 84, 102, A 3-74, no. 48. Furthermore, the unnamed critiques forwarded to the EC, 28 Aug and 15 Oct 1947, in: DBt PA, 2/510. See also the detailed petition *Bitte der Evangelischen Kirche zur Währungsreform* on behalf of the Chairman of the Protestant Church in Germany sent to the Allied Control Council, 13 Dec 1947, in: ADL, NL Franz Blücher, A 3-74, no. 13.

Chapter 5

1 ‘*What are we significantly concerned about day and night?! – Currency Reform. Will it happen today or tomorrow? Everyone is worried about it. Some are afraid, some cannot wait.*’, in: *Nürnberger Nachrichten*, edition Fürth, 9 June 1948.

2 E.g. unnamed letter sent to the EC on Christmas 1947, in: DBt PA, 2/510; complaint by Kurt Scheringer to President of the EC, Erich Köhler, Passau, 1 March 1948, in: ACDP, NL Paul Binder, I-105-022; letter by Hellmut Sommer to General Sir Brian Robertson *et al.*, 25 May 1948, in: Ibid..

3 Ziemer, G., *Deutscher Exodus: Vertreibung und Eingliederung von 15 Millionen Ostdeutschen*, Stuttgart, 1973, p. 94. Ziemer's figures are based on those published by the StBA in Wiesbaden in 1958.

4 *Der Geldordnung entgegen*, in: *Wirtschafts-Zeitung*, 7 May 1948.

5 *Praktische Arbeit Gebot der Stunde*, in: *Frankfurter Rundschau*, 6 March 1948.

6 Eckart, P., *Denn sie wissen nicht...*, in: *Wiesbadener Kurier*, 5 March 1948; *Kleinigkeiten*, in: *Frankfurter Neue Presse*, 19 April 1948.

7 E.g. *Vorwiegend positives Echo auf Frankfurt*, in: *Die Neue Zeitung*, 12 Jan 1948.

8 Report no. 107 (29 March 1948), in: Merritt, A. J.; Merritt, R. L. (eds.), l.c., pp. 220 f.

9 E.g. letter by Werner Berndt to Franz Blücher, 16 March 1948 (reply on 25 March 1948), in: ADL, NL Franz Blücher, A 3-73, 80/81.

10 Report no. 98 (6 March 1948), in: Merritt, A. J.; Merritt, R. L. (eds.), l.c., pp. 207 f.

11 Purport in a letter (written in English) by Hellmut Sommer to then UK's Minister for Germany, Francis Packenham, 25 May 1948, in: DBt PA, 2/510.

12 Galbraith, J. K., l.c., 1948, pp. 94 ff.

13 *Sprung in die Marktwirtschaft*, in: *Wirtschafts-Zeitung*, 7 May 1948; *Lockerung der Zwangswirtschaft*, in: *Wirtschafts- und Finanzzeitung*, 13 May 1948; *Wissenschaft und Marktwirtschaft*, in: *Der Tagesspiegel*, 16 May 1948.

14 Dönhoff, M., l.c., pp. 149 f.

15 Sommer, G., *Ein offenes Wort*, in: *Rheinischer Merkur*, 5 June 1948.

16 E.g. joint declaration by the *Deutscher Caritasverband*, the *Hauptausschuss für Arbeiterwohlfahrt* and the *Hilfswerk der Evangelischen Kirchen in Deutschland*, sent to Erich Köhler, on 21 April 1948; petition by the *Deutscher Städtetag* forwarded amongst others to Erhard on 29 April 1948; request by the *Gewerkschaftsrat* sent to Pünder and Köhler, 1 June 1948, in: DBt PA, 2/509.

17 Issue dated 15 July 1947.

18 Proposal *10 Thesen zur Währungsreform* forwarded to the EC, 2 May 1948, in: DBt PA, 2/509.

19 *Entschliessung der volkswirtschaftlichen Hochschullehrer Deutschlands*, n.l., n.d., in: BA, Z1, no. 703.

20 Report no. 90 (23 Jan 1948), in: Merritt, A. J.; Merritt, R. L. (eds.), l.c., p. 197.

21 See appendix 15, pp. 173–6.

22 *Pfeile gegen Erhard*, in: *Nordsee Zeitung*, n.d. (according to the context, the year 1948 can be assumed).

23 *Sprung in den freien Markt?*, in: *Die Gegenwart*, 1 April 1948, pp. 34 f.; *Zwei Angestellte – ein Referent*, in: *Darmstädter Echo*, 29 April 1948.

24 DGB proposal *Grundgesetz für Westdeutschland*, in: *Der Bund* II, 25 Sep 1948, p. 5.

25 *Die Beratungen in Bonn*, in: Ibid., 6 Nov 1948, p. 2.

26 *Überraschungen in Bonn*, in: *Die Neue Zeitung*, 11 Nov 1948, p. 1; *Tiefer Pessimismus im Bonner Rat*, in: Ibid., 13 Nov 1948, p. 1.

27 *Zentralverband der Fliegegeschädigten*, *Wir warnen*, Stuttgart, 1 April 1948, p. 2, in: BA, Z32, no. 43.

28 E.g. request by Curt Albrecht sent to the EC, 14 June 1948, in: DBt PA, 2/510. Eventually, there were more than 250 proposals from officials and individuals for the currency reform alone.

29 Memorandum entitled *Betrachtungen zur kommenden Währungs-Reform* by Hellmut Sommer addressing the President of the EC, Erich Köhler, all prime ministers and presidents of parliaments in the western *Länder*, the chairmen of the chambers of industry and commerce, the *Bankenrat* and the *Bank Deutscher Länder* (founded on 1 March 1948), the principals of the universities, the party chairmen, the unions, selected newspapers and the military governors, 25 May 1948, in: DBt PA, 2/510.

30 Internal document of AG CDU/CSU, Frankfurt am Main, 18 June 1948, p. 2 in: ACDP, NL Paul Binder, I-105-022. See also the response by Erich Köhler, 4 June 1948, in: DBt PA, 2/510.

31 Letter to Paul Binder, Frankfurt am Main, 24 June 1948, in: Ibid..

32 Woller, H., *Gesellschaft und Politik in der amerikanischen Besatzungszone – Die Region Ansbach und Fürth*, in: *Quellen und Darstellungen zur Zeitgeschichte*, edited by the IfZ, vol. 25, Munich, 1986, p. 294.

33 Newspaper article, in: *Fränkische Landeszeitung*, 19 June 1948.

34 *Military Government Gazette* 25, Law no. 61, pp. 848 ff. Regarding the terms and conditions of the German Currency Reform of 1948, see Tribe, K., *The 1948 Currency Reform – Structure and Purpose*, Keele University, Department of Economics, *Working Paper Series* no. 98/10, Staffordshire, 1998.

35 Davidson, E., *The Death and Life of Germany. An Account of the American Occupation*, Columbia, 1999, p. 224; also in: MacDonogh, G., l.c., p. 521.

36 Böttcher, K. W., *Die Übergangskrise der D-Mark*, in: FH, Jan 1949, p. 73.

37 Erhard, L., *Prosperity through Competition*, London, 1958, p. 13 (original title *Wohlstand für alle* translated by Jacques Rueff and André Piettre).

38 *Military Government Gazette* 25, Law no. 63, p. 863.

39 Colm, G.; Dodge, J. M.; Goldsmith, R. W., *A Plan for the Liquidation of War Finance and the Financial Rehabilitation of Germany*, in: *Zeitschrift für die gesamte Staatswissenschaft* 111, Tübingen, 1955, pp. 204–43.

40 Roeper, H., *Die D-Mark. Vom Besatzungskind zum Weltstar*, Frankfurt am Main, 1978, pp. 24 f.

41 Mendershausen, H.; Matchett, G., *Analysis of Size Distribution of Cash and Bank Deposits*, reprinted in: Möller, H. (ed.), l.c., pp. 457 ff.; Tribe, K., l.c., 1998, p. 4.

42 Neumann, E. P.; Noelle, E., l.c., 1954, pp. 147, 152.

43 Ibid., p. 151.

44 Report no. 133 (10 Aug 1948), in: Merritt, A. J.; Merritt, R. L. (eds.), l.c., pp. 251 f. See also *Kommentare*, in: *Nordsee Zeitung*, 21 June 1948.

45 Report no. 139 (22 Sep 1948), in: Ibid., p. 258 f.

46 Neumann, E. P.; Noelle, E., l.c., 1954, p. 148.

47 Report no. 133 (10 Aug 1948), in: Merritt, A. J.; Merritt, R. L. (eds.), l.c., pp. 251 f.

48 *Hungrige Augen*, in: *Die 50er Jahre*, l.c., p. 107.

49 BayHStA, *Regierung von Ober- und Mittelfranken, Berichterstattung 1948*, in: Woller, H., l.c., p. 297.

50 *Bayern in Zahlen*, Heft 4/1950, p. 204, in: Woller, H., l.c., p. 304.

51 *Fresswelle nach der Fettlücke*, in: *Die 50er Jahre*, l.c., p. 101.

52 Resolutions by the *Landesgewerkschaft Freie Berufe Hessen* on 25 June and by the DGB districts Ennepe-Ruhr, 7 July, Nordmark on 23 July, Lippstadt on 21 Aug and Moers/Rheinhausen on 22 Sep 1948, in: DBt PA, 2/509, 727.

53 Noelle, E.; Neumann, E. P. (eds.), l.c., pp. 154 f.

54 *Nürnberger Nachrichten*, 3 Nov 1948. See also Ambrosius, G., l.c., pp. 187 f. Furthermore, the internal party dispute between the Deputy Chairman of the CDU in North Wuerttemberg, Paul Bausch, and the Deputy Director of the Administration for Economics, Edmund Kaufmann, printed in: *Soziale Marktwirtschaft*, in: *Wirtschaftsverwaltung*, (*Sonderdruck*), n.d.. Further, the critique by the Christian Democratic Workers' Representation; cf. *Generalstreik?*, in: DUD, 8 Nov 1948, in: ACDP, Slg. BGS, VII-005-59/1.

55 Erhard, L., *Die deutsche Wirtschaftspolitik im Blickfeld europäischer Politik*, in: Hunold, A. (ed.), *Wirtschaft ohne Wunder*, Erlenbach-Zurich, 1953, p. 142.

56 *Kritik von links und rechts*, in: *Nordsee Zeitung*, n.d..

57 Petitions and resolutions sent to the EC, in: DBt PA, 2/509. In connection with this, see also the monthly reports by various mayors to the Bavarian Military Government, in: *Stadtverwaltung* (StVW) *Ansbach*, EAP 022-95/19.

58 *Die Aera Erhard*, in: *Volks-Wirtschaft*, 29 July 1948; *Freie Leistungsauslese?*, in: *Telegraf*, 7 Aug 1948; *Gegen Erhards Wirtschaftskurs*, in: *Westfälische Rundschau*, 10 Aug 1948; *„Echtes Geld"*, in: *Nordsee Zeitung*, n.d..

59 For particular polling days, see appendix 14, p. 172.

60 Neumann, E. P.; Noelle, E., l.c., 1954, p. 192; *Mehrgleisige Frankfurter Wirtschaftspolitik*, in: *Die Neue Zeitung*, 12 Oct 1948.

61 *Unpopulärer Wirtschaftsrat*, in: *Westdeutsches Tageblatt*, 3 July 1948; *Pressestimmen*, in: *Welt am Sonntag*, 22 Aug 1948.

62 E.g. *Ein offenes Wort*, in: *Rheinischer Merkur*, 5 June 1948.

63 Noelle, E.; Neumann, E. P. (eds.), l.c., p. 152.

64 See appendix 15/16, pp. 173–80.

65 E.g. *Wirtschaft und Verfassung*, in: *Neuer Vorwärts*, 2 Oct 1948.

66 Minutes of the EC's meeting no. 35, 64, 23 Feb and 24 May 1948 respectively, in: Salzmann, R. (ed.), l.c., pp. 143, 200; *Die Kritik am Frankfurter Wirtschaftsrat*, in: *Mitteilungen der Christlich-Sozialen Union*, 29 May 1948.

67 *Demokratie im Wirtschaftsrat*, in: *Weser-Kurier*, 26 Aug 1948; Rasch, E., *Zurück zur Zwangswirtschaft? – Mehr Respekt vor der Frankfurter Leistung*, in: *Neues Tageblatt*, 16 Oct 1948; *Von Altwein bis Zwicknagel – Die soziale Struktur des Wirtschaftsrates*, in: *Frankfurter Neue Presse*, 2 Nov 1948.

68 EMNID survey *Öffentliche Meinung und Jedermann-Programm*, 1 Nov 1948, in: ADL, NL Franz Blücher, A 3-7, 42-44. In connection with this, see also Noelle, E.; Neumann, E. P. (eds.), l.c., p. 156.

69 *Für und Wider Bewirtschaftung*, in: *Die Neue Zeitung*, 28 Oct 1948. See also Laitenberger, V., l.c., pp. 73 f.

70 Beier, G., *Der Demonstrations- und Generalstreik vom 12. November 1948*, Frankfurt am Main/Cologne, 1975, p. 89.

71 *Der grosse Auftakt*, in: *Der Bund* II, 20 Nov 1948, p. 2.

72 StBA, *Wirtschaft und Statistik*, 1949/1950, pp. 932 ff.; Borchardt, K.; Buchheim, C., *Die Wirkung der Marshall-Plan-Hilfe in Schlüsselbranchen der deutschen Wirtschaft*, in: VfZ 35/2, Munich, 1987, pp. 327 f.

73 Abelshauser, W., l.c., 1975, pp. 62–3.

74 *Gespaltener Markt*, in: *Allgemeine Zeitung*, 3 Dec 1948; Rupp, F., *Westdeutsche Wirtschaftspolitik – kritisch gesehen*, in: *Neue Zeitung*, 24 Dec 1948.

75 *Zentral gelenkte Wissenschaft*, in: *Das Volk*, 24 July 1948; *Die Schule des freien Marktes*, in: *Die Gegenwart*, 25 July 1948, pp. 20/21; *Diktatur des Konsumenten*, in: *Die Welt*, 27 July 1948.

Chapter 6

1 Konrad Adenauer in his first government policy statement on 20 Sep 1949, in: DRA, l.c., no. 2.

2 EMNID survey, in: *Ruhrnachrichten*, 9 July 1949.

3 Report no. 175 (June 1949), in: Merritt, A. J.; Merritt, R. L. (eds.), l.c., pp. 294–6.

4 EMNID survey, in: *Nordsee Zeitung*, 16 March 1949.

5 Report no. 189 (21 Sep 1949), in: Merritt, A. J.; Merritt, R. L. (eds.), l.c., p. 312.

6 *Der Wasserkopf in Frankfurt*, in: *Niedersächsische Volksstimme*, 9 March 1949.

7 *Gefährliche Wirtschaft*, in: *Die Freiheit*, 14 Jan 1949; complaint by Ilse Westphal sent to the bizonal Administration for Finance, 28 March 1949, in: DBt PA, 2/510; *Restordnung oder Neuordnung*, in: *Rheinische Zeitung*, 20 July 1949; *Die soziale Marktordnung Professor Erhards*, in: *Volksblatt*, 27 July 1949; *Klagen über westdeutsche Wirtschaftspolitik*, in: *Stuttgarter Zeitung*, 27 July 1949; *Die sagenhafte „soziale" Marktwirtschaft*, in: *Rheinische Zeitung*, 30 July 1949; *Pendelnde Wirtschaftspolitik*, in: *Nordwestdeutsche Rundschau*, 6 Aug 1949. In connection with this, see also the records of the then Secretary General of the *Länderrat*, Heinrich Troeger, in: *Interregnum: Tagebuch des Generalsekretärs des Länderrats der Bizone 1947-1949*, edited by Wolfgang Benz and Constantin Goschler, Munich, 1985, p. 119.

8 Leaflet *Die Wirtschaftspolitik Professor Erhards – Ein Segen für das Volk*, n.d.; *Bürohaus Börsenstrasse Nr. 2 – Unten Blumen und Kunst, oben hohe Politik*, in: *Allgemeine Zeitung*, 25 March 1949; *Vor einem Jahre: die D-Mark trat an*, in: *Nordsee Zeitung*, 18 June 1949.

9 E.g. complaint written by Oskar Blank to the delegate Theophil Kaufmann (CDU), Munich, 21 April 1949, in: ACDP, NL Theophil Kaufmann, I-071-012/8.

10 Asmussen, H., *Auch der Staat muss anständig handeln*, in: *Die Welt*, 28 May 1949 (letters patent to Hermann Pünder).

11 Mey, H., *Marktwirtschaft und Demokratie – Überlegungen zur Nachwirkung von Kontinuität und Neubeginn in der Gründungsphase der Bundesrepublik 1945-49*, in: VfZ 19, Munich, 1971, pp. 160–86; Tenbruck, F. H., *Alltagsnormen und Lebensgefühle in der Bundesrepublik*, in: Löwenthal, R.; Schwarz, H.-P. (eds.), *Die Zweite Republik. 25 Jahre Bundesrepublik – Eine Bilanz*, Stuttgart, 1974, pp. 289–310.

12 EMNID survey, in: *Frankfurter Rundschau*, 10 Sep 1949.

13 Reports no. 169 (6 May 1949) and 183-S (26 July 1949), in: Merritt, A. J.; Merritt, R. L. (eds.), l.c., pp. 287 and 307 respectively.

14 *Die Unlust an der Politik*, in: *Weser-Kurier*, 26 July 1949.

15 *Die Neue Zeitung*, 12 March 1949, p. 2; *Der Bund* III, 26 March 1949, p. 1; *Zum Grundgesetz*, in: *Der Bund* III, 7 May 1949, p. 2.

16 Report no. 170 (16 May 1949), in: Merritt, A. J.; Merritt, R. L. (eds.), l.c., pp. 288 f.

17 Report no. 191 (9 Dec 1949), in: Merritt, A. J.; Merritt, R. L. (eds.), l.c., pp. 314–17.

18 Ibid., p. 316.

19 Government policy statement on 20 Sep 1949, in: DRA, l.c., no. 2; printed in: Adenauer, K., l.c. 1975, pp. 153–69.

20 See appendix 15, pp. 173–6; StBA, *Statistisches Jahrbuch* 1953, p. 50.

21 Cerratti, R., l.c., p. 191.

22 *New York Times*, 17 July 1949, in: AdsD, holding Kurt Schumacher, no. Q 19.

23 See appendix 16, pp. 177–80.

24 IfD, l.c., pp. 45 ff.; report no. 90 (23 Jan 1948), in: Merritt, A. J.; Merritt, R. L. (eds.), l.c., p. 197.

25 Radio broadcasting address Kurt Schumacher, 21 April 1949, in: DRA, *Stimmen des 20. Jahrhundert: Nach bestem Wissen und Gewissen – Die Beratungen zum Grundgesetz im Parlamentarischen Rat 1948/49*, Frankfurt am Main, 1998, no. 17.

26 Noelle, E.; Neumann, E. P. (eds.), l.c., p. 104; IfD, l.c., pp. 53–8.

27 Ibid., pp. 60–8.

28 Art. 15 GG, in: BGBl. I.

29 *Das Soziale Klima* (1950), in: BA, Zsg 132/154.

30 Ibid., p. 2.

31 IfD, l.c., p. 33.

32 Opinion survey published in: *Neue Ruhrzeitung*, 25 May 1949 and *Hamburger Echo*, 25 June 1949. In connection with this, see also IfD, l.c., pp. 35–45.

33 CDU-leaflet *Freiheit in Arbeit und Beruf*, n.d.; Albers, J., *Der christliche Arbeiter bejaht Frankfurt*, in: *Rheinische Post*, 4 June 1949.

34 *Merkwürdigkeiten aus der VfW*, in: *Industriekurier*, 26 June 1949; *Klassenkampf-Situation in Westdeutschland*, in: *Der Sozialdemokrat*, 16 July 1949.

35 E.g. articles on Schumacher's stump speeches, in: *Ruhrnachrichten*, 3 Aug 1949; *Bemerkungen der Woche*, in: *Der Volkswirt*, no. 32, 12 Aug 1949, p. 4. See also Narr, W.-D., l.c., p. 114.

36 Neumann, E. P.; Noelle, E., l.c., 1954, p. 192; survey, in: *Der Spiegel*, 5 March 1949. The development in popularity among politicians at that time was also documented by an EMNID survey commissioned by the SPD party executive in June 1949. Accordingly, 13.07 per cent of the interviewees responded in favour of Schumacher, 13.0 per cent were for Erhard, and 11.15 per cent voted for Adenauer; cf. Gallup, in: AdsD, *Pressedokumentation* (PD).

37 See appendix 15/16, pp. 173–80.

38 Tennstädt, F., *Der Wähler*, Allensbach, 1957, p. 17.

39 Alt, F., *Der Prozess der ersten Regierungsbildung unter Konrad Adenauer. Eine monographische Untersuchung der Bildung der ersten Bundesregierung 1949*, Bonn, 1970.

40 Art. 122 GG.

41 *Vereinigtes Wirtschaftsgebiet aufgelöst*, in: *Süddeutsche Zeitung*, 20 Sep 1949.

42 *Abschliessender Bericht des Präsidenten des Wirtschaftsrates des Vereinigten Wirtschaftsgebietes über die Gesetzgebung des Wirtschaftsrates*, Frankfurt am Main, 7 Sep 1949, in: DBt PA, 2/316.

43 Report no. 191 (9 Dec 1949), in: Merritt, A. J.; Merritt, R. L. (eds.), l.c., p. 317.

44 Art. 20 para. 1 and 2 GG, in: BGBl. I.

45 Gardner, J., l.c., p. 289.

46 IfD, l.c., p. 76; Noelle, E.; Neumann, E. P. (eds.), l.c., p. 249.

47 Report no. 191 (9 Dec 1949), in: Merritt, A. J.; Merritt, R. L. (eds.), l.c., p. 316.

48 IfD, l.c., p. 7; Noelle, E.; Neumann, E. P. (eds.), l.c., p. 160.

49 Hafter, R., *Guter Start in Westdeutschland*, in: NZZ, 16 Aug 1949, p. 1.

50 Hielscher, E., *Leidensweg der deutschen Währungsreform*, Munich, 1948, p. 10.

51 *Soziale Marktwirtschaft*, in: *Wirtschafts-Zeitung*, 3 Sep 1949; *Die Chance der Sozialen Marktwirtschaft*, in: *Münchner Allgemeine Zeitung*, 4 Sep 1949; *Pressestimmen zur Wirtschaftspolitik*, in: *Aachener Nachrichten*, 6 Sep 1949; Dirks, W., *Zankapfel Wirtschaftspolitik*, in: *Neue Presse*, 13 Sep 1949; Weisser, G., *Wohin wird die westdeutsche Wirtschaft gesteuert?*, in: *Hamburger Echo*, 14 Oct 1949; Konradin, P., *Die Reise geht nach Utopia*, in: *Hannoversche Presse*, no. 147, 22 Oct 1949; *Der andere Weg*, in: *Württembergische Abend-Zeitung*, 28 Oct 1949; Gleitze, B., *Gefahren der freien Marktwirtschaft*, in: *Lübecker Freie Presse*, 1 Nov 1949.

Conclusion

1 Schumpeter, J. A., *Capitalism, Socialism and Democracy*, London, 1943, pp. 61, 167.

BIBLIOGRAPHY

MANUSCRIPTS AND ARCHIVAL SOURCES

Archiv der Christlich-Demokratische Politik (ACDP), Sankt Augustin

Bequests (*Nachlässe*) and Private Papers

NL Curt Becker
NL Paul Binder
NL Theodor Blank
NL Franz Böhm
NL Wilhelm Brese
NL Fritz Dengler
NL Bruno Dörpinghaus
NL Andreas Hermes
NL Margot Kalinke
NL Theophil Kaufmann
NL Erich Köhler
NL Adolf Lampe
NL Hans-Joachim von Merkatz
NL Alfred Müller-Armack
NL Fritz Neef
NL Michael Rott
NL Georg Strickrodt

Newspapers, Magazines and Press Services

Die Gegenwart

Additional Sources

VII-005 Sammlung
Plakatsammlung

Archiv für Christlich-Soziale Politik (ACSP), Munich

Bequests and Private Papers

NL Wilhelm Arnold
NL Anton Besold
NL Franz Elsen
NL Josef Müller
NL Hannes Schinagl
NL Hanns Seidel
NL Franz-Josef Strauss
NL Max Zwicknagel

Holdings

HA Werner Dollinger
DS 1/3
DS 3187
LGF-PV
Z-LL
Z-BTF

Additional Sources

Flugblattsammlung
Plakatsammlung

Archiv des Liberalismus (ADL), Gummersbach

Bequests and Private Papers

NL Franz Blücher
NL Everhard Bungartz

Additional Sources

Plakatsammlung

Archiv der Ludwig-Erhard-Stiftung (ALES), Bonn

Bequests and Private Papers

NL Ludwig Erhard

Archiv der sozialen Demokratie (AdsD), Bonn

Bequests and Private Papers

NL Gerhard Kreyssig
NL Erik Nölting (unsystematic)
NL Georg Reuter (DGB Archiv)
NL Willi Richter (DGB Archiv)
NL Erwin Schoettle
NL Waldemar von Knoeringen
NL Georg-August Zinn

Holdings

SPD Party Executive (old holding)
Kurt Schumacher
Landtagsfraktion Niedersachsen
Minutes 1946–9

Newspapers, Magazines and Press Services

SPD – *Sozialdemokratischer Pressedienst* signatory MF 1324

Film Nr. 001
Jahrgang 1 (1946)
Jahrgang 2 (1947)

Film Nr. 002
Jahrgang 2 (1947)
Jahrgang 3 (1948)

Film Nr. 003
Jahrgang 3 (1948)
Jahrgang 3 (1948)

Film Nr. 004
Jahrgang 3 (1948)
Jahrgang 4 (1949)

Film Nr. 005
Jahrgang 4 (1949)
Jahrgang 4 (1949)

Additional Sources

Zeitungsausschnittarchiv des Parteivorstandes der SPD Band I
K 2 Wirtschaftspolitik
K 21 Enteignung, Sozialisierung, Verstaatlichung
K 232 Wirtschaftsdemokratie
K 29 Verschiedenes
K 41 Währung

Flugblattsammlung
Plakatsammlung
Pressedokumentation
Sammlung Zeitgeschichte

Archives de l'Occupation Française en Allemagne et en Autriche (AOC), Colmar

Série: Bade

Bayerisches Hauptstaatsarchiv (BayHStA), Munich

Abteilung V Nachlässe und Sammlungen

Bequests and Private Papers

NL Hans Ehard
NL Anton Pfeiffer
Abteilung II Bestände ab 1800
Bayerischer Bevollmächtigter beim Länderrat in Stuttgart
Bayerischer Bevollmächtigter beim Vereinigten Wirtschaftsgebiet in Frankfurt

Additional Sources

Pressearchiv 1946–59 (Bayerische Staatskanzlei)
Akten der Bayerischen Staatskanzlei
Akten des Bayerischen Staatsministeriums für Wirtschaft und Verkehr
Berichte des Landesarbeitsamtes 1948
Regierung von Ober- und Mittelfranken Berichterstattung 1947/1948

Bundesarchiv (BA), Koblenz

Bequests and Private Papers

NL Franz Blücher
NL Carl Goerdeler
NL Friedrich Holzapfel
NL Jakob Kaiser
NL Johannes Popitz
NL Hermann Pünder
NL Fritz Schäffer
NL Erich Welter

Holdings

B102	Bundesministerium für Wirtschaft
Z1	Länderrat des amerikanischen Besatzungsgebietes
Z3	Wirtschaftsrat des VWG (incl. supplement Köhler)
Z4	Länderrat des VWG
Z6 I	Büro des Direktors Schlange-Schöningen
Z8	Verwaltung für Wirtschaft des VWG
Z13	Direktorialkanzlei des Verwaltungsrats des VWG
Z17	Frankfurter Pressekonferenz
Z32	Sonderstelle Geld und Kredit bei der Verwaltung für Finanzen
Z35	Deutsches Büro für Friedensfragen
Z46	Allies Control Authority, Office of Records and Archives
Zsg 1-98	Wirtschaftspolitische Gesellschaft von 1947
Zsg 132/154	Sammlung IfD Allensbach

Deutsche Bundesbank – Historisches Archiv (BuBa HA), Frankfurt a. Main

B331-HMS

Deutscher Bundestag, Parlamentsarchiv (DBt PA), Bonn/Berlin

Abteilung Wissenschaftliche Dokumentation (Bestand 1, 2)

Protokolle und Materialien:
Zonenbeirat der Britischen Besatzungszone
Länderrat des Amerikanischen Besatzungsgebietes
Wirtschaftsrat des Vereinigten Wirtschaftsgebietes
Länderrat des Vereinigten Wirtschaftsgebietes
Verwaltungsrat des Vereinigten Wirtschaftsgebietes

Deutsches Historisches Museum (DHM), Berlin

Sammlung Plakate Bundesrepublik Deutschland
Lebendiges virtuelles Museum Online (LeMO)

Digitales Archiv Marburg (DigAM), Marburg

Bestand KPD Hessen

Hessisches Hauptstaatsarchiv (HHStA), Wiesbaden

Bestand KPD Hessen

Institut für Stadtgeschichte Frankfurt (IStGF), Frankfurt a. Main

Akten zum Wirtschaftsrat

Institut für Demoskopie (IfD), Allensbach

Bericht über die erste Umfrage der wirtschaftspolitischen Gesellschaft von 1947 über die deutsche Situation, Allensbach, 1949 (provided as a loan by the IfD)

Institut für Zeitgeschichte (IFZ), Munich

Bequests and Private Papers

NL Wilhelm Hoegner
NL Hans Möller

Holdings

OMGUS files
Pressesammlung
Presseausschnittsammlung

Institut Universitaire de Hautes Études Internationales (IUHEI), Bibliothèque, Genève

Archiv Wilhelm Röpke: Correspondance Röpke – Rappard, 1937-1966

Landesarchiv Baden-Württemberg (LABW) / Staatsarchiv Freiburg (StAF), Freiburg

C 25/2

Landesarchiv Berlin (LAB), Berlin

Klingelhöfer Papers

Nordrhein-Westfälisches Hauptstaatsarchiv (HStAD), Düsseldorf

NL Guido Ziersch
RW 26-1026
RW 189-193
RWN 116
RWV 26-14

Presse und Informationsamt der Bundesregierung (BPA), Berlin

Pressesammlung

Stadtarchiv Köln (StAK), Cologne

NL Leo Schwering

Stadtverwaltung (StVW), Ansbach

EAP 022-95/19, 95/20

Stadtverwaltung (StVW), Fürth

EAP 4

Statistisches Bundesamt Deutschland (StBA), Wiesbaden

Bevölkerungsstatistik B15 (nach Alters- und Geburtsjahren) 1950
Statistisches Jahrbuch 1953
Wirtschaft und Statistik 1949/1950
Die deutschen Vertriebenen in Zahlen Teil II – 40 Jahre Eingliederung in der Bundesrepublik Deutschland

Stiftung Bundeskanzler-Adenauer-Haus (StBKAH), Rhöndorf

Bequests and Private Papers

NL Konrad Adenauer

Additional Sources

Press documentation

Stiftung Deutsches Rundfunkarchiv (DRA), Frankfurt a. Main

DRA, 76 U 3459/4, WDR doc. 564/2

The following sources are radio broadcast admissions on compact disc:

DRA, *Stimmen des 20. Jahrhunderts:*
1945 – Kapitulation und Wiederaufbau, Frankfurt am Main, 1995.
Überleben im Nachkriegsdeutschland, Frankfurt am Main, 2000.
Wir sind wieder wer, Frankfurt am Main, 1997.
Nach bestem Wissen und Gewissen – Die Beratungen zum Grundgesetz im Parlamentarischen Rat 1948/49, Frankfurt am Main, 1998.

PRINTED PRIMARY SOURCES

Editions and Document Collections

Akten zur Vorgeschichte der Bundesrepublik Deutschland 1945–9, edited by the *Bundesarchiv* and the *Institut für Zeitgeschichte*
Volume 1, September 1945–December 1946, edited by Walter Vogel and Christoph Weisz, Munich etc., 1976
Volume 2, January–June 1947, edited by Wolfram Werner, Munich etc., 1979
Volume 3, June–December 1947, edited by Günter Plum, Munich etc., 1982
Volume 4, January–December 1948, edited by Christoph Weisz, Hans-Dieter Kreikamp and Bernd Steger, Munich etc., 1983
Volume 5, January–September 1949, edited by Hans-Dieter Kreikamp, Munich etc., 1981.

Die CDU/CSU im Frankfurter Wirtschaftsrat. Protokolle der Unionsfraktion 1947-1949, edited by Rainer Salzmann, Düsseldorf, 1988.

Documents on Germany under Occupation 1945-1954, selected and edited by Beate Ruhm von Oppen, London/New York/Toronto, 1955.

Dokumente zur parteipolitischen Entwicklung in Deutschland seit 1945, edited by Ossip K. Flechtheim, vols. I–IX, Berlin, 1962–71.

Elections and Political Parties in Germany, 1945-1952, edited by Policy Reports Secretary Office of Executive Secretary, n.l., 1952.

Germany, 1947-1949; the story in documents, edited by US Dept. of State, Washington, 1950.

Gründungsurkunde Programme seit 1945 edited by the CSU, n.l., n.d.

Konrad Adenauer und die CDU der britischen Besatzungszone 1946-1949. Dokumente zur Gründungsgeschichte der CDU Deutschlands, edited by Helmuth Pütz, Bonn, 1975.

Protokoll der Verhandlungen des Parteitages der Sozialdemokratischen Partei Deutschlands vom 9. bis 11. Mai 1946 in Hannover, Hamburg, 1947.

Protokoll der Verhandlungen des Parteitages der Sozialdemokratischen Partei Deutschlands vom 29. Juni bis 2. Juli 1947 in Nürnberg, Hamburg, n.d.

Protokoll der Verhandlungen des Parteitages der Sozialdemokratischen Partei Deutschlands vom 11. bis 14. September 1948 in Düsseldorf, Hamburg, n.d., Berlin/Bonn, 1976.

Die SPD-Fraktion im Frankfurter Wirtschaftsrat 1947-1949: Protokolle, Aufzeichnungen, Rundschreiben, edited by Christoph Stamm, Bonn, 1993.

Die Unionsparteien 1946-1950. Protokolle der Arbeitsgemeinschaft der CDU/CSU Deutschlands und der Konferenzen der Landesvorsitzenden, edited by Brigitte Kaff, Düsseldorf, 1991.

Verhandlungen des Bayerischen Landtags, Stenographische Berichte, Beilagen, Sprech- und Sachverzeichnis, Munich, 1945–9.

Der Weg in die Soziale Marktwirtschaft: Referate, Protokolle, Gutachten der Arbeitsgemeinschaft Erwin von Beckerath 1943-1947, edited by Christine Blumenberg-Lampe, Stuttgart, 1986.

Der Wirtschaftsrat des Vereinigten Wirtschaftsgebietes 1947-1949, edited by the Office of the Economic Council, n.l., n.d.

Der Wissenschaftliche Beirat bei der VfW des VWGs; Gutachten 1948 - Mai 1950, edited by the *Bundeswirtschaftsministerium*, Göttingen, n.d.

Wörtliche Berichte über die 1.-40. Vollversammlung des Wirtschaftsrates des Vereinigten Wirtschaftsgebietes (Zweizonen-Wirtschaftsrat) in Frankfurt am Main, 8 vols., Wiesbaden/Frankfurt am Main, 1947–9.

Wörtliche Berichte und Drucksachen des Wirtschaftsrates des Vereinigten Wirtschaftsgebietes 1947-1949, by the *Institut für Zeitgeschichte* and the *Deutschen Bundestag, Wissenschaftliche Dienste*, edited by Christoph Weisz and Hans Woller, Munich etc., 1977.

Volume 1, Erschließungsband
Volume 2, Wörtliche Berichte 1–22 (25.06.1947-01.10.1948)
Volume 3, Wörtliche Berichte 23–40 (19.10.1948-08.08.1949)
Volume 4, Drucksachen 1–637
Volume 5, Drucksachen 638–1182
Volume 6, Drucksachen 1183–1672

Acts and Decrees

Amtsblatt der Hohen Alliierten Kommission in Deutschland, No. 1, edited by G. P. Glain, Bonn-Petersberg, 23 September 1949.

Amtsblatt des Kontrollrats in Deutschland edited by the Allied Secretariat, Nr. 11, Berlin, 31 October 1946.

Amtsblatt der Militärregierung Deutschland. Britisches Kontrollgebiet, No. 3, n.d.

A Decade of American Foreign Policy : Basic Documents, 1941-49 Prepared at the Request of the Senate Committee on Foreign Relations by the Staff of the Committee and the Department of State, Washington, DC, Government Printing Office, 1950.

Entscheidungen des Bundesverfassungsgerichts, Amtliche Sammlung._Gesetz- und Verordnungsblatt des Wirtschaftsrats des Vereinigten Wirtschaftsgebietes (from Nr. 19/48 onwards titled *Gesetzblatt der Verwaltung des Vereinigten Wirtschaftsgebietes*).

Öffentlicher Anzeiger für das Vereinigte Wirtschaftsgebiet, edited by the *Rechtsamt des Vereinigten Wirtschaftsgebiets.*

Mitteilungsblatt des Verwaltungsamts für Wirtschaft des amerikanischen und britischen Besatzungsgebiets, edited by the *Verwaltungsamt für Wirtschaft in Minden.*

SHAEF Law No. 191 of the USA, in: *Gazette US Military Government Germany*, 24 November 1944.

The Psychological Warfare Division, Supreme Headquarters Allied Expeditionary Force. An Account of its Operations in the Western European Campaign 1944-1945, Bad Homburg, 1945.

Newspapers, Magazines and Press Services

Aachener Nachrichten
Abendpost
Allgemeine Zeitung
Arbeiterzeitung (Schaffhausen)
Der Bund
Il Contadino Svizzero
Darmstädter Echo
Der Gerade Weg – Organ der Christlich-Sozialen Union
Deutsche Zeitung
Deutschland-Union-Dienst (*DUD*)
Echo vom Zürichberg (Oerlikon)
Express (Biel)
Feuille d'Avis de Neuchâtel

Frankfurter Allgemeine Zeitung
Frankfurter Neue Presse
Frankfurter Rundschau
Fränkische Landeszeitung
Freie Presse
Freiheit
Die Freiheit
Gazette de Lausanne
Die Gegenwart
Hamburger Echo
Handelsblatt
Hannoversche Presse
Hannoversche Volksstimme
Hessische Nachrichten
Hochwacht (Winterthur)
Industriekurier
Informationsblatt der Kommunistischen Partei
Journal de Genève
Journal de Montreux
Kasseler Zeitung
Lübecker Freie Presse
Mainzer Allgemeine Zeitung
Mitteilungen der Christlich Sozialen Union
Münchner Allgemeine
National Zeitung (Basel)
Neue Presse
Neues Deutschland
Neues Tageblatt
Neuer Vorwärts – Zentralorgan der Sozialdemokratischen Partei Deutschlands
Neues Winterthurer Tagblatt
Neue Zeit
Die Neue Zeitung
Neue Zürcher Nachrichten
Neue Zürcher Zeitung
Niedersächsische Volksstimme
Nordsee Zeitung
Nordwestdeutsche Rundschau
Nürnberger Nachrichten
ORDO, Jahrbuch für die Ordnung von Wirtschaft und Gesellschaft
Ostschweiz (St. Gallen)
Das Parlament
Rhein-Neckar-Zeitung Heidelberg
Rheinische Post
Rheinische Zeitung
Rheinischer Merkur
Ruhrnachrichten
Saarbrücker Zeitung
Salzburger Nachrichten
Schleswig-Holsteinische Volkszeitung
Schwäbische Zeitung
Schwäbische Landeszeitung
Schweizer Monatshefte
Seeländer Volksstimme (Biel)
Der Sozialdemokrat
Sozialdemokratischer Pressedienst
Stuttgarter Zeitung
La Suisse
Süddeutsche Zeitung
Tagesanzeiger (Zurich)
Der Tagesspiegel
Die Tat
Telegraf
Textil-Zeitung
Thurgauer Zeitung (Frauenfeld)
La Tribune de Genève
Union in Deutschland (see also *DUD*)
Union im Norden
Union im Wahlkampf
Vaterland (Luzern)
Das Volk
Der Volkswirt
Volks-Wirtschaft (Sozialdemokratischer Pressedienst)
Vossische Zeitung
Die Welt
Die Weltwoche
Welt am Sonntag
Weser-Kurier Bremen
Westfälische Rundschau
Westdeutsches Tageblatt
Wiesbadener Kurier
Der Wirtschaftsspiegel
Wirtschaftsverwaltung
Wirtschafts-Zeitung
Wirtschafts- und Finanzzeitung
Württembergische Abend-Zeitung
Die Zeit
Zeitschrift für Schweizer Statistik & Volkswirtschaft

Newspaper Articles and Booklets

Agartz, V., *Unternehmertum – Trotz Planung*, in: *Wirtschafts Zeitung*, 24 May 1946.
Agartz, V., *Um den Neubau der Wirtschaft*, in: *Rheinische Zeitung*, 27 July 1947.
Barbier, H. D., *Die Freiheit als Sozialprogramm*, in: *Frankfurter Allgemeine Zeitung*, 1 February 1997.
Binder, P., *Sozialisierung und Planwirtschaft*, in: *Schwäbische Zeitung*, no. 7, vol. 4, 23 January 1948.
Binder, P., *Deutschlands Rückkehr in die Wirtschaft*, in: *Schwäbische Zeitung*, no. 27, vol. 4, 2 April 1948.
Böhm, F., *Schutz vor den „Großen"?* in: *Frankfurter Allgemeine Zeitung*, 17 April 1953.
Böttcher, K. W., *Die Übergangskrise der D-Mark*, in: *Frankfurter Hefte*, January 1949.
Braichet, R., *Le Problème Allemand*, in: *Feuille d'Avis de Neuchâtel*, 24 May 1945.
Clifford, A., n.t., in: *Daily Mail*, 28 July 1946.
Dehler, T., n.t., in: *Die Neue Zeitung*, vol. 4, issue 17, Munich, 11 July 1948.
Dirks, W., *Zankapfel Wirtschaftspolitik – Der Wahlkampf unter falscher Alternative*, in: *Frankfurter Neue Presse*, 13 September 1949.
Ehard, H., *Vor einer neuen Fehlentwicklung? Kritik am Frankfurter Wirtschaftsrat*, in: *Süddeutsche Zeitung*, no. 84, 4 October 1947.
Erhard, L., *Ein Notweg*, in: *Das Tage-Buch*, 1931.
Erhard, L., *Werbewirtschaft und Werbegestaltung*, in: *Die deutsche Fertigware*, Teil A, Heft 3, 1937, pp. 51–60.
Erhard, L., *Zur Jahreswende 1945/46*, in: *Die Neue Zeitung*, 31 December 1945.
Erhard, L., *Ausblicke*, in: *Deutsche Zeitung und Wirtschafts Zeitung*, 17 May 1946.
Erhard, L., *Politischer Föderalismus und wirtschaftlicher Zentralismus*, in: *Die Neue Zeitung*, 9 October 1946.
Erhard, L., *Freie Wirtschaft und Planwirtschaft*, in: *Die Neue Zeitung*, 14 October 1946.
Erhard, L., *Politischer Föderalismus und wirtschaftlicher Zentralismus. Aufgaben und Grenzen zentraler Wirtschaftsverwaltungsstellen*, in: *Der Wirtschaftsspiegel*, issue 2, vol. 1/2, January/February 1947.
Erhard, L., *Ist eine dezentralisierte Planwirtschaft möglich?*, in: *Die Neue Zeitung*, 26 May 1947.
Erhard, L., *Sprachverwirrung um die Wirtschaftsordnung*, in: *Die Neue Zeitung*, 23 June 1947.
Erhard, L., *Wirtschaftspolitik im Zeichen der Währungsreform und der Aktivierung des Marshallplans*, in: *Wirtschaftsverwaltung* 1, May 1948, pp. 4–15.
Erhard, L., *Soziale Marktwirtschaft*, in: *Die Neue Zeitung*, 8 January 1950.
Erhard, L., *Marktwirtschaft und Werbung gehören untrennbar zusammen*, in: *Wirtschaft und Werbung*, 12 December 1952.
Erhard, L., *Was uns trennte, was uns einte*, in: *Deutsche Zeitung*, 26 December 1975.
Eucken, W., *Wirtschaftspolitik am toten Punkt*, in: *Neue Zürcher Zeitung*, 20 July 1948a.
Eucken, W., *Der Kurs der Wirtschaftspolitik*, in: *Wirtschafts Zeitung*, 4 December 1948.
Eucken, W., *Von der alten zur neuen Wirtschaftspolitik*, in: *Frankfurter Allgemeine Zeitung*, 31 December, 1949.
Fack, F. U., *„Ich brauche mich Ihnen nicht vorzustellen"*, in: *Frankfurter Allgemeine Zeitung*, 1 February 1997.
Frentzel-Wagner, H., *Bremsklötze weg!*, in: *Die Zeit*, 28 August 1947.

Frenzel, C., *Die Entscheidung von Minden*, in: *Schwäbische Landeszeitung*, 28 January 1947.
Gleitze, B., *Gefahren der freien Marktwirtschaft*, in: *Lübecker Freie Presse*, 1 November 1949.
Götz, H. H., *Er suchte kompetente Gesprächspartner*, in: *Frankfurter Allgemeine Zeitung*, 1 February 1997.
Grote-Mißmahl, U., *Gewerkschaftliche Forderungen*, in: *Die Freiheit*, 16 June 1949.
György, P., *Gondolatok egy könyvsiker felett*, in: *Magyar Nemzet*, 26 February 1944.
Hafter, R., *Die Politik der Besatzungsmächte in Deutschland – Frischer Wind im Frankfurter Wirtschaftsrat*, in: *Neue Zürcher Zeitung*, 22 April 1948.
Hafter, R., *Die neue Währung in Westdeutschland – Scharfe Reaktion von russischer Seite – Erste Etappe der Reform*, in: *Neue Zürcher Zeitung*, 20 June 1948.
Hafter, R., *Der Wahlkampf in Westdeutschland – Die Parteiprogramme*, in: *Neue Zürcher Zeitung*, 27 July 1949.
Hafter, R., *Der Wahlkampf in Westdeutschland – Kontradiktorische Versammlung in Frankfurt*, in: *Neue Zürcher Zeitung*, 13 August 1949.
Hafter, R., *Guter Start in Westdeutschland*, in: *Neue Zürcher Zeitung*, 16 August 1949.
Hafter, R., *Die Möglichkeiten einer Koalition im westdeutschen Bundestag*, in: *Neue Zürcher Zeitung*, 19 August 1949.
Himpele, F., *Unpopulärer Wirtschaftsrat*, in: *Westdeutsches Tageblatt*, no. 56, 3 July 1947.
Huebner, R., *Werbung für alle*, in: *Frankfurter Allgemeine Zeitung*, 20 January 1953.
Ilau, H., *Künstliche Verwirrung*, in: *Frankfurter Allgemeine Zeitung*, 13 June 1953.
Jeske, J., *Die Marktwirtschaft – das war er*, in: *Frankfurter Allgemeine Zeitung*, 1 February 1997.
Kaufmann, E., *Soziale Marktwirtschaft*, in: *Wirtschaftsverwaltung*, n.d.
Konradin, P., *Die Reise geht nach Utopia*, in: *Hannoversche Presse*, 22 October 1949.
Kriedemann, H., *Positive Wirtschaftspolitik*, in: *Volks-Wirtschaft – Sozialdemokratischer Pressedienst*, vw/III/34, 26 August 1948.
Kriedemann, H., *Freie Wirtschaft und die Folgen*, in: *Sozialdemokratischer Pressedienst*, III/106, 3 September 1948.
Kriedemann, H., *Deutsche Wirtschaft 1948*, in: *Sozialdemokratischer Pressedienst Sonderdienst*, 21 December 1948.
Kriedemann, H., *Bilanz der „freien Wirtschaft"*, in: *Sozialdemokratischer Pressedienst*, IV/54, 9 May 1949.
Kronberger, P., *Warum Wirtschaftsdemokratie*, in: *Frankfurter Rundschau*, 9 April 1946.
Kronberger, P., *6760 Milliarden Kriegskosten – Beweis für die Notwendigkeit sozialistischer Planwirtschaft*, in: *Hannoversche Presse*, 11 October 1946.
Ladame, P.-A., *La crise de notre temps et le néo-libéralisme du professeur Röpke*, in: *La Tribune de Genève*, 29 June 1945.
Langer, W., *Wer ist denn eigentlich dieser Ludwig Erhard?*, in: *Frankfurter Allgemeine Zeitung*, 1 February 1997.
Leineweber, P., *Die Deutsche Wirtschaft am Jahresende – Der Ruf nach der Wirtschaftsfreiheit*, in: *Freie Presse*, 24 December 1946.
Miksch, L., *Gedanken zur Wirtschaftsordnung*, in: *Der Wirtschaftsspiegel*, issue 2, vol. 18, November 1947.
Miksch, L., *Das Problem der künftigen Wirtschaftsformen: Gedanken zur Wirtschaftsordnung*, in: *Der Wirtschaftsspiegel*, 1947a, pp. 401–55.

Miksch, L., *Wirtschaftspolitik in der Demokratie*, in: *Die Zeit*, 3 July 1947b.
Miksch, L., *Die Zinspolitik am Scheideweg*, in: *Neue Zürcher Zeitung*, 6 September 1948c.
Mötteli, C., *Das Problem der internationalen Ordnung – Zur Neuauflage eines Buches von Wilhelm Röpke*, in: *Neue Zürcher Zeitung*, 5 August 1954.
Montag, A., *Die Aera Erhard*, in: *Volks-Wirtschaft – Sozialdemokratischer Pressedienst*, vw/III/30, 29 July 1948.
Mülbach, P., *Gefährliche „Wirtschaft"*, in: *Die Freiheit*, 14 January 1949.
Müller-Armack, A., *Soziale Marktwirtschaft*, in: *Der Wirtschaftsspiegel*, issue 2, vol. 21, December 1947.
Müller-Armack, A., *Soziale Marktwirtschaft*, in: *Telegraf*, 31 July 1947.
Müller-Armack, A., *Sicherung der Marktwirtschaft*, in: *Der Tagesspiegel*, 28 September 1948.
Muthesius, V., *Diktatur des Konsumenten*, in: *Die Welt*, 27 July 1948.
Nell-Breuning, O. v., *Die Währungsbereinigung in Deutschland II*, in: *Neue Zürcher Zeitung*, 15 November 1948.
Neumann, C., *Marktwirtschaft unverletzlich!*, in: *Industriekurier*, 12 December 1948.
N.N., *Ausblick in die Nachkriegswirtschaft*, in: *Tagesanzeiger* (Zurich), 22 January 1942.
N.N., *Wirtschaft im und nach dem Krieg*, in: *Hochwacht* (Winterthur), 30 January 1942.
N.N., *Prospettive economiche del dopo-guerra*, in: *Il Contadino Svizzero*, February 1942.
N.N., *Die Gesellschaftskrisis der Gegenwart*, in: *Vaterland* (Luzern), 16 March 1942.
N.N., *Die Gesellschaftskrisis der Gegenwart*, in: *Thurgauer Zeitung* (Frauenfeld), 31 March 1942.
N.N., *Der Dritte Weg*, in: *Ostschweiz* (St. Gallen), 4 April 1942.
N.N., *La Crise de Notre Temps*, in: *Gazette de Lausanne*, 18 May 1942.
N.N., *Die Gesellschaftskrisis der Gegenwart*, in: *Tagesanzeiger* (Zurich), 6 June 1942.
N.N., *Der Dritte Weg*, in: *Seeländer Volksstimme* (Biel), 11 June 1942.
N.N., *Prof. W. Röpke nach Amerika berufen*, in: NZZ, 9 February 1943.
N.N., *Berufung von Prof. W. Röpke*, in: *Neues Winterthurer Tagblatt*, 9 February 1943.
N.N., *Le professeur Röpke appelé à New York*, in: *Gazette de Lausanne*, 9 February 1943.
N.N., *De Genève à New York*, in: *Journal de Genève*, 9 February 1943.
N.N., *Wilhelm Röpke verlässt Genf*, in: *Express* (Biel), 9 February 1943.
N.N., *Wissenschaftliche Nachrichten*, in: *National Zeitung* (Basel), 10 February 1943.
N.N., *Wilhelm Röpke geht nach New York*, in: *Neue Zürcher Nachrichten*, 10 February 1943.
N.N., *Geht Professor Röpke nach Amerika?*, in: *Die Tat*, 10 February 1943.
N.N., *Röpke nach New York berufen*, in: *Bund*, 10 February 1943.
N.N., *Le professeur Wilhelm Röpke*, in: *La Suisse*, 10 February 1943.
N.N., *Wilhelm Röpke nach Amerika berufen*, in: *Echo vom Zürichberg* (Oerlikon), 11 February 1943.
N.N., *L'Example de la Suisse*, in: *Journal de Genève*, 4 June 1943.
N.N., *La société saine et malade*, in: *Journal de Genève*, 30 November 1943.
N.N., *Une conférence de M. Röpke sur „La société saine et malade"*, in: *La Tribune de Genève*, 1 December 1943.
N.N., *Antiroepke*, in: *Arbeiter Zeitung* (Schaffhausen), 21 April 1944.
N.N., *So etwas wie ein geistiger Führer…*, in: *Das Volk* (Olten), 24 June 1944.
N.N., *Wirtschaft von morgen*, in: *Die Weltwoche*, 29 September 1944.
N.N., *Le Professeur Röpke*, in: *Journal de Montreux*, 5 December 1944.

N.N., *77 Prozent bevorzugen die überparteiliche Zeitung*, in: *Deutsche Zeitung*, 25 November 1946.
N.N., *Das ganze Volk wird entscheiden*, in: *Hannoversche Volksstimme*, 14 February 1947.
N.N., *Gegen das Volk*, in: *Rheinische Zeitung*, 8 March 1947.
N.N., *Im Westen „sozialisiert" die CDU*, in: *Telegraf*, 30 March 1947.
N.N., *„Soziale Marktwirtschaft"*, in: *Telegraf*, 31 July 1947.
N.N., *Das Streiflicht*, in: *Süddeutsche Zeitung*, no. 81, 23 September 1947.
N.N., *Der Prüfstein*, in: *Die Neue Zeitung*, no. 79, 3 October 1947.
N.N., *Hinweg mit dem Länder-Egoismus – Partikularistische Engherzigkeit gefährdet die Arbeit des Zweizonen-Wirtschaftsrates*, in: *Telegraf*, no. 234/2, 7 October 1947.
N.N., *Neubau oder Wiederaufbau?*, in: *Süddeutsche Zeitung*, 4 November 1947.
N.N., *Vorwiegend positives Echo auf Frankfurt*, in: *Die Neue Zeitung*, 12 January 1948.
N.N., *Die Kritik am Frankfurter Wirtschaftsrat*, in: *Mitteilungen der Christlich Sozialen Union*, no. 11, 29 May 1948.
N.N., *Kommentare*, in: *Nordsee Zeitung*, 21 June 1948.
N.N., *Zentral gelenkte Wissenschaft*, in: *Das Volk*, 24 July 1948.
N.N., *„Freie" Leistungsauslese*, in: *Telegraf*, 7 August 1948.
N.N., *Gegen Erhards Wirtschaftskurs*, in: *Westfälische Rundschau*, 10 August 1948.
N.N., *Pressestimmen*, in: *Welt am Sonntag*, 22 August 1948.
N.N., *Bayern proklamiert Planwirtschaft*, in: *Aachener Nachrichten*, 27 August 1948.
N.N., *Restordnung oder Neuordnung*, in: *Rheinische Zeitung*, 20 July 1949.
N.N., *Die soziale Marktordnung Professor Erhards*, in: *Volks-Wirtschaft*, 27 July 1949.
N.N., *Die sagenhafte „soziale" Marktwirtschaft*, in: *Rheinische Zeitung*, 30 July 1949.
N.N., *Pendelnde Wirtschaftspolitik*, in: *Nordwestdeutsche Rundschau*, 6 August 1949.
N.N., *Soziale Marktwirtschaft*, in: *Wirtschafts Zeitung*, 3 September 1949.
N.N., *Die Chance der sozialen Marktwirtschaft*, in: *Münchner Allgemeine*, 4 September 1949.
N.N., *Pressestimmen zur Wirtschaftspolitik*, in: *Aachener Nachrichten*, 6 September 1949.
N.N., *Der andere Weg*, in: *Württembergische Abend-Zeitung*, 28 October 1949.
Rittershausen, H., *Politische Tendenzen in Westdeutschland*, in: *Neue Zürcher Zeitung*, 14 April 1949.
Röpke, W., *Grundfragen rationeller Wirtschaftspolitik*, in: *Zeitschrift für Schweizer Statistik & Volkswirtschaft*, no. 1, 1941.
Röpke, W., *Die Grundlagen der Nationalökonomie I*, in: *Neue Zürcher Zeitung*, 22 February 1942.
Röpke, W., *Grundlagen der Nationalökonomie II*, in: *Neue Zürcher Zeitung*, 24 February 1942.
Röpke, W., *Internationale Wirtschaftsprobleme nach dem Kriege*, in: *Neue Zürcher Zeitung*, n.d.
Röpke, W., *Das Echo eines Buches I-IV*, in: *Neue Zürcher Zeitung*, 23–6 July 1942.
Röpke, W., *Weltwirtschaft und internationale Geldordnung nach dem Kriege – Der „Dritte Weg" in der Weltwirtschaft*, in: *Schweizer Monatshefte*, no. 10, 10 January 1943.
Röpke, W., *Gerechte Rohstoffverteilung zwischen den Völkern*, in: *Neue Zürcher Zeitung*, 14 June 1944.
Röpke, W., *Ein neuer Typ der Wirtschaftspolitik*, in: *Stuttgarter Zeitung*, 27 February 1946.

Röpke, W., *Vereinigte Staaten von Deutschland*, in: *Neue Zürcher Zeitung*, 21 September 1946.

Röpke, W., *Sozialismus in Deutschland?*, in: *Neue Zürcher Zeitung*, 12 April 1947.

Röpke, W., *Um die deutsche Wirtschaftsheilung I*, in: *Neue Zürcher Zeitung*, 19 February 1948a.

Röpke, W., *Um die deutsche Wirtschaftsheilung II*, in: *Neue Zürcher Zeitung*, 20 February 1948b.

Röpke, W., *Kollektivistischer Starrkrampf in Deutschland*, in: *Neue Zürcher Zeitung*, 1 June 1948c.

Röpke, W., *Die Rettung Westdeutschlands*, in: *Neue Zürcher Zeitung*, 30 June 1948d.

Rupp, F., *Westdeutsche Wirtschaftspolitik – kritisch gesehen*, in: *Die Neue Zeitung*, 24 December 1948.

Rüstow, A., *Die Bewältigung des Wohlstandes*, in: *Frankfurter Allgemeine Zeitung*, 7 December 1960.

Schäfer, O., *Für die Wirtschaftsdemokratie*, in: *Hessische Nachrichten*, 3 November 1945.

Schiller, K., *Wirtschaft am Scheidewege*, in: *Schleswig-Holsteinische Volkszeitung*, 13 April 1946.

Schröder, E., *Wirtschaftspolitische Gesellschaft in Deutschland*, in: *Neue Zürcher Zeitung*, 1 January 1948.

Schumacher, K., *Deutschland und Europa*, in: *Sozialdemokratischer Pressedienst*, no. 16, 7 August 1946.

Schumpeter, J., *Der Übergang zum Sozialismus*, in: *Wirtschafts Zeitung*, 26 July 1946.

Schwarz, H.-P., *Ludwig Erhard – ein grosser Unzeitgemässer*, in: *Frankfurter Allgemeine Zeitung*, 1 February 1997.

Skopp, P., *Wirtschaft und Verfassung – Auf dem Wege zur Wirtschaftsdemokratie*, in: *Neuer Vorwärts*, 2 October 1948.

Sommer, G., *Ein offenes Wort*, in: *Rheinischer Merkur*, 5 June 1948.

SPD (ed.), *Was wir wollen*, n.l., 1949.

SPD (ed.), *„Für ein freies Deutschland in einem neuen Europa", Wahlaufruf der Sozialdemokratischen Partei Deutschlands, Sonderversand*, in: *SPD-Pressedienst*, 1949.

SPD Hamburg (ed.), *Leitsätze der Sozialdemokratischen Partei Deutschlands zur Gestaltung einer sozialistischen deutschen Wirtschaftsverfassung*, Hamburg, 1946.

Stampfer, F., *Klare Wirtschaftspolitik*, in: *Der Sozialdemokrat*, 25 January 1947.

Stampfer, F., *Zwang und Arbeit*, in: *Sozialdemokratischer Pressedienst*, III/139, 15 November 1948.

Wallenberger, H., *Fragen der Pressefreiheit*, in: *Die Neue Zeitung*, 8 July 1946.

Weber, A., *Der künftige Daseinsrahmen*, in: *Wirtschafts Zeitung*, 14 June 1946.

Weisser, G., *Wohin wird die westdeutsche Wirtschaft gesteuert?*, in: *Hamburger Echo*, 14 October 1949.

WipoG, *Marktwirtschaft als politisches Element*, in: *Der Wirtschaftsspiegel*, 15 December 1947.

Woerdehoff, B., *Die Adenauersche Mumie*, in: *Die Zeit*, 6 February 1987.

SECONDARY WORKS

Monographs

Abelshauser, W., *Wirtschaft in Westdeutschland, 1945-1948: Rekonstruktion und Wachstumsbedingungen in der amerikanischen und britischen Zone*, Stuttgart, 1975.

Abelshauser, W., *Wirtschaftsgeschichte der Bundesrepublik Deutschland (1945-1980)*, Frankfurt am Main, 1983.

Abelshauser, W., *Die verhinderte Neuordnung? Wirtschaftsordnung und Sozialstaatsprinzip in der Nachkriegszeit*, in: Gagel, W. (ed.), *Die Entstehung der Bundesrepublik Deutschland*, Stuttgart, 1984, pp. 58–77.

Abromeit, H., *Das Politische in der Werbung. Wahlwerbung und Wirtschaftswerbung in der Bundesrepublik*, Opladen, 1972.

Adorno, T. W., *Was bedeutet Aufarbeitung der Vergangenheit?*, in: Idem, *Erziehung zur Mündigkeit*, edited by G. Kadelbach, Frankfurt am Main, 1971, pp. 10–26.

Agartz, V., *Sozialistische Wirtschaftspolitik*, presentation given on the party convention of the SPD in 1946, edited by the SPD Greater-Hesse, Frankfurt am Main, 1946.

Albert, M., *Capitalism versus Capitalism*, New York, 1993.

Albig, W., *Public Opinion*, New York/London, 1939.

Albrecht, C.; Behrmann, G. C.; Bock, M.; Homann, H.; Tenbruck, F. H., *Die intellektuelle Gründung der Bundesrepublik. Eine Wirkungsgeschichte der Frankfurter Schule*, Frankfurt am Main/New York, 1999.

Albrecht, W. (ed.), *Kurt Schumacher. Reden – Schriften – Korrespondenzen 1945-1952*, Berlin/Bonn, 1985a.

Albrecht, W. (ed.), *Kurt Schumacher als deutscher und europäischer Sozialist*, Bonn, 1988.

Alt, F., *Der Prozess der ersten Regierungsbildung unter Konrad Adenauer. Eine monographische Untersuchung der Bildung der ersten Bundesregierung 1949*, Bonn, 1970.

Altmann, R.; Gross, J., *Gespräch über Erhard*, in: Schröder, G.; Müller-Armack, A.; Hohmann, K.; Gross, J.; Altmann, R. (eds.), *Ludwig Erhard – Beiträge zu seiner politischen Biographie, Festschrift zum 75. Geburtstag*, Frankfurt am Main, 1972.

Altrichter, H., *Sozialismus oder Marktwirtschaft? Die Diskussion um die wirtschaftliche Neuordnung in den Westzonen 1945-1948*, in: Ruffmann, K.H.; Altrichter, H. (eds.), *„Modernisierung" versus „Sozialismus". Formen und Strategien sozialen Wandels im 20. Jahrhundert*, Erlangen, 1983, pp. 187–227.

Ambrosius, G., *Die Durchsetzung der sozialen Marktwirtschaft in Westdeutschland 1945–9*, Stuttgart, 1977.

Ambrosius, G., *Funktionswandel und Strukturveränderung der Bürokratie 1945–9: Das Beispiel Wirtschaftsverwaltung*, in: Winkler, H. A. (ed.), *Politische Weichenstellungen im Nachkriegsdeutschland 1945-1953*, Göttingen, 1979, pp. 167–207.

Aristotle; Gigon, O. (ed.), *Politik*, Munich, 1986.

Arnold, F., *Anschläge. 220 politische Plakate als Dokumente der deutschen Geschichte 1900-1980*, Ebenhausen, 1985.

Balabkins, N., *Germany under Direct Controls: Economic Aspects of Industrial Disarmament, 1945-1948*, New Brunswick, 1964.

Bark, D. L.; Gress, D. R., *A History of West Germany – From Shadow to Substance, 1945-1963*, vol. I, Oxford, 1989.

Barry, N. P., *Political and Economic Thought of German Neo-Liberalism*, in: Peacock, A.; Willgerodt, H. (eds.), *German Neo-Liberals and the Social Market Economy*, London, 1989.

Baumgärtel, M. (ed.), *Geschichte einer Volkspartei: 50 Jahre CSU 1945-1995*, edited by the *Hanns-Seidel-Stiftung*, Munich, 1995.

Bausch, H., *Rundfunkpolitik nach 1945*, vol. 1, 1945–62, Munich, 1980.

Becker, F., *Kleine Geschichte der CDU*, edited by the *Konrad-Adenauer-Stiftung*, Stuttgart, 1995.

Becker, H. P., *Die soziale Frage im Neoliberalismus*, Heidelberg/Leuven, 1965.

Becker, J.; Stammen, T.; Waldmann, P. (eds.), *Vorgeschichte der Bundesrepublik Deutschland – Zwischen Kapitulation und Grundgesetz*, Munich, 1979.

Becker, W., *CDU und CSU 1945-1950. Vorläufer, Gründung und regionale Entwicklung bis zum Entstehen der CDU-Bundespartei*, Mainz, 1987.

Becker, W., *Historische Grundlagen der christlich-demokratischen Parteibildung nach 1945*, in: Buchstab, G.; Otto, K. (eds.), *Die Gründung der Union. Tradition, Entstehung und Repräsentanten*, Munich, 1990.

Becker, W.; Morsey, R. (eds.), *Christliche Demokratie in Europa. Grundlagen und Entwicklungen seit dem 19. Jahrhundert*, Cologne/Vienna, 1988.

Beier, G., *Der Demonstrations- und Generalstreik vom 12. November 1948*, Frankfurt am Main/Cologne, 1975.

Belloc, H.; Chesterton, C., *The Party System*, London, 1921.

Benz, W.; Graml, H. (eds.), *Aspekte deutscher Aussenpolitik im 20. Jahrhundert*, Stuttgart, 1976.

Benz, W. (ed.), *Die Bundesrepublik Deutschland. Geschichte in drei Bänden*, vol. 3, Frankfurt am Main, 1983.

Benz, W., *Von der Besatzungsherrschaft zur Bundesrepublik. Stationen einer Staatsgründung 1946-1949*, Frankfurt am Main, 1985.

Benz, W., *Die Geschichte der Bundesrepublik Deutschland. Politik, Wirtschaft, Gesellschaft, Kultur*, Frankfurt am Main, 1989.

Benz, W., *Deutschland unter alliierter Besatzung 1945–9/1955*, Berlin, 1999.

Benz, W., *Die Gründung der Bundesrepublik Deutschland – Von der Bizone zum souveränen Staat*, Munich, 1999a.

Berghahn, V. R., *Modern Germany: Society, Economy and Politics in the Twentieth Century*, Cambridge, 1982.

Berghahn, V. R., *Ideas into Politics: The Case of Ludwig Erhard*, in: Bullen, R. J.; Pogge von Strandmann, H. J. O.; Polonsky, A. B. (eds.), *Ideas into Politics*, London, 1984.

Berghahn, V. R., *The Americanisation of West German Industry, 1945-1973*, Leamington Spa, 1986.

Berghahn, V. R., *Modern Germany*, Cambridge, 1987.

Berghahn, V. R.; Vitolis, S. (eds.), *Gibt es einen deutschen Kapitalismus? Tradition und globale Perspektiven der sozialen Marktwirtschaft*, Frankfurt am Main, 2006.

Berg-Schlosser, D., *Die Konstituierung des Wirtschaftssystems*, in: Becker, J.; Stammen, T.; Waldmann, P., *Vorgeschichte der Bundesrepublik Deutschland – Zwischen Kapitulation und Grundgesetz*, Munich, 1979.

Berg-Schlosser, D., *Ludwig Erhard*, in: Bernecker, W. L.; Dotterweich, V. (eds.), *Persönlichkeit und Politik in der Bundesrepublik Deutschland. Politische Portraits*, vol. 1, Göttingen, 1982, pp. 113–22.

Berg-Schlosser, D.; Rytlewski, R. (eds.), *Political Culture in Germany*, London, 1993.

Bergsträsser, L., *Geschichte der politischen Parteien in Deutschland*, Munich/Vienna, 1965.

Best, J., *Public Opinion: Micro and Macro*, Homewood, 1973.

Beyme, K. v., *The Political System of the Federal Republic of Germany*, Aldershot, 1983.

Biedenkopf, K. H., *Ludwig Erhards Ringen um eine politische Gesamtordnung*, in: Hohmann, K.; Schönwitz, D.; Weber, H. J.; Wünsche, H. F. (eds.), *Grundtexte zur Sozialen Marktwirtschaft*, vol. 2, *Das Soziale in der Sozialen Marktwirtschaft*, Stuttgart/New York, 1988, pp. 453–70.

Bismarck, Ph. v., *Soziale Marktwirtschaft. Das Geschenk der Stunde Null*, Freiburg/Basel/Vienna, 1992.

Bittel, K. (ed.), *Das Potsdamer Abkommen und andere Dokumente*, Berlin, 1959.

Bitter, G., *Zur Typologie des deutschen Zeitungswesens in der Bundesrepublik Deutschland*, Munich, 1951.

Blesgen, D. J., *Erich Preiser. Wirken und wirtschaftspolitische Wirkungen eines deutschen Nationalökonomen (1900 - 1967)*, Berlin/Heidelberg, 2000.

Blum, R., *Soziale Marktwirtschaft. Wirtschaftspolitik zwischen Neoliberalismus und Ordoliberalismus*, Tübingen, 1969.

Blumenberg-Lampe, C., *Das Wirtschaftspolitische Programm der "Freiburger Kreise"*, Berlin, 1973.

Blumenberg-Lampe, C. (ed.), *Einführung in die Edition*, in: *Der Weg in die Soziale Marktwirtschaft: Referate, Protokolle, Gutachten der Arbeitsgemeinschaft Erwin von Beckerath 1943-1947*, Stuttgart, 1986.

Blumenberg-Lampe, C., *Oppositionelle Nachkriegsplanung: Wirtschaftswissenschaftler gegen den Nationalsozialismus*, in: Eckhard, J.; Martin, B.; Mück., M.; Ott, H. (eds.), *Die Freiburger Universität in der Zeit des Nationalsozialismus*, Freiburg/Würzburg, 1991, pp. 207–19.

Blumer, H., *Collective Behaviour*, New York, 1946.

Blümle, G.; Goldschmidt, N., *Zur Normativität ordoliberalen Denkens*, in: Külp, B.; Vanberg, V. (eds.), *Freiheit und wettbewerbliche Ordnung. Gedenkband zur Erinnerung an Walter Eucken*, Freiburg/Berlin/Munich, 2000.

Böhm, F., *Wettbewerb und Monopolkampf. Eine Untersuchung zur Frage des wirtschaftlichen Kampfrechts und zur Frage der rechtlichen Struktur der geltenden Wirtschaftsordnung*, Berlin, 1933.

Böhm, F., *Die Ordnung der Wirtschaft als geschichtliche Aufgabe und rechtsschöpferische Leistung*, Stuttgart/Berlin, 1937.

Böhm, F., *Reden und Schriften*, Karlsruhe, 1960.

Böhm, F., *Freiheit und Ordnung in der Marktwirtschaft*, Baden-Baden, 1980.

Borchardt, K., *Zur Geschichte des Bayerischen Staatsministeriums für Wirtschaft und Verkehr*, Stuttgart, 1987.

Bösch, F., Frei, N. (eds.), *Medialisierung und Demokratie im 20. Jahrhundert*, Göttingen, 2006.

Bosl, K., *Bayerische Geschichte*, Munich, 1990.

Bourdieu, P., *Public Opinion Does Not Exist*, in: Mattelart, A.; Siegelaub, S. (eds.), *Communication and Class Struggle*, vol. I, New York, 1979, pp. 124–30.

Bracher, K. D.; Eschenburg, Th.; Fest, J.; Jäckel, E., *Geschichte der Bundesrepublik Deutschland*, 5 vols., Stuttgart/Wiesbaden/Mannheim, 1981–7.

Braunthal, J., *Kurt Schumacher und die Sozialistische Internationale*, in: Scholz, A.; Oschilewski, W. G. (eds.), *Turmwächter der Demokratie – Ein Lebensbild von Kurt Schumacher*, vol. I, Berlin, 1954.

Brettschneider, F., *Öffentliche Meinung und Politik – Eine empirische Studie zur Responsivität des Deutschen Bundestages zwischen 1949 und 1990*, Opladen, 1995.

Brockway, F., *The New Leader*, in: Scholz, A.; Oschilewski, W. G. (eds.), *Turmwächter der Demokratie – Ein Lebensbild von Kurt Schumacher*, vol. II, Berlin, 1953.

Broyer, S., *Retour à l'économie de marché: les débats du conseil scientifique attaché à l'administration économique de la Bizone*, in: Commun, P. (ed.), *L'ordoliberalisme allemande. Aux sources de l'économie sociale de marché*, Cergy-Pontoise, 2003, pp. 201–21.

Bryce, J., *The American Commonwealth*, Indianapolis, 1888.

Buchanan, J., *The Economics and the Ethics of Constitutional Order*, Ann Arbor, 1991.

Buchheim, C., *Die Wiedereingliederung Westdeutschlands in die Weltwirtschaft, 1945-1958*, Munich, 1990.

Buchstab, G.; Otto, K. (eds.), *Die Gründung der Union. Tradition, Entstehung und Repräsentanten*, Munich, 1990.

Byrnes, J. F., *Restatement of US Policy in Germany*, Stuttgart, 6 September 1946 (US Government Print Office, Department of State publication, 2616, 1946)

Cantril, H.; Strunk, M., *Public Opinion 1935-1946*, Princeton, 1951.

Clay, L. D., *Decision in Germany*, Garden City/New York, 1950.

Cockett, R., *Thinking the Unthinkable – Think-Tanks and the Economic Counter-Revolution 1931-1983*, London, 1994.

Commun, P., *La contribution d'Alfred Müller-Armack à l'initiation d'un ordre économique libéral en Europe de 1958 à 1963*, in: Bitsch, M.-Th. (ed.), *Le couple France Allemagne et les institutions européennes. Une postérité pour le plan Schuman?*, Bruxelles, 2001, pp. 171–91.

Dahl, R. A., *Polyarchy. Participation and Opposition*, New Haven/London, 1971.

Dahrendorf, R., *Society and Democracy in Germany*, Garden City/New York, 1969.

Davidson, E., *The Death and Life of Germany. An Account of the American Occupation*, Columbia, Missouri, 1999.

Deissler, D., *Die entnazifizierte Sprache – Sprachpolitik und Sprachregelung in der Besatzungszeit*, Frankfurt am Main/Berlin/Bern/Bruxelles/New York/Oxford/Vienna, 2006.

Deter, G., *Ursprung und Entwicklung der Sozialen Marktwirtschaft*, in: Rüther, G. (ed.), *Soziale Marktwirtschaft. Entstehung, Grundlagen, Instrumente*, Bonn, 1994.

Deuerlein, E., *Die Einheit Deutschlands. Ihre Erörterung und Behandlung auf den Kriegs- und Nachkriegskonferenzen 1941-1949. Darstellung und Dokumentation*, Frankfurt am Main/Berlin, 1957a.

Deuerlein, E., *CDU/CSU 1945-1957. Beiträge zur Zeitgeschichte*, Cologne, 1957b.

Deuerlein, E. (ed.), *Potsdam 1945. Quellen zur Konferenz der „Grossen Drei"*, Munich, 1963.

Deuerlein, E., *Deutschland nach dem Zweiten Weltkrieg 1945-1955*, Konstanz, 1964.

Dewey, J., *The Public and Its Problems*, Athens, 1927.
Dicey, A. V., *Lectures on the Relation between Law and Public Opinion in England during the Nineteenth Century*, London, 1963.
Diekmannshenke, H.; Meißner, I. (eds.), *Politische Kommunikation im Historischen Wandel*, Tübingen, 2001.
Dietze, C. v., *Richtlinien künftiger Agrarpreispolitik*, 1943, in: *Der Weg in die Soziale Marktwirtschaft: Referate, Protokolle, Gutachten der Arbeitsgemeinschaft Erwin von Beckerath 1943-1947*, edited by Christine Blumenberg-Lampe, Stuttgart, 1986.
Dietze, C. v., *Nationalökonomie und Theologie*, Tübingen/Stuttgart, 1947.
Doering-Manteuffel, A., *Die Bundesrepublik Deutschland in der Ära Adenauer. Aussenpolitik und innere Entwicklung 1949-1963*, Darmstadt, 1983.
Dönhoff, M., *Von gestern nach übermorgen – Zur Geschichte der Bundesrepublik Deutschland*, Hamburg, 1981.
Donnison, F. S. V., *Civil Affairs and Military Government, North West Europe 1944-1946*, London, 1961.
Dorondo, D. R., *Bavaria and German Federalism: Reich to Republic, 1918-33, 1945-49*, New York, 1992.
Dreher, K., *Der Weg zum Kanzler. Adenauers Griff nach der Macht*, Düsseldorf, 1972.
Dworkin, R., *Is Democracy Possible Here? – Principles for a New Political Debate*, Princeton, 2006.
Ebinger, S., *Alexander Rüstow und die Soziale Marktwirtschaft*, Würzburg, 1988.
Edinger, L. J., *Kurt Schumacher. Persönlichkeit und politisches Verhalten*, Cologne, 1967.
Edinger, L. J., *West German Politics*, New York, 2006.
Eick, J. (ed.), *So nutzt man den Wirtschaftsteil einer Tageszeitung*, Frankfurt, 1971.
Elster, J. (ed.), *Rational Choice*, Oxford, 1986.
Elster, J., *Nuts and Bolts for the Social Sciences*, Cambridge, 1989.
Erhard, L., *Kriegsfinanzierung und Schuldenkonsolidierung. Faksimiledruck der Denkschrift von 1943/44*, Frankfurt am Main/Berlin/Vienna, 1977, preface, p. VII.
Erhard, L., *Die deutsche Wirtschaftspolitik im Blickfeld europäischer Politik*, in: Hunold, A. (ed.), *Wirtschaft ohne Wunder*, Erlenbach-Zurich, 1953.
Erhard, L. *Wohlstand für alle*, Düsseldorf, 1957 (new edition Gütersloh, 1963)
Erhard, L., *Prosperity through Competition*, London, 1958.
Erhard, L., *Wirken und Reden*, Ludwigsburg, 1966.
Erhard, L., *Wirtschaftspolitische Erfordernisse nach Beendigung des Krieges*, in: Stützel, W.; Watrin, C.; Willgerodt, H.; Hohmann, K. (eds.), *Grundtexte zur Sozialen Marktwirtschaft. Zeugnisse aus 200 Jahren ordnungspolitischer Diskussion*, Stuttgart/New York, 1981.
Erhard, L., *Wirtschaftspolitik als Teil der Gesellschaftspolitik*, in: Hohmann, K. (ed.), *Ludwig Erhard. Gedanken aus fünf Jahrzehnten, Reden und Schriften*, Düsseldorf/Vienna/New York, 1988.
Erhard, L., *Das Ordnungsdenken in der Marktwirtschaft*, in: Hohmann, K. (ed.), *Ludwig Erhard. Gedanken aus fünf Jahrzehnten, Reden und Schriften*, Düsseldorf/Vienna/New York, 1988a.
Erhard, L., *Franz Oppenheimer, dem Lehrer und Freund* (1964), in: Hohmann, K. (ed.), *Ludwig Erhard. Gedanken aus fünf Jahrzehnten, Reden und Schriften*, Düsseldorf/Vienna/New York, 1988b.

Erhard, L., *Deutsche Wirtschaftspolitik – Der Weg der Sozialen Marktwirtschaft*, Düsseldorf/Vienna/New York/Moscow, 1992 (originally published in 1962).

Eschenburg, T., *„Aus persönlichem Erleben: Zur Kurzfassung der Denkschrift 1943/44" zur Kriegsschrift Ludwig Erhards „Kriegsfinanzierung und Schuldenkonsolidierung"*, Frankfurt am Main, 1977.

Eschenburg, T., *Jahre der Besatzung 1945–9*, Stuttgart/Wiesbaden, 1983.

Etzioni, A., *The Active Society. A Theory of Societal and Political Processes*, London/New York, 1968.

Eucken, W., *Kapitaltheoretische Untersuchungen. Mit einer Einleitung in die Sammlung: Was leistet die nationalökonomische Theorie?*, Jena, 1934.

Eucken, W., *Grundlagen der Nationalökonomie*, Jena, 1940.

Eucken, W., *Wettbewerb als Grundprinzip der Wirtschaftsverfassung*, in: Schmölders, G. (ed.), *Der Wettbewerb als Mittel volkswirtschaftlicher Leistungssteigerung und Leistungsauslese*, Berlin, 1942.

Eucken, W., *The Foundations of Economics – History and Theory in the Analysis of Economic Reality*, Berlin/New York, 1992 (reprint of the first English edition published by William Hodge, London, 1950).

Eucken, W., *Grundsätze der Wirtschaftspolitik*, Tübingen, 1952.

Eynern, G. v., *Soziale Marktwirtschaft. Analyse eines wissenschaftlichen und politischen Schlagworts*, in: *Beiträge zur empirischen Konjunkturforschung. Festschrift zum 25jährigen Bestehen des Deutschen Institute für Wirtschaftsforschung*, Berlin, 1951, pp. 121–47.

Fack, F. U.; Fromme, F., K.; Nonnenmacher, G. (eds.), *Das deutsche Modell, Freiheitlicher Rechtsstaat und Soziale Marktwirtschaft*, Munich, 1991.

Fait, B.; Mintzel, A.; Schlemmer, Th. (eds.), *Die CSU 1945-1948. Protokolle und Materialien zur Frühgeschichte der Christlich-Sozialen Union*, 3 vols., Munich, 1993.

Fait, B., *Demokratische Erneuerung unter dem Sternenbanner – Amerikanische Kontrolle und Verfassungsgebung in Bayern 1946*, ch. 11, Düsseldorf, 1998.

Faul, E. (ed.), *Wahlen und Wähler in Westdeutschland*, Villingen, 1960.

Fischer, H. D., *Die grossen Zeitungen. Portraits der Weltpresse*, Munich, 1966.

Fischer, H.-D., *Parteien und Presse in Deutschland seit 1945*, Bremen, 1971.

Fischer, H.-D. (ed.), *Deutsche Zeitungen des 17. bis 20. Jahrhunderts (Publizistik-Historische Beiträge, Band 2)*, Munich, 1972.

Fischer, H.-D., *Reeducations- und Pressepolitik unter britischem Besatzungsstatus. Die Zonenzeitung „Die Welt" 1946-1950. Konzeption, Artikulation und Rezeption*, Düsseldorf, 1978.

Frederiksen, O. J., *The American Military Occupation of Germany, 1945-1953*, Washington, D.C., Goverment Printing Office, 1953.

Frei, N., *Hörfunk und Fernsehen*, in: Benz, W. (ed.), *Die Bundesrepublik Deutschland. Geschichte in drei Bänden*, vol. 3, Frankfurt am Main, 1983, pp. 319–57.

Galbraith, J. K., *The German Economy*, in: Harris, S.E., *Foreign Economic Policy for the United States*, Cambridge, Mass., 1948

Gallup, G. H., *Public Opinion in a Democracy*, Princeton, 1939.

Gallup, G.; Rae, S. F., *The Pulse of Democracy: The Public Opinion Poll and How It Works*, New York, 1940.

Gather, G., *Wirtschaft – Politik – Gesellschaft. Die Wirtschaftspolitische Gesellschaft 1947/71 und das Bildungswerk Offene Welt. Ulrich von Pufendorf zum 70. Geburtstag, 12. Oktober 1971*, Frankfurt am Main, 1971, pp. 10–15.

Gelberg, K-U., *Hans Ehard – Die Föderalistische Politik des Bayerischen Ministerpräsidenten 1946-1954*, Düsseldorf, 1992.

Giersch, H.; Paqué, H.; Schmieding, H., *The Fading Miracle: Four Decades of Market Economy in Germany*, Cambridge, Mass., 1992.

Gillessen, G., *Die Frankfurter Zeitung im Dritten Reich*, Berlin, 1986.

Gimbel, J., *Amerikanische Besatzungspolitik in Deutschland 1945–9*, Frankfurt am Main, 1968.

Gimbel, J., *Byrnes und die Bizone – Eine amerikanische Entscheidung zur Teilung Deutschlands?*, in: Benz, W.; Graml, H. (eds.), *Aspekte deutscher Aussenpolitik im 20. Jahrhundert*, Stuttgart, 1976, pp. 193–210.

Glasser, T. L.; Salmon, C. T. (eds.), *Public Opinion and the Communication of Consent*, New York, 1995.

Glynn, C. J., *Public Opinion*, Oxford, 1999.

Görtemaker, M., *Geschichte der Bundesrepublik Deutschland: Von der Gründung bis zur Gegenwart*, Munich, 1999.

Goldschmidt, N., *Entstehung und Vermächtnis ordoliberalen Denkens. Walter Eucken und die Notwendigkeit einer kulturellen Ökonomik*, Münster, 2002.

Goldschmidt, N.; Wohlgemuth, M. (eds.), *Die Zukunft der Sozialen Marktwirtschaft – Sozialethische und Ordnungsökonomische Grundlagen*, Freiburg im Breisgau, 2004.

Goldschmidt, N., *Zur Theorie der Sozialpolitik. Implikationen aus ordnungsökonomischer Perspektive*, in: Goldschmidt, N.; Wohlgemuth, M. (eds.), *Die Zukunft der Sozialen Marktwirtschaft – Sozialethische und Ordnungsökonomische Grundlagen*, Freiburg im Breisgau, 2004, pp. 63–95.

Goldschmidt, N., *Die Rolle Walter Euckens im Widerstand: Freiheit, Ordnung und Wahrhaftigkeit als Handlungsmaximen*, in: Goldschmidt, N. (ed.), *Wirtschaft, Politik und Freiheit*, Freiburg im Breisgau, 2005.

Goldschmidt, N. (ed.), *Wirtschaft, Politik und Freiheit*, Freiburg im Breisgau, 2005.

Gotto, K., *Die deutschen Katholiken und die Wahlen in der Adenauer-Ära*, in: Langner, A. (ed.), *Katholizismus im politischen System der Bundesrepublik, 1949-1963*, Paderborn, 1978, pp. 22-25.

Götz, H. H., *Die geistigen Väter der sozialen Marktwirtschaft*, in: Eick, J. (ed.), *So nutzt man den Wirtschaftsteil einer Tageszeitung*, Frankfurt am Main, 1971.

Graml, H., *Die Alliierten und die Teilung Deutschlands. Konflikte und Entscheidungen 1941-1948*, Frankfurt am Main, 1985.

Grebing, H., *Zur Problematik der personellen und programmatischen Kontinuität in den Organisationen der Arbeiterbewegung in Westdeutschland 1945/46*, in: *Herkunft und Mandat. Beiträge zur Führungsproblematik in der Arbeiterbewegung*, Frankfurt am Main/Cologne, 1976, pp. 171–94.

Grebing, H., *Lehrstücke in Solidarität. Briefe und Biographien deutscher Sozialisten 1945–9*, Stuttgart, 1983.

Grebing, H., *Flüchtlinge und Parteien in Niedersachsen. Eine Untersuchung der politischen Meinungs- und Willensbildungsprozesse während der ersten Nachkriegszeit 1945-1952/53*, Hanover, 1990.

Grebing, H., *Von der Traditionskompanie zur Staatspartei. Die Modernisierung der Sozialdemokratie in den 1950er und 1960er Jahren im regionalen Vergleich*, in: Kocka, J.; Puhle, H.-J.; Tenfelde, K., *Von der Arbeiterbewegung zum modernen Sozialstaat. Festschrift für Gerhard A. Ritter zum 65. Geburtstag*, Munich, 1994, pp. 205–21.

Greiss, F., *Erhards Soziale Marktwirtschaft und die Waage*, in: Schröder, G.; Müller-Armack, A.; Hohmann, K.; Gross, J.; Altmann, R. (eds.), *Ludwig Erhard – Beiträge zu seiner politischen Biographie, Festschrift zum 75. Geburtstag*, Frankfurt am Main, 1972, pp. 89–110.

Greuner, R., *Lizenzpresse. Auftrag und Ende. Der Einfluss der anglo-amerikanischen Besatzungspolitik auf die Wiedererrichtung eines imperialistischen Pressewesens in Westdeutschland*, Berlin, 1962.

Grimmer-Solem, E., *The Rise of Historical Economics and Social Reform in Germany 1864-1894*, New York, 2003.

Grossekettler, H., *On Designing an Economic Order. The Contributions of the Freiburg School*, in: Walker, D. A. (ed.), *Perspectives on the History of Economic Thought*, vol. II, Aldershot, 1989, pp. 38–84.

Grossekettler, H., *Die Wirtschaftsordnung als Gestaltungsaufgabe. Entstehungsgeschichte und Entwicklungsperspektiven des Ordoliberalismus nach 50 Jahren Sozialer Marktwirtschaft*, Hamburg/Münster, 1997.

Grossekettler, H., *Adolf Lampe, die Transformationsprobleme zwischen Friedens- und Kriegswirtschaften und die Arbeitsgemeinschaft Erwin von Beckerath*, in: Goldschmidt, N. (ed.), *Wirtschaft, Politik und Freiheit*, Freiburg im Breisgau, 2005.

Gutmann, G.; Hochstrate, H.-J.; Schlüter, R., *Die Wirtschaftsverfassung der Bundesrepublik Deutschland. Entwicklung und ordnungspolitische Grundlagen*, Stuttgart, 1964.

Gutmann, G., *Individuelle Freiheit, Macht und Wirtschaftslenkung. Zur neoliberalen Konzeption einer marktwirtschaftlichen Ordnung*, in: Cassel, D.; Gutmann, G.; Thieme, H. J. (eds.), *25 Jahre Marktwirtschaft in der Bundesrepublik Deutschland. Konzeption und Wirklichkeit*, Stuttgart, 1972.

Gutmann, G., *Soziale Marktwirtschaft als Gesellschaftsidee. Zur anthropologischen und ethischen Grundlegung einer ordnungspolitischen Konzeption*, in: Gauger, J.-D.; Weigelt, K. (eds.), *Soziales Denken in Deutschland zwischen Tradition und Innovation*, Bonn, 1990.

Gutscher, J. M., *Die Entwicklung der FDP von ihren Anfängen bis 1961*, Meisenheim, 1967.

Habermas, J., *Strukturwandel der Öffentlichkeit: Untersuchungen zu einer Kategorie der bürgerlichen Gesellschaft*, Frankfurt am Main, 1999[6].

Hagemann, W., *Grundzüge der Publizistik. Als Einführung in die Lehre von der sozialen Kommunikation*, Münster, 1966.

Hampe, P. (ed.), *Währungsreform und Soziale Marktwirtschaft*, Munich, 1989.

Hardmann, C., *Die Wahlkampfwerbung von Parteien in der Bundesrepublik Deutschland*, Cologne, 1992.

Harris, S. E. (ed.), *Postwar Economic Problems*, New York, 1943.

Hartmann, P. C., *Bayerns Weg in die Gegenwart*, Regensburg, 1989.

Hartwell, R. M., *A History of the Mont Pèlerin Society*, Indianapolis, 1995.

Haselbach, D., *Autoritärer Liberalismus und Soziale Marktwirtschaft. Gesellschaft und Politik im Ordoliberalismus*, Baden-Baden, 1991.

Haselbach, D., *Franz Oppenheimer's Theory of Capitalism and of a Third Path*, in: Koslowski, P. (ed.), *The Theory of Capitalism in the German Economic Tradition. Historism, Ordo-Liberalism, Critical Theory, Solidarism*, Berlin, 2000, pp. 54–86.

Häußermann, E., *Konrad Adenauer und die Presse vor 1933*, in: Stehkämper, H. (ed.), *Konrad Adenauer. Oberbürgermeister von Köln*, Cologne, 1976.
Hayek, F. A. v., *The Road to Serfdom*, Chicago, 1944.
Hayek, F. A. v., *Der Weg zur Knechtschaft*, Erlenbach-Zurich, 1945.
Hayek, F. A. v., *Individualismus und wirtschaftliche Ordnung*, Salzburg, 1976.
Hayek, F. A. v., *Die Verfassung der Freiheit*, Tübingen, 1983.
Hayek, F. A. v., *Was ist und was heisst "sozial"?*, in: Hunold, A. (ed.), *Masse und Demokratie*, Erlenbach-Zurich/Stuttgart, 1957
Heck, B., *Adenauer und die Christlich-Demokratische Union Deutschlands*, in: *Konrad Adenauer und seine Zeit. Politik und Persönlichkeit des ersten Bundeskanzlers. Beiträge von Weg- und Zeitgenossen*, vol. I, Stuttgart, 1976.
Heck, B. (ed.), *Die CDU und ihr Programm – Programme, Erklärungen, Entschliessungen*, Melle/Sankt Augustin, 1979.
Hegel, G. W. F., *Philosophy of Right* (translated with notes by T. M. Knox), London, 1821 (1971).
Heidenheimer, A. J., *Adenauer and the CDU. The Rise of the Leader and the Integration of the Party*, The Hague, 1960.
Heitzer, H., *Die CDU in der britischen Zone: Gründung, Organisation, Programm und Politik 1945–9*, Düsseldorf, 1988.
Hennessy, B. C., *Public Opinion*, Belmont, 1970.
Hennis, W., *Meinungsforschung und repräsentative Demokratie. Zur Kritik politischer Umfragen*, Tübingen, 1957.
Hesiod, *Theogony, Works and Days, Testimonia*, edited and translated by G. W. Most, Cambridge, Mass./London, 2006.
Heusgen, C., *Ludwig Erhards Lehre von der Sozialen Marktwirtschaft: Ursprünge, Kerngehalt, Wandlungen*, Bern, 1981.
Hielscher, E., *Leidensweg der deutschen Währungsreform*, Munich, 1948.
Hindess, B., *Choice, Rationality and Social Theory*, London, 1988.
Hintze, P. (ed.), *Die CDU Parteiprogramme: Eine Dokumentation der Ziele und Aufgaben*, Bonn, 1995.
Hodenberg, C. v., *Konsens und Krise: Eine Geschichte der westdeutschen Medienöffentlichkeit 1945-1973*, Göttingen, 2006.
Höpfinger, R., *Bayerische Lebensbilder 2 – Biografien, Erinnerungen, Zeugnisse: Franz Josef Strauß, Ludwig Bölkow, Sepp Hort*, edited by the *Hanns-Seidel-Stiftung*, Munich, 2004.
Hohmann, K. (ed.), *Ludwig Erhard. Gedanken aus fünf Jahrzehnten, Reden und Schriften*, Düsseldorf/Vienna/New York, 1988.
Hrbek, R., *Die SPD – Deutschland und Europa. Die Haltung der Sozialdemokratie zum Verhältnis von Deutschland-Politik und Westintegration (1945-1957)*, Bonn, 1972.
Hubensteiner, B., *Bayerische Geschichte, Staat und Volk, Kunst und Kultur*, Munich, 1985.
Hume, D., *Of the First Principles of Government*, in: Hendel, Ch. W. (ed.), *David Hume's Political Essays*, New York, 1953.
Hunold, A. (ed.), *Wirtschaft ohne Wunder*, Erlenbach-Zurich, 1953.
Hunold, A. (ed.), *Masse und Demokratie*, Erlenbach-Zurich, 1957.
Hurwitz, H., *Die Pressepolitik der Alliierten*, in: Pross, H. (ed.), *Deutsche Presse seit 1945*, Bern/Munich/Vienna, 1965.

Hurwitz, H., *Die Stunde Null der deutschen Presse. Die amerikanische Pressepolitik in Deutschland 1945–9*, Cologne, 1972.

Huster, E.-U., *Die Politik der SPD 1945-1950*, Frankfurt am Main/New York, 1978.

Hutchings, V. L., *Public Opinion and Democratic Accountability – How Citizens Learn about Politics*, Princeton, 2003.

Jahn, H. E., *An Adenauers Seite. Sein Berater erinnert sich*, Munich/Vienna, 1987.

John, A., *Ahlen und das Ahlener Programm. Dokumente, Ereignisse, Erinnerungen*, Ahlen, 1977.

Judt, T., *Postwar: A History of Europe since 1945*, London, 2007.

Juling, P., *Programmatische Entwicklung der FDP 1946 bis 1969. Einführung und Dokumente*, in: Kaak, H. (ed.), *Studien zum politischen System der Bundesrepublik Deutschland*, Meisenheim am Glan, 1977, pp. 9–87.

Jürgensen, K., *Die Gründung des Landes Schleswig-Holstein nach dem Zweiten Weltkrieg. Der Aufbau der Demokratischen Ordnung in Schleswig-Holstein unter dem ersten Ministerpräsidenten Theodor Steltzer 1945-1947*, Neumünster, 1969.

Kaden, A., *Einheit oder Freiheit. Die Wiedergründung der SPD 1945/46*, Hanover, 1964.

Kahn, E.; Naphtali, F., *Wie liest man den Handelsteil einer Tageszeitung*, Frankfurt am Main, 1922.

Kardorff, U. v., *Aufzeichnungen 1942-1945*, Munich, 1994.

Kasper, W.; Streit, M., *Lessons from the Freiburg School. The Institutional Foundations of Freedom and Prosperity, Center for Independent Studies*, Australia, 1993.

Katzenstein, P. J., *Policy and Politics in West Germany: The Growth of a Semisovereign State*, Philadelphia, 1987.

Kettenacker, L., *Germany since 1945*, Oxford, 1997.

Kleinhenz, G. D., *Wirtschafts- und Sozialpolitik: Die Verwirklichung einer Sozialen Marktwirtschaft durch die Landespolitik der CSU*, in: Baumgärtel, M. (ed.), *Geschichte einer Volkspartei: 50 Jahre CSU 1945-1995*, edited by the *Hanns-Seidel-Stiftung*, Munich, 1995.

Kleinmann, H.-O., *Geschichte der CDU*, Stuttgart, 1993.

Klönne, A.; Klaus, B.; Stiller, K. Th., *Die Deutsche Arbeiterbewegung. Geschichte – Ziele – Wirkungen*, Düsseldorf/Cologne, 1980.

Klotzbach, K., *Der Weg zur Staatspartei. Programmatik, praktische Politik und Organisation der deutschen Sozialdemokratie 1945-1965*, Berlin/Bonn, 1982.

Klump, R., *Wege zur Sozialen Marktwirtschaft – Die Entwicklung ordnungspolitischer Konzeptionen in Deutschland vor der Währungsreform*, in: Streissler, E., (ed.), *Studien zur Entwicklung der ökonomischen Theorien XVI. Die Umsetzung wirtschaftspolitischer Grundkonzeptionen in die kontinentaleuropäische Praxis des 19. und 20. Jahrhunderts*, part I, Berlin, 1997, pp. 129–60.

Klump, R., *Der Beitrag der Freiburger Kreise zum Konzept der sozialen Marktwirtschaft*, in: Goldschmidt, N. (ed.), *Wirtschaft, Politik und Freiheit*, Freiburg im Breisgau, 2005.

Koch, S., *Parteien in der Region. Eine Zusammenhangsanalyse von lokaler Mitgliederpräsenz, Wahlergebnis und Sozialstruktur*, Opladen, 1994.

Koerfer, D., *Kampf ums Kanzleramt, Erhard und Adenauer*, Stuttgart, 1987, p. 783.

Korda, R. M., *Für Bürgertum und Business. 'Die Frankfurter Allgemeine Zeitung'*, in: Thomas, M. W. (ed.), *Porträts der deutschen Presse. Politik und Profit*, Berlin, 1980, pp. 81–96.

Kordes, W.; Pollmann, H., *Das Presse- und Informationsamt der Bundesregierung (Ämter und Organisation der Bundesrepublik Deutschland, Band 18)*, Düsseldorf, 1985.
Koslowski, P., *Solidarism, Capitalism, and Economic Ethics in Heinrich Pesch*, in: Idem (ed.), *The Theory of Capitalism in the German Economic Tradition: Historism, Ordo-Liberalism, Critical Theory, Solidarism*, Berlin/New York, 2000, pp. 371–94.
Koslowski, P., *Das Ausgleichsprinzip der Sozialen Marktwirtschaft zwischen Solidarität und Korporatismus*, in: Goldschmidt, N.; Wohlgemuth, M. (eds.), *Die Zukunft der Sozialen Marktwirtschaft – Sozialethische und Ordnungsökonomische Grundlagen*, Freiburg im Breisgau, 2004, pp. 57–61.
Koszyk, K., *Deutsche Presse im 19. Jahrhundert. Geschichte der deutschen Presse*, vol. II, Berlin, 1966.
Koszyk, K., *Kontinuität oder Neubeginn. Massenkommunikation in Deutschland 1945–9*, Siegen, 1981.
Koszyk, K., *Pressepolitik für Deutsche 1945–9. Geschichte der deutschen Presse Teil IV* (*Abhandlungen und Materialien zur Publizistik*, vol. 10), Berlin, 1986.
Kowitz, R., *Alfred Müller-Armack: Wirtschaftspolitik als Berufung. Zur Entstehungsgeschichte der Sozialen Marktwirtschaft und dem politischen Wirken des Hochschullehrers*, Cologne, 1998.
Kraus, A., *Geschichte Bayerns. Von den Anfängen bis zur Gegenwart*, Munich, 1988.
Krautkrämer, E., *Deutsche Geschichte nach dem Zweiten Weltkrieg. Eine Darstellung der Entwicklung von 1945 bis 1949 mit Dokumenten*, Hildesheim, 1962.
Krieger, W., *Germany*, in: Reynolds, D. (ed.), *The Origins of the Cold War in Europe. International Perspectives*, New Haven/London, 1994.
Kuklick, B., *American Policy and the Division of Germany*, Ithaca, 1972.
Lampe, A., *Zur Theorie des Sparprozesses und der Kreditschöpfung*, Jena, 1926.
Lampe, A., *Binnenhandel und Binnenhandelspolitik*, in: Weber, A. (ed.), *Volkswirtschaftslehre. Eine Einführung. Band 4: Handels- und Verkehrspolitik*, Munich/Leipzig, 1933, pp. 1–146.
Lampe, A., *Allgemeine Wehrwirtschaftslehre*, Jena, 1938.
Langguth, G. (ed.), *Politik und Plakat – 50 Jahre Plakatgeschichte am Beispiel der CDU*, Bonn, 1995.
Langner, A., *Wirtschaftliche Ordnungsvorstellungen im deutschen Katholizismus 1945-1963*, in: Idem (ed.), *Katholizismus, Wirtschaftsordnung und Sozialpolitik 1945-1963*, Paderborn/Munich/Vienna/Zurich, 1980, pp. 27 ff.
Lasswell, H. D., *Democracy Through Public Opinion*, Menasha, 1941.
Lazarsfeld, P. F., *Am Puls der Gesellschaft. Zur Methodik der empirischen Soziologie*, Vienna/Frankfurt am Main/Zurich, 1968.
Lazarsfeld, P. F.; Berlson, B.; Gaudet, H., *The People's Choice*, New York, 1948.
Lenz, F., *Wirtschaftsplanung und Planwirtschaft*, Berlin, 1947.
Leuschner, U., *Die Geschichte der FDP – Metamorphosen einer Partei zwischen rechts, sozialliberal und neokonservativ*, Münster, 2005.
Lijphart, A., *Democracies. Patterns of Majoritarian and Consensus Government in Twenty-One Countries*, New Haven/London, 1984.
Lippmann, W., *Public Opinion*, New York, 1922.
Lippmann, W., *The Phantom Public*, New York, 1925.

Lippmann, W., *Die Gesellschaft freier Menschen, mit Einführung von Wilhelm Röpke. Deutsche Übersetzung von Dr. E. Schneider*, Bern, 1945, p. 510 (original title: *The Good Society*).

Locke, J., *An Essay Concerning Human Understanding*, New York, 1959.

Löffler, B., *Soziale Marktwirtschaft und administrative Praxis. Das Bundeswirtschaftsministerium unter Ludwig Erhard*, Wiesbaden, 2002.

Löffler, M., *Presserecht. Kommentar zum Reichsgesetz über die Presse und zum Presserecht der Länder sowie zu den sonstigen die Presse betreffenden Vorschriften*, Stuttgart, 1955.

Löffler, M., *Der Verfassungsauftrag der Presse*, in: Wilke, J. (ed.), *Pressefreiheit*, Darmstadt, 1984, pp. 343–56.

Lösche, P.; Walter, F., *Die SPD. Klassenpartei, Volkspartei, Quotenpartei*, Darmstadt, 1992.

Lowell, A. L., *Public Opinion and Popular Government*, New York, 1913.

Luhmann, N., *Politische Theorie im Wohlfahrtsstaat*, Munich, 1981.

Lutz, F. A., *Das Grundproblem der Geldverfassung*, Stuttgart, 1936.

MacDonogh, G., *After the Reich. From the Fall of Vienna to the Berlin Airlift*, London, 2007.

Mannhart, F., *Entwicklung und Strukturwandel der Tagespresse in der Bundesrepublik Deutschland seit 1945 und ihre Position im öffentlichen Raum*, Munich, 1957.

Marsh, C., *The Survey Method: The Contribution of Surveys to Sociological Explanation*, London, 1982.

Marsh, D.; Stoker, G. (eds.), *Theory and Methods in Political Science*, New York, 1995.

März, J., *Die moderne Zeitung. Ihre Einrichtungen und ihre Betriebsweise*, Munich, 1951.

Matz, E., *Die Zeitungen der US-Armee für die deutsche Bevölkerung (1944-1946)*, Münster, 1969.

McLuhan, M., *The Medium Is the Massage: An Inventory of Effects, with Quentin Fiore*, New York/London, 1967.

Meehan, P., *A Strange Enemy People: Germans under the British, 1945–1950*, London, 2001.

Mehnert, K.; Schulte, H., *Deutschland-Jahrbuch 1949*, Essen, 1949.

Merkl, P. H., *The Origin of the West German Republic*, New York/Oxford, 1963.

Merritt, A. J.; Merritt, R. L. (eds.), *Public Opinion in Occupied Germany. The OMGUS Surveys, 1945–9*, Urbana/Chicago/London, 1970.

Merritt, A. J.; Merritt, R. L. (eds.), *Public Opinion in Semisovereign Germany. The HICOC Surveys, 1949-1955*, Urbana/Chicago/London, 1980.

Mettler, B., *Demokratisierung und Kalter Krieg. Zur amerikanischen Informations- und Rundfunkpolitik in Westdeutschland 1945–9*, Berlin, 1975.

Miksch, L., *Wettbewerb als Aufgabe. Grundsätze einer Wettbewerbsordnung*, Stuttgart/Berlin, 1937 (2nd edition Godesberg, 1947).

Miksch, L., *Wettbewerb und Wirtschaftsverfassung*, in: *Grundtexte zur Sozialen Marktwirtschaft* 1, edited by the *Ludwig-Erhard-Stiftung*, Stuttgart/Jena/New York, 1947/1981.

Mill, J. S., *On Liberty*, London, 1859.

Miller, S., *Kurt Schumacher, Vorsitzender der Sozialdemokratischen Partei Deutschlands, im Urteil von Zeitgenossen*, in: Kocka, J. *et al.* (eds.), *Von der Arbeiterbewegung zum modernen Sozialstaat*, Munich etc., 1994.

Miller, S.; Potthoff, H., *Kleine Geschichte der SPD. Darstellung und Dokumente 1848-1990*, Bonn, 1991.

Miller, W., *The Survey Method in the Social and Political Sciences: Achievements, Failures, Prospects*, London, 1983.

Mintzel, A., *Die CSU in Bayern*, in: Dittberner, J.; Ebbinghausen, R. (eds.), *Parteiensystem in der Legitimationskrise. Studien und Materialien zur Soziologie der Parteien in der Bundesrepublik Deutschland*, Opladen, 1973, pp. 349–426.

Mintzel, A., *Geschichte der CSU. Ein Überblick*, Opladen, 1977a.

Mintzel, A., *Gesellschaft, Staat und Parteiorganisation. Ein analytisches Stenogramm der Entwicklung Bayerns und der CSU*, in: Narr, W.-D. (ed.), *Auf dem Weg zum Einparteienstaat*, Opladen, 1977b, pp. 173–212.

Mintzel, A., *Political and Socio-economic Developments in the Postwar Era: The Case of Bavaria, 1945-1989*, in: Rohe, K. (ed.), *Elections, Parties and Political Traditions: Social Foundations of German Parties and Party Systems 1867-1987* (German Historical Perspectives 4), New York/Oxford, 1990, pp. 145–78.

Mintzel, A., *Die Christlich-Soziale Union in Bayern*, in: Mintzel, A.; Oberreuter, H. (eds.), *Parteien in der Bundesrepublik Deutschland (Bundeszentrale für politische Bildung)*, Bonn, 1992, pp. 217–65.

Mirowski, P.; Plehwe, D. (eds.), *The Road from Mont Pèlerin – The Making of the Neoliberal Thought Collective*, Cambridge, Mass., 2009.

Moeller, R. G. (ed.), *West Germany under Construction: Politics, Society, and Culture in the Adenauer Era*, Ann Arbor, 1997.

Molitor, B., *Wirtschaftspolitik*, Munich/Vienna, 1992.

Möller, H. (ed.), *Zur Vorgeschichte der Deutschen Mark. Die Währungsreformpläne 1945-1948*, Basel/Tübingen, 1961.

Mommsen, W., *Deutsche Parteiprogramme – Eine Auswahl vom Vormärz bis zur Gegenwart*, Munich, 1951.

Monroe, A. D., *Public Opinion in America*, New York, 1975.

Morsey, R., *Die Bundesrepublik Deutschland: Entstehung und Entwicklung bis 1969*, Munich, 1995.

Möschel, W., *Wirtschaftsverfassung*, in: Goldschmidt, N.; Wohlgemuth, M. (eds.), *Die Zukunft der Sozialen Marktwirtschaft – Sozialethische und Ordnungsökonomische Grundlagen*, Freiburg im Breisgau, 2004, pp. 175–89.

Mötteli, C., *Die deutsche Wirtschaft im Herbst 1947*, in: Schwarz, U.; Mötteli, C., *Deutschland im Herbst 1947*, Zurich, 1947.

Müchler, G., *CDU/CSU. Das schwierige Bündnis*, Munich, 1976.

Müller, G., *Die Grundlegung der westdeutschen Wirtschaftsordnung im Frankfurter Wirtschaftsrat*, Frankfurt am Main, 1982.

Müller-Armack, A., *Wirtschaftslenkung und Marktwirtschaft*, Hamburg, 1946.

Müller-Armack, A., *Zur Diagnose unserer wirtschaftlichen Lage*, Bielefeld, 1947.

Müller-Armack, A., *Wirtschaftslenkung und Marktwirtschaft*, Hamburg, 1947.

Müller-Armack, A., *Religion und Wirtschaft*, Bern/Stuttgart, 1950a.

Müller-Armack, A., *Soziale Marktwirtschaft – Handwörterbuch der Sozialwissenschaften*, vol. 9, Göttingen, 1956.

Müller-Armack, A., *Wirtschaftsordnung und Wirtschaftspolitik, Studien und Konzepte zur Sozialen Marktwirtschaft und zur Europäischen Integration*, Freiburg im Breisgau, 1966.

Müller-Armack, A., *Auf dem Weg nach Europa. Erinnerungen und Ausblicke*, Tübingen/Stuttgart, 1971.

Müller-Armack, A., *Die Konzeption der Sozialen Marktwirtschaft*, in: Altvater, E.; Arndt, H.; Besters, H. (eds.), *Unsere Wirtschaft: Basis, Dschungel, Dogma? – Marktwirtschaft in der gegenwärtigen Auseinandersetzung*, Cologne, 1974.

Müller-Armack, A., *Die Grundformel der Sozialen Marktwirtschaft*, in: *Soziale Marktwirtschaft als nationale und internationale Ordnung, Symposium I*, edited by the *Ludwig-Erhard-Stiftung*, Stuttgart, 1978.

Müller-Armack, A., *Genealogie der Sozialen Marktwirtschaft. Frühschriften und weiterführende Konzepte*, Bern/Stuttgart, 1981.

Müller-Armack, Andreas, *Das Konzept der Sozialen Marktwirtschaft – Grundlagen, Entwicklung, Aktualität*, in: Grosser, D.; Lange, Th.; Müller-Armack, A.; Neuss, B. (eds.), *Soziale Marktwirtschaft. Geschichte – Konzept – Leistung*, Mainz, 1988.

Müller-Vogg, H., *Public Relations für die Soziale Marktwirtschaft. Die Öffentlichkeitsarbeit der Bundesvereinigung der Deutschen Arbeitgeberverbände, des Bundesverbandes der Deutschen Industrie und des Instituts der Deutschen Wirtschaft zwischen 1966 und 1974*, Munich, 1979.

Muthesius, V., *Erinnerungen an den "Befreiungskrieg"*, in: Schröder, G.; Müller-Armack, A.; Hohmann, K.; Gross, J.; Altmann, R. (eds.), *Ludwig Erhard – Beiträge zu seiner politischen Biographie, Festschrift zum 75. Geburtstag*, Frankfurt, 1972, p. 159.

Muthesius, V., *Augenzeuge von drei Inflationen. Erinnerungen und Gedanken eines Wirtschaftspublizisten*, Frankfurt, 1973, p. 101.

Naphtali, F., *Wirtschaftsdemokratie – Ihr Wesen, Weg und Ziel*, Frankfurt, 1928.

Närger, H. A., *Der Wirtschaftsrat des Vereinigten Wirtschaftsgebietes. Entwicklung, Verfassung und staatsrechtliche Würdigung* (status of 1 January 1949), Munich, 1949.

Narr, W.-D., *CDU – SPD. Programm und Praxis seit 1945*, Stuttgart, 1966.

Nawroth, E., *Die Sozial- und Wirtschaftsphilosophie des Neoliberalismus*, Heidelberg/Leuven, 1962.

Neumann, E. P.; Noelle, E., *Antworten. Politik im Kraftfeld der öffentlichen Meinung*, Allensbach, 1954.

Nicholls, A. J., *Ludwig Erhard and German Liberalism – An Ambivalent Relationship?*, in: Jarausch, K; Jones, L. E. (eds.), *In Search of Liberal Germany: Studies in the History of German Liberalism from 1789 to the Present*, Providence, RI/Oxford, 1990.

Nicholls, A. J., *Freedom with Responsibility – The Social Market Economy in Germany, 1918-1963*, Oxford, 1994.

Nicholls, A. J., *The Bonn Republic – West German Democracy 1945-1990*, London/New York, 1997.

Nipperdey, H. C., *Die soziale Marktwirtschaft in der Verfassung der Bundesrepublik. Vortrag vor der jur. Studiengesellschaft in Karlsruhe am 5. März 1954*, Karlsruhe, 1954.

Nipperdey, Th., *Deutsche Geschichte 1866-1918. Erster Band: Arbeitswelt und Bürgergeist*, Munich 1993.

Noelle, E.; Neumann, E. P. (eds.), *Jahrbuch der Öffentlichen Meinung 1947-1955*, Allensbach, 1956.

Noelle-Neumann, E., *Die Schweigespirale. Öffentliche Meinung – unsere soziale Haut*, Munich/Zurich, 1980.

Nölting, E., *Freiheit und Bindung in der sozialistischen Wirtschaft. Referat auf der wirtschaftspolitischen Tagung am 19./20.6.1947 in Bad Wildungen*, in: Weber, A., *Erik Nölting, Sozialistische Wirtschaftsordnung. Beiträge zur Diskussion*, Hamburg, 1948.

Norris, P., *A Virtuous Circle – Political Communication in Postindustrial Societies*, Cambridge, 2000.

Oncken, H., *Politik, Geschichtsschreibung und öffentliche Meinung*, in: Idem, *Historisch-Politische Aufsätze und Reden*, vol. 1, Munich/Berlin, 1914.

Oppenheimer, F., *System der Soziologie* (III/1). *Band 3: Theorie der reinen und politischen Ökonomie, Teil 1: Grundlagen*, Jena, 1910.

Oppenheimer, F., *Weder so – noch so. Der dritte Weg*, Potsdam, 1933.

Oron, J. H., *The Captive Press in the Third Reich*, Princeton/New Jersey, 1964.

Ortlieb, H. D., *Wandlungen des Sozialismus. Fünf Aufsätze zur Gegenwartslage des Sozialismus*, Hamburg, 1947.

Oswalt, W., *Liberale Opposition gegen den NS-Staat: Zur Entwicklung von Walter Euckens Sozialtheorie*, in: Goldschmidt, N. (ed.), *Wirtschaft, Politik und Freiheit*, Freiburg im Breisgau, 2005.

Ott, H., *Der „Freiburger Kreis"*, in: Lill, R.; Kißener, M. (eds.), *20. Juli 1944 in Baden und Württemberg*, Konstanz, 1994, pp. 125–53.

Overesch, M., *Deutschland 1945–9. Vorgeschichte und Gründung der Bundesrepublik*, Königstein im Taunus etc., 1979.

Park, R., *The Crowd and the Public*, Chicago, 1904.

Paupié, K., *Frankfurter Zeitung (1856-1943)*, in: Fischer, H.-D. (ed.), *Deutsche Zeitungen des 17. bis 20. Jahrhunderts (Publizistik-Historische Beiträge, Band 2)*, Munich, 1972, pp. 241–56.

Peacock, A.; Willgerodt, H. (eds.), *Germany's Social Market Economy: Origins and Evolution*, London, 1989.

Pelton, F. D. (alias Franz Oppenheimer), *Sprung über ein Jahrhundert*, Bern/Leipzig, 1935.

Peterson, E. N., *The American Occupation of Germany – Retreat to Victory*, Detroit, 1977.

Peukert, H., *Das sozialökonomische Werk Wilhelm Röpkes. Teil 1*, Frankfurt am Main, 1992.

Peukert, H., *Walter Eucken (1891-1950) and the Historical School*, in: Koslowski, P. (ed.), *The Theory of Capitalism in the German Economic Tradition*, Berlin, 2000, pp. 93–145.

Peukert, H., *Die wirtschafts- und sozialpolitischen Zielsetzungen des Freiburger Kreises*, in: Goldschmidt, N. (ed.), *Wirtschaft, Politik und Freiheit*, Freiburg im Breisgau, 2005, pp. 267–88.

Pirker, T., *Die blinde Macht. Die Gewerkschaftsbewegung in Westdeutschland*, vol. 1, Munich, 1960.

Pirker, T., *Die SPD nach Hitler. Die Geschichte der Sozialdemokratischen Partei Deutschlands 1945-1964*, Munich, 1964.

Pitkin, H. F., *The Concept of Representation*, Berkeley/Los Angeles, 1967.

Pleyer, P., *Deutscher Nachkriegsfilm 1946-1948, Studien zur Publizistik*, Münster, 1965.

Plumpe, W., *Die Entstehungsphase des industriellen Spitzenverbandes im britischen und amerikanischen Besatzungsgebiet nach dem Zweiten Weltkrieg im Spiegel der öffentlichen Meinung*, manuscript, Bochum, 1979.

Popper, K. R., *The Open Society and its Enemies*, London, 1945.
Preece, R. J. C., *Land Elections in the German Federal Republic*, London, 1968.
Price, V., *Public Opinion*, Newbury Park, 1992.
Pritzkoleit, K., *Wem gehört Deutschland? Eine Chronik von Besitz und Macht*, Vienna/Munich/Basel, 1957.
Pross, H. (ed.), *Deutsche Presse seit 1945*, Bern/Munich/Vienna, 1965.
Pross, H., *Zeitungsreport. Die Deutsche Presse im 20. Jahrhundert*, Weimar, 2000.
Prowe, D., *Unternehmer, Gewerkschaften und Staat in der Kammerneuordnung in der britischen Besatzungszone bis 1950*, in: Petzina, D.; Euchner, W. (eds.), *Wirtschaftspolitik im britischen Besatzungsgebiet 1945–9*, Düsseldorf, 1984, pp. 235–54.
Ptak, R., *Neoliberalism in Germany: Revisiting the Ordoliberal Foundations of the Social Market Economy*, in: Mirowski, P.; Plehwe, D. (eds.), *The Road from Mont Pèlerin – The Making of the Neoliberal Thought Collective*, Cambridge, Mass., 2009, pp. 98–138.
Pulzer, P. G. J., *German Politics, 1945-1995*, Oxford, 1995.
Pünder, H., *Die Entstehung der Sozialen Marktwirtschaft*, in: Schröder, G.; Müller-Armack, A.; Hohmann, K.; Gross, J.; Altmann, R. (eds.), *Ludwig Erhard – Beiträge zu seiner politischen Biographie, Festschrift zum 75. Geburtstag*, Frankfurt am Main, 1972.
Pünder, T., *Das Bizonale Interregnum. Die Geschichte des Vereinigten Wirtschaftsgebiets 1946-1949*, Waiblingen, 1966.
Radunski, P., *Moderne Wahlkampfführung als politische Kommunikation*, Munich, 1980.
Rasch, H., *Grundlagen der Wirtschaftsverfassung*, Bad Godesberg, 1948.
Rausch, H., *Politisches Bewusstsein und politische Einstellungen im Wandel*, in: Weidenfeld, W. (ed.), *Die Identität der Deutschen*, Munich, 1983, pp. 119–53.
Recker, M.-L., *Wahlen und Wahlkämpfe in der Bundesrepublik Deutschland, 1949-1969*, in: Ritter, G. A. (ed.), *Wahlen und Wahlkämpfe in Deutschland: Von den Anfängen im 19. Jahrhundert bis zur Bundesrepublik*, Düsseldorf, 1997.
Riedl, A., *Liberale Publizistik für Soziale Marktwirtschaft – Die Unterstützung der Wirtschaftspolitik Ludwig Erhards in der Frankfurter Allgemeinen Zeitung und in der Neuen Zürcher Zeitung 1948/49 bis 1957*, Regensburg, 1992.
Risse, R., *Alltag mit Erhard*, in: Schröder, G.; Müller-Armack, A.; Hohmann, K.; Gross, J.; Altmann, R. (eds.), *Ludwig Erhard – Beiträge zu seiner politischen Biographie, Festschrift zum 75. Geburtstag*, Frankfurt am Main, 1972, pp. 591–8.
Ritter, W., *Kurt Schumacher. Eine Untersuchung seiner politischen Konzeption und seiner Gesellschafts- und Staatsauffassung*, Hannover, 1964.
Roeper, H., *Die D-Mark. Vom Besatzungskind zum Weltstar*, Frankfurt am Main, 1978.
Röpke, W., *Die Gesellschaftskrisis der Gegenwart*, Erlenbach-Zurich, 1942.
Röpke, W., *Civitas Humana – Grundfragen der Gesellschafts- und Wirtschaftsordnung*, Erlenbach-Zurich, 1944.
Röpke, W., *Internationale Ordnung*, Zurich, 1945a.
Röpke, W., *Die Deutsche Frage*, Erlenbach-Zurich, 1945b.
Röpke, W., *The German Question*, London, 1946 (transl. by E. W. Dickes).
Röpke, W., *Die Ordnung der Wirtschaft*, Frankfurt am Main, 1948.
Röpke, W., *Mass und Mitte*, Erlenbach-Zurich, 1950.

Röpke, W., *Die Gesellschaftskrisis der Gegenwart*, Erlenbach-Zurich, 1952.
Röpke, W., *A Humane Economy – The Social Framework of the Free Market*, Chicago, 1960.
Röpke, W., *Jenseits von Angebot und Nachfrage*, Bern/Stuttgart, 1979.
Rosenau, J. N., *Public Opinion and Foreign Policy*, New York, 1961.
Rousseau, J. J., *The Social Contract*, New York, 1762.
Rübsam-Haug, D., *Widerstand und Nachkriegsplanung. Der „Freiburger Kreis" als Beispiel kirchlich-akademischen Widerstandes gegen den Nationalsozialismus*, in: Schnabel, Th. (ed.), *Formen des Widerstandes im Südwesten 1933-1945. Scheitern und Nachwirken*, Ulm, 1994, pp. 113–23.
Rüstow, A., *Das Versagen des Wirtschaftsliberalismus*, Heidelberg, 1950a.
Rüstow, A., *Ortsbestimmung der Gegenwart*, Erlenbach-Zurich, 1950b.
Rüstow, A., *Soziale Marktwirtschaft als Gegenprogramm gegen Kommunismus und Bolschewismus*, in: Hunold, A. (ed.), *Wirtschaft ohne Wunder*, Erlenbach-Zurich, 1953.
Rüstow, A., *Paläoliberalismus, Kommunismus und Liberalismus*, in: Greiss, F.; Meyer, F. W. (eds.), *Wirtschaft, Gesellschaft und Kultur*, Berlin, 1961.
Rüther, D., *Der Widerstand des 20. Juli auf dem Weg in die Soziale Marktwirtschaft. Die wirtschaftspolitischen Vorstellungen der bürgerlichen Opposition gegen Hitler*, Paderborn, 2002.
Rüther, D., *Der Einfluss Freiburger Nationalökonomen auf die wirtschaftspolitischen Vorstellungen und Planungen der Widerstandsbewegung des 20. Juli 1944 – dargestellt am Beispiel der „Volkswirtschaftsfibel" von 1941/42*, in: Goldschmidt, N. (ed.), *Wirtschaft, Politik und Freiheit*, Freiburg im Breisgau, 2005.
Sarcinelli, U., *Politikvermittlung und demokratische Kommunikationskultur*, in: Idem (ed.), *Politikvermittlung. Beiträge zur politischen Kommunikationskultur*, Bonn, 1987.
Sartori, G., *The Theory of Democracy Revisited*, Chatham, 1987.
Schachtner, R., *Die deutschen Nachkriegswahlen*, Munich, 1956.
Schara, S., *Die SPD im Frankfurter Wirtschaftsrat 1947 bis 1949*, Cologne, 1988.
Schildt, A., *Hegemon der häuslichen Freiheit: Rundfunk in den 50er Jahren*, in: Schildt, A; Sywottek, A., *Modernisierung im Wiederaufbau: Die westdeutsche Gesellschaft der 50er Jahre*, Bonn, 1998.
Schindelbeck, D.; Ilgen, V., *„Haste was, biste was!" Werbung für die Soziale Marktwirtschaft*, Darmstadt, 1999.
Schlecht, O., *Die Vereinbarkeit von politischer und wirtschaftlicher Ordnung*, in: *Vorträge und Aufsätze*, Nr. 106, edited by the *Walter Eucken Institute*, Tübingen, 1986.
Schlecht, O., *Die Soziale Marktwirtschaft ist der Dritte Weg, Ein Model macht Karriere*, in: Fack, F. U.; Fromme, F. K.; Nonnenmacher, G. (ed.), *Das deutsche Modell, Freiheitlicher Rechtsstaat und Soziale Marktwirtschaft*, Munich, 1991.
Schmidt, F., *Presse in Fesseln – Eine Schilderung de NS-Pressetrusts*, Berlin, 1948.
Schmidt, K.-D., *Soziale Gerechtigkeit durch unternehmerische Initiative: Der Bund Katholischer Unternehmer, 1949-1990*, Munich, 1994.
Schmölders, G., *Ludwig Erhard und die Mont Pèlerin Society*, in: Schröder, G.; Müller-Armack, A.; Hohmann, K.; Gross, J.; Altmann, R. (eds.), *Ludwig Erhard – Beiträge zu seiner politischen Biographie, Festschrift zum 75. Geburtstag*, Frankfurt am Main, 1972.

Schockenhoff, V., *Wirtschaftsverfassung und Grundgesetz: Die Auseinandersetzungen in den Verfassungsberatungen 1945–9*, Frankfurt am Main/New York, 1986.

Scholz, A.; Oschilewski, W. G. (eds.), *Turmwächter der Demokratie – Ein Lebensbild von Kurt Schumacher*, vols. I and II, Berlin, 1953/1954.

Schröder, G.; Müller-Armack, A.; Hohmann, K.; Gross, J.; Altmann, R. (eds.), *Ludwig Erhard – Beiträge zu seiner politischen Biographie, Festschrift zum 75. Geburtstag*, Frankfurt am Main, 1972.

Schulin, E., *Einleitung*, in: Rübsam, D.; Schadeck, H. (eds.), *Der „Freiburger Kreis". Widerstand und Nachkriegsplanung 1933-1945*, Freiburg, 1990, pp. 7-16.

Schulz, K., D., *Unternehmerinteresse und Wirtschaftssystem. Beiträge der Unternehmer zur politischen Entwicklung der Bundesrepublik Deutschland*, Frankfurt am Main, 1986.

Schumacher, K., *Aufgaben und Ziele der deutschen Sozialdemokratie* (presentation given at the party convention of the SPD in 1946), edited by the SPD Greater-Hesse, Frankfurt am Main, 1946.

Schumacher, K., *Die Wandlungen um den Klassenkampf*, in: Idem, *Reden und Schriften*, Berlin, 1962, pp. 297 ff.

Schumpeter, J. A., *Capitalism, Socialism and Democracy*, London, 1943.

Schumpeter, J. A., *Capitalism in the Postwar World*, in: Harris, S. E. (ed.), *Postwar Economic Problems*, New York, 1943, pp. 113–26.

Schwarz, H.-P., *Vom Reich zur Bundesrepublik. Deutschland im Widerstreit der aussenpolitischen Konzeptionen in den Jahren der Besatzungsherrschaft 1945–9*, Neuwied, 1966.

Schwarz, H.-P., *Die Ära Adenauer. Gründerjahre der Republik 1949-1957. Geschichte der Bundesrepublik Deutschland, Band 2*, Wiesbaden, 1981.

Schweitzer, C.-C.; Karsten, D.; Spencer, R.; Cole, R. T.; Kommers, D.; Nicholls, A. (eds.), *Politics and Government in Germany, 1944-1994*, Oxford, 1995.

Schwering, L., *Frühgeschichte der Christlich-Demokratischen Union*, Recklinghausen, 1963.

Schwering, L., *Auf der Suche nach dem neuen Kurs – Zur Erinnerung an die Gründung der CDU im Rheinland vor 25 Jahren*, Cologne, 1970.

Seidel, H., *Wirtschaftspolitik und Soziale Ethik*, Munich 1952.

Seidel, H., *Zeitprobleme. Gesammelte Aufsätze und Vorträge*, Aschaffenburg, 1960a.

Seidel, H., *Weltanschauung und Politik. Ein Beitrag zum Verständnis der Christlich-Sozialen Union in Bayern*, Munich, 1960b.

Seidel, H., *Vom Mythos der öffentlichen Meinung*, Aschaffenburg, 1961.

Sering, P. (alias Richard Löwenthal), *Jenseits des Kapitalismus*, Lauf, 1946.

Siebert, H., *Prinzipien der deutschen Wirtschaftsordnung - ökonomische Aspekte*, in: Kirchhof, P.; Kommers, D. P. (eds.), *Deutschland und sein Grundgesetz. Themen einer deutsch-amerikanischen Konferenz*, Baden-Baden 1993.

Siebert, H., *The German Economy – Beyond the Social Market*, Princeton/Oxford, 2005.

Siegler, H. V., *Dokumente zur Deutschlandfrage. Von der Atlantik-Charta 1941 bis zur Berlin-Sperre 1961*, 3 vols., Bonn/Vienna/Zurich, 1961.

Sombart, W., *Der moderne Kapitalismus. Historisch-systematische Darstellung des gesamteuropäischen Wirtschaftslebens von seinen Anfängen bis zur Gegenwart*, Munich/Leipzig, 1922.

Spicka, M. E., *Selling the Economic Miracle – Economic Reconstruction and Politics in West Germany, 1949-1957*, New York/Oxford, 2007.

Splichal, S., *Public Opinion and Democracy: Vox Populi – Vox Dei?*, Cresskill, New Jersey, 2001.
Stammen, T., *Programme der Politischen Parteien in Deutschland*, Munich, 1996.
Starbatty, J., *Alfred Müller-Armacks Beitrag zur Theorie und Politik der Sozialen Marktwirtschaft*, in: *Soziale Marktwirtschaft im vierten Jahrzehnt ihrer Bewährung*, edited by the *Ludwig-Erhard-Stiftung*, Stuttgart/New York, 1982.
Starbatty, J., *Ordoliberalismus*, in: Dichtl, E.; Issing, O. (eds.), *Geschichte der Nationalökonomie*, Munich, 1994.
Starr, J. R., *DeNazification, Occupation and Control of Germany, March-July 1945*, Salisbury, N.C., 1977.
Sternberger, D., *Block und Koalition. Eine Studie zur Entstehung der deutschen Parteiensysteme nach 1945*, in: Sternberger, D. (ed.), *Lebende Verfassung. Studien über Koalition und Opposition*, Meisenheim am Glan, 1956.
Sternberger, D., *Lebende Verfassung. Studien über Koalition und Opposition*, Meisenheim am Glan, 1956.
Stolper, G., *German Realities*, New York, 1948.
Stöss, R.; Schmollinger, H. W., *Die Parteien und die Presse der Parteien und Gewerkschaften in der Bundesrepublik Deutschland, 1945-1974*, Munich, 1975.
Strauß, W., *Entwicklung und Aufbau des Vereinigten Wirtschaftsgebiets*, Heidelberg, 1948.
Streissler, E., *Soziale Marktwirtschaft und parlamentarische Demokratie – Die ökonomischen Aspekte*, in: *Soziale Marktwirtschaft und Parlamentarische Demokratie*, edited by the *Ludwig-Erhard-Stiftung*, vol. 28, Stuttgart/New York, 1990.
Streit, M. E., *The Freiburg School of Law and Economics*, in: Boettke, P. J. (ed.), *The Elgar Companion to Austrian Economics*, Aldershot, 1994, pp. 508–15.
Streit, M. E., *Freiburger Beiträge zur Ordnungsökonomik*, Tübingen, 1995.
Sueskind, W. E., *Der politische Rohstoff*, in: Moras, J.; Paeschke, H. (eds.), *Deutscher Geist zwischen Gestern und Morgen*, Deutsche Verlagsanstalt, Stuttgart, 1954.
Tenbruck, F. H., *Alltagsnormen und Lebensgefühle in der Bundesrepublik*, in: Löwenthal, R.; Schwarz, H.-P. (eds.), *Die Zweite Republik. 25 Jahre Bundesrepublik – Eine Bilanz*, Stuttgart, 1974.
Tennstädt, F., *Der Wähler*, Allensbach, 1957.
Thieme, H, J., *Soziale Marktwirtschaft: Ordnungskonzeption und wirtschaftspolitische Gestaltung*, Munich, 1994.
Thomas, M. W. (ed.), *Porträts der deutschen Presse. Politik und Profit*, Berlin, 1980.
Tocqueville, A. de, *Democracy in America*, New York, 1840.
Tomin, W., *Die Geschichte der SPD in Hamburg 1945 bis 1950*, Hamburg, 1995.
Tönnies, F., *Kritik der öffentlichen Meinung*, Berlin, 1922.
Tooze, A., *The Wages of Destruction – The Making and Breaking of the Nazi Economy*, London, 2006.
Treue, W., *Widerstand von Unternehmern und Nationalökonomen*, in: Schmädeke, J.; Steinbach, P. (eds.), *Der Widerstand gegen den Nationalsozialismus*, Munich/Zurich, 1944, pp. 917–37.
Tribe, K., *Strategies of Economic Order: German Economic Discourse, 1750-1950*, Cambridge, 1995.
Tribe, K., *Liberalism and Neoliberalism in Britain, 1930-1980*, in: Mirowski, P.; Plehwe, D. (eds.), *The Road from Mont Pèlerin – The Making of the Neoliberal Thought Collective*, Cambridge, Mass., 2009, pp. 68–97.

Trippen, N., *Josef Kardinal Frings (1887-1978): Sein Wirken für das Erzbistum Köln und für die Kirche in Deutschland*, vol. I, Paderborn, 2003.

Troeger, H., *Interregnum: Tagebuch des Generalsekretärs des Länderrats der Bizone 1947-1949*, edited by W. Benz and C. Goschler, Munich, 1985.

Uertz, R., *Christentum und Sozialismus in der frühen CDU. Grundlagen und Wirkungen der christlich-sozialen Ideen in der Union 1945-49*, Stuttgart, 1981.

Uhl, B., *Die Idee des Christlichen Sozialismus in Deutschland 1945-1947*, Mainz, 1975.

Vanberg, V., *Constitutionally Constrained and Safeguarded Competition in Markets and Politics*, in: Idem, *The Constitution of Markets. Essays in Political Economy*, London/New York, 2001, pp. 1–16.

Vanberg, V., *Soziale Sicherheit, Müller Armacks 'Soziale Irenik' und die ordoliberale Perspektive*, in: Hasse, R. H.; Quaas, F. (eds.), *Wirtschaftsordnung und Gesellschaftskonzept*, Bern, 2002, pp. 227–60.

Vanberg, V., *Die Verfassung der Freiheit: Zum Verhältnis von Liberalismus und Demokratie*, in: Berthold, N.; Gundel, E. (eds.), *Theorie der sozialen Ordnungspolitik*, Stuttgart, 2003, pp. 35–51.

Van Hook, J. C., *Rebuilding Germany: The Creation of the Social Market Economy, 1945-1957*, Cambridge, 2004.

Vogel, B.; Nohlen, D.; Schultze, R.-O., *Wahlen in Deutschland: Theorie – Geschichte – Dokumente 1848-1970*, Berlin/New York, 1971.

Vogel, W., *Westdeutschland 1945-1950. Der Aufbau von Verfassungs- und Verwaltungseinrichtungen über den Ländern der drei westlichen Besatzungszonen*, vol. I, *Geschichtlicher Überblick; oberste beratende Stellen und Einrichtungen für Gesetzgebung, Verwaltung und Rechtsprechung; einzelne Verwaltungszweige: Ernährung, Landwirtschaft und Forsten*, Koblenz, 1956.
vol. II, *Einzelne Verwaltungszweige: Wirtschaft, Marshallplan, Statistik*, Boppard, 1964.
vol. III, *Einzelne Verwaltungszweige: Finanzen; Post und Verkehr; Arbeit und Soziales; Flüchtlinge, Suchdienst und Kriegsgefangene; Justiz, Inneres*, Boppard, 1963.

Vogelsang, T., *Das geteilte Deutschland*, Munich, 1969.

Wandel, E., *Die Entstehung der Bank deutscher Länder und die deutsche Währungsreform 1948. Die Rekonstruktion des westdeutschen Geld- und Währungssystems 1945–9 unter Berücksichtigung der amerikanischen Besatzungspolitik*, Frankfurt am Main, 1980.

Watrin, C., *Zur sozialen Dimension marktwirtschaftlicher Ordnungen*, in: Hohmann, K.; Schönwitz, D.; Weber, H. J.; Wünsche, H. F. (eds.), *Grundtexte zur Sozialen Marktwirtschaft, Band 2, Das Soziale in der Sozialen Marktwirtschaft*, Stuttgart/New York, 1988, pp. 411–15.

Watrin, C., *Der Weg zur Freiheit*, Freiburg im Breisgau, 1991.

Watrin, C., *Die Tradition Freiheitlicher und Sozialer Politik*, in: *Soziale Marktwirtschaft als historische Weichenstellung – Bewertungen und Ausblicke. Eine Festschrift zum 100. Geburtstag von Ludwig Erhard* edited by the *Ludwig-Erhard-Stiftung*, Bonn, 1998, pp. 3–21.

Weber, A., *Bürokratie, Planwirtschaft und Sozialismus*, in: Weber, A.; Nölting, E. (eds.), *Sozialistische Wirtschaftsordnung. Beiträge zur Diskussion*, Hamburg, 1948.

Weber, A., *Erik Nölting, Sozialistische Wirtschaftsordnung. Beiträge zur Diskussion*, Hamburg, 1948.

Weber, M., *Wirtschaft und Gesellschaft*, Tübingen, 1922.

Weiss, K. G., *Wahrheit und Wirklichkeit. Der Weg aus den Weltkriegen in die Soziale Marktwirtschaft und eine künftige Weltordnung*, Homburg-Saarplatz, 1996.

Welter, E., *Die Wirtschaftspolitische Bildungsaufgabe*, in: Hunold, A. (ed.), *Wirtschaft ohne Wunder*, Zurich, 1953, pp. 340–56.

Welty, E., *Die Entscheidung in die Zukunft. Grundsätze und Hinweise zur Neuordnung im deutschen Lebensraum*, Heidelberg, 1946.

Wessels, J.-W., *Economic Policy and Microeconomic Performance in Inter-War Europe. The Case of Austria, 1918-1938*, Stuttgart, 2007.

Wettstein, K. P., *Die Politik der sozialdemokratischen Fraktion im Zweizonen-Wirtschaftsrat (1947-1949) unter besonderer Berücksichtigung ihrer wirtschaftspolitischen Konzeption*, Heidelberg, 1966.

Winkler, H. A. (ed.), *Politische Weichenstellungen im Nachkriegsdeutschland 1945-1953*, Göttingen, 1979.

Winkler, H. A., *Der lange Weg nach Westen*, vol. II, *Deutsche Geschichte vom Dritten Reich bis zur Wiedervereinigung*, Munich, 2000.

Wiskemann, E., *A Great Swiss Newspaper. The Story of the Neue Zürcher Zeitung*, London/New York/Toronto, 1959.

Wolfrum, E., *Französische Besatzungspolitik und deutsche Sozialdemokratie. Politische Neuansätze in der „vergessenen" Zone bis zur Bildung des Südweststaates 1945-1952*, Düsseldorf, 1991.

Wünsche, H. F., *Ludwig Erhards Gesellschafts- und Wirtschaftskonzeption, Soziale Marktwirtschaft als politische Ökonomie*, Bonn/Stuttgart, 1986.

Wulff, M., *Die neoliberale Wirtschaftsordnung. Versuch einer dynamischen Analyse der Konzeption und Realität*, Tübingen, 1976.

Wünsche, H. F., *Welcher Marktwirtschaft gebührt das Beiwort „sozial"?* in: Hohmann, K.; Schönwitz, D.; Weber, H. J.; Wünsche, H. F. (eds.), *Grundtexte zur Sozialen Marktwirtschaft, Band 2, Das Soziale in der Sozialen Marktwirtschaft*, Stuttgart/New York, 1988, pp. 21–31.

Wünsche, H. F., *Der Einfluss Oppenheimers auf Erhard und dessen Konzeption von der Sozialen Marktwirtschaft*, in: Caspari, V.; Schefold, B. (eds.), *Franz Oppenheimer und Adolph Lowe, Zwei Wirtschaftswissenschaftler der Frankfurter Universität*, Marburg, 1996, pp. 141–61.

Wünsche, H. F., *Erhards Soziale Marktwirtschaft. Von Eucken programmiert, von Müller-Armack inspiriert?*, in: *Soziale Marktwirtschaft als historische Weichenstellung – Bewertungen und Ausblicke. Eine Festschrift zum 100. Geburtstag von Ludwig Erhard* edited by the *Ludwig-Erhard-Stiftung*, Bonn, 1998, pp. 131–69.

Ziemke, E. F., *The US Army in the Occupation of Germany, 1944-1946*, Washington, D.C., 1975.

Zink, H., *The United States in Germany, 1944-1955*, Princeton/Toronto/London/New York, 1957.

Zmirak, J., *Wilhelm Röpke, Swiss Localist, Global Economist*, Wilmington, DE, 2001.

Zorn, W., *Bayerns Geschichte im 20. Jahrhundert. Von der Monarchie zum Bundesland*, Munich, 1986.

Zweig, K., *The Origins of the Social Market Economy – The Leading Ideas and their Intellectual Roots*, London, 1980.

Chronicles and Reference Books

Deuerlein, E.; Gruner, W. D., *Die politische Entwicklung Bayerns 1945 bis 1972*, in: Spindler, M. (ed.), *Handbuch der bayerischen Geschichte*, vol. 4/1, Munich, 1974.

Koszyk, K.; Pruys, K. H. (eds.), *Handbuch der Massenkommunikation*, Munich/New York/London/Paris, 1981a.

Löwenthal, R.; Schwarz, H.-P. (eds.), *Die Zweite Republik. 25 Jahre Bundesrepublik – Eine Bilanz*, Stuttgart, 1974.

Mintzel, A., *Die Christlich-Soziale Union in Bayern e.V.*, in: Stöss, R. (ed.), *Parteienhandbuch. Die Parteien der Bundesrepublik Deutschland 1945-1980*, vol. I, Opladen, 1983.

Potthoff, H.; Wenzel, R., *Handbuch politischer Institutionen und Organisationen 1945–9*, Düsseldorf, 1983.

Memoirs and (Auto-) Biographies

Adenauer, K., *Erinnerungen 1945-1953*, Stuttgart, 1965.

Adenauer, K., *Reden 1917-1967. Eine Auswahl*, edited by H.-P. Schwarz, Stuttgart, 1975.

Adenauer, K., *Briefe 1947-1949*, edited by H. P. Mensing, Berlin, 1983.

Adenauer, K., *Briefe 1949-1951*, edited by H. P. Mensing, Berlin, 1984.

Adenauer, K.; Poppinga, A. (ed.) *"Seid wach für die kommenden Jahre". Grundsätze, Erfahrungen, Einsichten*, Bergisch Gladbach, 1997.

Albrecht, W., *Kurt Schumacher. Ein Leben für den demokratischen Sozialismus*, Bonn, 1985.

Alsheimer, H. (ed.), *Ludwig Erhard: Der Weg unseres Landes aus den Trümmern des Krieges – Spuren seines Wirkens in Frankfurt am Main-Höchst und Bad Homburg vor der Höhe*, Bad Homburg vor der Höhe, Frankfurt am Main, Hofheim im Taunus, 1997.

Bayer, A.; Baumgärtel, M. (eds.), *Weltanschauung und politisches Handeln – Hanns Seidel zum 100. Geburtstag*, edited by the *Hanns-Seidel-Stiftung*, Munich, 2001.

Conze, W., *Jakob Kaiser. Politiker zwischen Ost und West 1945–9*, Stuttgart/Berlin/Cologne/Mainz, 1969.

Groß, H. F., *Hanns Seidel 1901-1961: Eine politische Biographie*, edited by the *Hanns-Seidel-Stiftung*, Munich, 1992.

Hentschel, V., *Ludwig Erhard – Ein Politikerleben*, Berlin, 1998.

Laitenberger, V., *Ludwig Erhard. Der Nationalökonom als Politiker*, Göttingen, 1986.

Lukomski, J. M., *Ludwig Erhard. Der Mensch und der Politiker*, Düsseldorf, 1965.

Merseburger, P., *Der schwierige Deutsche. Kurt Schumacher*, Stuttgart, 1995.

Schlüter-Ahrens, R., *Der Volkswirt Jens Jessen. Leben und Werk*, Marburg, 2001.

Schwarz, H.-P., *Adenauer. Der Aufstieg. 1876-1952*, vol. I, Stuttgart, 1986.

Schwarz, H.-P., *Adenauer. Der Staatsmann. 1952-1967*, vol. II, Stuttgart, 1991.

Schwarz, H.-P., *Konrad Adenauer: A German Politician and Statesman in a Period of War, Revolution, and Reconstruction*, vol. 2, Providence, 1997.

Weseman, F., *Kurt Schumacher*, Frankfurt am Main, 1952.

Williams, Ch., *Adenauer – The Father of the New Germany*, London, 2000.

Serial Publications

Abelshauser, W., *Freiheitlicher Sozialismus oder Soziale Marktwirtschaft? Die Gutachtertagung über Grundfragen der Wirtschaftsplanung und Wirtschaftslenkung am 21. und 22. Juni 1946*, in: *Vierteljahreshefte für Zeitgeschichte* 24/4, Munich, 1976, p. 415.

Albers, J., *Die Aufgabe der Christlich Demokratischen Union im Leben des deutschen Volkes*, in: *Schriftenreihe der Christlich-Demokratischen Union des Rheinlandes* 2, Cologne, 1945, pp. 5 ff.

Altmann, R., Erb, D., *Soziale Marktwirtschaft als gesellschaftliche Ordnungspolitik*, in: *Ludwig Erhard und seine Politik, Symposium XIII*, edited by the *Ludwig-Erhard-Stiftung*, Stuttgart/New York, 1985.

Baur, E. J., *Public Opinion and the Primary Group*, in: *American Sociological Review* 25, Columbus, OH, 1960, pp. 209–10.

Berndt, A.; Goldschmidt, N., *Leonhard Miksch (1901-1950). Leben und Werk*, in: *Institute for Economic Research, Department of Mathematical Economics, Discussion Paper*, no. 24a, Freiburg im Breisgau, 2000.

Berndt, A.; Goldschmidt, N., *„Wettbewerb als Aufgabe" – Leonhard Mikschs Beitrag zur Ordnungstheorie und -politik*, in: *ORDO* 51, Stuttgart, 2000, pp. 33–74.

Blumer, H., *Public Opinion and Public Opinion Polling*, in: *American Sociological Review* 13, Columbus, OH, 1948, pp. 542–9.

Böhm, F., *Die Idee des Ordo im Denken Walter Euckens*, in: *ORDO* 3, Stuttgart, 1950.

Borchardt, K.; Buchheim, C., *Die Wirkung der Marshall-Plan-Hilfe in Schlüsselbranchen der deutschen Wirtschaft*, in: *Vierteljahreshefte für Zeitgeschichte* 35/2, Munich, 1987, pp. 317–48.

Bourdieu, P., *Public Opinion Does Not Exist*, in: *Sociology in Question*, London, 1993, pp. 149–57.

Broyer, S., *The Social Market Economy: Birth of an Economic Style*, in: *Discussion Paper FS I*, pp. 96–318, *Wissenschaftszentrum Berlin für Sozialforschung*, Berlin, 1996.

Bücker, V., *Der Kölner Kreis und seine Konzeption für ein Deutschland nach Hitler*, in: *Historisch-politische Mitteilungen* 2, Cologne, 1995, pp. 49–82.

Colm, G.; Dodge, J. M.; Goldsmith, R. W., *A Plan for the Liquidation of War Finance and the Financial Rehabilitation of Germany*, in: *Zeitschrift für die gesamte Staatswissenschaft* 111, Tübingen, 1955, pp. 204–43.

Commun, P., *Erhards Bekehrung zum Ordoliberalismus: Die grundlegende Bedeutung des wirtschaftspolitischen Diskurses in Umbruchszeiten*, in: *Freiburg Discussion Papers on Constitutional Economics* 4/4, Freiburg im Breisgau, 2004.

Dathe, U.; Goldschmidt, N., *Wie der Vater, so der Sohn? Neuere Erkenntnisse zu Walter Euckens Leben und Werk anhand des Nachlasses von Rudolf Eucken in Jena*, in: *ORDO* 54, Stuttgart, 2003, pp. 49–74.

Dirks, W., *Die Zweite Republik*, in: *Frankfurter Hefte* 1/ 1, Frankfurt am Main, 1946, pp. 23 ff.

Dirks, W., *Das Abendland und der Sozialismus*, in: *Frankfurter Hefte*, 1/ 3, Frankfurt am Main, 1946, pp. 67–76.

Dirks, W., *Das Wort Sozialismus*, in: *Frankfurter Hefte*, 1/ 7, Frankfurt am Main, 1946, pp. 639 ff.

Dornbusch, R., *The End of the German Miracle*, in: *Journal of Economic Literature* 31/2, Pittsburgh, PA, 1993, pp. 881–5.

Dowe, D. (ed.), *Kurt Schumacher und der „Neubau" der deutschen Sozialdemokratie nach 1945, Referate und Podiumsdiskussion eines Kolloquiums des Gesprächskreises Geschichte der Friedrich-Ebert-Stiftung in Bonn am 12./13. Oktober 1995, Heft 13*, Bonn, 1996.
Dürr, E., *Die Soziale Marktwirtschaft*, in: *Wirtschaftswissenschaftliches Studium*, 6, 1988.
Ehni, H. P., *Sozialistische Neubauforderung und Proklamation des "Dritten Weges". Richtungen sozialdemokratischer Wirtschaftspolitik 1945-1947*, in: *Archiv für Sozialgeschichte* 13, Bonn, 1973, pp. 131–89.
Eschenburg, T., *Regierung, Bürokratie und Parteien 1945–9 – Ihre Bedeutung für die politische Entwicklung der Bundesrepublik*, in: *Vierteljahreshefte für Zeitgeschichte* 24/1, Munich, 1976, pp. 58–74.
Eucken, W., *Staatliche Strukturwandlungen und die Krisis des Kapitalismus*, in: *Weltwirtschaftliches Archiv* 36, Berlin/Heidelberg, 1932, pp. 297–21.
Eucken, W., *Die Überwindung des Historismus*, in: *Schmollers Jahrbuch* 62, Berlin, 1938, pp. 63–86.
Eucken, W., *Wissenschaft im Stile Schmollers*, in: *Weltwirtschaftliches Archiv* 52, Berlin/Heidelberg, 1940a, pp. 468–506.
Eucken, W., *Das ordnungspolitische Problem*, in: *ORDO* 1, Stuttgart, 1948, pp. 56–90.
Eucken, W., *Die Wettbewerbsordnung und ihre Verwirklichung*, in: *ORDO* 2, Stuttgart, 1949, pp. 1–99.
Eucken, W., *Wettbewerb, Monopol und Unternehmer*, in: *Wirtschaft und Gesellschaft*, Bad Nauheim, 1953.
Eynern, G. v., *Freiheit in der Planwirtschaft*, in: *Das Sozialistische Jahrhundert* I, 7/8, Berlin, 1947.
Gimbel, J., *Byrnes' Stuttgarter Rede und die amerikanische Nachkriegspolitik in Deutschland*, in: *Vierteljahreshefte für Zeitgeschichte* 20, Munich, 1972, pp. 39–62.
Goldschmidt, N., *Die Entstehung der Freiburger Kreise*, in: *Historisch-Politische Mitteilungen* 4, Cologne, 1997, pp. 1–17.
Goldschmidt, N., *Christlicher Glaube, Wirtschaftstheorie und Praxisbezug: Walter Eucken und die Anlage 4 der Denkschrift des Freiburger Bonhoeffer-Kreises*, in: *Historisch-Politische Mitteilungen* 5, Cologne, 1998, pp. 33–48.
Goldschmidt, N.; Arnold, B., *Leonhard Miksch (1901-1950) – A Forgotten Member of the Freiburg School*, in: *Freiburg Discussion Papers on Constitutional Economics* 03/02, Freiburg im Breisgau, 2003.
Goldschmidt, N., *Alfred Müller-Armack and Ludwig Erhard: Social Market Liberalism*, in: *CREPHE-CREA Histoire du Libéralisme en Europe*, Brochure No. 21, Paris, 2004.
Grebing, H., *„Neubau" statt „Wiederaufbau" der SPD – die Lehren aus der Weimarer Republik*, in: Dowe, D. (ed.), *Kurt Schumacher und der „Neubau" der deutschen Sozialdemokratie nach 1945, Referate und Podiumsdiskussion eines Kolloquiums des Gesprächskreises Geschichte der Friedrich-Ebert-Stiftung in Bonn am 12./13. Oktober 1995, Heft 13*, Bonn, 1996, pp. 73–89.
Grossekettler, H., *Wissenschaftliche Politikberatung. Beiträge von Ministerien als politikberatende Institutionen*, in: *Volkswirtschaftliche Diskussionsbeiträge der Westfälischen Wilhelms-Universität* No. 355, Münster, 2004.
Hagen, M., *Das politische Plakat als zeitgeschichtliche Quelle*, in: *Geschichte und Gesellschaft*, 3/78, Göttingen, 1978, pp. 414 ff.

Harrison, T., *What is Public Opinion?*, in: *Political Quarterly* 11, Oxford, 1940, pp. 368–83.

Heinen, R., *Die rechtlichen und tatsächlichen Grundlagen des Neubaus der deutschen Presse*, in: *Mitteilungen des Nordwestdeutschen Zeitungsverleger-Vereins e.V. für die britische Zone*, 2/ 5, Düsseldorf, 1947.

Henke, K-D.; Woller, H., *Lehrjahre der CSU – Eine Nachkriegspartei im Spiegel vertraulicher Berichte an die Amerikanische Militärregierung*, in: *Schriftenreihe der Vierteljahreshefte für Zeitgeschichte* 48, Stuttgart, 1984.

Henning, F.-W., *Konrad Adenauer und die Soziale Marktwirtschaft bis 1956*, in: Pohl, H. (ed.), *Adenauers Verhältnis zu Wirtschaft und Gesellschaft*, in: *Rhöndorfer Gespräche*, vol. 12, Bonn, 1992, pp. 10–32.

Herbst, S., *Surveys in the public sphere: Applying Bourdieu's critique of opinion polls*, in: *International Journal of Public Opinion Research* 4/3, Oxford, 1992, pp. 220–29.

Herbst, L., *Krisenüberwindung und Wirtschaftsneuordnung. Ludwig Erhards Beteiligung an den Nachkriegsplanungen am Ende des Zweiten Weltkrieges*, in: *Vierteljahreshefte für Zeitgeschichte* 25, Munich, 1977, pp. 304–40.

Hieronymi, O., *Wilhelm Röpke, The Social Market Economy and Today's Domestic and International Order*, in: *Cahiers HEI 2002, no. 6, Colloque Wilhelm Röpke (1899-1966), The Relevance of his Teaching Today: Globalization and the Social Market Economy*, Geneva, 2002.

Hofmann, J., *The CDU Press of the German Federal Republic*, in: *Gazette*, 5/ 1, Leiden, 1959, pp. 31 ff.

Huber, F., *Re-education durch Rundfunk. Die Umerziehungspolitik der britischen Besatzungsmacht in Deutschland am Beispiel des NWDR 1945-1948*, in: Rüden, P. v.; Wagner, H.-U. (eds.), *Nordwestdeutsche Hefte zur Rundfunkgeschichte; Sonderheft*, Hamburg, 2006.

Jarren, O., *Politik und politische Kommunikation in der modernen Gesellschaft*, in: *Aus Politik und Zeitgeschichte*, 39/94, Bonn, pp. 3 ff.

Jasay, A. de, *Soziale Marktwirtschaft: Sozialismus in anderer Form?*, in: *Adjektivlose oder Soziale Marktwirtschaft?*, edited by the *Ludwig-Erhard-Stiftung*, Bonn, 1993.

Kaiser, J., *Um Deutschlands Schicksal*, in: *Deutschland und die Union, Die Berliner Tagung 1946. Reden und Aussprache*, in: *Schriftenreihe der CDU Berlin: Wege in die neue Zeit*, 4, Berlin, 1946, pp. 9 ff.

Kluge, U., *Der "Freiburger Kreis" 1938-1945 – Personen, Strukturen und Ziele kirchlich-akademischen Widerstandsverhaltens gegen den Nationalsozialismus*, in: *Freiburger Universitätsblätter* 27/ 102, pp. 19–40, Freiburg im Breisgau, 1988.

Knower, F. H., *Experimental Studies of Change in Attitudes: I. A Study of the Effect of Oral Argument on Changes of Attitudes*, in: *Journal of Abnormal and Social Psychology* 6(1), Washington, D.C., 1935, pp. 315–47.

Knowles, C., *British Occupation of Germany 1945-1946*, Postgraduate Student Conference, German Historical Institute, London, 2007.

Koch, W., *Der Wissenschaftliche Beirat beim Bundesminister für Wirtschaft*, in: *Probleme der normativen Ökonomik und der wirtschaftspolitischen Beratung. Schriften des Vereins für Socialpolitik – Gesellschaft für Wirtschafts- und Sozialwissenschaften*, vol. 29, Frankfurt am Main, 1963, pp. 405–20.

Kogon, E., *Der Weg zu einem Sozialismus der Freiheit in Deutschland*, in: *Frankfurter Hefte*, 2/ 9, Frankfurt am Main, 1947, pp. 877–96.

Koszyk, K., *German Newspapers with Socialist Tendency since 1945*, in: *Gazette*, 5/1, Leiden, 1959, pp. 41 ff.

Koszyk, K., *Die Inhaltsanalyse der deutschen Presse*, in: *Publizistik* 7, 1962, pp. 142–6.

Kreikamp, H.-D., *Die amerikanische Deutschlandpolitik im Herbst 1946 und die Byrnes-Rede in Stuttgart*, in: *Vierteljahreshefte für Zeitgeschichte* 29, Munich, 1981a.

Laitenberger, V., *Auf dem Weg zur Währungs- und Wirtschaftsreform. Ludwig Erhards Wirtschaftspolitik im Frühjahr 1948*, in: *Politik und Zeitgeschichte* 23, Bonn, 1988, pp. 29–44.

Lampe, A., *Umriss einer allgemeinen Theorie der Wirtschaftspolitik*, in: *Jahrbücher für Nationalökonomie und Statistik* 163, Stuttgart, 1951, pp. 81–213.

Lampert, H.; Bossert, A., *Die Soziale Marktwirtschaft – eine theoretisch unzulänglich fundierte ordnungspolitische Konzeption?*, in: *Hamburger Jahrbuch für Wirtschafts- und Gesellschaftspolitik* 32, Hamburg, 1987, pp. 109–30.

Lampert, H., *Die Soziale Marktwirtschaft in der Bundesrepublik Deutschland. Ursprung, Konzeption, Entwicklung und Probleme*, in: *Aus Politik und Zeitgeschichte* 17, Bonn, 1988.

Lange-von Kulessa, J.; Renner, A., *Die Soziale Marktwirtschaft Alfred Müller-Armacks und der Ordoliberalismus der Freiburger Schule – Zur Unvereinbarkeit zweier Staatsauffassungen*, in: *ORDO* 49, Stuttgart, 1998, pp. 79–104.

Lenel, H. O., *Die sogenannten Freibuger Kreise.*, in: *ORDO* 39, Stuttgart, 1988, pp. 287–94.

Lösche, P., *Abschied von der Klassenpartei – Das Ringen der SPD um die Mittelschichten*, in: Dowe, D. (ed.), *Kurt Schumacher und der „Neubau" der deutschen Sozialdemokratie nach 1945, Referate und Podiumsdiskussion eines Kolloquiums des Gesprächskreises Geschichte der Friedrich-Ebert-Stiftung in Bonn am 12./13. Oktober 1995, Heft 13*, Bonn, 1996, pp. 93–112.

Mahrenholz, E. G., *Medien und Macht – Wie sichern wir Pluralismus und Transparenz?*, in: *Bertelsmann Briefe* 129, Gütersloh, 1993.

Mey, H., *Marktwirtschaft und Demokratie – Überlegungen zur Nachwirkung von Kontinuität und Neubeginn in der Gründungsphase der Bundesrepublik 1945-49*, in: *Vierteljahreshefte für Zeitgeschichte* 19, Munich, 1971, pp. 160–86.

Miksch, L., *Wirtschaftsmoral und Wirtschaftsordnung*, in: *Wirtschaftsverwaltung* 1/14, 1948a, pp. 2–5.

Miksch, L., *Zur Theorie des Gleichgewichts*, in: *ORDO* 1, Stuttgart, 1948b, pp. 175–96.

Miksch, L., *Die Wirtschaftspolitik des Als-Ob*, in: *Zeitschrift für die gesamte Staatswissenschaft* 105, Tübingen, 1949, pp. 310–38.

Mintzel, A., *Die CSU. Anatomie einer konservativen Partei 1945-1972*, in: *Schriften des Zentralinstituts für sozialwissenschaftliche Forschungen der Freien Universität Berlin*, vol. 26, Opladen, 1975.

Moeller, H., *Liberalismus*, in: *Jahrbücher für Nationalökonomie und Statistik* 162, Stuttgart, 1950, pp. 214–40.

Morsey, R., *Die Bildung der ersten Regierungskoalition 1949. Adenauers Entscheidungen von Frankfurt und Rhöndorf am 20. und 21. August 1949*, in: *Historisches Jahrbuch* 97/98, Freiburg/Munich, 1978, pp. 418–38.

Morsey, R., *Konrad Adenauer und der Weg zur Bundesrepublik Deutschland 1946-1949*, in: Idem (ed.), *Konrad Adenauer und die Bundesrepublik Deutschland*, in: *Rhöndorfer Gespräche*, vol. 3, Stuttgart/Zurich, 1979.

Morsey, R., *Die Rhöndorfer Weichenstellung vom 21. August 1949. Neue Quellen zur Vorgeschichte der Koalitions- und Regierungsbildung nach der Wahl zum ersten Deutschen Bundestag*, in: *Vierteljahreshefte für Zeitgeschichte* 28, Munich, 1980, pp. 508 ff.

Müchler, G., *Zum frühen Verhältnis von CDU und CSU*, in: *Politische Studien* 23/202, Munich, 1972, pp. 595–613.

Müller-Armack, A., *Soziale Irenik*, in: *Weltwirtschaftliches Archiv* 64, Berlin/Heidelberg, 1950, pp. 181–203.

Müller-Armack, *The Social Market Economy as an Economic and Social Order*, in: *Review of Social Economy* 36, Washington, D.C., 1978a.

Neidhardt, F. (ed.), *Öffentlichkeit, öffentliche Meinung, soziale Bewegungen*, in: *Kölner Zeitschrift für Soziologie und Sozialpsychologie*, Sonderheft 34/94, Opladen, 1994.

Neumann, F., *Military Government and the Revival of Democracy in Germany*, in: *Columbia Journal of International Affairs* 2, 1948, pp. 3–20.

Nicholls, A. J., *Das andere Deutschland – Die "Neoliberalen"*, in: *Zeitschrift für Wirtschaftspolitik* 33, Stuttgart, 1984, pp. 241–59.

Niethammer, L., *Die Amerikanische Besatzungsmacht zwischen Verwaltungstradition und politischen Parteien in Bayern 1945*, in: *Vierteljahreshefte für Zeitgeschichte* 15/2, Munich, 1967, pp. 153–210.

Noelle-Neumann, E., *The Spiral of Silence: A Theory of Public Opinion*, in: *Journal of Communication* 24, Oxford, 1974, pp. 43–51.

Nölting, E., *Freiheit und Bindung in der sozialistischen Wirtschaft*, in: Idem; Kromphardt, W., *Marktspaltung und Kernplanung in der Volkswirtschaft*, in: *Dortmunder Schriften zur Sozialforschung* 3, Dortmund, 1947.

Oberender, P., *Der Einfluß ordnungstheoretischer Prinzipien Walter Euckens auf die deutsche Wirtschaftspolitik nach dem Zweiten Weltkrieg: Eine ordnungspolitische Analyse*, in: *ORDO* 40, Stuttgart, 1989.

Pennock, J. R., *Responsiveness, Responsibility, and Majority Rule*, in: *American Political Science Review 46*, Los Angeles, CA, 1952, pp. 790–807.

Pohl, H. (ed.), *Adenauers Verhältnis zu Wirtschaft und Gesellschaft*, in: *Rhöndorfer Gespräche*, vol. 12, Bonn, 1992.

Potthoff, H., *Kurt Schumacher – Sozialdemokraten und Kommunisten*, in: Dowe, D. (ed.), *Kurt Schumacher und der „Neubau" der deutschen Sozialdemokratie nach 1945, Referate und Podiumsdiskussion eines Kolloquiums des Gesprächskreises Geschichte der Friedrich-Ebert-Stiftung in Bonn am 12./13. Oktober 1995, Heft 13*, Bonn, 1996, pp. 133–48.

Price, V.; Neijens, P., *Deliberative Polls: Toward Improved Measures of 'Informed' Public Opinion?*, in: *International Journal of Public Opinion Research* 10/2, 1998, pp. 145–75.

Prowe, D., *Economic Democracy in Post-World War II Germany: Corporatist Crisis Response, 1945-1948*, in: *Journal of Modern History* 57, Chicago, 1985, pp. 451–82.

Reich, N., *Germany's Labor and Economic Recovery*, in: *Proceedings of the Academy of Political Science* 26/2, 1955, pp. 47–64.

Rieter, H.; Schmolz, M., *The Ideas of German Ordoliberalism 1938-1945: Pointing the Way to a New Economic Order*, in: *The European Journal of the History of Economic Thought* 1, London, 1993, pp. 87–114.

Röpke, W., *Blätter der Erinnerung an Walter Eucken*, in: *ORDO*, Düsseldorf/Munich, 1961.

Rohe, K. (ed.), *Elections, Parties and Political Traditions: Social Foundations of German Parties and Party Systems 1867-1987* (German Historical Perspectives 4), New York/Oxford, 1990.

Roth, K. H., *Das Ende eines Mythos. Ludwig Erhard und der Übergang der deutschen Wirtschaft von den Annexion zur Nachkriegsplanung 1939-1945*, in: *Zeitschrift für Sozialgeschichte des 20. und 21. Jahrhunderts* 10, Hamburg, 1995.

Rürup, R., *Kurt Schumacher – Persönlichkeit und politische Konzeption*, in: *Neue politische Literatur* 11, Darmstadt, 1966, pp. 424–34.

Rüstow, A., *Interessenpolitik oder Staatspolitik*, in: *Schriften des Vereins für Socialpolitik* 187, Munich, 1933.

Rüstow, A., *Zwischen Kapitalismus und Kommunismus*, in: *ORDO* 2, Stuttgart, 1949.

Sänger, F., *Zur Geschichte der „Frankfurter Zeitung"*, in: *Publizistik* 22, 1977, pp. 275–94.

Sally, R., *Ordoliberalism and the Social Market: Classical Political Economy from Germany*, in: *New Political Economy* 1, Cambridge, 1996, pp. 233–57.

Sarcinelli, U., *Politikvermittlung und Demokratie in der Mediengesellschaft – Beiträge zur politischen Kommunikationskultur*, in: *Schriftenreihe der Bundeszentrale für politische Bildung* 352, Bonn/Wiesbaden, 1998.

Schlecht, O., *Die Genesis des Konzepts der Sozialen Marktwirtschaft*, in: Hohmann, K.; Schönwitz, D.; Weber, H. J.; Wünsche, H. F. (eds.), *Grundtexte zur Sozialen Marktwirtschaft*, vol. 2, *Das Soziale in der Sozialen Marktwirtschaft*, Stuttgart/New York, 1988, pp. 131–45.

Schmollinger, H. W., *Die Deutsche Partei*, in: Stöss, R. (ed.), *Parteien-Handbuch. Die Parteien der Bundesrepublik Deutschland 1945-1980*, (*Schriften des Zentralinstituts für Sozialwissenschaftliche Forschung der Freien Universität Berlin vol. 38*), Opladen, 1986, pp. 1025–111.

Schüller, A., *Der ordnungspolitische Weg der Bundesrepublik – Entwicklung und Perspektiven*, in: *Zeitschrift für Wirtschaftspolitik* 39, Stuttgart, 1990, pp. 57–75.

Schulz, G., *Die CDU – Merkmale ihres Aufbaus*, in: Lange, M. G.; Schulz, G.; Schütz, K. *et al.*, *Parteien in der Bundesrepublik. Studien zur Entwicklung der deutschen Parteien bis zur Bundestagswahl 1953*, in: *Schriften des des Instituts für politische Wissenschaften*, vol. 6, Stuttgart/Düsseldorf, 1953.

Schulz, G., *Konrad Adenauers gesellschaftspolitische Vorstellungen*, in: Pohl, H. (ed.), *Adenauers Verhältnis zu Wirtschaft und Gesellschaft*, in: *Rhöndorfer Gespräche*, vol. 12, Bonn, 1992, pp. 154–81.

Schütz, W. J., *Deutsche Tagespresse in Tatsachen und Zahlen. Ergebnisse einer Strukturuntersuchung des gesamten deutschen Zeitungswesens*, in: *Publizistik* 1, 1956, pp. 31–48.

Schütz, K., *Die Sozialdemokratie im Nachkriegsdeutschland*, in: Lange, M. G.; Schulz, G.; Schütz, K. *et al.*, *Parteien in der Bundesrepublik. Studien zur Entwicklung der deutschen Parteien bis zur Bundestagswahl 1953*, in: *Schriften des Instituts für politische Wissenschaften*, vol. 6, Stuttgart/Düsseldorf, 1953.

Schwarz, H.-P., *Geschichtsschreibung und politisches Selbstverständnis. Die Geschichte der Bundesrepublik Deutschland – Herausforderung für die Forschung*, in: *Politik und Zeitgeschichte* 36, Bonn, 1982, pp. 3–16.

Semler, J., *Wirtschaftslage und Wirtschaftsgestaltung*, in: *Fragen der Zeit, Schriftenreihe der Christlich-Sozialen Union Bayerns* 1, Munich, 1946.

Siebrecht, V., *Die Arbeitspolitik nach der Währungsreform*, in: *Frankfurter Hefte* 3/6, Frankfurt am Main, 1948.

Speier, H., *Historical Development of Public Opinion*, in: *American Journal of Sociology* 55, 1950, pp. 376–88.

Steger, B., *Konstruktionsfehler der bizonalen "Verfassung". Vorschläge Edmund Kaufmanns zur Überwindung struktureller Mängel des Vereinigten Wirtschaftsgebiets 1947/1948*, in: *Vierteljahreshefte für Zeitgeschichte* 29, Munich, 1982, pp. 286 ff.

Stoltenberg, G., *Konrad Adenauer und die Soziale Marktwirtschaft*, in: *Die Politische Meinung* 45/373, edited by the *Konrad-Adenauer-Stiftung*, Sankt Augustin, 2000.

Streit, M. E., *Economic Order, Private Law and Public Policy. The Freiburg School of Law and Economics in Perspective*, in: *Journal of Institutional and Theoretical Economics* 148, Bad Feilnbach, 1992, pp. 675–704.

Tribe, K., *The 1948 Currency Reform – Structure and Purpose*, Keele University, Department of Economics, *Working Paper Series* no. 98/10, Staffordshire, 1998.

Tuchtfeldt, E., *Soziale Marktwirtschaft und Globalsteuerung*, in: *Ludwig-Erhard-Stiftung* (ed.), *Grundtexte zur Sozialen Marktwirtschaft*, vol. 1: *Zeugnisse aus zweihundert Jahren ordnungspolitischer Diskussion*, Stuttgart/New York, 1981.

Vanberg, V., *'Ordnungstheorie' as Constitutional Economics – The German Conception of a 'Social Market Economy'*, in: *ORDO* 39, Stuttgart, 1988, pp. 17–1.

Vanberg, V., *Die normativen Grundlagen von Ordnungspolitik*, in: *ORDO* 48, Stuttgart, 1997, pp. 707–26.

Vanberg, V., *The Freiburg School: Walter Eucken and Ordoliberalism*, in: *Freiburg Discussion Papers on Constitutional Economics* 04/11, Freiburg im Breisgau, 2004.

Vetter, E. G., *Wirtschaftspublizistik*, in: *Handwörterbuch der Betriebswirtschaft* I/3.4., Stuttgart, 1976, pp. 4644–51.

Vogelsang, T., *Die Bemühungen um eine deutsche Zentralverwaltung 1945/46*, in: *Vierteljahreshefte für Zeitgeschichte* 18/4, Munich, 1970, pp. 510–28.

Watrin, C., *Principles of the Social Market Economy - its Origins and Early History*, in: *Zeitschrift für die gesamte Staatswissenschaft* 135, Tübingen, 1979.

Weber, A., *Sozialistische Marktwirtschaft*, in: *Das Sozialistische Jahrhundert* 4/1, Berlin, 1950.

Weber, M., *Die Protestantische Ethik und der Geist des Kapitalismus*, orig. in: *Archiv für Sozialwissenschaft u. Sozialpolitik* 20 (1904), pp. 1–54 and 21 (1905), pp. 1–110 (Reprint: Munich, 2004).

Welty, E., *Christlicher Sozialismus*, in: *Die neue Ordnung* 1, 1946/47, pp. 39 ff., 132 ff.

Wengst, U., *Die CDU/CSU im Bundestagswahlkampf 1949*, in: *Vierteljahreshefte für Zeitgeschichte* 34/ 1, Munich, 1986, pp. 1–52.

Woller, H., *Gesellschaft und Politik in der amerikanischen Besatzungszone – Die Region Ansbach und Fürth*, in: *Quellen und Darstellungen zur Zeitgeschichte*, edited by the *Institut für Zeitgeschichte*, vol. 25, Munich, 1986.

Zimmermann, K., *Erste Reichstagung der Christlich-Demokratischen Union in Godesberg am 14., 15. und 16. Dezember 1945*, in: *Schriftenreihe der Christlich-Demokratischen Union des Rheinlandes* 3, Cologne, 1946, pp. 7 ff.

Zorn, R., *Von der regulierten Marktwirtschaft*, in: *Sozialistische Monatshefte*, 4/1 and 4/2, Stuttgart, 1949.

UNPUBLISHED THESES

Berberich, W., *Die historische Entwicklung der Christlich-Sozialen Union in Bayern bis zum Eintritt in die Bundesrepublik*, doctoral thesis, Würzburg, 1965.

Boos, V., *Bypassing Regional Identity: A Study of Identifications and Interests in Scottish and Catalan Press Commentary on European Integration, 1973-1993*, doctoral thesis, Florence, 2005.

Brado, W., *Das Presserecht nach 1945*, doctoral thesis, Heidelberg, 1955.

Cerratti, R., *The Development of the Free Democratic Party in West Germany, 1945-1956*, doctoral thesis, Oxford, 1982.

Gardner, J., *The Public Debate about the Formulation of the Basic Law of the Federal Republic of Germany, 1948-1949*, doctoral thesis, Oxford, 2004.

Glossner, C. L., *Bertelsmann und das Dritte Reich. Eine Untersuchung der Verlagshistorie im Nationalsozialistischen Regime*, Université de Fribourg Presse, diploma thesis, Fribourg, 2000.

Glossner, C. L., *Quo Vadit Germany? The Formation of the German Economic Model of Governance between Liberal Socialism and Social Liberalism in the Economic Council 1947-1949*, M.Phil. thesis, Oxford, 2004.

Hädler, Ch., *Die Versorgung der deutschen Tagespresse mit Zeitungsdruckpapier*, doctoral thesis, Nuremberg, 1961.

Köser, H., *Die Grundsatzdebatte in der SPD von 1945/46 bis 1958/59*, doctoral thesis, Freiburg, 1971.

Lampe, A., *Versuche zur Theorie des Unternehmergewinns*, doctoral thesis, Munich, 1922.

Ptak, R., *Vom Ordoliberalismus zur Sozialen Marktwirtschaft – Stationen des Neoliberalismus in Deutschland*, doctoral thesis, Hamburg, 2003.

Schmidt, M. E., *Die Ordnungsfrage in der Wirtschaftspolitik der deutschen Sozialdemokratie nach den Programmen der SPD*, doctoral thesis, Freiburg im Breisgau, 1956.

Schreyer, K., *Bayern – ein Industriestaat*, doctoral thesis, Munich, 1969.

Tan, P. S. M., *Idea Factories: American Policies for German Higher Education and Reorientation, 1944-1949*, D.Phil. thesis, Oxford, 2000.

Vieritz, J., *Die SPD im Meinungsbild der ersten Kriegsjahre in Briefen an Kurt Schumacher 1945–9*, state examination thesis, University of Göttingen, 1988.

Wellmann, H., *Die Soziale Marktwirtschaft im Spiegel von Meinungsumfragen*, doctoral thesis, Cologne, 1962.

Welsch, E.-J., *Die hessischen Lizenzträger und ihre Zeitungen*, doctoral thesis, Dortmund, 2002.

Wenzel, R., *Konrad Adenauer und die Gestaltung der Wirtschafts- und Sozialordnung in Westdeutschland 1945-1951/52*, doctoral thesis, Augsburg, 1981.

Wuerstlein, G., *Zur Problematik der deutschen Presse nach 1945*, doctoral thesis, Erlangen, 1971.

INDEX

www.ingramcontent.com/pod-product-compliance
Ingram Content Group UK Ltd.
Pitfield, Milton Keynes, MK11 3LW, UK
UKHW020122290926
15471UKWH00003B/233

9 781780 764214